Hodgson Mill
Whole Grain Baking

Hodgson Mill
Whole Grain Baking

400 Healthy and Delicious Recipes for Muffins, Breads, Cookies, and More

The Bakers at Hodgson Mill

www.hodgsonmill.com

FAIR WINDS
PRESS
BEVERLY, MASSACHUSETTS

Text © 2007 Fair Winds Press

First published in the USA in 2007 by
Fair Winds Press, a member of
Quayside Publishing Group
100 Cummings Center
Suite 406-L
Beverly, MA 01915–6101

11 10 09 08 07   1 2 3 4 5

ISBN-13: 978-1-59233-261-8
ISBN-10: 1-59233-261-7

Library of Congress Cataloging-in-Publication Data available

Cover design by Laura Herrmann Couallier
Book design by Leslie Haimes
Photography by Madeline Polss

Printed and bound in USA

Thank you to all of our wonderful recipe testers—
Kate Nowinski, Maria Herrera, Linda Fund, Mary Connelly, Jennifer Gauthier,
Dwayne Ridgaway, Charlene Patton, and Sharon Davis.

CONTENTS

INTRODUCTION

Welcome to the Hodgson Mill Whole Grain Baking cookbook. Since 1882 we've been grinding whole grains and making wholesome foods that are full of natural flavor but free of artificial preservatives, additives, and colorings. We are still grinding grain in the Ozark Mountains of Missouri, only ten miles from the original water mill, and the same commitment to quality and consumer satisfaction that began in 1882 endures today.

WHY BAKE WITH WHOLE GRAINS?

For starters, baking with whole grains gives you and your family more nutrition in every bite. A whole grain has three edible parts—the endosperm, germ, and the bran. Each part contributes one or more essential components of a healthy diet. The endosperm, or inner part of the kernel, is basically a carbohydrate, which we need for energy. The germ is a nutritional powerhouse, packed with B vitamins, Vitamin E, zinc, iron, copper, selenium, and magnesium. The germ also contains phytochemicals, which, if consumed regularly, may help reduce the risk of developing cancer or cardiovascular disease. The bran, or outer layer of the kernel, provides necessary dietary fiber.

Whole grains can also play a role in weight control, as they fill you up more than refined grains, according to a 2003 Harvard School of Public Health study. Researchers found that women who ate more whole grains consistently weighed less than those who chose refined grains. Whole grains take longer to digest, so they keep you feeling fuller, longer. If you're not hungry, you're not as tempted to nibble, and this helped the women in the study maintain their weight.

In addition to packing a strong nutritional punch, another good reason to bake with whole grains is their nutty flavor and pleasing texture. Unlike the pale, bland taste of baked goods made with refined grains, which, ironically, may cause us to overeat because they don't satisfy the taste buds, whole grain baked goods give our taste buds a welcome workout.

The 2005 Dietary Guidelines for Americans suggest consuming at least three or more one-ounce servings of whole grains every day, depending on age and gender. The USDA recommends that small children consume 3 to 5 ounces of whole grains, women 5 to 6 ounces, and men 6 to 8 ounces. A 1-ounce serving is equal to one slice of 100 percent whole grain bread. Consuming the recommended amount of whole grains a day is even easier, now that you have this book full of delicious whole grain recipes.

From easy breads to make in an automatic bread machine, to handmade breads, coffee cakes, muffins, cookies, cakes, flatbreads, pizzas, and griddle-baked pancakes, this cookbook is full of great ways to make your baked goods more delicious and nutritious. If you're new to whole grain baking, there are recipes that introduce you to the flavor and texture in familiar ways. **One great way to start is to simply substitute 1 cup (125 g) of Hodgson Mill Stone Ground Whole Grain White Whole Wheat Flour for 1 cup (125 g) of all-purpose flour in bread, cake, cookie, and pizza crust recipes. Remove 1 tablespoon (8 g) of flour per cup and add 1 additional tablespoon (15 ml) of liquid in recipe per cup. This substitution works for all of the whole grain flours listed below.** For the accomplished whole grain baker, recipes like Pumpernickel Bread, Bran Muffins, and Whole Grain Belgian Waffles will help you celebrate the taste and texture of the whole grain.

ALTERNATIVE FLOURS

Baking with whole grains is also a wonderful way to explore a whole new world of flours, each of them made by grinding and milling the different grains or combining those grains with other grains or flours. Here are some of our favorites:

Buckwheat: Buckwheat is considered a cereal plant, so it's not technically a grain. Our 100 percent stone ground whole grain buckwheat flour is perfect for made-from-scratch buckwheat pancakes or crêpes. Hearty and flavorful, buckwheat flour is also a wonderful alternative to all-purpose flour in a savory gravy or as a sauce thickener. And because buckwheat contains no gluten, it can be a tasty alternative for anyone who is gluten intolerant.

50/50 Flour: Our whole grain 50/50 flour is a unique blend of equal parts 100 percent stone ground wheat flour and all-purpose unbleached, unenriched white flour. This is a perfect flour to use when you want to begin eating more whole wheat foods, as this flour can be used in any recipe calling for all-purpose flour.

Brown Rice Flour: Ground from brown rice kernels, this stone ground whole grain flour has a neutral flavor and a light, somewhat sandy texture. Brown rice is known for its deep, rich flavor and heartier texture compared to white rice, but it's also higher in protein and fiber. You can use brown rice flour in snacks and soups, or for homemade gluten- and wheat-free baby or dietetic foods. For gluten-free baking, brown rice flour is usually mixed with finer flours and starches like corn starch, potato flour, or tapioca flour to even out the texture, and xanthan gum to add body.

Rye Flour: Stone ground whole grain rye contains less gluten than wheat, so is usually used in combination with wheat flour to make bread. Rye flour is wheat-free, high in fiber, and great tasting. Because rye flour is pale grayish brown in color, rye bread dough usually contains unsweetened cocoa powder and molasses to give it a deep, dark color.

Spelt Flour: Whole spelt grain is an ancient precursor of modern wheat varieties. Spelt is a favorite food among athletes in endurance training because the whole grain is an excellent source of complex carbohydrates and nutrients. Spelt flour also has more amino acids and minerals than wheat flour, as well as the whole grain health benefits. If you want to substitute 1 cup (125 g) of spelt flour for 1 cup (125 g) of all-purpose flour in a recipe, add 1 additional tablespoon (15 g) of spelt flour. Just make sure you remove 1 tablespoon (8 g) of flour per cup and add 1 tablespoon (15 ml) of liquid in recipe per cup.

White Whole Wheat Flour: Stone ground whole grain white whole wheat flour has been popular for centuries in Eastern Europe and Australia, but red wheat is more common in the US and other parts of the Western world. White whole wheat (which is actually tan in color) is milder and sweeter in flavor and has a lighter texture than whole wheat flour, but has all the same health benefits. It can be substituted 1 cup (125 g) for 1 cup (125 g) with any type of flour.

Whole Wheat Graham Flour: Named after nineteenth-century health reformer Dr. Sylvester Graham, stone ground whole grain whole wheat graham flour contains wheat kernels ground under specific and exacting conditions that ensure that the bran, germ, and endosperm remain in the flour. The end result is the finest texture whole wheat flour available with no preservatives and no additives.

Whole Wheat Pastry Flour: Our stone ground whole grain pastry flour is finely stone-ground using traditional methods that retain all of the grain's natural oils and vitamins. This pastry flour is great for cookies, cakes, and other treats that require a fine, soft flour. Just make sure you remove 1 tablespoon (8 g) of flour per cup and add 1 tablespoon (15 ml) of liquid in recipe per cup.

Yellow or White Corn Meal, Plain: Our whole grain corn meals offer all the natural corn bran and germ for robust taste, superior texture, and top nutritional benefit. You can use it to replace up to ¼ of all-purpose flour for corn meal pancakes, cookies, or other baked goods.

COMBINATION PRODUCTS

Many baking recipes call for a combination of whole grain, bread, and/or all-purpose flours. Here are more of our favorites:

Best For Bread Flour: To make this flour we use a very high-protein (high-gluten) wheat and mill it slowly. This guarantees that your bread will bake into superior loaves, unsurpassed in flavor and texture. This flour is ideal for use with electric bread baking machines.

All-Purpose, Unbleached Naturally White Flour: Our all-purpose flour is both unbleached and unenriched, which is a difficult combination to find in most all-purpose white flours. We remove the bran and the germ from the wheat kernel, leaving only the endosperm. This flour is particularly healthy and convenient for anyone on iron-restricted diets.

Oat Bran Flour: Our naturally wheat-free oat bran flour is specially milled to emphasize the natural benefits of oat bran, resulting in a wholesome and flavorful flour. Oat bran has many health benefits, including its ability to lower cholesterol and the fact that it's a great source of fiber.

Oat Bran Flour Blend: This mixture of a unique blend of equal parts 100 percent oat bran flour and unbleached, unenriched white flour gives bread its familiar texture and rise, and this blend can be used in any recipe calling for all-purpose flour by replacing up to half of the flour quantity with Oat Bran Flour Blend.

Soy Flour: To make this soy flour we gently grind soybeans into a fine flour that is packed with nutrients such as isoflavones, which have been shown to reduce the risk of heart disease and cancer. You can use soy flour in all of your favorite baked goods to add a pleasant flavor and texture, while also boosting their nutritional profile by adding protein, iron, and calcium. As a general rule, soy flour can replace up to ¼ of the main flour in your nonyeast raised favorite recipes. In yeast recipes, just place 2 tablespoons (16 g) of soy flour in your measuring cup before measuring all-purpose flour or another flour called for in the recipe. To make your own soy milk using soy flour, see the recipe note on page 128.

Vital Wheat Gluten: This powdered ingredient is a protein blend found in wheat. Gluten develops during kneading, helps make dough elastic, and allows bread to rise by trapping gases created by the yeast. Some flours, especially whole grains, do not contain enough gluten for a satisfactory rise, so Vital Wheat Gluten should be added to the recipe.

BAKING WITH WHOLE GRAIN CEREALS

You can also bake with finely ground or partially cooked whole grain cereals, like our Cracked Wheat, Multi Grain, and Bulgur Wheat with Soy Hot Cereals. You could also use some of our other wholesome cereals and products, such as Wheat Germ, Untoasted Wheat Bran, Unprocessed Milled Flax Seed, and Oat Bran Hot Cereal. Usually, the method in the recipe calls for softening the cereal grains with a liquid before incorporating it into the batter or dough. For a taste and texture treat, try substituting 1 cup (125 g) of cooked breakfast cereal for 1 cup (125 g) bread flour in your favorite bread recipe.

GETTING STARTED

Any experienced baker will tell you that you do not need expensive equipment to begin baking your own breads, coffee cakes, cookies, and cakes at home. Most of the items you need are probably already in your kitchen. Here's the equipment we suggest having on hand:

Baking sheets. The (17 x 12 x 1-inch [42.5 x 30 x 2.5-cm]) large baking sheet or (15 x 10 5 1-inch [37.5 x 25 x 2.5-cm]) jelly-roll pan can be lined with parchment paper for easy removal of baked goods and even easier cleanup.

Bread pans. Most common are metal pans in two sizes: 9 x 5 x 3-inch (22.5 x 12.5 x 7.5-cm) or $8^{1}/2$ x $4^{1}/2$-inch (21.3 x 11.3-cm). Glass bread pans are also okay, but remember to lower the oven temperature by 25°F (3.8°C). Dark pans usually darken the crust.

Cake pans. Most common are round metal pans in 8- or 9-inch (20- or 22.5-cm) sizes, but you can also use Bundt, jellyroll, and 9 x 13 x 2-inch (22.5 x 32.5 x 5-cm) baking pans.

Oven

Yardstick or ruler

Large wooden spoon

Long-handled dough whisk. This wooden-handled utensil has a wire head shaped like an old-fashioned Victorian carpet beater, but it's the best for mixing whole grain dough.

Instant-read thermometer. Used for checking water temperature before proofing yeast, making sure liquids are heated to the proper temperature before adding them to the dough, and/or checking whether baked bread is done.

Timer

Wire cooling rack

Measuring cups, dry and liquid

Measuring spoons

Mixing bowls, two large size

Rubber spatula

Rolling pin

Saucepans (small, medium, and large sizes)

Serrated (or bread) **knife** for dividing dough

Other equipment that is not absolutely necessary but is nice to have includes the following:

Bread board for kneading dough

Electric knife

Electric stand mixer with paddle and dough hook attachments for mixing dough

Pastry brush

Plastic wrap

Baking tiles. You place handmade bread dough on these tiles to bake in a hot oven.

An assortment of bread pans (for baguettes, brioches, bread sticks, etc.)

Food processor

OTHER BAKING INGREDIENTS

In addition to whole grain flours, you will also need the following ingredients on hand: butter, vegetable oil, eggs, spices, sugars (granulated, brown, and confectioners'), unsweetened cocoa powder, bottled milk, nonfat dry milk, and applesauce or canned pumpkin. Other necessary ingredients will vary from recipe to recipe and may include items such as caraway, sesame, or poppy seeds, molasses, honey, or rolled oats.

BAKING WITH YEAST

Yeast is a living organism. A package of yeast contains thousands of microscopic living plants that depend on a specific temperature range to grow. The process of yeast fermentation in bread dough involves consuming sugar and starch and converting them into carbon dioxide and alcohol, which in turn gives yeast-risen baked goods their volume and flavor. Hodgson Mill offers two types of yeast: Active Dry Yeast and Fast-Rise Yeast. Each $5/16$-ounce packet contains $2^{1}/2$ teaspoons (10 g) of yeast, which is 25 percent more for higher loaves!

Our Active Dry Yeast is a dry, granular form of yeast used in conventional bread baking. This type of yeast is usually dissolved in a liquid that is warmed to 105°F to 115°F (42°C to 46°C) and allowed to activate before being combined with other ingredients.

Our Fast-Rise Yeast is a highly active strain of dry yeast. The particles are very fine, which allows up to 50 percent faster rising time. Many recipes suggest mixing Fast-Rise Yeast with the dry ingredients before adding the liquids. This is the type of yeast you'll use in automatic bread machine recipes; in most of those machines, the yeast is the last ingredient added to the bread pan.

If necessary, you can usually substitute Fast-Rise Yeast or bread machine yeast for active dry yeast in almost any recipe. There's no need to proof the yeast first—just mix the Fast-Rise Yeast in with the dry ingredients, but still incorporate the water or liquid (that would have been used to proof the active dry yeast) with the other liquid ingredients so the dough has enough moisture. Your bread dough will rise 50 percent faster than with active dry yeast.

GLUTEN-FREE BAKING

Some people cannot tolerate the gluten, or protein, in wheat that provides the elasticity needed for baked goods to rise. The challenge in gluten-free baking is finding a combination of flours and binders that approximate the role gluten plays in normal wheat flour. Fortunately, Hodgson Mill offers a wide variety of specialty gluten-free flours, starches, mixes, and meals. These include Stone Ground Whole Grain Brown Rice Flour; Pure Corn Starch; Whole Grain Yellow or White Corn Meal, Plain; Stone Ground Buckwheat Flour; Soy Flour; Whole Grain Multi Purpose Baking Mix; Milled Flax Seed; and Whole Grain Apple Cinnamon Muffin Mix with Milled Flax Seed. These whole grain products can be combined with ingredients such as xanthan gum (a thickener, stabilizer, and emulsifier made from corn syrup), potato starch, or tapioca flour, all of which are available at health food stores or better grocery stores.

When baking gluten-free items, be sure to check the labels and use gluten-free baking powder, unsweetened cocoa powder, instant mashed potatoes, etc. When in doubt, check the label or contact the company for more information. Note: Some people who cannot tolerate gluten are also allergic to eggs and dairy products. Each gluten-free recipe suggests alternatives for making the recipe dairy- and egg-free.

For more information on whole grain baking and a complete listing of Hodgson Mill products, visit us at www.hodgsonmill.com or call 800.525.0177.

Happy baking!

1 cup (125 g) Hodgson Mill Stone Ground Whole Grain White Whole Wheat or 50/50 Flour

1 cup (125 g) Hodgson Mill Best For Bread Flour

$1/2$ teaspoon (1.5 g) dry mustard powder

1 cup (4 ounces [115 g]) grated sharp Cheddar

1 package ($5/16$ ounce) or $2^1/2$ teaspoons (10 g) Hodgson Mill Fast-Rise Yeast

FOR THE TOPPING:

Milk for brushing

$1/4$ cup (25 g) finely grated Parmesan cheese

Place milk, egg, sugar, salt, flours, mustard powder, Cheddar, and yeast in bread pan of bread machine. Select dough cycle and start machine.

Line baking sheet with parchment paper. At end of cycle, transfer dough to floured surface and cut in half. Roll each half out to 12 x 8-inch (30 x 20-cm) rectangle. Cut each rectangle into 12 (8 x 1-inch [20 x 2.5-cm]) strips. Tie each strip into loose knot and place on prepared baking sheet. Cover and let rise in a warm place for 30 minutes.

Preheat oven to 375°F (190°C). For topping, brush rolls with milk and sprinkle with Parmesan cheese.

Bake rolls 12 minutes or until golden.

Yield: 16 rolls

Each with: 98 Calories; 3g Fat (29.9% calories from fat); 5g Protein; 12g Carbohydrate; 1g Dietary Fiber; 21 mg Cholesterol; 210mg Sodium.

Variation: To make dough by hand, whisk sugar, salt, flours, mustard powder, Cheddar, and yeast together in large bowl. Add milk and egg and stir together to make soft dough. Transfer to floured surface and knead gently until dough is not sticky, 2 to 3 minutes. Return to bowl, cover, and let rise in a warm place until doubled in bulk, about 1 hour. Proceed with baking steps.

 *Spoon Rolls*

Spongy-textured spoon rolls, which get a double lift from yeast and self-rising flour, helped busy people in the 1930s and 40s put dinner on the table. Today, they're still a welcome accompaniment to a last-minute soup or a slow-cooker stew. This dough can be covered and stored in the refrigerator for up to a week, ready to be baked at the last minute.

 1 package ($5/16$ ounce) or $2^1/2$ teaspoons (10 g) Hodgson Mill Active Dry Yeast
 2 cups (470 ml) warm (105°F to 115°F [40.5°C to 46°C]) water
 12 tablespoons ($1^1/2$ sticks [167 g]) unsalted butter, melted
 $1/4$ cup (50 g) sugar
 1 large egg, beaten
 2 cups (250 g) Hodgson Mill 50/50 or Stone Ground Whole Grain White Whole Wheat Flour
 2 cups (250 g) self-rising flour

Preheat the oven to 400°F (200°C). Grease two 12-cup muffin pans and set aside.

Sprinkle yeast over warm water in large bowl and set aside until foamy, about 5 minutes.

With wooden spoon, stir butter, sugar, and egg into yeast mixture until well blended. Beat in the flours, 1 cup (125 g) at a time, until thoroughly blended. Continue beating until well blended.

Spoon batter into prepared muffin cups, filling them about half-full.

Bake 15 minutes, or until rolls have risen and browned. Serve hot.

Yield: 24 rolls

Each with: 133 Calories; 6g Fat (40.7% calories from fat); 3g Protein; 17g Carbohydrate; 1g Dietary Fiber; 23mg Cholesterol; 136mg Sodium.

Gluten-Free Yeast Rolls

Soft, yeasty, and mellow, these tender and moist rolls are true cousins of those made with wheat.

3 large eggs or equivalent egg substitute

1 teaspoon (5 ml) cider vinegar

3 tablespoons (45 ml) vegetable oil, such as canola

$^1/_2$ cup (125 g) unsweetened applesauce

$1^1/_3$ cups (315 ml) water

1 cup (125 g) Hodgson Mill Whole Grain Multi Purpose Baking Mix

1 cup (125 g) Hodgson Mill Stone Ground Whole Grain Brown Rice Flour

1 cup (130 g) tapioca flour or potato starch

$^1/_2$ cup (65 g) Hodgson Mill Pure Corn Starch

4 teaspoons (28 g) xanthan gum

3 tablespoons (42 g) packed brown sugar

$^1/_2$ teaspoon (3 g) salt

1 package ($^5/_{16}$ ounce) or $2^1/_2$ teaspoons (10 g) Hodgson Mill Fast-Rise Yeast

Whisk eggs, vinegar, and oil together in large bowl. Whisk in applesauce and water and pour into bread pan. Add baking mix, rice flour, tapioca flour, corn starch, xanthan gum, brown sugar, and salt. Add yeast. Select dough cycle and start machine.

Preheat oven to 350°F (180°C). Grease two 6-cup muffin tins.

When cycle is complete, stop machine. Carefully spoon dough into prepared muffin tin and smooth tops with spatula.

Bake 20 to 25 minutes or until instant-read thermometer inserted in center of roll registers at least 190°F (87.7°C). Turn out onto wire rack to cool.

Yield: 12 rolls

Each with: 204 Calories; 6g Fat (23.0% calories from fat); 4g Protein; 38g Carbohydrate; 2g Dietary Fiber; 47mg Cholesterol; 105mg Sodium.

Note: To make this recipe dairy- and egg-free, use vegetable oil and egg substitute.

Gluten-Free Cinnamon Rolls

Make this very wet and spongy dough in the bread machine, then use a special technique for creating the cinnamon rolls.

FOR THE DOUGH:

3 large eggs or equivalent egg substitute

1 teaspoon (5 ml) cider vinegar

3 tablespoons (45 ml) vegetable oil, such as canola

$^1/_2$ cup (125 g) unsweetened applesauce

1$^1/_3$ cups (315 ml) water

1 cup (125 g) Hodgson Mill Whole Grain Multi Purpose Baking Mix

1 cup (125 g) Hodgson Mill Stone Ground Whole Grain Brown Rice Flour

1 cup (130 g) tapioca flour or potato starch

$^1/_2$ cup (65 g) Hodgson Mill Pure Corn Starch

4 teaspoons (28 g) xanthan gum

3 tablespoons (42 g) packed brown sugar

$^1/_2$ teaspoon (3 g) salt

1 package ($^5/_{16}$ ounce) or 2$^1/_2$ teaspoons (10 g) Hodgson Mill Fast-Rise Yeast

FOR THE FILLING:

3 tablespoons (45 ml) melted butter or margarine

2 teaspoons (4.6 g) ground cinnamon

$^1/_2$ cup (100 g) sugar

$^3/_4$ cup (110 g) raisins

FOR THE GLAZE:

1 cup (100 g) confectioners' sugar

$^1/_4$ teaspoon (1.3 ml) gluten-free vanilla extract

1 tablespoon (15 ml) 2 percent milk or soy milk

For dough, whisk eggs, vinegar, and oil together in large bowl. Whisk in applesauce and water and pour into bread pan. Add baking mix, rice flour, tapioca flour, corn starch, xanthan gum, brown sugar, and salt. Add yeast. Select dough cycle and start machine.

Grease two (6-cup) muffin tins. Spray two 20 inch (50 cm) -long pieces of wax or parchment paper with nonstick spray and place on flat surface.

When cycle is complete, stop machine. Scoop half of dough onto prepared paper. Spray spatula with nonstick spray. With spatula, spread wet dough out to 10 x 14-inch (25 x 35-cm) rectangle.

For filling, drizzle melted butter over surface of dough. Mix cinnamon and sugar together in bowl. Sprinkle mixture evenly over dough followed by raisins.

Roll up, jelly-roll style, lifting a long end of the paper up and gently nudging or scraping dough into roll. Spray knife or dough scraper with non-stick spray and cut roll into 6 (1^1/2-inch [3.8-cm]) pieces. Place cinnamon rolls, spiral side up, in prepared muffin tin. Cover and let rise for 30 minutes.

Preheat oven to 350°F (180°C). Bake 15 to 18 minutes or until risen and lightly browned. Transfer to wire rack to cool.

For glaze, whisk confectioners' sugar, vanilla, and milk together and drizzle over warm rolls.

Yield: 12 rolls

Each with: 330 Calories; 8g Fat (21.9% calories from fat); 4g Protein; 63g Carbohydrate; 2g Dietary Fiber; 55mg Cholesterol; 136mg Sodium.

 ## Gluten-Free Quick Cinnamon Rolls

Gluten-free doughs—even ones that use baking powder as a leavener, as in this recipe—have to be very wet in order to rise properly and have good texture, so making these rolls requires a bit of patience. However, the tender results are well worth it. Because the dough is so wet, you will need a dough scraper.

FOR THE DOUGH:

^{3}/4 cup (93.8 g) Hodgson Mill Stone Ground Whole Grain Brown Rice Flour

^{3}/4 cup (97.5 g) Hodgson Mill Pure Corn Starch

2 teaspoons (3 g) gluten-free baking powder

^{1}/2 teaspoon (4 g) xanthan gum

^{1}/2 teaspoon (3 g) salt

1 tablespoon (13 g) sugar

2 large eggs or equivalent egg substitute

^{1}/3 cup (80 ml) vegetable oil, such as canola

^{1}/2 cup (120 ml) 2 percent milk or soy milk

FOR THE FILLING:

   3 tablespoons (45 ml) melted butter or margarine

   2 teaspoons (4.6 g) ground cinnamon

   1/2 cup (100 g) sugar

   3/4 cup (110 g) raisins

FOR THE GLAZE:

   1 cup (100 g) confectioners' sugar

   1/4 teaspoon (1.3 ml) gluten-free vanilla extract

   1 tablespoon (15 ml) 2 percent milk or soy milk

Preheat oven to 400°F (200°C). Grease 6-cup muffin tin. Line baking sheet with parchment paper. Spray 20 inch (50 cm) -long piece of wax or parchment paper with nonstick spray and place on flat surface.

For dough, sift flour, corn starch, baking powder, xanthan gum, salt, and sugar together in medium bowl. In separate bowl, whisk eggs, oil, and milk together. Blend egg mixture into dry ingredients until just moistened.

Scoop dough onto prepared paper. Spray spatula with nonstick spray. With spatula, spread wet dough into 10 x 14-inch (25 x 35-cm) rectangle.

For filling, drizzle melted butter over surface of dough. Mix cinnamon and sugar together in bowl. Sprinkle mixture evenly over dough, followed by raisins.

Roll up, jelly-roll style, lifting a long end of the paper up and gently nudging or scraping dough into roll. Spray dough scraper with non-stick spray and cut roll into 6 (1 1/2-inch [3.9-cm]) pieces. Place cinnamon rolls, spiral side up, in prepared muffin tin.

Bake 15 to 18 minutes or until risen and lightly browned. Transfer to wire rack to cool.

For glaze, whisk confectioners' sugar, vanilla, and milk together and drizzle over warm rolls.

Yield: 6 rolls

Each with: 520 Calories; 21g Fat (35.3% calories from fat); 5g Protein; 81g Carbohydrate; 1g Dietary Fiber; 82mg Cholesterol; 444mg Sodium.

Gluten-Free Wild Rice Popovers

Like the classic Yorkshire pudding, these popovers are best enjoyed right out of the oven and are a wonderful accompaniment to a beef or mushroom dish. They don't rise quite as high as wheat-based popovers, but their savory flavor is fabulous. For the highest and lightest popovers, remember to preheat the popover pan in the oven before adding the batter.

1/2 cup (82.5 g) cooked wild rice

1/2 cup (62.5 g) Hodgson Mill Stone Ground Whole Grain Brown Rice Flour or Whole Grain Multi Purpose Baking Mix

1/4 cup (32.5 g) Hodgson Mill Pure Corn Starch

1/2 teaspoon (3 g) salt

1 teaspoon (2.3 g) ground white pepper

4 large eggs or equivalent egg substitute

1 cup (235 ml) 2 percent milk or soy milk

1 tablespoon (15 ml) gluten-free Worcestershire or soy sauce

Preheat oven to 400°F (200°C). Heavily grease a muffin or popover tin and heat in oven.

Place wild rice in food processor or blender and process until cut into very small pieces. Pour rice flour or mix and corn starch into bowl. Stir in salt and pepper to blend. Whisk in eggs, milk, and Worcestershire sauce to form smooth batter. Stir in processed wild rice.

Remove pan from oven. Quickly pour about 1/3 cup (80 ml) batter into each prepared popover or muffin cup. Return to oven. Bake 22 to 25 minutes or until puffed and golden.

Yield: 12 popovers

Each with: 76 Calories; 2g Fat (24.0% calories from fat); 3g Protein; 11 g Carbohydrate; trace Dietary Fiber; 64mg Cholesterol; 130mg Sodium.

Note: To make this recipe dairy- and egg-free, use egg substitute and soy milk.

Gluten-Free Sandwich Rolls

For hamburgers or other sandwiches, these gluten-free rolls have that mellow, yeasty flavor of white bread. Because the dough is batter-like, the rolls form in 4-inch (10-cm) mini pie pans, which you can buy at kitchenware shops.

2 packages ($^5/16$ ounce each) or 5 teaspoons (20 g) Hodgson Mill
　　Active Dry Yeast

$^1/2$ cup (120 ml) warm (105°F to 115°F [43.3°C to 46°C]) water

2 cups (250 g) Hodgson Mill Stone Ground Whole Grain Brown Rice Flour

2 cups (250 g) tapioca flour

$^1/4$ cup (50 g) sugar

4 teaspoons (28 g) xanthan gum

$1^1/2$ teaspoons (9 g) salt

$1^1/2$ cups (355 ml) 2 percent milk or soy milk

4 tablespoons (60 ml) melted butter or vegetable oil, such as canola

1 teaspoon (5 ml) gluten-free vinegar

3 large eggs or equivalent egg substitute

Sprinkle yeast over water in small bowl and set aside until foamy, about 5 minutes.

Combine flours, sugar, xanthan gum, and salt in large bowl. Whisk together milk, melted butter, vinegar, and eggs in medium bowl. Mix yeast, then egg mixture, into dry ingredients in a large bowl, to form smooth batter. Beat for 2 minutes.

Grease 12 (4-inch [10-cm]) miniature pie pans. Spoon batter into prepared pans. Cover and let rise in a warm place until doubled in bulk, about 1 hour.

Preheat oven to 350°F (180°C). Bake 15 to 20 minutes or until instant-read thermometer inserted in center of roll registers at least 190°F (87.7°C). Turn out onto wire racks to cool.

Yield: 12 sandwich rolls

Each with: 227 Calories; 6g Fat (24.0% calories from fat); 5g Protein; 39g Carbohydrate; 1g Dietary Fiber; 59mg Cholesterol; 335mg Sodium.

Add It: If desired, brush rolls with a mixture of egg and water, then sprinkle with sesame, caraway, or poppy seeds before baking.

Variation: Make the dough in the bread machine by placing water, oil, vinegar, eggs, flours, xanthan gum, and salt in bread pan. Substitute Hodgson Mill Fast-Rise

Yeast in place of active dry and add that last to bread pan. Select dough cycle and start machine. When cycle is complete, proceed with baking steps.

Note: To make this recipe dairy- and egg-free, use vegetable oil, egg substitute, and soy milk.

Whole Wheat Parker House Rolls

Softened with milk, egg, and honey and brushed with butter before baking, these homey rolls taste wonderful hot out of the oven.

1 package ($^5/16$ ounce) or $2^1/2$ teaspoons (10 g) Hodgson Mill Active Dry Yeast

$^1/4$ cup (60 ml) warm (105°F to 115°F [43.3°C to 46°C]) water

1 cup (235 ml) warm (105°F to 115°F [43.3°C to 46°C]) milk

1 large egg

$^1/4$ cup (80 g) honey

1 tablespoon (18 g) salt

3 cups (375 g) Hodgson Mill Organic Stone Ground Whole Grain Whole Wheat Graham Flour

6 tablespoons (85 g) butter, melted

Sprinkle yeast over water in large bowl and set aside until foamy, about 5 minutes.

Grease two 8-inch (20-cm) round cake pans. Beat milk, egg, honey, and salt into yeast mixture until well blended. Beat in flour, 1 cup (125 g) at a time, to form soft dough. Turn out onto floured surface and pat or roll to 1-inch (2.5-cm) thickness. Cut 18 rolls out with 3-inch (7.5-cm) biscuit cutter. Gather scraps, re-roll, and cut again. Spread melted butter on dough circles and fold in half. Arrange rolls, folded side down, in cake pans. Cover and let rise in a warm place until doubled in bulk, about 1 hour.

Preheat oven to 400°F (200°C). Bake 15 to 20 minutes or until rolls are browned and instant-read thermometer inserted in roll registers at least 190°F (87.7°C). Turn out onto wire racks to cool.

Yield: 18 rolls

Each with: 128 Calories; 5g Fat (34.3% calories from fat); 3g Protein; 19g Carbohydrate; 2g Dietary Fiber; 23mg Cholesterol; 404mg Sodium.

Whole Wheat Hamburger Buns

The perfect burger deserves the perfect bun, and this is it.

2 packages (^{5}/16 ounce each) or 5 teaspoons (20 g) Hodgson Mill
    Active Dry Yeast

^{1}/4 cup (60 ml) warm (105°F to 115°F [43.3°C to 46°C]) water

2 cups (475 ml) hot water

2^1/2 cups (312.5 g) Hodgson Mill Stone Ground Whole Wheat Graham Flour

^{1}/4 cup (32 g) nonfat dry milk

^{1}/4 cup (60 ml) vegetable oil, such as canola

^{1}/4 cup (80 g) honey

1 teaspoon (6 g) salt

3 cups (375 g) Hodgson Mill All-Purpose, Unbleached Naturally White Flour

FOR THE TOPPING:

Vegetable oil for brushing

Sprinkle yeast over warm water in small bowl and set aside until foamy, about
5 minutes.

Pour hot water over whole wheat flour in large bowl and stir. Add dry milk, oil,
honey, and salt; stir well. Let cool 5 minutes to 105°F to 115°F (43.3°C to 46°C)
and then add yeast mixture.

Beat with electric mixer for 3 minutes. Turn dough out onto floured surface. Knead
in all-purpose flour to form soft dough (about 5 minutes or until smooth and elastic).
Place dough in large, oiled bowl and turn to coat. Cover and let rise in a warm
place until doubled in bulk, about 1 hour.

Punch dough down, cover, and let rise in a warm place again for 1 hour.

Preheat oven to 375°F (190°C). Line 2 baking sheets with parchment paper. Turn
dough out onto floured surface and roll out to ^{1}/2-inch (1.2-cm) thickness. Cut with
floured doughnut cutter without the hole or a small can the size of a bun. Gather
scraps, re-roll, and cut again. Place buns 2 inches (5 cm) apart on baking sheet.
Cover and let rise in a warm place 30 minutes.

Bake 25 minutes or until risen and browned and instant-read thermometer inserted
in bun registers at least 190°F (87.7°C). Transfer to wire racks to cool and brush
tops with oil.

Yield: 18 buns

Each with: 173 Calories; 3g Fat (16.7% calories from fat); 5g Protein; 33g Carbohydrate; 3g Dietary Fiber; trace Cholesterol; 128mg Sodium.

 ## *Whole Wheat Bagels*

This recipe will give you a new appreciation for the artisan approach needed for delicious, authentic bagels. These are mixed, kneaded, formed, broiled, boiled, and baked! You can wrap and freeze any extra bagels for up to 3 months.

2 packages (^{5}/16 ounce each) or 5 teaspoons (20 g) Hodgson Mill Active Dry Yeast

2 cups (470 ml) warm (105°F to 115°F [43.3°C to 46°C]) water

2 tablespoons (40 g) honey

2 cups (250 g) Hodgson Mill Stone Ground Whole Wheat Graham Flour

3 cups (375 g) Hodgson Mill All-Purpose, Unbleached Naturally White Flour

^{1}/4 cup (60 ml) vegetable oil, such as canola

1^1/2 teaspoons (9 g) salt

3^1/2 quarts (3.3 L) water

1 teaspoon (6 g) salt

FOR THE TOPPING:

Sesame seeds

Sprinkle yeast over warm water in large bowl and set aside until foamy, about 5 minutes.

Add honey, stirring well. Stir in whole wheat flour and salt. Gradually stir in enough all-purpose flour to form soft dough. Turn dough out onto heavily floured surface (dough will be sticky), and knead by hand until smooth and elastic, 8 to 10 minutes, or use dough hook on electric stand mixer for 5 to 8 minutes. Place dough in large, oiled bowl, turning to coat. Cover and let rise in a warm place until doubled in bulk, about 1^1/2 hours.

Lightly grease 2 baking sheets. Punch dough down, turn out onto floured surface, and divide into 12 equal pieces. Roll each piece into smooth ball. Cut hole in center of each ball with 1-inch (2.5-cm) cutter or a floured finger. Gently pull dough away from center to make a 1 to 1^1/2-inch (2.5 to 3.8-cm) hole. Place shaped bagels on lightly greased baking sheets. Cover and let rise in a warm place 15 minutes.

Preheat broiler. Broil bagels, 5 inches (12.5 cm) from heat, 2 minutes on each side or until lightly browned. Preheat oven to 425°F (220°C).

Bring water and 1 teaspoon (6 g) salt to a boil in a large pot. Reduce heat, and simmer bagels 3 minutes on each side. Place bagels back on lightly greased baking sheets. Sprinkle with sesame seeds; lightly press seeds into bagels.

Bake for 20 to 25 minutes or until golden brown and an instant-read thermometer inserted near center of bagel registers at least 190°F (87.7°C).

Yield: 12 bagels

Each with: 223 Calories; 5g Fat (19.0% calories from fat); 6g Protein; 41 g Carbohydrate; 4g Dietary Fiber; 0mg Cholesterol; 454mg Sodium.

Variation: Instead of sesame seeds, use poppy seeds, dried herbs, or toasted onion for toppings.

 ## *Wheat Germ Refrigerator Rolls*

The beauty of refrigerator rolls is that the dough or formed rolls can be made ahead, kept cool in the refrigerator, and used within 3 days, which makes these great rolls for entertaining. But don't keep the dough any longer than 3 days—the dough becomes bitter after that.

> 2 packages ($5/16$ ounce each) or 5 teaspoons (20 g) Hodgson Mill
>   Active Dry Yeast
> 3 tablespoons (42 g) packed light or dark brown sugar
> 1 tablespoon (18 g) salt
> $3^{1}/2$ cups (437.5 g) Hodgson Mill All-Purpose, Unbleached Naturally White Flour
> 4 tablespoons ($^{1}/2$ stick [55 g]) butter, cut in small pieces
> 2 cups (470 ml) 2 percent milk
> 2 large eggs
> 1 cup (130 g) Hodgson Mill Wheat Germ, Untoasted
> 2 to $2^{1}/2$ cups (250 to 312.5 g) Hodgson Mill Stone Ground Whole Wheat Graham
>   Flour

FOR THE TOPPING:
> Vegetable oil for brushing
> 1 large egg, beaten
> Additional wheat germ for sprinkling

In large mixing bowl, stir together the yeast, sugar, salt, and 2 cups (250 g) all-purpose flour until smooth. Stir in butter. Heat milk in saucepan over medium heat until warm (105°F to 115°F [43.3°C to 46°C]).

Stir warm milk into flour-yeast mixture and beat with electric mixer on medium speed for 2 minutes, scraping the sides of the bowl occasionally. Add remaining 1^1/2 cups (187.5 g) all-purpose flour and stir until blended. Add eggs and beat at high speed for 1 minute, or until the mixture is thick and elastic. Stir in wheat germ. Gradually stir in just enough whole wheat flour (about 2 cups [250 g]) to make soft dough that pulls away from the sides of the bowl.

Turn the dough onto a lightly floured surface and knead by hand 8 to 10 minutes or with dough hook attachment on electric mixer 5 to 8 minutes, until dough is smooth and elastic. Cover dough with plastic wrap, then with a clean tea towel and let rest 20 minutes.

Oil two 9-inch (22.5-cm) round pans. Punch down the dough. Divide it in half. Divide each half into 10 equal portions, and form each into a smooth ball. Arrange 20 balls in the oiled pans. Brush tops with a little vegetable oil. Cover loosely with plastic wrap and refrigerate overnight.

Remove rolls from the refrigerator 1 hour before serving time. Uncover pans and let stand at room temperature 30 minutes.

Preheat oven to 400°F (200°C). Brush the tops of the rolls with the beaten egg and sprinkle with wheat germ. Bake 25 to 30 minutes.

Yield: 20 rolls

Each with: 185 Calories; 4g Fat (19.2% calories from fat); 7g Protein; 31 g Carbohydrate; 4g Dietary Fiber; 36mg Cholesterol; 364mg Sodium.

 ## *Spelt Crescent Rolls*

Dark reddish brown, the spelt grain has recently been rediscovered. It has more protein and nutrients than wheat, but not as much gluten. You can wrap and freeze extra rolls for up to 3 months. To reheat, simply place on baking sheet, covered with foil, and warm in 350°F (180°C) oven.

1 package (^{5}/16 ounce) or 2^1/2 teaspoons (10 g) Hodgson Mill
    Active Dry Yeast

1^1/4 cups (295 ml) water

2 tablespoons (40 g) honey

2 tablespoons (26 g) sugar

1/4 teaspoon (3 g) salt

5 cups (625 g) Hodgson Mill Organic Whole Grain Spelt Flour

Sprinkle yeast over water in large bowl and set aside until foamy, about 5 minutes.

Stir in honey and sugar until well blended. Add salt and enough flour (4 to 5 cups [500 to 625 g]) to make a dough. Transfer dough to floured surface and knead by hand 8 to 10 minutes or with electric mixer fitted with dough hook attachment for 5 to 8 minutes, until smooth and elastic. Place dough in large, oiled bowl, cover and let rise in a warm place for 30 minutes.

Line 3 baking sheets with parchment paper. Punch down dough and transfer to floured surface. Divide into thirds. Cut each third in half. Roll out each piece to a 14-inch (35-cm) circle. Cut into 8 wedges with a sharp knife or pizza cutter. Starting with large end, roll up into crescent shapes. Place on prepared baking sheets and let rise in a warm place until doubled in bulk, about 1 hour.

Preheat oven to 350°F (180°C). Bake 30 to 35 minutes or until instant-read thermometer inserted in center of roll registers at least 190°F (87.7°C).

Yield: 48 rolls

Each with: 41 Calories; trace Fat (7.1% calories from fat); 2g Protein; 10g Carbohydrate; 2g Dietary Fiber; 0mg Cholesterol; 11 mg Sodium.

 ## *Onion Rye Dinner Rolls*

Hearty and satisfying, these rye rolls go well with a grilled steak dinner.

1/3 cup (53.3 g) minced onion

3 tablespoons (45 ml) vegetable oil

1 cup (235 ml) 2 percent milk

2 tablespoons (40 g) molasses

1 teaspoon (6 g) salt

1 tablespoon (8 g) unsweetened cocoa powder

2 tablespoons (28 g) butter

2 packages (5/16 ounce each) or 5 teaspoons (20 g) Hodgson Mill Active Dry Yeast

1/2 cup (120 ml) lukewarm (110°F [43.3°C]) water

3 cups (375 g) Hodgson Mill All-Purpose, Unbleached Naturally White Flour

2 teaspoons (5.4 g) caraway seeds

$^1/_2$ cup (65 g) Hodgson Mill Wheat Germ, Untoasted

1 to 1$^1/_4$ cups (125 to 156.3 g) Hodgson Mill Stone Ground Whole Grain Rye Flour

FOR THE EGG GLAZE:

1 large egg

2 teaspoons (10 ml) water

Sauté onion in vegetable oil over medium-high heat until golden, about 10 minutes. Set aside to cool.

Scald milk in saucepan over medium-high heat until bubbles form around perimeter of pan. Stir in molasses, salt, unsweetened cocoa powder, and butter and continue stirring until butter melts. Set aside to cool to lukewarm (110°F [43.3°C]).

Sprinkle yeast over water in large bowl and set aside until foamy, about 5 minutes.

Combine milk mixture with yeast mixture. Add all-purpose flour and beat vigorously for 1 minute or until batter is very smooth. Stir in caraway seeds, onion, wheat germ, and enough rye flour so dough is firm enough to knead. Turn dough onto floured surface. Knead by hand for 8 to 10 minutes or in electric mixer fitted with dough hook attachment for 5 to 8 minutes, or until smooth and elastic. Place in large, oiled bowl, turning to coat. Cover and let rise in a warm place until doubled in bulk, about 1 hour.

Line 2 large baking sheets with parchment paper. Punch down dough. Transfer to floured surface. Roll by hand into long rope about 1$^1/_2$-inches (3.8-cm) thick. Cut into 1$^1/_2$-inch (3.8-cm) pieces and shape into buns. Place 2 inches (5 cm) apart on prepared baking sheets. Cover and let rise in a warm place until doubled in bulk, about 45 minutes.

Preheat oven to 400°F (200°C). For glaze, beat egg with water and brush tops of the buns.

Bake 12 to 15 minutes or until nicely browned and instant-read thermometer inserted in center of roll registers at least 190°F (87.7°C).

Yield: 18 dinner rolls

Each with: 153 Calories; 5g Fat (25.7% calories from fat); 5g Protein; 25g Carbohydrate; 3g Dietary Fiber; 15mg Cholesterol; 143mg Sodium.

Onion Rye Dinner Rolls in the Bread Machine

This is similar to the made-by-hand recipe, but is more streamlined and makes a smaller batch of rolls. You simply add ingredients to the bread machine and start on the dough cycle, then form the rolls by hand.

1/4 cup (40 g) minced onion

2 tablespoons (28 ml) vegetable oil

1/4 cup (60 ml) 2 percent milk

1/4 cup (60 ml) lukewarm (110°F [43.3°C]) water

2 tablespoons (28 g) butter, melted

2 tablespoons (40 g) molasses

1 teaspoon (6 g) salt

1 tablespoon (8 g) unsweetened cocoa powder

2 cups (250 g) Hodgson Mill All-Purpose, Unbleached Naturally White Flour or Best For Bread Flour

1 cup (125 g) Hodgson Mill Stone Ground Whole Grain Rye Flour

1/4 cup (32.5 g) Hodgson Mill Wheat Germ, Untoasted

2 teaspoons (5.4 g) caraway seeds

1 package (5/16 ounce) or 2 1/2 teaspoons (10 g) Hodgson Mill Fast-Rise Yeast

FOR THE EGG GLAZE:

1 large egg

2 teaspoons (10 ml) water

Sauté onion in vegetable oil over medium-high heat until golden, about 10 minutes. Set aside to cool.

Place ingredients in bread pan according to manufacturer's directions. Select dough cycle and start the machine.

When cycle is complete, form dough into long rope about 1 1/2 to 2-inches (3.8 to 5-cm) wide. Cut into 1 1/2-inch (3.8-cm) pieces and shape into buns. Place 2 inches (5 cm) apart on oiled or parchment-lined baking sheet. Cover with towel and let rise in a warm place until doubled, about 1 hour.

Preheat oven to 400°F (200°C). For glaze, beat egg with water and brush tops of rolls.

Bake 12 to 15 minutes or until nicely browned.

Yield: 12 to 14 dinner rolls

Each with: 160 Calories; 5g Fat (25.8% calories from fat); 4g Protein; 27g Carbohydrate; 3g Dietary Fiber; 6mg Cholesterol; 201 mg Sodium.

Variation: Use finely minced green onion for the onion and add 1 teaspoon (5 g) ground white pepper for an even more savory roll.

 High-Fiber Onion Rye Buns

For a great ham or steak sandwich, the bun also has to be delicious, and this one is. There is just enough rye to make it interesting, and just enough all-purpose flour to make it soft.

1 cup (235 ml) 2 percent milk

2 tablespoons (40 g) honey

1 teaspoon (6 g) salt

3 tablespoons (42 g) butter

1 package ($^5/16$ ounce) or $2^1/2$ teaspoons (10 g) Hodgson Mill Active Dry Yeast

$^1/2$ cup (120 ml) lukewarm (110°F [43.3°C]) water

3 cups (375 g) Hodgson Mill All-Purpose, Unbleached Naturally White Flour

2 tablespoons (5.4 g) caraway seeds

6 tablespoons (60 g) minced onion

$^1/2$ cup (65 g) Hodgson Mill Wheat Germ, Untoasted

1 to $1^1/4$ cups (125 to 156.3 ml) Hodgson Mill Stone Ground Whole Grain Rye Flour

FOR THE GLAZE:

1 large egg

2 teaspoons (10 ml) water

Scald milk in saucepan over medium-high heat until bubbles form around the perimeter. Stir in honey, salt, and butter and set aside until warm (105°F to 115°F [43.3°C to 46°C]). Sprinkle yeast over water in bowl and set aside to proof until foamy, about 5 minutes.

Stir yeast into milk mixture. Add all-purpose flour and beat vigorously for 1 minute or until batter is very smooth. Beat in caraway seeds, onion, wheat germ, and enough rye flour so that the dough is firm enough to knead. Turn dough out onto floured surface and knead for 8 minutes by hand or in electric mixer fitted with dough hook attachment for about 5 minutes.

Place dough in large, oiled bowl and turn to coat. Cover and let rise in a warm place until doubled in bulk, about 1 hour.

Line 2 baking sheets with parchment paper. Punch dough down. Transfer dough to floured surface. Roll out dough with your hands into a long rope about 1 to 1 1/2 inches (3.8-cm) long. Cut into 18 pieces and shape into buns. Place buns on prepared baking sheets.

Preheat oven to 400°F (200°C). For glaze, beat the egg with water in bowl and brush tops of the buns. Bake 12 to 15 minutes or until nicely browned and instant-read thermometer inserted in center of bun registers 190°F (87.7°C).

Yield: 18 buns

Each with: 135 Calories; 3g Fat (17.2% calories from fat); 4g Protein; 25g Carbohydrate; 3g Dietary Fiber; 6mg Cholesterol; 145mg Sodium.

 ## *Easy Whole Wheat Refrigerator Rolls*

What's easy about these rolls? You make up the dough in a saucepan and keep the dough in the refrigerator for up to 3 days, then form and bake the rolls when you want. Minimal mess, minimal clean-up, and all on your own schedule!

1 1/2 cups (355 ml) 2 percent milk

2 packages (5/16 ounce each) or 5 teaspoons (20 g) Hodgson Mill
    Active Dry Yeast

1/4 cup (60 ml) warm (105°F to 115°F [43.3°C to 46°C] water

1/2 cup (1 stick [112 g]) butter, cut into pieces

1/2 cup (160 g) honey

2 large eggs, beaten

1 teaspoon (6 g) salt

3 cups (375 g) Hodgson Mill Stone Ground Whole Wheat Graham Flour

2 cups (250 g) Hodgson Mill All-Purpose, Unbleached Naturally White Flour

Scald milk in 4-quart saucepan over medium heat until bubbles form around the perimeter. Set aside to reach to 105°F to 115°F (43.3°C to 46°C). Sprinkle yeast in water in small bowl and set aside until foamy, about 5 minutes.

Beat in butter, honey, yeast, eggs, salt, and flours until dough is smooth. Cover with lid and refrigerate for up to 3 days.

When ready to bake, remove dough 3 or 4 hours before serving. Grease two 8 x x 2-inch (20 x 20 x 5-cm) square baking pans. Transfer dough to floured surface and knead lightly. Roll out to $^1/2$-inch (0.6-cm) thickness. Cut into 20 squares. Place in prepared pans. Cover and let rise in a warm place until doubled in bulk, about 2 hours.

Preheat oven to 375°F (190°C). Bake 12 to 15 minutes or until lightly browned and an instant-read thermometer inserted in center of roll registers 190°F (87.7°C).

Yield: 20 rolls

Variation: Brush rolls with melted butter before baking, if desired.

Each with: 185 Calories; 6g Fat (26.6% calories from fat); 5g Protein; 31 g Carbohydrate; 3g Dietary Fiber; 32mg Cholesterol; 169mg Sodium.

 ## Insta-Bake Pecan Rolls

Rich with butter, brown sugar, and pecans, these rolls can be served for breakfast, lunch, or dinner—but they can also serve as dessert. Leavened with baking powder, these rolls are rich and cake-like.

FOR THE TOPPING:

$^1/2$ cup (115 g) packed light or dark brown sugar

$^1/2$ cup (1 stick [112 g]) butter or margarine

$^1/4$ cup (55 g) pecan halves or crushed pecans

FOR THE DOUGH:

2 cups (250 g) Hodgson Mill Whole Wheat Insta-Bake Mix

$^2/3$ cup (160 ml) 2 percent milk

FOR THE FILLING:

2 tablespoons (28 g) butter or margarine, softened

$^1/4$ cup (60 g) packed light or dark brown sugar

1 teaspoon (2.3 g) ground cinnamon

Preheat oven to 425°F (220°C). Place brown sugar, butter, and pecans in bottom of 11 x 7 x $1^1/2$-inch (27.5 x 17.5 x 3.8-cm) baking pan. Place pan in oven until butter melts, about 5 minutes. Remove from oven and stir mixture together.

mix together baking mix with milk and beat by hand 20 strokes to
ugh. Transfer to floured surface, shape into ball, and knead 5 times. Pat
5 x 9-inch (37.5 x 22.5-cm) rectangle. Spread surface with butter and
n brown sugar and cinnamon. Roll up tightly, jelly-roll style, starting with
Pinch seams closed.

into 12 pieces. Place each piece in pan over topping, spiral side up, with
1/2 inch (1.2 cm) between rolls.

Bake 15 minutes or until golden brown. Invert pan onto serving platter to serve.
Leave pan over rolls for 30 seconds to let topping release, then remove pan.

Yield: 12 rolls

Each with: 228 Calories; 12g Fat (45.6% calories from fat); 3g Protein; 29g Carbohydrate; 2g Dietary
Fiber; 27mg Cholesterol; 255mg Sodium.

 ## *Whole Wheat, Soy, and Tofu Cinnamon Rolls*

With whole wheat, soy, and tofu, these cinnamon rolls can actually be good for you.
Cinnamon is a healing, comforting spice, while soy and tofu are a good source of
protein.

FOR THE DOUGH:

    3 cups (375 g) Hodgson Mill Stone Ground Whole Wheat Graham Flour
    1 cup (125 g) Hodgson Mill Soy Flour
    2 packages (5/16 ounce each) or 5 teaspoons (20 g) Hodgson Mill Active Dry Yeast
    1 1/4 tablespoons (16.3 g) granulated sugar
    1 teaspoon (6 g) salt
    4 ounces (100 g) firm tofu
    1 1/2 cups (295 ml) warm (105°F to 115°F [43.3°C to 46°C]) water

FOR THE FILLING:

    1/2 cup (115 g) packed light or dark brown sugar
    1 cup (145 g) raisins
    1 teaspoon (2.3 g) ground cinnamon

Stir together flours, yeast, sugar, and salt in large mixing bowl. In a small bowl,
mash tofu with a fork and whisk together with warm water. Make well in center of

dry ingredients and pour in water-tofu mixture. Stir ingredients well with spoon or fork so that flour is moistened.

Transfer dough to very lightly floured surface and knead 5 times by hand. Place dough in large, oiled bowl and turn to coat. Cover and let rise in a warm place until doubled in bulk, about 2 hours, or cover and refrigerate overnight.

Line baking sheet with parchment paper. Divide dough in half. On very lightly floured surface, roll each half to a $10^1/2$-inch (26.3-cm) square. Sprinkle with half of the brown sugar and raisins, leaving a $1/2$-inch (1.2-cm) perimeter. Sprinkle with cinnamon. Roll up tightly, jelly-roll style, starting with a long end. Pinch seam closed. With seam side down, slice each roll into 8 equal pieces. Place on prepared baking sheet with spiral side up. For single rolls, place about 3 inches (7.5 cm) apart on baking sheet; for pull-apart rolls, place about $1/2$ inch (1.2 cm) apart. Cover and let rise in a warm place about 45 minutes.

Preheat oven to 400°F (200°C). Bake 20 minutes, or until golden brown on edges and bottom. Transfer rolls to a wire rack to cool.

Yield: 16 rolls

Each with: 161 Calories; 1g Fat (3.8% calories from fat); 7g Protein; 35g Carbohydrate; 5g Dietary Fiber; 0mg Cholesterol; 138mg Sodium.

Add It: Make a glaze by whisking 1 cup (100 g) confectioners' sugar with 2 tablespoons (28 ml) 2 percent or soy milk and 1 teaspoon (5 ml) vanilla extract. Drizzle over cooled rolls.

Brown 'n Serve Rolls

Don't even think about buying those sad rolls from the grocery store when you can have these homemade, yeasty, whole grain beauties. By partially baking the rolls ahead of time, you can freeze these to make your own convenience bread.

2 packages ($5/16$ ounce each) or 5 teaspoons (20 g) Hodgson Mill
    Active Dry Yeast
$3/4$ cup (175 ml) warm (105°F to 115 °F [43.3°C to 46°C]) water
$1/3$ cup (66.6 g) sugar
1 teaspoon (6 g) salt
$3/4$ cup (175 ml) warm (105°F to 115°F [43.3°C to 46°C]) milk
$1/2$ cup (1 stick [112 g]) butter, cut into pieces and softened

3 large eggs, beaten

3 cups (375 g) Hodgson Mill Stone Ground Whole Wheat Graham Flour

2/3 cup (41.6 g) Hodgson Mill All-Purpose, Unbleached Naturally White Flour

Sprinkle yeast over water in large bowl. Set aside until foamy, about 5 minutes.

Beat in sugar, salt, milk, butter, and eggs by hand or with electric mixer, then whole wheat flour. Beat in enough all-purpose flour to make soft dough that doesn't cling to sides of the bowl. Cover and let rise in a warm place until doubled in bulk, about 1 hour.

Grease 24 muffin cups. Punch dough down, and spoon into prepared muffin cups, filling them two-thirds full. Cover and let rise in a warm place until doubled again, about 20 minutes.

Preheat oven to 250°F (120°C). Bake 25 minutes. Turn out onto wire racks to cool thoroughly. Wrap well and freeze for up to 3 months.

When rolls are ready for final baking, thaw and place on greased cookie sheet, then bake in a preheated 400°F (200°C) oven for 10 to 12 minutes.

Yield: 24 rolls

Each with: 121 Calories; 5g Fat (35.3% calories from fat); 3g Protein; 17g Carbohydrate; 2g Dietary Fiber; 35mg Cholesterol; 139mg Sodium.

 ## *Chive Rolls* (See photo on page 226.)

While the soup is simmering, whip up these light, moist, savory rolls. The Insta-Bake mix already has leavening and salt in it, so you can save time by not having to measure these ingredients. The recipe can also be easily doubled.

1 cup (125 g) Hodgson Mill Whole Wheat Insta-Bake Mix

3/4 cup (175 ml) 2 percent milk

3 tablespoons (42 g) good quality mayonnaise

2 tablespoons (6 g) snipped fresh chives

1/2 teaspoon (1.2 g) ground white pepper

Preheat oven to 350°F (180°C). Grease 6 muffin cups.

Whisk all ingredients together in bowl. Spoon dough into prepared muffin cups, filling them two-thirds full.

Bake 20 to 25 minutes, or until risen and lightly browned. Serve warm.

Yield: 6 rolls

Each with: 134 Calories; 7g Fat (44.7% calories from fat); 3g Protein; 16g Carbohydrate; 2g Dietary Fiber; 5mg Cholesterol; 199mg Sodium.

 ## *Farmhouse Rolls*

The same wonderful Parker House-style rolls that great-grandmother made on the farm can now be made an easier way. Using instant or bread machine yeast takes some of the guesswork out of making yeast rolls, as you don't have to "proof" the yeast in water first. Just stir it in with the dry ingredients. This old-fashioned egg bread dough is very versatile and forgiving of any treatment—it really doesn't matter if you knead it too much or not at all, and it can be refrigerated at any stage. It also makes wonderful cinnamon rolls or even tasty egg bread loaves, if you want to branch out later on.

$1^1/2$ cups (355 ml) boiling water

$2/3$ cup (148 g) vegetable shortening

2 large eggs, beaten

$1/2$ cup (100 g) sugar

1 teaspoon (6 g) salt

3 cups (375 g) Hodgson Mill All-Purpose, Unbleached Naturally White Flour

2 packages ($5/16$ ounce each) or 5 teaspoons (20 g) Hodgson Mill Fast-Rise Yeast

$1^1/2$ to 2 cups (192 to 250 g) Hodgson Mill Stone Ground Whole Grain White Whole Wheat Flour

4 tablespoons ($1/2$ stick [55 g]) unsalted butter, melted

In the bowl of electric mixer or large bowl, pour boiling water over shortening and let stand until lukewarm (90°F [32.2°C]).

Using paddle attachment or wooden spoon, beat eggs, sugar, salt, and 1 cup (125 g) all-purpose flour into the shortening mixture. Add yeast and beat again. Add enough of the remaining flours, $1/2$ cup (62.5 g) at a time and alternating between all-purpose and whole wheat flour, until dough is too stiff for beaters. Switch to the dough hook or turn the dough out onto a floured surface and knead in the rest of the flours until smooth and elastic, about 5 minutes.

Place dough in a large, oiled bowl and turn to coat. Cover and let rise in a warm place until doubled in bulk, about $1^1/2$ hours or in the refrigerator overnight.

Punch dough down and turn out onto a floured surface. Divide in half. Roll each half out to $^1/_2$-inch (1.3-cm) thickness. With a 3-inch (7.5-cm) biscuit cutter or a round cookie cutter, cut out 16 circles of dough. Gather scraps, re-roll, and cut again. Brush each circle of dough with melted butter and fold over to make a semicircle. Pinch closed. Place rolls with seams upright, touching, in ungreased cake pans, cover with plastic wrap, and let rise in a warm place again until doubled in bulk. (At this point, the unbaked rolls could be refrigerated for up to 24 hours, but be sure to let them rise in a warm place before baking.)

Preheat oven to 350°F (180°C). Bake 17 to 20 minutes, or until slightly browned. Serve warm.

Yield: 32 rolls

Each with: 124 Calories; 6g Fat (42.6% calories from fat); 2g Protein; 16g Carbohydrate; 1g Dietary Fiber; 16mg Cholesterol; 71 mg Sodium.

Variation: To make the dough with an automatic bread machine, add the ingredients to the bread pan following the manufacturer's directions. Select the dough cycle and start the machine. Stop the machine after first rise. Form dough into rolls, and proceed with rolling and baking steps.

Easy Butter Flake Wheat Rolls

If you're new to whole grain baking or making yeast rolls, try this easy recipe, which uses our whole grain mix.

   1 package (16 ounces [455 g]) Hodgson Mill Honey Whole Wheat Bread Mix
   6 tablespoons (85 g) butter, melted

Make dough according to package instructions and let rise in a warm place until doubled.

Roll dough into a $^1/_4$-inch (0.6-cm) thick rectangle. Brush dough with melted butter. Cut rectangle into strips $1^1/_2$-inch (3.8-cm) wide. Stack 5 strips, one on top of another, to make a pile of 5 strips. Repeat with remaining strips. Cut each pile into $1^1/_2$-inch (3.8-cm) blocks. Stick each block on end in muffin cup. Cover and let rise in a warm place until doubled in bulk, about 1 hour.

Preheat oven to 400°F (200°C). Bake 15 to 20 minutes or until the rolls are a rich golden color. Turn out rolls onto wire rack to cool slightly. Serve warm.

Yield: 12 rolls

Each with: 84 Calories; 3g Fat (27.3% calories from fat); 3g Protein; 13g Carbohydrate; 2g Dietary Fiber; 16mg Cholesterol; 157mg Sodium.

 Multi Grain Rolls

Cooking whole grains to soften them before adding them to bread dough is an ancient technique that still works well today. The utensil of choice for blending and stirring whole grain doughs like this one is a long-handled dough whisk, which looks a little like a Victorian wire carpet beater. A sturdy wooden spoon or the paddle attachment on a stand mixer also work well.

2 cups (470 ml) water
2 cups (250 g) Hodgson Mill Multi Grain Cereal with Flaxseed and Soy, uncooked
$^1/_2$ cup (1 stick [112 g]) butter, cut into pieces
3 cups (375 g) Hodgson Mill Stone Ground Whole Wheat Graham Flour
2 packages ($^5/_{16}$ ounce each) or 5 teaspoons (20 g) Hodgson Mill Fast-Rise Yeast
$^1/_2$ cup (65 g) nonfat dry milk
2 cups (470 ml) water
$^1/_3$ cup (115 g) honey
3 large eggs
1 tablespoon (18 g) salt
1 to 2 cups (125 to 250 g) Hodgson Mill All-Purpose,
    Unbleached Naturally White Flour

Bring water to a boil in a large saucepan. Stir in cereal and cook, stirring constantly, for 5 to 7 minutes or until cereal is soft. Remove from heat, stir in butter, and set aside.

Combine whole wheat flour, yeast, and dry milk in mixing bowl. Mix well.

Add water and honey to cooked cereal and let mixture cool to 120°F (48.9°C). Stir cereal mixture into ingredients in mixer and beat about 1 minute. Cover and let dough rest 10 minutes to make a sponge.

Stir in eggs and salt. Beat in all-purpose flour, 1 cup (125 g) at a time, until dough begins to make a ball, and pulls away from sides of bowl. Transfer dough to floured surface and knead by hand or in bowl with dough hook attachment until smooth and elastic, about 5 to 6 minutes. Dough should be pliable, smooth, and elastic, but not sticky.

Line 2 baking sheets with parchment paper. Lightly oil hands. Pinch off 1/4-cup (55-g) portions and roll into balls. Place close together, but not touching, on prepared baking sheets. Cover and let rise in a warm place until doubled in bulk, about 1 hour.

Preheat oven to 350°F (180°C). Bake 18 to 22 minutes until golden brown or until instant-read thermometer inserted in center registers at least 190°F (87.7°C).

Yield: 4 to 5 dozen large rolls

Each with: 199 Calories; 6g Fat (27.2% calories from fat); 6g Protein; 31 g Carbohydrate; 3g Dietary Fiber; 43mg Cholesterol; 409mg Sodium.

Note: Recipe may be halved. Extra rolls can be wrapped and frozen for up to 3 months.

Variation: Substitute 2 cups (250 g) Hodgson Mill Cracked Wheat, Oat Bran, or Bulgur Wheat with Soy Cereal for Multi Grain.

 ## *Whole Grain Maple Mustard Pan Rolls*

These interesting rolls—perfect for brunch or with a ham—get their flavor from authentic maple syrup and good Dijon mustard. Even the glaze gets in the act with maple syrup and mustard seeds. Use your instant-read thermometer to make sure milk mixture is the correct temperature before stirring in the yeast.

1 1/4 cups (295 ml) 2 percent milk

3/4 stick (6 tablespoons [85 g]) unsalted butter, cut into pieces

1/4 cup (60 ml) pure maple syrup

2 packages (5/16 ounce each) or 5 teaspoons (20 g) Hodgson Mill Active Dry Yeast

3 cups (375 g) Hodgson Mill Stone Ground Whole Grain White Whole Wheat Flour

3 cups (375 g) Hodgson Mill All-Purpose, Unbleached Naturally White Flour

1 tablespoon (18 g) salt

1 large whole egg

1 large egg yolk

1/2 cup (125 g) whole-grain or coarse-grained Dijon mustard

FOR THE GLAZE:

    2 tablespoons (28 g) unsalted butter, melted and cooled

    1 tablespoon (15 ml) pure maple syrup

    1 large egg, beaten lightly

    1 teaspoon (3.7 g) mustard seeds for sprinkling

In a saucepan over medium heat, heat milk, butter, and syrup just until warm (about 105°F [40.5°C]) and butter begins to melt. Remove from heat, stir in yeast, and set aside until foamy, about 5 minutes.

In bowl of electric mixer or a large bowl if kneading by hand, whisk flours and salt together. In a small bowl, whisk whole egg, yolk, and mustard together.

With dough hook of electric mixer or dough whisk (if whisking by hand), stir milk mixture and egg mixture into flour mixture to form a sticky dough. Knead by hand about 15 minutes or dough hook about 5 minutes, until dough is smooth and elastic (it should be soft). Place dough in large, oiled bowl and turn to coat. Cover and let rise in a warm place until doubled in bulk, about 1 hour.

For glaze, stir together butter, syrup, and egg with fork in small bowl. Grease a 13 x 9 x 2-inch (32.5 x 22.5 x 5-cm) baking pan. Punch down dough and divide into 20 pieces. Form each piece into smooth ball and place in pan. Brush rolls with about half of glaze and let rise in a warm place, covered loosely with plastic wrap, 1 hour, or until doubled in bulk.

Preheat oven to 400°F (200°C). Brush rolls with remaining glaze and sprinkle with seeds. Bake rolls in middle of oven 20 minutes, or until golden brown, and cool in pan on a rack 20 minutes.

Yield: 20 rolls

Each with: 220 Calories; 7g Fat (25.8% calories from fat); 5g Protein; 38g Carbohydrate; 3g Dietary Fiber; 19mg Cholesterol; 133mg Sodium.

 Almond-Glazed Banana Blueberry Sweet Rolls

With the sweet flavor of banana in the dough and a hint of almond in the glaze, these rolls just might replace the traditional cinnamon rolls on your family's must-have-for-breakfast list! You don't have to mention the benefits of whole grains or the antioxidants in the blueberries, but you know they're there.

FOR THE DOUGH:

1 cup (235 ml) 2 percent milk

4 tablespoons ($1/2$ stick [55 g]) butter

2 packages ($5/16$ ounce each) or 5 teaspoons (20 g) Hodgson Mill
Active Dry Yeast

$1/2$ cup (120 ml) warm (105°F to 115°F [40.5°C to 46°C]) water

$1/4$ cup (50 g) sugar

$1/2$ cup (115 g) sour cream, regular or light

1 teaspoon (6 g) salt

1 cup (125 g) Hodgson Mill Oat Bran Hot Cereal, uncooked

1 large egg

$1/2$ cup (112.5 g) mashed banana (1 medium)

3 cups (375 g) Hodgson Mill All-Purpose, Unbleached Naturally White Flour

$1^1/2$ cups (187.5 g) Hodgson Mill Stone Ground Whole Grain White Whole Wheat
Flour

FOR THE FILLING:

$1/2$ cup (115 g) packed light or dark brown sugar

1 teaspoon (2.3 g) ground cinnamon

$1/2$ cup (75 g) sliced almonds

$1/2$ cup (75 g) Hodgson Mill Dried Wild Blueberries

2 tablespoons (28 g) butter, melted

FOR THE GLAZE:

1 cup (100 g) confectioners' sugar

7 teaspoons (35 ml) 2 percent milk

$1/4$ teaspoon (0.6 ml) almond extract

For dough, heat milk and butter in saucepan over medium heat until mixture reaches 135°F (57.2°C). Sprinkle yeast over warm water in small bowl and set aside until foamy, about 5 minutes.

Pour milk mixture into a large mixing bowl and add sugar, sour cream, salt, and oat bran hot cereal. Let mixture sit for 5 minutes to soften cereal.

Add egg, mashed banana, and yeast mixture to oat bran mixture and mix well with electric mixer or dough whisk. Add both flours and blend to make soft dough. Turn onto lightly floured surface and knead until smooth, 10 minutes by hand or 4 minutes in an electric mixer with a fitted dough hook attachment. Place dough in oiled bowl, turning once to coat. Cover and let rise in a warm place until doubled in bulk, about 1 hour.

For filling, combine brown sugar, cinnamon, sliced almonds, and blueberries in bowl. Punch down dough and turn out onto lightly floured surface. Divide dough in half and let rest for 10 minutes.

Line 2 baking sheets with parchment paper. Roll out each dough half to 15 x 10-inch (37.5 x 25-cm) rectangle. Brush surface of each dough with half of melted butter and sprinkle with half of filling. Roll up, jelly-roll style, starting with a long side. Pinch edges to seal. Cut roll in 1 to 1^1/2-inch (2.5 to 3.8-cm) slices. Place slices, spiral side up, on prepared baking sheets. Cover and let rise in warm place until almost doubled in bulk, about 45 minutes.

Preheat oven to 375°F (190°C). Bake 15 minutes or until golden brown. Transfer to wire racks to cool.

For glaze, combine ingredients and mix well. Drizzle glaze over warm rolls.

Yield: 24 to 30 rolls

Each with: 220 Calories; 7g Fat (25.8% calories from fat); 5g Protein; 38g Carbohydrate; 3g Dietary Fiber; 19mg Cholesterol; 133mg Sodium.

 ## *Savory Herb and Oat Bran Rolls*

The oats add moisture and the herbs add a savory tang to these yeasty rolls.

1^1/2 cups (355 ml) skim milk

1^1/2 cups (187.5 g) Hodgson Mill Oat Bran Hot Cereal, uncooked

1^1/2 teaspoons (9 g) salt

^{1}/2 cup (100 g) sugar

3 tablespoons (42 g) olive oil

2 packages (^{5}/16 ounce each) or 5 teaspoons (20 g) Hodgson Mill Active Dry Yeast

^{1}/2 cup warm (105°F to 115°F [40.5°C to 46°C]) water

5^1/2 cups (687.5 g) Hodgson Mill 50/50 Flour

1 large egg

1 tablespoon (14 g) dried herb blend of your choice

^{1}/2 cup (100 g) grated Asiago or Parmesan cheese

FOR THE GLAZE:

   1 large egg, beaten

Scald milk in large saucepan over medium-high heat until bubbles form around the perimeter. Pour milk into large bowl and stir in cereal, salt, sugar, and olive oil. Let cool to 105°F to 115°F (40.5°C to 46°C). Sprinkle yeast over warm water in bowl and set aside until foamy, about 5 minutes.

Stir 2 cups (250 g) flour into milk mixture and mix well by hand or with electric mixer. Beat in egg and yeast mixture, then dried herbs and cheese. Add enough of remaining flour to make soft dough. Place dough in large, oiled bowl, turning once to coat. Cover and let rise in a warm place until doubled in bulk, about 1 hour.

Punch down dough, cover, and let rise in a warm place for second time for 1 hour.

Turn dough onto lightly floured surface. Shape into ball, cover, and let rest 10 minutes.

Preheat oven to 375°F (190°C). Line 2 baking sheets with parchment paper. Divide ball into four portions. Then cut each portion into 6 pieces. Shape into smooth balls. Place balls of dough on prepared baking sheet, about 2 inches (5 cm) apart. Snip balls with kitchen shears almost to center in 3 places to make cloverleaf rolls. Brush with egg for glaze. Bake 15 to 20 minutes, until rolls are golden brown.

Yield: 24 rolls

Each with: 174 Calories; 3g Fat (16.7% calories from fat); 7g Protein; 30g Carbohydrate; 3g Dietary Fiber; 17mg Cholesterol; 178mg Sodium.

 Honey White Whole Wheat Rolls

With white whole wheat and all-purpose flours, milk, butter, and honey, these rolls are light and feathery. Serve warm with your best butter and preserves. You can wrap and freeze extra rolls for up to 3 months.

   1 cup (235 ml) 2 percent milk
   1/4 cup (50 g) honey
   2 teaspoons (12 g) salt
   1/2 cup (1 stick [112 g]) butter
   2 packages (5/16 ounce each) or 5 teaspoons (20 g) Hodgson Mill Active Dry Yeast
   1/2 cup (120 ml) warm (105°F to 115°F [40.5°C to 46°C]) water
   2 cups (250 g) Hodgson Mill Stone Ground Whole Grain White Whole Wheat Flour

3 large eggs, beaten

3 to 3¹/2 cups (375 to 437.5 g) Hodgson Mill All-Purpose, Unbleached Naturally White Flour

Scald milk in large saucepan over medium-high heat until bubbles form around the perimeter. Pour milk into large bowl and stir in honey, salt, and butter. Let cool to 105°F to 115°F (40.5°C to 46°C). Sprinkle yeast over warm water in bowl and set aside until foamy, about 5 minutes.

Stir white whole wheat flour into milk mixture and blend well by hand with dough whisk or with electric mixer. Stir in yeast mixture and eggs. Add enough all-purpose flour to make soft dough. Transfer dough to floured surface. Knead dough until smooth and satiny, 10 minutes by hand or 5 minutes in an electric mixer fitted with dough hook attachment. Place dough in large, oiled bowl, turning once to coat. Cover and let rise in warm place until doubled, about 2 hours.

Turn dough onto lightly floured surface and roll into 1-inch (2.5-cm) balls and place on prepared baking sheets. Cover and let rise in warm place until doubled in bulk, about 1 hour.

Preheat oven to 375°F (190°C). Bake 10 minutes or until rolls are lightly browned. Turn out onto wire racks to cool.

Yield: 24 rolls

Each with: 144 Calories; 5g Fat (28.7% calories from fat); 4g Protein; 22g Carbohydrate; 2g Dietary Fiber; 34mg Cholesterol; 229mg Sodium.

 ## *Whole Wheat Buttermilk Crescent Rolls*

A mixture of flours and tangy buttermilk give these rolls a wonderful texture and flavor. Wrap and freeze extras for up to 3 months.

2 cups (470 ml) buttermilk or 2 percent milk soured with vinegar or lemon juice (see note)

¹/2 cup (1 stick [112 g]) butter, cut into pieces

1 teaspoon (6 g) salt

¹/2 cup (100 g) sugar

1 cup (125 g) Hodgson Mill Oat Bran Hot Cereal, uncooked

¹/2 teaspoon (0.7 g) baking soda

2 packages (⁵/16 ounce each) or 5 teaspoons (20 g) Hodgson Mill Active Dry Yeast

$^1/_2$ cup warm (105°F to 115°F [40.5°C to 46°C]) water

2 cups (250 g) Hodgson Mill Stone Ground Whole Wheat Graham Flour

1 large egg

2 cups (250 g) Hodgson Mill Best For Bread Flour

$2^1/_2$ cups (312.5 g) Hodgson Mill Naturally White, Unbleached,
    All-Purpose Flour

Heat buttermilk and butter in large saucepan over medium heat until butter melts (buttermilk may curdle). Add salt, sugar, cereal, and baking soda to the buttermilk mixture and let stand 5 minutes to soften cereal. Sprinkle yeast over warm water in bowl and set aside until foamy, about 5 minutes.

Transfer buttermilk mixture to large bowl. Stir in 2 cups (250 g) whole wheat flour by hand or with electric mixer. Pour in yeast mixture and egg and mix thoroughly. Add enough bread and all-purpose flours to make soft dough. Transfer dough to floured surface. Knead dough until smooth and satiny, 10 minutes by hand or 4 minutes in an electric mixer fitted with dough hook attachment. Place dough in large, oiled bowl, turning once to coat. Cover and let rise in warm place until doubled, about 1 hour.

Punch dough down. Turn dough onto lightly floured surface and divide into 4 pieces. Let rest 5 minutes.

Line 2 baking sheets with parchment paper. Roll each piece into 9-inch (22.5-cm) circle. Brush each circle with melted butter and cut into 8 wedges with sharp knife or pizza wheel. Starting with large end, roll up each wedge into crescent shape and place on prepared baking sheets, point side down.

Preheat oven to 375°F (190°C). Bake 15 minutes or until rolls are lightly browned. Turn out onto wire racks to cool.

Yield: 32 rolls

Each with: 144 Calories; 4g Fat (21.7% calories from fat); 4g Protein; 25g Carbohydrate; 2g Dietary Fiber; 14mg Cholesterol; 135mg Sodium.

Note: If you don't have buttermilk, substitute by pouring 4 teaspoons (20 ml) vinegar or lemon juice in a 2-cup (470-ml) measure. Fill to top with milk and let sit for 2 minutes, then use in recipe.

2

Automatic Bread
Machine Breads

Baking whole grain breads in an automatic bread machine is the easiest way to achieve a perfect result every time. Even accomplished bread bakers agree that mixing and kneading the dough on the dough cycle of the bread machine—even if you end up baking the loaf in the oven—gives you a superior product. This is because the bread machine mixes the dough thoroughly and systematically, usually better than you can do by hand. The whole wheat cycle is greater for heavier doughs, giving an extra knead and rising time.

You can convert most handmade bread recipes for use in a bread machine by following what bread machine manufacturers recommend: Place the wet ingredients in the bread pan first, followed by the flours and the other dry ingredients, then add Fast-Rise Yeast or the bread machine yeast last. Bread machine yeast is specially formulated so that it doesn't need to proof in water until foamy, as active dry yeast does, before use in a bread recipe. (Alternatively, you can also use bread machine yeast in handmade breads. Simply eliminate the proofing step and mix the bread machine yeast in with the flours, but add the amount of water needed for proofing to the recipe.) If mixture seems dry at the beginning of cycle, add 1 or 2 tablespoons of additional liquid. Hodgson Mill bread mixes and whole grain flours are not intended for rapid cycle use. Most recipes use whole wheat or basic cycle.

If your bread machine doesn't bake a regular-shaped loaf but that's what you'd like, then use the Variation for each recipe. Select the dough cycle on your machine that will mix, then knead the dough and let it rise until doubled in bulk in the bread pan. When the cycle is complete, punch down, work out any air bubbles (a rolling pin works great), and form the dough into a loaf. Place it in the prepared pan, allow second rise to top of pan and bake the loaf in the oven.

Potato Cheese Bread

This moist, tender bread is comfort food at its finest.

  1^1/2 cup (355 ml) warm (105°F to 115°F [40.5°C to 46°C]) water

  3 tablespoons (45 ml) vegetable oil, such as canola

  ^{1}/2 cup (28 g) instant dry potato flakes

  2 teaspoons (12 g) salt

  1 tablespoon (13 g) sugar

  ^{1}/2 cup (50 g) grated cheese, such as sharp Cheddar, Parmesan, or Asiago

  2 cups (250 g) Hodgson Mill Organic Stone Ground Whole Grain Whole Wheat
    Graham Flour

  2 cups (250 g) Hodgson Mill Best For Bread Flour

  4 teaspoons (12 g) Hodgson Mill Vital Wheat Gluten

  1 package (^{5}/16 ounce) or 2^1/2 teaspoons (10 g) Hodgson Mill
    Active Dry Yeast

Place ingredients in bread pan according to manufacturer's instructions. Select whole wheat cycle and start the machine.

Yield: One 2-pound (910-g) loaf

Each with: 1565 Calories; 43g Fat (23.8% calories from fat); 52g Protein; 258g Carbohydrate; 18g Dietary Fiber; 0mg Cholesterol; 4340mg Sodium.

Variation: Set machine on dough cycle. When cycle is complete, form dough into a loaf and place in greased 9 x 5 x 3-inch (22.5 x 12.5 x 7.5-cm) pan. Allow second rise to top of pan and bake in 350°F (180°C) oven for 35 to 40 minutes or until instant-read thermometer inserted in center registers at least 190°F (87.7°C). Turn out onto wire rack to cool.

 Gluten-Free Herb and Olive Loaf

This is a wonderful, savory loaf. The pumpkin adds moisture and a golden color, but the true flavor stars of this bread are the rosemary and olive. This bread rises high and bakes to a dark golden brown, with a mellow flavor and tender crumb.

  3 large eggs or equivalent egg substitute

  1 teaspoon (5 ml) cider vinegar

  3 tablespoons (45 ml) olive oil

  ^{1}/2 cup (112.5 g) canned pumpkin (not pumpkin pie filling)

1 1/3 cups (315 ml) water

1 cup (125 g) Hodgson Mill Whole Grain Multi Purpose Baking Mix

1 cup (125 g) Hodgson Mill Stone Ground Whole Grain Brown Rice Flour

1 cup (130 g) tapioca flour or potato starch

1/2 cup (65 g) Hodgson Mill Pure Corn Starch

4 teaspoons (28 g) xanthan gum

3 tablespoons (45 g) packed light or dark brown sugar

1 teaspoon (6 g) salt

2 teaspoons (2.4 g) dried rosemary

1 cup (100 g) pitted kalamata olives, finely chopped

1/2 cup (50 g) grated Parmesan, Asiago, or Pecorino Romano cheese or grated soy-based cheese

1 package (5/16 ounce) or 2 1/2 teaspoons (10 g) Hodgson Mill Fast-Rise Yeast

Whisk eggs, vinegar, and olive oil together in large bowl. Whisk in pumpkin and water and pour into bread pan. Start machine on dough cycle. Add baking mix, rice flour, potato and corn starch, xanthan gum, brown sugar, and salt. Add rosemary, olives, and cheese. Add yeast.

When cycle is complete, stop machine, then turn to bake cycle. Alternatively, carefully spoon dough into greased 9 x 5 x 3-inch (22.5 x 12.5 x 7.5-cm) loaf pan and smooth top with spatula. Allow second rise to top of pan and bake in 350°F (180°C) oven for 45 to 50 minutes or until instant-read thermometer inserted in center registers at least 190°F (87.7°C). Turn out onto wire rack to cool.

Yield: One 1-pound (455-g) loaf

Each with: 2892 Calories; 105g Fat (31.1% calories from fat); 65g Protein; 457g Carbohydrate; 21 g Dietary Fiber; 592mg Cholesterol; 4668mg Sodium.

 Gluten-Free Whole Grain White Bread

Made with a combination of soy, garbanzo bean (chickpea), millet, and brown rice flours, as well as potato and corn starch, this bread rises high and bakes to a golden brown, with a mellow flavor and tender crumb.

3 large eggs or equivalent egg substitute

1 teaspoon (5 ml) cider vinegar

3 tablespoons (45 ml) olive oil

1/2 cup (125 g) unsweetened applesauce

1^1/3 cups (315 ml) warm (105°F to 115°F [40.5°C to 46° C]) water

1 cup (125 g) Hodgson Mill Whole Grain Multi Purpose Baking Mix

1 cup (125 g) Hodgson Mill Stone Ground Whole Grain Brown Rice Flour

1 cup (130 g) tapioca flour or potato starch

^{1}/2 cup (65 g) Hodgson Mill Pure Corn Starch

4 teaspoons (28 g) xanthan gum

3 tablespoons (45 g) packed light or dark brown sugar

^{1}/2 teaspoon (3 g) salt

1 package (^{5}/16 ounce) or 2^1/2 teaspoons (10 g) Hodgson Mill
   Fast-Rise Yeast

Whisk eggs, vinegar, and olive oil together in large bowl. Whisk in applesauce and water and pour into bread pan. Start machine on dough cycle. Add baking mix, rice flour, potato and corn starch, xanthan gum, brown sugar, and salt. Add yeast.

When cycle is complete, stop machine, then turn to bake cycle. Alternatively, carefully spoon dough into greased 9 x 5 x 3-inch (22.5 x 12.5 x 7.5-cm) loaf pan and smooth top with spatula. Allow second rise to top of pan and bake in 350°F (180°C) oven for 45 to 50 minutes or until instant-read thermometer inserted in center registers at least 190°F (87.7°C). Turn out onto wire rack to cool.

Yield: One 1-pound (455-g) loaf

Each with: 2448 Calories; 66g Fat (22.9% calories from fat); 48g Protein; 452g Carbohydrate; 18g Dietary Fiber; 561mg Cholesterol; 1260mg Sodium.

Note: To make this recipe dairy- and egg-free, use vegetable oil and egg substitute.

White Whole Wheat and Cornbread

This bread, which uses sugar in place of molasses, is a modern version of anadama bread, a delicious loaf that originated in New England colonial days. Its hearty flavor and texture makes great sandwiches and toast. The dough will be more batter-like than most bread doughs.

3 tablespoons (45 ml) vegetable oil, such as canola

1 cup (235 ml) 2 percent milk

3/4 cup (175 ml) warm (105°F to 115°F [40.5°C to 46°C]) water

1 large egg

1 1/2 teaspoons (9 g) salt

3 tablespoons (39 g) sugar

2 1/2 cups (312.5 g) Hodgson Mill Best For Bread Flour

1 cup (125 g) Hodgson Mill Stone Ground Whole Grain White Whole Wheat Flour

1/2 cup (70 g) Hodgson Mill Stone Ground Whole Grain Yellow Corn Meal, Plain

1 package (5/16 ounce) or 2 1/2 teaspoons (10 g) Hodgson Mill Fast-Rise Yeast

Place ingredients in bread pan according to manufacturer's instructions. Select whole wheat cycle and start the machine.

Yield: One 1 1/2-pound (682.5-g) loaf

Each with: 2318 Calories; 54g Fat (20.2% calories from fat); 79g Protein; 402g Carbohydrate; 29g Dietary Fiber; 205mg Cholesterol; 3430mg Sodium.

Variation: Set machine on dough cycle. When cycle is complete, form dough into a loaf and place in greased 9 x 5 x 3-inch (22.5 x 12.5 x 7.5-cm) pan. Allow second rise to top of pan and bake in 350°F (180°C) oven for 42 to 45 minutes or until instant-read thermometer inserted in center registers at least 190°F (87.7°C). Turn out onto wire rack to cool.

 Golden Flax Bread with White Whole Wheat

Milled flax seed adds omega-3s to this delicious bread.

1 cup (235 ml) warm (105°F to 115°F [40.5°C to 46°C]) water

2 tablespoons (28 g) butter

3 tablespoons (60 g) molasses

1 teaspoon (6 g) salt

2 tablespoons (14 g) Hodgson Mill Milled Flax Seed

1 tablespoon (21 g) Hodgson Mill Vital Wheat Gluten, optional

1 cup (125 g) Hodgson Mill Stone Ground Whole Grain White Whole Wheat Flour

1 1/2 cups (187.5 g) Hodgson Mill Best For Bread Flour

1 1/2 tablespoons (12 g) nonfat dry milk

1 1/2 teaspoons (6 g) Hodgson Mill Fast-Rise Yeast

Place ingredients in bread pan according to manufacturer's instructions. Select basic or whole wheat cycle with a light or medium color setting and start the machine.

Yield: One 1^1/2-pound (682.5-g) loaf

Each with: 2135 Calories; 30g Fat (12.5% calories from fat); 117g Protein; 362g Carbohydrate; 24g Dietary Fiber; 97mg Cholesterol; 3389mg Sodium.

Variation: Start the bread on the dough cycle. Spoon the dough into greased 9 x 5 x 3-inch (22.5 x 12.5 x 7.5-cm) loaf pan. Allow second rise to top of pan and bake at 350°F (180°C) for 42 to 45 minutes or until an instant-read thermometer inserted in the center registers at least 190°F (87.7°C). Turn out onto wire rack to cool.

 ## *Olive and Roasted Red Pepper Loaf*

Enjoy slices of this savory loaf toasted or brushed with olive oil and sizzled on the grill over charcoal.

   1 cup (235 ml) warm (105°F to 115°F [40.5°C to 46°C]) water

   1 tablespoon (15 ml) vegetable oil, such as canola

   1 teaspoon (6 g) salt

   3 tablespoons (24 g) nonfat dry milk

   1 tablespoon (13 g) sugar

   3 tablespoons (34 g) drained, diced red bell peppers or pimentos

   2 tablespoons (12.5 g) sliced, pitted ripe olives, drained

   1 cup (125 g) Hodgson Mill Best For Bread Flour

   2 cups (250 g) Hodgson Mill Stone Ground Whole Grain White Whole Wheat Flour

   1 package (^{5}/16 ounce) or 2^1/2 teaspoons (10 g) Hodgson Mill Fast-Rise Yeast

Place ingredients in bread pan according to manufacturer's instructions. Select whole wheat cycle and start the machine.

Yield: One 1^1/2-pound (682.5-g) loaf

Each with: 1506 Calories; 20g Fat (11.5% calories from fat); 60g Protein; 287g Carbohydrate; 30g Dietary Fiber; 4mg Cholesterol; 2454mg Sodium.

Variation: Set machine on dough cycle. When cycle is complete, form dough into a loaf and place in greased 9 x 5 x 3-inch (22.5 x 12.5 x 7.5-cm) pan. Allow second rise to top of pan and bake in 350°F (180°C) oven for 42 to 45 minutes or until instant-read thermometer inserted in center registers at least 190°F (87.7°C). Turn out onto wire rack to cool.

Honey Whole Wheat Cinnamon Raisin Bread

> 1 cup (220 ml) warm (105°F to 115°F [40.5°C to 46°C]) water
> 1 box (16 ounces [455 g]) Hodgson Mill Honey Whole Wheat Bread Mix
> 1 teaspoon (2.3 g) ground cinnamon
> 3 tablespoons (45 g) packed light or dark brown sugar
> 2 tablespoons (28 g) butter, in pieces, or (28 ml) vegetable oil, such as canola
> Yeast packet from bread mix

Place ingredients in bread pan according to manufacturer's directions. Select whole wheat setting and start the machine.

Yield: One 1½-pound (682.5-g) loaf

Variation: Set machine on dough cycle. When cycle is complete, form dough into a loaf and place in greased 9 x 5 x 3-inch (22.5 x 12.5 x 7.5-cm) pan. Allow second rise to top of pan and bake in 350°F (180°C) oven for 42 to 45 minutes or until instant-read thermometer inserted in center registers at least 190°F (87.7°C). Turn out onto wire rack to cool.

Each with: 2039 Calories; 30g Fat (13.8% calories from fat); 72g Protein; 348g Carbohydrate; 30g Dietary Fiber; 62mg Cholesterol; 2457mg Sodium.

Onion and Black Pepper Bread

Easy additions like onion and black pepper make this bread even more savory. It's great to use for hors d'oeuvres or with Brie for a gourmet grilled cheese.

> 1 cup (235 ml) warm (105°F to 115°F [40.5°C to 46°C]) water
> 1 tablespoon (14 g) butter, softened, or (15 ml) vegetable oil, such as canola
> 1 teaspoon (6 g) salt
> 1½ cups (187.5 g) Hodgson Mill Best For Bread Flour
> 1½ cups (187.5 g) Hodgson Mill Stone Ground Whole Grain White Whole Wheat
>   or 50/50 Flour
> 1 tablespoon (8 g) nonfat dry milk

1 tablespoon (13 g) sugar

1^1/2 teaspoons (4.5 g) minced, dry onions

^{3}/4 teaspoon (1.5 g) ground black pepper

^{1}/4 teaspoon (0.8 g) garlic powder

2 teaspoons (8 g) Hodgson Mill Fast-Rise Yeast

Place ingredients in bread pan according to manufacturer's instructions. Select whole wheat cycle and start the machine.

Yield: One 1^1/2-pound (682.5-g) loaf

Each with: 1418 Calories; 15g Fat (8.9% calories from fat); 55g Protein; 282g Carbohydrate; 26g Dietary Fiber; 33mg Cholesterol; 2327mg Sodium.

Variation: You can easily make this bread in smaller, cylindrical loaves that are perfect for cocktail or bridge party fare. Heavily grease four 10^3/4-ounce (300-g) clean empty soup cans or two 8^1/4 x 3^1/2-inch (18.1 x 8.8-cm) tin bread molds, opened at only one end. Set machine on dough cycle. When the cycle is complete, divide dough into four or two portions. Place in greased molds. Set aside to rise until dough is within 1 inch (2.5 cm) of top of cans or molds, about 30 minutes. Bake in 375°F (190°C) oven for 30 to 35 minutes or until instant-read thermometer inserted in center registers at least 190°F (87.7°C). Turn out onto wire rack to cool. Slice into rounds to serve.

 Buckwheat and Banana·Bread (See photo on page 227.)

In this recipe, mashed banana adds smooth texture and moisture without the sweet flavor of a quick bread. Hearty yet possessing a tender crumb, this bread is delicious for toast or sandwiches.

1^1/4 cups (295 ml) warm (105°F to 115°F [40.5°C to 46°C]) water

3 tablespoons (24 g) nonfat dry milk

1^1/2 teaspoons (9 g) salt

1^1/2 tablespoons (25 ml) vegetable oil, such as canola

1^1/2 tablespoons (30 g) honey

^{1}/2 cup (112.5 g) mashed banana (about 1 medium)

^{3}/4 cup (93.7 g) Hodgson Mill Stone Ground Whole Grain Buckwheat Flour

1^1/2 cups (187.5 g) Hodgson Mill Stone Ground Whole Wheat Graham, 50/50, or White Whole Wheat Flour

2 cups (250 g) Hodgson Mill Best For Bread Flour

1/3 cup (48.3 g) raisins, optional

1 package (5/16 ounce) or 2 1/2 teaspoons (10 g) Hodgson Mill Fast-Rise Yeast

Place ingredients in bread pan according to manufacturer's instructions. Select whole wheat and start the machine.

Yield: One 1 1/2-pound (682.5-g) loaf

Each with: 2212 Calories; 14g Fat (5.3% calories from fat); 70g Protein; 480g Carbohydrate; 47g Dietary Fiber; 4mg Cholesterol; 9770mg Sodium.

Variation: Set machine on dough cycle. When cycle is complete, form dough into a loaf and place in greased 9 x 5 x 3-inch (22.5 x 12.5 x 7.5-cm) pan. Allow second rise to top of pan and bake in 350°F (180°C) oven for 35 to 40 minutes or until instant-read thermometer inserted in center registers at least 190°F (87.7°C).

 ## *Gluten-Free Buckwheat and Banana Bread*

Made with naturally gluten-free buckwheat flour, this loaf stays moist with the addition of banana.

3 large eggs or equivalent egg substitute

1 teaspoon (5 ml) cider vinegar

3 tablespoons (45 ml) vegetable oil, such as canola

1/2 cup (112.5 g) mashed banana (about 1 medium)

1 1/3 cups (315 ml) warm (105°F to 115°F [40.5°C to 46°C]) water

1 cup (125 g) Hodgson Mill Stone Ground Whole Grain Buckwheat Flour

1 cup (125 g) Hodgson Mill Stone Ground Whole Grain Brown Rice Flour

1 cup (130 g) tapioca flour or potato starch

1/2 cup (65 g) Hodgson Mill Pure Corn Starch

4 teaspoons (28 g) xanthan gum

3 tablespoons (45 g) packed light or dark brown sugar

1 1/2 teaspoons (9 g) salt

1 package (5/16 ounce) or 2 1/2 teaspoons (10 g) Hodgson Mill Fast-Rise Yeast

Whisk eggs, vinegar, and vegetable oil together in large bowl. Whisk in mashed banana and water and pour into bread pan. Start machine on dough cycle. Add flours, potato and corn starch, xanthan gum, brown sugar, and salt. Add yeast.

When cycle is complete, stop machine, then turn to bake cycle. Alternatively, carefully spoon dough into greased 9 x 5 x 3-inch (22.5 x 12.5 x 7.5-cm) loaf pan and smooth top with spatula. Bake in 350°F (180°C) oven for 45 to 50 minutes or until instant-read thermometer inserted in center registers at least 190°F (87.7°C). Turn out onto wire rack to cool.

Yield: One 1-pound (455-g) loaf

Each with: 2502 Calories; 63g Fat (21.8% calories from fat); 41g Protein; 464g Carbohydrate; 20g Dietary Fiber; 561mg Cholesterol; 3391mg Sodium.

Note: To make this recipe dairy- and egg-free, use egg substitute and vegetable oil.

 ## *Yeasted Cornbread*

With corn meal for texture, this golden bread makes fabulous morning toast.

> 3^1/2 cups (427.5 g) Hodgson Mill Best For Bread Flour
> ^{1}/2 cup (70 g) Hodgson Mill Stone Ground Whole Grain Yellow Corn Meal, Plain
> 1 teaspoon (6 g) salt
> 3 tablespoons (42 g) sugar
> 3 tablespoons (45 ml) vegetable oil, such as canola or shortening
> 1 cup (235 ml) 2 percent milk
> ^{1}/2 cup (120 ml) warm (105°F to 115°F [40.5°C to 46°C]) water
> 1 large egg
> 1 package (^{5}/16 ounce) or 2^1/2 teaspoons (10 g) Hodgson Mill
>   Fast-Rise Yeast

Place ingredients in bread pan according to manufacturer's instructions. Select basic/white bread cycle and start the machine.

Yield: One 1^1/2-pound (682.5-g) loaf

Each with: 2318 Calories; 52g Fat (19.4% calories from fat); 79g Protein; 406g Carbohydrate; 21 g Dietary Fiber; 205mg Cholesterol; 2383mg Sodium.

Variation: Set machine on dough cycle. When cycle is complete, form dough into a loaf and place in greased 9 x 5 x 3-inch (22.5 x 12.5 x 7.5-cm) pan. Allow second rise to top of pan and bake in 350°F (180°C) oven for 35 to 40 minutes or until instant-read thermometer inserted in center registers at least 190°F (87.7°C). Turn out onto wire rack to cool.

Gluten-Free Yeasted Cornbread

Moist and delicious with just the right texture, this bread makes wonderful morning toast.

 3 large eggs or equivalent egg substitute
 1 teaspoon (5 ml) cider vinegar
 3 tablespoons (45 ml) vegetable oil, such as canola
 $1/2$ cup (112.5 g) canned pumpkin (not pumpkin pie filling)
 $1^1/3$ cups (315 ml) warm (105°F to 115°F [40.5°C to 46°C]) water
 1 cup (140 g) Hodgson Mill Stone Ground Whole Grain Yellow Corn Meal, Plain
 1 cup (125 g) Hodgson Mill Stone Ground Whole Grain Brown Rice Flour
 1 cup (130 g) tapioca flour or potato starch
 $1/2$ cup (65 g) Hodgson Mill Pure Corn Starch
 4 teaspoons (28 g) xanthan gum
 3 tablespoons (45 g) packed light or dark brown sugar
 1 teaspoon (6 g) salt
 1 package ($5/16$ ounce) or $2^1/2$ teaspoons (10 g) Hodgson Mill Fast-Rise Yeast

Whisk eggs, vinegar, and vegetable oil together in large bowl. Whisk in pumpkin and water and pour into bread pan. Start machine on dough cycle. Add corn meal, flour, potato and corn starch, xanthan gum, brown sugar, and salt. Add yeast.

When cycle is complete, stop machine, then turn to bake cycle. Or, carefully spoon dough into greased 9 x 5 x 3-inch (22.5 x 12.5 x 7.5-cm) loaf pan and smooth top with spatula. Bake in 350°F (180°C) oven for 45 to 50 minutes or until instant-read thermometer inserted in center registers at least 190°F (87.7°C). Turn out onto wire rack to cool.

Yield: One 1-pound (455-g) loaf

Each with: 2595 Calories; 62g Fat (21.1% calories from fat); 46g Protein; 480g Carbohydrate; 22g Dietary Fiber; 561 mg Cholesterol; 2331 mg Sodium.

Note: To make this recipe dairy- and egg-free, use egg substitute.

Swedish Limpa Bread

This traditional Scandinavian bread is especially tasty as part of a holiday smorgasbord or buffet. It also makes wonderful open-faced sandwiches. To make flat ale, open a dark beer and stir until the bubbles are dispersed. Scoop off the residual foam before measuring the ale.

REGULAR LOAF

$1/4$ cup (60 ml) warm (105°F to 115°F [40.5°C to 46°C]) water

$1 3/4$ cups (218.8 g) Hodgson Mill Best For Bread Flour

$1/4$ cup (31.3 g) Hodgson Mill Stone Ground Whole Grain Rye Flour

1 tablespoon (8 g) nonfat dry milk

1 teaspoon (6 g) salt

1 tablespoon (14 g) butter

$3/4$ tablespoon (15 g) honey

$3/4$ tablespoon (15 g) molasses

$1/2$ cup (120 ml) flat ale (see headnote)

$1/4$ teaspoon (0.5 g) ground cardamom

$1/4$ teaspoon (0.5 g) anise seed

$1/2$ tablespoon (2.5 g) dried orange peel or fresh orange zest

1 teaspoon (4 g) Hodgson Mill Fast-Rise Yeast

LARGE LOAF

$1/2$ cup (120 ml) warm (105°F to 115°F [40.5°C to 46°C]) water

$2 1/2$ cups (312.5 g) Hodgson Mill Best For Bread Flour

$1/2$ cup (62.5 g) Hodgson Mill Stone Ground Whole Grain Rye Flour

2 tablespoons (16 g) nonfat dry milk

$1 1/2$ teaspoons (9 g) salt

2 tablespoons (28 g) butter

1 tablespoon (20 g) honey

1 tablespoon (20 g) molasses

$3/4$ cup (175 ml) flat ale or non-alcoholic beer (see headnote)

$1/2$ teaspoon (1 g) ground cardamom

$1/2$ teaspoon (1 g) anise seed

1 tablespoon (5 g) dried orange peel or fresh orange zest

2 teaspoons (8 g) Hodgson Mill Fast-Rise Yeast

For both recipes: Place ingredients in bread pan according to manufacturer's instructions. Select basic/white bread cycle and start the machine.

Yield: One 1-pound (455-g) regular or 1^1/2-pound (682.5-g) large loaf

Each with: 1077 Calories; 13g Fat (10.3% calories from fat); 36g Protein; 212g Carbohydrate; 13g Dietary Fiber; 33mg Cholesterol; 2338mg Sodium.

Variation: Set machine on dough cycle. When the cycle is complete, form dough into a loaf and place in greased 9 x 5 x 3-inch (22.5 x 12.5 x 7.5-cm) pan. Allow second rise to top of pan and bake in 350°F (180°C) oven for 35 to 40 minutes or until instant-read thermometer inserted in center registers at least 190°F (87.7°C).

 ## Sun Nut Bread

Sunflower seeds and honey flavor this whole wheat bread, giving you the best of the prairie.

REGULAR LOAF

^{3}/4 cup (175 ml) warm (105°F to 115°F [40.5°C to 46°C]) water

1^3/4 cups (218.8 g) Hodgson Mill Best For Bread Flour

^{1}/2 cup (62.5 g) Hodgson Mill Stone Ground Whole Grain Whole
    Wheat Graham Flour

1 tablespoon (8 g) nonfat dry milk

^{1}/4 teaspoon (1.5 g) salt

1 tablespoon (14 g) butter

2 tablespoons (40 g) honey

^{1}/4 cup (32.5 g) roasted, shelled sunflower seeds

1^1/4 teaspoons (5 g) Hodgson Mill Fast-Rise Yeast

LARGE LOAF

1^1/4 cups (295 ml) warm water (105°F to 115°F [40.5°C to 46°C])

2^1/2 cups (312.5 g) Hodgson Mill Best For Bread Flour

^{3}/4 cup (94 g) Hodgson Mill Stone Ground Whole Grain Whole
    Wheat Graham Flour

2 tablespoons (16 g) nonfat dry milk

^{1}/2 teaspoon (3 g) salt

2 tablespoons (28 g) butter

2 tablespoons (40 g) honey

$^1/_2$ cup (70 g) shelled sunflower seeds

2 teaspoons (8 g) Hodgson Mill Fast-Rise Yeast

For both recipes: Place ingredients in bread pan according to manufacturer's instructions. Select basic/white bread cycle and start the machine.

Yield: One 1-pound (455-g) regular or 1$^1/_2$-pound (682.5-g) large loaf

Each with: 1383 Calories; 32g Fat (19.8% calories from fat); 46g Protein; 245g Carbohydrate; 18g Dietary Fiber; 33mg Cholesterol; 733mg Sodium.

Note: If using unsalted sunflower seeds, increase the salt by a pinch.

Variation: Set machine on dough cycle. When cycle is complete, form dough into a loaf and place in greased 9 x 5 x 3-inch (22.5 x 12.5 x 7.5-cm) pan. Allow second rise to top of pan and bake in 350°F (180°C) oven for 35 to 40 minutes or until instant-read thermometer inserted in center registers at least 190°F (87.7°C).

 ## Spelt Bread

Spelt is an ancient grain with a mellow flavor. Because it doesn't have as much natural gluten as wheat, you need to add vital wheat gluten to the dough in order to ensure the loaf rises properly.

$^7/_8$ cup (205.6 ml) water

2 tablespoons (30 ml) vegetable oil, such as canola

1 tablespoon (20 g) honey

2 tablespoons (40 g) molasses

1 teaspoon (6 g) salt

2 cups (250 g) Hodgson Mill Organic Whole Grain Spelt Flour

1 cup (125 g) Hodgson Mill Best For Bread Flour

1 tablespoon (7 g) Hodgson Mill Vital Wheat Gluten

1 package ($^5/_{16}$ ounce) or 2$^1/_2$ teaspoons (10 g) Hodgson Mill Fast-Rise Yeast

Place ingredients in bread pan according to manufacturer's directions. Select basic cycle and medium color settings, then start the machine.

Yield: One 1^1/2-pound (682.5-g) loaf

Each with: 1549 Calories; 35g Fat (17.6% calories from fat); 65g Protein; 308g Carbohydrate; 46g Dietary Fiber; 0mg Cholesterol; 2174mg Sodium.

Variation: Set machine on dough cycle. When cycle is complete, form dough into a loaf and place in greased 9 x 5 x 3-inch (22.5 x 12.5 x 7.5-cm) pan. Allow second rise to top of pan and bake in 350°F (180°C) oven for 35 to 40 minutes or until instant-read thermometer inserted in center registers at least 190°F (87.7°C). Turn out onto wire rack to cool.

 ## *Gluten-Free Potato Soy Bread*

Made with a combination of soy, garbanzo bean (chickpea), millet, and brown rice flours as well as potato and corn starch, this bread rises high and bakes to a golden brown, with a mellow flavor and tender crumb.

3 large eggs or equivalent egg substitute

1 teaspoon (5 ml) cider vinegar

3 tablespoons (45 ml) olive oil

^{1}/2 cup (112.5 g) mashed potatoes

1^1/3 cups (315 ml) warm (105°F to 115°F [40.5°C to 46°C]) water

1 cup (125 g) Hodgson Mill Whole Grain Multi Purpose Baking Mix

1 cup (125 g) Hodgson Mill Stone Ground Whole Grain Brown Rice Flour

1 cup (130 g) tapioca flour or potato starch

^{1}/2 cup (62.5 g) Hodgson Mill Soy Flour

4 teaspoons (28 g) xanthan gum

3 tablespoons (45 g) packed light or dark brown sugar

^{1}/2 teaspoon (3 g) salt

1 package (^{5}/16 ounce) or 2^1/2 teaspoons (10 g) Hodgson Mill Fast-Rise Yeast

Whisk eggs, vinegar, and olive oil together in large bowl. Whisk in mashed potatoes and water and pour into bread pan. Start machine on dough cycle. Add baking mix, rice flour, potato starch, soy flour, xanthan gum, brown sugar, and salt. Add yeast.

When cycle is complete, stop machine, then turn to bake cycle. Or carefully spoon dough into greased 9 x 5 x 3-inch (22.5 x 12.5 x 7.5-cm) loaf pan and smooth top with spatula. Allow second rise to top of pan and bake in 350°F (180°C) oven for 45 to 50 minutes or until instant-read thermometer inserted in center registers at least 190°F (87.7°C). Turn out onto wire rack to cool.

Yield: One 1-pound (455-g) loaf

Each with: 2218 Calories; 68g Fat (25.7% calories from fat); 78g Protein; 364g Carbohydrate; 31 g Dietary Fiber; 563mg Cholesterol; 1503mg Sodium.

Note: To make this recipe dairy- and egg-free, use vegetable oil and egg substitute.

 ## *Potato Wheat Soy Bread*

With potato for moisture, and wheat and soy for health and flavor, this bread is a winner. Make sure all the ingredients—especially the mashed potatoes—are at room temperature before you start the recipe. (Cold mashed potatoes are not as easy to work into the dough.)

> 1 teaspoon (6 g) salt
>
> 1 tablespoon (15 g) packed light or dark brown sugar
>
> 1 package (^{5}/16 ounce) or 2^1/2 teaspoons (10 g) Hodgson Mill
>   Fast-Rise Yeast
>
> ^{1}/2 cup + 3 tablespoons (165 ml) soy or 2 percent milk
>
> 1 cup (125 g) Hodgson Mill Stone Ground Whole Grain Whole Wheat Graham
>   Flour
>
> ^{3}/4 cup (93.8 g) Hodgson Mill Best For Bread Flour
>
> ^{1}/4 cup (31.3 g) Hodgson Mill Soy Flour
>
> ^{1}/4 cup (56.3 g) mashed potatoes

Place ingredients in bread pan according to manufacturer's directions. Select basic cycle or whole wheat cycle and light crust setting, then start the machine.

Yield: One 1-pound (455-g) loaf

Each with: 954 Calories; 6g Fat (5.7% calories from fat); 47g Protein; 191 g Carbohydrate; 29g Dietary Fiber; 1 mg Cholesterol; 2295mg Sodium.

Variation: Set machine on dough cycle. When cycle is complete, form dough into a loaf and place in greased 9 x 5 x 3-inch (22.5 x 12.5 x 7.5-cm) pan. Allow second rise to top of pan and bake in 350°F (180°C) oven for 35 to 40 minutes or until instant-read thermometer inserted in center registers at least 190°F (87.7°C). Turn out onto wire rack to cool.

Saucy Apple Bread

With apples, applesauce, and honey, this loaf makes a great breakfast, snack, or tea bread.

REGULAR LOAF

$1/2$ cup (120 ml) apple cider

$1^1/3$ cups (167 g) Hodgson Mill Best For Bread Flour

$3/4$ cup + 1 tablespoon (109 g) Hodgson Mill Stone Ground Whole Grain Whole Wheat Graham Flour

1 teaspoon (6 g) salt

2 tablespoons + $1^1/2$ teaspoons (22 g) yogurt (plain)

2 tablespoons + $1^1/2$ teaspoons (22 g) honey

$1/4$ teaspoon (1.2 ml) vanilla extract

2 tablespoons + $1^1/2$ teaspoons (30 g) walnuts, chopped

2 tablespoons + $1^1/2$ teaspoons egg, beaten

$1/3$ cup (81.6 g) unsweetened applesauce

$1/3$ cup (50 g) Granny Smith apple, unpeeled and diced

$3/4$ teaspoon (3 g) Hodgson Mill Fast-Rise Yeast

LARGE LOAF

$3/4$ cup (175 ml) apple cider

2 cups (250 g) Hodgson Mill Best For Bread Flour

$1^1/4$ cups (156.3 g) Hodgson Mill Stone Ground Whole Grain Whole Wheat Graham Flour

$1^1/2$ teaspoons (9 g) salt

$1/4$ cup (60 g) yogurt (plain)

$1/4$ cup (60 g) honey

$1/2$ teaspoon (2.5 ml) vanilla extract

$1/4$ cup (40 g) walnuts, chopped

1 large egg, beaten

$1/2$ cup (125 g) unsweetened applesauce

$1/2$ cup (75 g) Granny Smith apple, unpeeled and diced

$1^1/4$ teaspoons (5 g) Hodgson Mill Fast-Rise Yeast

For both recipes: Place ingredients in bread pan according to manufacturer's directions. Select basic cycle and start the machine.

Yield: One 1-pound (455-g) regular or 1½-pound (682.5-g) large loaf

Each with: 1388 Calories; 18g Fat (11.3% calories from fat); 45g Protein; 278g Carbohydrate; 24g Dietary Fiber; 166mg Cholesterol; 2232mg Sodium.

Variation: Set machine on dough cycle. When cycle is complete, form dough into a loaf and place in greased 9 x 5 x 3-inch (22.5 x 12.5 x 7.5-cm) pan. Allow second rise to top of pan and bake in 350°F (180°C) oven for 35 to 40 minutes or until instant-read thermometer inserted in center registers at least 190°F (87.7°C). Turn out onto wire rack to cool.

Pumpernickel Bread

This classic German bread has a dark color and dense texture, and is meant to be sliced thin. Also, the top may be slightly honeycombed.

Because the whole wheat and rye flours used in this recipe are low in gluten, this dough needs extra kneading. If your machine does not have a whole wheat cycle, use this technique: After the machine has completed its first knead, simply reset and restart the machine on the regular bake cycle.

REGULAR LOAF

³/4 cup (175 ml) warm (105°F to 115°F [40.5°C to 46°C]) water

1 cup (125 g) Hodgson Mill Best For Bread Flour

¹/3 cup (41.7 g) Hodgson Mill Stone Ground Whole Grain Whole Wheat Graham Flour

²/3 cup (83.3 g) Hodgson Mill Stone Ground Whole Grain Rye Flour

1 tablespoon (8 g) nonfat dry milk

1 tablespoon + ³/4 teaspoon (24.5 g) sugar

1 teaspoon (6 g) salt

1 tablespoon + ³/4 teaspoon (24.5 g) butter, softened

2 tablespoons (18 g) Hodgson Mill Whole Grain Yellow Corn Meal Mix, Self-Rising

5 teaspoons (13 g) unsweetened cocoa powder

2 tablespoons + 1¹/2 teaspoons (30 g) molasses

¹/4 teaspoon (0.6 g) instant coffee powder

1 teaspoon (2.1 g) caraway seeds

1¹/2 teaspoons (6 g) Hodgson Mill Fast-Rise Yeast

LARGE LOAF

$1^1/4$ cups (295 ml) warm (105°F to 115°F [40.5°C to 46°C]) water

$1^1/2$ cups (187.5 g) Hodgson Mill Best For Bread Flour

$1/2$ cup (62.5 g) Hodgson Mill Stone Ground Whole Wheat Graham Flour

1 cup (125 g) Hodgson Mill Stone Ground Whole Grain Rye Flour

1 tablespoon + $1^1/2$ teaspoons (12 g) nonfat dry milk

2 tablespoons (28 g) sugar

$1^1/2$ teaspoons (9 g) salt

2 tablespoons (28 g) butter, softened

$1/4$ cup (36 g) Hodgson Mill Whole Grain Yellow Corn Meal Mix, Self-Rising

$6^1/2$ teaspoons (17 g) unsweetened cocoa powder

3 tablespoons + $1^1/2$ teaspoons (70 g) molasses

$1/2$ teaspoon (1.2 g) instant coffee powder

2 teaspoons (4.2 g) caraway seeds

2 teaspoons (8 g) Hodgson Mill Fast-Rise Yeast

For both recipes: Place ingredients in bread pan according to manufacturer's instructions. Select whole wheat cycle and start the machine.

Yield: One 1-pound (455-g) regular or $1^1/2$-pound (682.5-g) large loaf

Each with: 1238 Calories; 21 g Fat (14.2% calories from fat); 37g Protein; 251g Carbohydrate; 28g Dietary Fiber; 45mg Cholesterol; 2391 mg Sodium.

Variation: You can make this bread in smaller, cylindrical loaves, which are perfect for cocktail or bridge party fare. Heavily grease four $10^3/4$-ounce (300-g) clean empty soup cans or two $8^1/4$ x $3^1/2$-inch (20.6 x 8.8-cm) tin bread molds, opened at only one end. Set machine on dough cycle. When kneading part of cycle is complete, stop the machine. Reset to dough cycle to allow for second knead and then let dough rise. When second cycle is complete, divide dough into four or two portions. Place in greased molds. Set aside to rise until dough is within 1 inch (2.5 cm) of top of cans or molds, about 30 minutes. Bake in 375°F (190°C) oven for 30 to 35 minutes or until instant-read thermometer inserted in center registers at least 190°F (87.7°C). Turn out onto wire rack to cool. Slice into rounds to serve.

Old-Fashioned Rye Bread

Great flavor and texture make this European bread ideal for ham sandwiches or toast. Make the dough in the bread machine, and then form it into round loaves and bake in the oven for a true Old World result.

1^1/2 cups (355 ml) warm (105°F to 115°F [40.5°C to 46°C]) water

3 tablespoons (45 g) packed light or dark brown sugar

2 teaspoons (12 g) salt

2 tablespoons (30 ml) vegetable oil

^{1}/2 cup (170 g) molasses

^{1}/4 cup (85 g) honey

2 teaspoons (3.4 g) grated orange peel

2^1/2 cups (312.5 g) Hodgson Mill Organic Stone Ground Whole Grain Rye Flour

2 cups (250 g) Hodgson Mill Organic Naturally White Unbleached All-Purpose Flour

2 packages (^{5}/16 ounce each) or 5 teaspoons (20 g) Hodgson Mill Fast-Rise Yeast

Hodgson Mill Stone Ground Whole Grain Yellow Corn Meal, Plain, for sprinkling

Place water, brown sugar, salt, oil, molasses, honey, orange peel, flours, and yeast in bread pan according to manufacturer's directions. Select dough cycle.

When cycle is complete, transfer dough to floured surface and shape into two round loaves. Place on slightly greased cookie sheet sprinkled with corn meal. Cover with damp cloth and let rise about 1 hour.

Preheat oven to 375°F (190°C).

Bake for 35 to 40 minutes or until instant-read thermometer inserted in center registers at least 190°F (87.7°C). Transfer to wire rack to cool.

Yield: One 1^1/2-pound (682.5-g) loaf

Each with: 2894 Calories; 38g Fat (10.7% calories from fat); 62g Protein; 647g Carbohydrate; 62g Dietary Fiber; 0mg Cholesterol; 4354mg Sodium.

Multi Grain and More Bread

You'll get even more whole grain goodness with this bread, which also includes multi grain cereal and wheat germ. For accent and crunch, sprinkle a few rolled oats on top after the final rise, just before baking.

REGULAR LOAF

$3/4$ cup (175 ml) warm (105°F to 115°F [40.5°C to 46°C]) water

$1^1/4$ cups (156.3 g) Hodgson Mill Best For Bread Flour

$1/4$ cup (31.3 g) Hodgson Mill Stone Ground Whole Grain Whole Wheat Graham Flour

1 tablespoon (8 g) nonfat dry milk

1 teaspoon (6 g) salt

1 tablespoon (7 g) Hodgson Mill Multi Grain Cereal with Flaxseed, uncooked

2 tablespoons (14 g) Hodgson Mill Wheat Germ, Untoasted

$1^1/2$ tablespoons (30 g) honey

1 teaspoon (4 g) Hodgson Mill Fast-Rise Yeast

Rolled oats for accent (optional)

LARGE LOAF

$1^1/4$ cups (295 ml) warm (105°F to 115°F [40.5°C to 46°C]) water

$2^1/4$ cups (281.3 g) Hodgson Mill Best For Bread Flour

$1/2$ cup (62.5 g) Hodgson Mill Stone Ground Whole Grain Whole Wheat Graham Flour

2 tablespoons (16 g) nonfat dry milk

$1^1/2$ teaspoons (9 g) salt

$1/2$ cup (62.5 g) Hodgson Mill Multi Grain Cereal with Flaxseed, uncooked

3 tablespoons (21 g) Hodgson Mill Wheat Germ, Untoasted

$2^1/2$ tablespoons (50 g) honey

2 teaspoons (8 g) Hodgson Mill Fast-Rise Yeast

Rolled oats for accent (optional)

For both recipes: Place all ingredients in bread pan according to manufacturer's directions. Select basic cycle and start the machine.

Yield: One 1-pound (455-g) regular or $1^1/2$-pound (682.5-g) large loaf

Each with: 823 Calories; 2g Fat (2.2% calories from fat); 33g Protein; 176g Carbohydrate; 15g Dietary Fiber; 1 mg Cholesterol; 2203mg Sodium.

Variation: Set machine on dough cycle. When cycle is complete, form dough into a loaf and place in greased 9 x 5 x 3-inch (22.5 x 12.5 x 7.5-cm) pan. Allow second rise to top of pan and bake in 350°F (180°C) oven for 35 to 40 minutes or until instant-read thermometer inserted in center registers at least 190°F (87.7°C). Turn out onto wire rack to cool.

 ## Mocha Java Bread

Like to dunk your toast in your morning coffee? Then this bread is for you with its hint of rich coffee flavor.

REGULAR LOAF

$3/4$ cup (175 ml) warm (105°F to 115°F [40.5°C to 46°C]) water

$1^3/4$ cups (218.8 g) Hodgson Mill Best For Bread Flour

1 tablespoon (8 g) nonfat dry milk

1 teaspoon (6 g) salt

1 tablespoon + $1^1/2$ teaspoons (21 g) butter, softened

$1/4$ cup (31.3 g) Hodgson Mill Stone Ground Whole Grain Rye Flour

1 tablespoon + $1^1/2$ teaspoons (22.5 g) packed light or dark brown sugar

1 large egg

1 tablespoon (7.2 g) instant mocha coffee mix with sugar

$1/4$ cup (40 g) chopped pecans

1 teaspoon (4 g) Hodgson Mill Fast-Rise Yeast

LARGE LOAF

1 cup + 2 tablespoons (263 ml) warm (105°F to 115°F [40.5°C to 46°C]) water

$2^1/3$ cups (291.7 g) Hodgson Mill Best For Bread Flour

2 tablespoons (16 g) nonfat dry milk

$1^1/2$ teaspoons (9 g) salt

2 tablespoons (28 g) butter, softened

$1/2$ cup (62.5 g) Hodgson Mill Stone Ground Whole Grain Rye Flour

2 tablespoons (30 g) packed light or dark brown sugar

1 large egg

2 tablespoons (14.4 g) instant mocha coffee mix with sugar

$1/2$ cup (80 g) chopped pecans

2 teaspoons (8 g) Hodgson Mill Fast-Rise Yeast

For both recipes: Place all ingredients in bread pan according to manufacturer's instructions. Select basic cycle and start the machine.

Yield: One 1-pound (455-g) regular or $1^1/2$-pound (682.5-g) large loaf

Each with: 1354 Calories; 43g Fat (27.3% calories from fat); 44g Protein; 215g Carbohydrate; 15g Dietary Fiber; 235mg Cholesterol; 2492mg Sodium.

Variation: Set machine on dough cycle. When cycle is complete, form dough into a loaf and place in greased 9 x 5 x 3-inch (22.5 x 12.5 x 7.5-cm) pan. Allow second rise to top of pan and bake in 350°F (180°C) oven for 35 to 40 minutes or until instant-read thermometer inserted in center registers at least 190°F (87.7°C). Turn out onto wire rack to cool.

Caraway Rye Bread

Enjoy this traditional light rye bread with caraway seeds spread with unsalted butter.

1 cup (235 ml) warm (105°F to 115°F [40.5°C to 46°C]) water

2 tablespoons (40 g) honey

2 tablespoons (40 g) molasses

1 tablespoon (14 g) butter

$1^1/2$ teaspoons (9 g) salt

2 teaspoons (4.2 g) caraway seeds

$1/2$ teaspoon (0.8 g) grated orange zest

1 cup (125 g) Hodgson Mill Organic Stone Ground Whole Grain Rye Flour

2 cups (250 g) Hodgson Mill Organic Naturally White Unbleached, All-Purpose Flour

2 tablespoons (14 g) Hodgson Mill Vital Wheat Gluten

1 package ($5/16$-ounce) or $2^1/2$ teaspoons (10 g) Hodgson Mill Fast-Rise Yeast

Place all ingredients in bread pan according to manufacturer's instructions. Select whole wheat setting and start the machine.

Yield: One $1^1/2$-pound (682.5-g) loaf

Each with: 1600 Calories; 16g Fat (8.4% calories from fat); 52g Protein; 346g Carbohydrate; 32g Dietary Fiber; 31 mg Cholesterol; 3339mg Sodium.

Variation: Set machine on dough cycle. When cycle is complete, form dough into a loaf and place in greased 9 x 5 x 3-inch (22.5 x 12.5 x 7.5-cm) pan. Allow second rise to top of pan and bake in 350°F (180°C) oven for 35 to 40 minutes or until instant-read thermometer inserted in center registers at least 190°F (87.7°C).

Italian Pesto Wheat Bread

Use prepared pesto from a jar or make your own in summer when the basil in your herb garden is lush, then freeze it in $^1/4$-cup (65-g) increments for easy use. Stir well before measuring to blend oil.

REGULAR LOAF

$^1/2$ cup + 2 tablespoons (148 ml) warm (105°F to 115°F [40.5°C to 46°C]) water

1 tablespoon (14 g) sugar

$^1/2$ teaspoon (3 g) salt

$^1/4$ cup (65 g) prepared pesto

$1^1/2$ cups (187.5 g) Hodgson Mill Best For Bread Flour

$^1/2$ cup (62.5 g) Hodgson Mill Stone Ground Whole Grain Whole Wheat Graham Flour

1 teaspoon (4 g) Hodgson Mill Fast-Rise Yeast

LARGE LOAF

1 cup (235 ml) warm (105°F to 115°F [40.5°C to 46°C]) water

1 tablespoon + $1^1/2$ teaspoons (21 g) sugar

$^3/4$ teaspoon (4.5 g) salt

$^1/3$ cup (86.6 g) prepared pesto

2 cups (250 g) Hodgson Mill Best For Bread Flour

1 cup (125 g) Hodgson Mill Stone Ground Whole Grain Whole Wheat Graham Flour

2 teaspoons (8 g) Hodgson Mill Fast-Rise Yeast

For both recipes: Place all ingredients in bread pan according to manufacturer's directions. Select basic cycle for regular loaf or whole wheat cycle for large loaf and start the machine.

Yield: One 1-pound (455-g) regular or $1^1/2$-pound (682.5-g) large loaf

Each with: 1166 Calories; 29g Fat (21.8% calories from fat); 42g Protein; 195g Carbohydrate; 15g Dietary Fiber; 17mg Cholesterol; 1513mg Sodium.

Variation: Set machine on dough cycle. When cycle is complete, form dough into a loaf and place in greased 9 x 5 x 3-inch (22.5 x 12.5 x 7.5-cm) pan. Bake in 350°F (180°C) oven for 35 to 40 minutes or until instant-read thermometer inserted in center registers at least 190°F (87.7°C).

 ## *Honey Whole Wheat Bread*

When you think about whole wheat bread, this is the look and the flavor you imagine. Simply put, it's wonderful!

1^1/8 cups (265 ml) warm (105°F to 115°F [40.5°C to 46°C]) water

3 tablespoons (60 g) honey

^{1}/3 teaspoon (2 g) salt

1^1/2 cups (187.5 g) Hodgson Mill Stone Ground Whole Grain Whole Wheat Graham Flour

1^1/2 cups (187.5 g) Hodgson Mill Best For Bread Flour

2 tablespoons (6 g) vegetable oil, such as canola

1^1/2 teaspoons (6 g) Hodgson Mill Fast-Rise Yeast

Place ingredients in bread pan according to manufacturer's directions. Select whole wheat and start the machine.

Yield: One 1-pound (455-g) loaf

Each with: 1655 Calories; 30g Fat (15.7% calories from fat); 45g Protein; 320g Carbohydrate; 31g Dietary Fiber; 0mg Cholesterol; 751 mg Sodium.

Variation: Set machine on dough cycle. When cycle is complete, form dough into a loaf and place in greased 9 x 5 x 3-inch (22.5 x 12.5 x 7.5-cm) pan. Allow second rise to top of pan and bake in 350°F (180°C) oven for 35 to 40 minutes or until instant-read thermometer inserted in center registers at least 190°F (87.7°C).

Honey Mustard Bread

Chicken broth and honey mustard flavor in bread? Yes, when you want a smooth, mellow flavor. Try this bread for a great chicken salad sandwich or cubed and toasted in a savory bread pudding.

REGULAR LOAF

$^1/_2$ cup (120 ml) warm (105°F to 115°F [40.5°C to 46°C]) water

1$^1/_2$ cups (187.5 g) Hodgson Mill Best For Bread Flour

$^1/_2$ cup (62.5 g) Hodgson Mill Stone Ground Whole Grain Whole Wheat Graham Flour

2 teaspoons (3.2 g) nonfat dry milk

2$^1/_2$ tablespoons (50 g) honey

$^1/_2$ teaspoon (3 g) salt

$^1/_4$ cup (60 ml) chicken broth

1$^2/_3$ tablespoons (26.3 g) Dijon mustard

1 teaspoon (1 g) snipped chives

1 teaspoon (4 g) Hodgson Mill Fast-Rise Yeast

LARGE LOAF

$^3/_4$ cup (175 ml) warm (105°F to 115°F [40.5°C to 46°C]) water

2 cups (250 g) Hodgson Mill Best For Bread Flour

1 cup (125 g) Hodgson Mill Stone Ground Whole Grain Whole Wheat Graham Flour

1 tablespoon (8 g) nonfat dry milk

$^1/_4$ cup (80 g) honey

1 teaspoon (6 g) salt

$^1/_2$ cup (120 ml) chicken broth

2$^1/_2$ tablespoons (37.5 g) Dijon mustard

2 teaspoons (2 g) snipped chives

2 teaspoons (8 g) Hodgson Mill Fast-Rise Yeast

For both recipes: Place all ingredients in bread pan according to manufacturer's directions. Select whole wheat cycle and start the machine.

Yield: One 1-pound (455-g) regular or 1^1/2-pound (682.5-g) large loaf

Each with: 1022 Calories; 2g Fat (2.1% calories from fat); 36g Protein; 226g Carbohydrate; 15g Dietary Fiber; 1mg Cholesterol; 1632mg Sodium.

Variation: Set machine on dough cycle. When cycle is complete, form dough into a loaf and place in greased 9 x 5 x 3-inch (22.5 x 12.5 x 7.5-cm) pan. Allow second rise to top of pan and bake in 350°F (180°C) oven for 35 to 40 minutes or until instant-read thermometer inserted in center registers at least 190°F (87.7°C).

 ## *High-Fiber Bran Bread*

You'll get high fiber and great flavor from stone ground wheat graham flour and wheat bran in this bread—it's a great way to start your day.

> 1^1/2 cups (355 ml) warm (105°F to 115°F [40.5°C to 46°C]) water
>
> 2 tablespoons (16 g) nonfat dry milk
>
> 2 tablespoons (28 ml) vegetable oil, such as canola
>
> 2 tablespoons (40 g) molasses
>
> 2 tablespoons (40 g) honey
>
> 1^1/2 teaspoons (9 g) salt
>
> 2^1/4 cups (281.3 g) Hodgson Mill Stone Ground Whole Grain Whole Wheat Graham Flour
>
> 1^1/4 cups (156.3 g) Hodgson Mill Best For Bread Flour
>
> 1 cup (125 g) Hodgson Mill Wheat Bran, Unprocessed
>
> 2 teaspoons (8 g) Hodgson Mill Fast-Rise Yeast

Place ingredients in bread pan according to manufacturer's directions. Select whole wheat and start the machine.

Yield: One 1^1/2-pound (682.5-g) loaf

Each with: 2081 Calories; 32g Fat (12.8% calories from fat); 64g Protein; 423g Carbohydrate; 70g Dietary Fiber; 3mg Cholesterol; 3330mg Sodium.

Variation: Set machine on dough cycle. When cycle is complete, form dough into a loaf and place in greased 9 x 5 x 3-inch (22.5 x 12.5 x 7.5-cm) pan. Allow second rise to top of pan and bake in 350°F (180°C) oven for 35 to 40 minutes or until instant-read thermometer inserted in center registers at least 190°F (87.7°C).

German Dark Rye Bread

This dark, moist rye bread is delicious with a grilled brat and horseradish or with an aged cheese.

1 cup + 2 tablespoons (263 ml) warm (105°F to 115°F [40.5°C to 46°C]) water

1/4 cup (80 g) honey

2 tablespoons (28 g) butter, softened, or (28 ml) vegetable oil, such as canola

1 1/2 teaspoons (3.1 g) caraway seeds (optional)

1 teaspoon (6 g) salt

2 cups (250 g) Hodgson Mill All-Purpose, Unbleached Naturally White Flour

2 tablespoons (15.6 g) unsweetened cocoa powder

1 cup (125 g) Hodgson Mill Stone Ground Whole Grain Rye Flour

2 tablespoons (14 g) Hodgson Mill Vital Wheat Gluten

1 1/4 teaspoons (5 g) Hodgson Mill Fast-Rise Yeast

Place ingredients in bread pan according to manufacturer's directions. Select whole wheat cycle and start the machine.

Yield: One 1 1/2-pound (682.5-g) loaf

Each with: 1734 Calories; 29g Fat (13.7% calories from fat); 53g Protein; 357g Carbohydrate; 35g Dietary Fiber; 62mg Cholesterol; 2380mg Sodium.

First Variation: For an even easier way to make Dark Rye, use 1 package (16 ounces) Hodgson Mill Caraway Rye Bread Mix. For a 1 1/2-pound (682.5-g) loaf, pour 1 cup (240 ml) water in your bread machine, along with 2 tablespoons (28 g) butter/margarine or (28 ml) vegetable oil, 3 tablespoons (60 g) molasses, and 3 tablespoons (24 g) unsweetened cocoa powder. Add the bread mix and yeast packet. Use the whole wheat bread setting.

Second Variation: Set machine on dough cycle. When cycle is complete, form dough into a loaf and place in greased 9 x 5 x 3-inch (22.5 x 12.5 x 7.5-cm) pan. Allow second rise to top of pan and bake in 350°F (180°C) oven for 35 to 40 minutes or until instant-read thermometer inserted in center registers at least 190°F (87.7°C).

Garlic and Sun-Dried Tomato Bread (See photo on page 228.)

Baked in a round loaf, this hearty bread makes delicious crostini. Simply slice, brush the cut sides of each slice with olive oil, and toast in oven or outdoors on the grill. Top with chopped fresh tomatoes and fresh basil.

12 sun-dried tomatoes

$3/4$ cup (175 ml) boiling water

$1/4$ cup (60 ml) warm (105°F to 115°F [40.5°C to 46°C]) water

$3/4$ teaspoon (4.5 g) salt

$1^1/2$ teaspoons (7.5 ml) vegetable oil, such as canola

$1/2$ cup (62.5 g) Hodgson Mill Stone Ground Whole Grain Whole Wheat Graham Flour

$2^1/2$ cups (312.5 g) Hodgson Mill Best For Bread Flour

2 teaspoons (8 g) sugar

$3/4$ teaspoon (1 g) dried rosemary, crushed

$1/4$ teaspoon (3 g) garlic powder

2 teaspoons (8 g) Hodgson Mill Fast-Rise Yeast

Fill medium bowl with $3/4$ cup (175 ml) boiling water, then soak 8 sun-dried tomatoes in water for 10 minutes or until plumped. Set aside 4 remaining sun-dried tomatoes for last step.

Drain, reserving water. Snip tomatoes into small pieces. Add the $1/4$ cup (60 ml) warm water to drained tomato water to make 1 cup (235 ml) liquid.

Place plumped tomatoes, 1 cup (235 ml) tomato/water liquid, salt, oil, flours, sugar, rosemary, garlic powder, and yeast in bread machine. Place remaining sun-dried tomatoes on top of dry ingredients. Select basic cycle, using light crust option, and start the machine.

Yield: One 1-pound (455-g) loaf

Each with: 1508 Calories; 22g Fat (12.7% calories from fat); 53g Protein; 291g Carbohydrate; 22g Dietary Fiber; 0mg Cholesterol; 2159mg Sodium.

Variation: Set machine on dough cycle. When cycle is complete, form dough into a round loaf and place on parchment paper-lined baking sheet. Allow for second rise and bake in 350°F (180°C) oven for 40 to 45 minutes or until instant-read thermometer inserted in center registers at least 190°F (87.7°C). Transfer to wire rack to cool.

Flax Prairie Bread

Flecked with deliciously healthy seeds, this bread provides omega-3 and whole grain benefits.

$1^1/4$ cups (295 ml) warm (105°F to 115°F [40.5°C to 46°C]) water

2 tablespoons (40 g) amber honey

2 tablespoons (28 ml) vegetable oil, such as canola

$1/3$ cup (47 g) Hodgson Mill Milled Flax Seed

1 cup (125 g) Hodgson Mill Stone Ground Whole Grain Whole Wheat Graham Flour

2 cups (250 g) Hodgson Mill Best For Bread Flour

$1^1/2$ teaspoons (9 g) salt

2 tablespoons (30 g) roasted sunflower seeds, hulled and unsalted

1 tablespoon (8 g) poppy seeds

2 teaspoons (8 g) Hodgson Mill Fast-Rise Yeast

Place ingredients in bread pan according to manufacturer's directions. Select whole wheat cycle and start the machine.

Yield: One $1^1/2$-pound (682.5-g) loaf

Each with: 1922 Calories; 54g Fat (24.1% calories from fat); 61g Protein; 319g Carbohydrate; 38g Dietary Fiber; 0mg Cholesterol; 3250mg Sodium.

Variation: Set machine on dough cycle. When cycle is complete, form dough into a loaf and place in greased 9 x 5 x 3-inch (22.5 x 12.5 x 7.5-cm) pan. Allow second rise to top of pan and bake in 350°F (180°C) oven for 50 to 55 minutes or until instant-read thermometer inserted in center registers at least 190°F (87.7°C). Turn out onto wire rack to cool.

 Cracked Wheat Sunflower Bread

Enjoy this high-rising bread with a soft crumb and nutty texture.

1 cup (235 ml) warm (105°F to 115°F [40.5°C to 46°C]) water

1 tablespoon (14 g) butter, softened, or 1 tablespoon (15 ml) vegetable oil, such as canola

1 tablespoon (20 g) honey

1 tablespoon (8 g) nonfat dry milk

1 teaspoon (6 g) salt

2¹/4 cups (281.3 g) Hodgson Mill Best For Bread Flour

¹/4 cup (31.3 g) Hodgson Mill Cracked Wheat Hot Cereal, uncooked

¹/4 cup (35 g) roasted sunflower seeds, hulled and unsalted

1 teaspoon (4 g) Hodgson Mill Fast-Rise Yeast

Place ingredients in bread pan according to manufacturer's directions. Select basic cycle and start the machine.

Yield: One 1¹/2-pound (682.5-g) loaf

Each with: 1425 Calories; 32g Fat (19.1% calories from fat); 53g Protein; 252g Carbohydrate; 17g Dietary Fiber; 33mg Cholesterol; 2343mg Sodium.

Variation: Set machine on dough cycle. When cycle is complete, form dough into a loaf and place in greased 9 x 5 x 3-inch (22.5 x 12.5 x 7.5-cm) pan. Allow second rise to top of pan and bake in 350°F (180°C) oven for 50 to 55 minutes or until instant-read thermometer inserted in center registers at least 190°F (87.7°C). Turn out onto wire rack to cool.

Cracked Wheat Bread

With a nubby texture from the cracked wheat cereal, this bread tastes great in a grilled cheese sandwich. (And, of course, use a good cheese to go with this delicious bread!)

1¹/3 cups (325 ml) warm (105°F to 115°F [40.5°C to 46°C]) water

¹/2 cup (62.5 g) Hodgson Mill Cracked Wheat Hot Cereal, uncooked

2 tablespoons (30 g) packed light or dark brown sugar

1 tablespoon (14 g) softened butter or 1 tablespoon (15 ml) vegetable oil, such as canola

1 cup (125 g) Hodgson Mill Stone Ground Whole Grain Whole Wheat Graham Flour

1³/4 cups (218.8 g) Hodgson Mill Best For Bread Flour

1¹/2 teaspoons (9 g) salt

2¹/4 teaspoons (9 g) Hodgson Mill Fast-Rise Yeast

Place ingredients in bread pan according to manufacturer's directions. Select whole wheat cycle and start the machine.

Yield: One 1^1/2-pound (682.5-g) loaf

Each with: 1557 Calories; 15g Fat (8.4% calories from fat); 54g Protein; 324g Carbohydrate; 34g Dietary Fiber; 31 mg Cholesterol; 3370mg Sodium.

Variation: Set machine on dough cycle. When cycle is complete, form dough into a loaf and place in greased 8^1/2 x 4^1/2 x 3-inch (21.5 x 11.25 x 7.5-cm) pan. Allow a full hour for dough to rise to top of pan and bake in 350°F (180°C) oven for 50 to 55 minutes or until instant-read thermometer inserted in center registers at least 190°F (87.7°C). Turn out onto wire rack to cool.

 ## *Whole Wheat Carrot Bread*

A golden, sunny bread with a mellow, sweet flavor, this tastes even better spread with an orange-flavored butter.

REGULAR LOAF

^{1}/2 cup (120 ml) warm (105°F to 115°F [40.5°C to 46°C]) water

1 teaspoon (6 g) salt

^{2}/3 cup (79.2 g) grated fresh carrots (about 1 large)

1 tablespoon (20 g) honey

2 tablespoons (30 g) plain, low-fat yogurt

1 tablespoon (20 g) molasses

1 tablespoon (13.6 g) vegetable oil

1^1/3 cups (16.6 g) Hodgson Mill Best For Bread Flour

^{2}/3 cup (82.5 g) Hodgson Mill Stone Ground Whole Grain Whole Wheat Graham Flour

2 teaspoons (5.3 g) nonfat dry milk

2 tablespoons (18 g) chopped walnuts (optional)

1 teaspoon (4 g) Hodgson Mill Fast-Rise Yeast

LARGE LOAF

^{3}/4 cup (175 ml) warm (105°F to 115°F [40.5°C to 46°C]) water

1^1/2 teaspoons (9 g) salt

1 cup (120 g) grated fresh carrots (about 1 and 1/3 large)

2 tablespoons (40 g) honey

^{1}/4 cup (60 g) plain, low-fat yogurt

2 tablespoons (40 g) molasses

1 tablespoon (13.6 g) vegetable oil

2¼ cups (281.3 g) Hodgson Mill Best For Bread Flour

1 cup (125 g) Hodgson Mill Stone Ground Whole Grain Whole Wheat Graham
    Flour

1 tablespoon (8 g) nonfat dry milk

¼ cup (36 g) chopped walnuts (optional)

2¼ teaspoons (9 g) Hodgson Mill Fast-Rise Yeast

For both recipes: Place ingredients in bread pan according to manufacturer's directions. Select whole wheat cycle and start the machine.

Yield: One 1-pound (455-g) regular or 1½-pound (682.5-g) large loaf

---

Each with: 1220 Calories; 25g Fat (17.6% calories from fat); 39g Protein; 224g Carbohydrate; 20g Dietary Fiber; 5mg Cholesterol; 2240mg Sodium.

Variation: Set machine on dough cycle. When cycle is complete, form dough into a loaf and place in greased 9 x 5 x 3-inch (22.5 x 12.5 x 7.5-cm) pan. Allow second rise to top of pan and bake in 350°F (180°C) oven for 30 to 35 minutes or until instant-read thermometer inserted in center registers at least 190°F (87.7°C). Turn out onto wire rack to cool.

 ## *Gluten-Free Brown Rice Flour Bread*

This hearty bread is great served with soup or stew. The dough will be batter-like.

1⅓ cups (315 ml) warm (105°F to 115°F [40.5°C to 46°C]) water

3 large eggs or equivalent egg substitute

1 teaspoon (5 ml) cider vinegar

3 tablespoons (45 ml) vegetable oil, such as canola oil

½ cup (125 g) unsweetened applesauce, ½ cup (112.5 g) mashed banana,
    or ½ cup (112.5 g) canned pumpkin

2 tablespoons (30 g) packed light or dark brown sugar

2 cups (250 g) Hodgson Mill Stone Ground Whole Grain Brown Rice Flour

1 cup (130 g) Hodgson Mill Pure Corn Starch

2 teaspoons (14 g) xanthan gum

1½ teaspoons (5 g) Hodgson Mill Fast-Rise Yeast

Place water, eggs, vinegar, oil, applesauce, and brown sugar in bread pan. In a bowl, mix together brown rice flour, corn starch, and xanthan gum and add to pan, along with yeast. Start on dough cycle.

When cycle is complete, stop machine, then turn to bake cycle. Alternatively, carefully spoon dough into greased 9 x 5 x 3-inch (22.5 x 12.5 x 7.5-cm) loaf pan and smooth top with spatula. Allow second rise to top of pan and bake in 350°F (180°C) oven for 45 to 50 minutes or until instant-read thermometer inserted in center registers at least 190°F (87.7°C). Turn out onto wire rack to cool.

Yield: One 1-pound (455-g) loaf

Each with: 2456 Calories; 62g Fat (22.2% calories from fat); 43g Protein; 446g Carbohydrate; 10g Dietary Fiber; 561mg Cholesterol; 189mg Sodium.

Note: To make this recipe dairy- and egg-free, use vegetable oil and egg substitute.

 ## *Basic Rye Bread*

Dark brown with a tender crumb and caraway seeds, this is the classic rye bread. It's great for ham sandwiches and Reubens.

    1 cup + 2 tablespoons warm (105°F to 115°F [40.5°C to 46°C]) water

    2 tablespoons (40 g) molasses

    1 tablespoon (15 ml) vegetable oil, such as canola

    1^1/2 teaspoons (9 g) salt

    2 cups (250 g) Hodgson Mill Best For Bread Flour

    1^1/2 cups (187.5 g) Hodgson Mill Stone Ground Whole Grain Rye Flour

    3 tablespoons (45 g) packed light or dark brown sugar

    1 tablespoon (8 g) unsweetened cocoa powder

    ^{3}/4 teaspoon (1.5 g) caraway seeds

    2 teaspoons (8 g) Hodgson Mill Fast-Rise Yeast

Place ingredients in bread pan according to manufacturer's directions. Select whole wheat cycle with light crust setting and start the machine.

Yield: One 1-pound (455-g) loaf

Each with: 1771 Calories; 21 g Fat (9.6% calories from fat); 55g Protein; 385g Carbohydrate; 42g Dietary Fiber; 0mg Cholesterol; 3278mg Sodium

Variation: Set machine on dough cycle. When cycle is complete, form dough into a loaf and place in greased 9 x 5 x 3-inch (22.5 x 12.5 x 7.5-cm) pan. Allow second rise to top of pan and bake in 350°F (180°C) oven for 55 to 60 minutes or until instant-read thermometer inserted in center registers at least 190°F (87.7°C). Turn out onto wire rack to cool.

 Gluten-Free Apple Cinnamon Bread (See photo on page 229.)

With the homey fragrance of cinnamon and both fresh and dried apples, this wonderful bread rises high and bakes to a golden brown. It has a mellow flavor and tender crumb, and it makes delicious French toast.

    3 large eggs or equivalent egg substitute
    1 teaspoon (5 ml) cider vinegar
    3 tablespoons (45 ml) vegetable oil, such as canola
    1/2 cup (125 g) unsweetened applesauce
    1 1/4 cups (355 ml) warm (105°F to 115°F [40.5°C to 46°C]) water
    1 teaspoon (2.3 g) ground cinnamon
    3 tablespoons (45 g) packed light or dark brown sugar
    1 large Granny Smith apple, peeled, cored, and grated
    1 cup (125 g) Hodgson Mill Whole Grain Apple Cinnamon Muffin Mix with Milled
        Flax Seed
    1 cup (125 g) Hodgson Mill Stone Ground Whole Grain Brown Rice Flour
    1 cup (130 g) tapioca flour or potato starch
    1/2 cup (65 g) Hodgson Mill Pure Corn Starch
    4 teaspoons (28 g) xanthan gum
    1 1/2 teaspoons (9 g) salt
    1 package (5/16 ounce) or 2 1/2 teaspoons (10 g) Hodgson Mill Fast-Rise Yeast

Whisk eggs, vinegar, and vegetable oil together in large bowl. Whisk in applesauce, water, cinnamon, brown sugar, and grated apple and pour into bread pan. Start machine on dough cycle. Add muffin mix, rice flour, potato starch, corn starch, xanthan gum, and salt. Add yeast.

When cycle is complete, stop machine, then turn to bake cycle. Alternatively, carefully spoon dough into greased 9 x 5 x 3-inch (22.5 x 12.5 x 7.5-cm) loaf pan and smooth top with spatula. Bake in 350°F (180°C) oven for 45 to 50 minutes or until instant-read thermometer inserted in center registers at least 190°F (87.7°C). Turn out onto wire rack to cool.

Yield: One 1-pound (455-g) loaf

Each with: 2619 Calories; 65g Fat (21.3% calories from fat); 52g Protein; 487g Carbohydrate; 23g Dietary Fiber; 561mg Cholesterol; 3712mg Sodium.

Note: To make this recipe dairy- and egg-free, use vegetable oil and egg substitute.

Apple Oat Bread

Mellow apple flavor blends with whole grain wheat and oats to make a memorable bread.

REGULAR LOAF

$1/2$ cup (120 ml) warm (105°F to 115°F [40.5°C to 46°C]) water

$1^1/3$ cups (166.6 g) Hodgson Mill Best For Bread Flour

$2/3$ cup (82.5 g) Hodgson Mill Stone Ground Whole Grain Whole Wheat Graham Flour

2 teaspoons (5.2 g) nonfat dry milk

1 teaspoon (6 g) salt

2 teaspoons (9.2 g) butter, softened, or 2 teaspoons (10 ml) vegetable oil, such as canola

$1/2$ cup (75 g) chopped fresh apple

1 tablespoon (15 ml) frozen apple juice concentrate, thawed

2 teaspoons (10 ml) fresh lemon juice

1 tablespoon (20 g) honey

2 tablespoons (30.6 g) yogurt

2 teaspoons (13.3 g) molasses

$1/4$ cup (31.3 g) Hodgson Mill Oat Bran Hot Cereal, uncooked

1 teaspoon (4 g) Hodgson Mill Fast-Rise Yeast

LARGE LOAF

$3/4$ cup (175 ml) warm (105°F to 115°F [40.5°C to 46°C]) water

2 cups (250 g) Hodgson Mill Best For Bread Flour

2 cups (250 g) Hodgson Mill Stone Ground Whole Grain Whole Wheat Graham Flour

1 tablespoon (8 g) nonfat dry milk

1^1/$_2$ teaspoons (9 g) salt

1 tablespoon (14g/15 ml) butter, softened, or 2 teaspoons (10 ml) vegetable oil, such as canola

^{3}/$_4$ cup (100 g) chopped fresh apple

2 tablespoons (30 ml) frozen apple juice concentrate, thawed

1 tablespoon (15 ml) lemon juice

2 tablespoons (40 g) honey

^{1}/$_4$ cup (61.3 g) yogurt

1 tablespoon (20 g) molasses

^{1}/$_2$ cup (62.5 g) Hodgson Mill Oat Bran Hot Cereal, uncooked

1^1/$_2$ teaspoons (6 g) Hodgson Mill Fast-Rise Yeast

For both recipes: Place all ingredients in bread pan according to manufacturer's instructions. Select whole wheat cycle and start the machine.

Yield: One 1-pound (455-g) regular or 1^1/$_2$-pound (682.5-g) large loaf

Each with: 1208 Calories; 13g Fat (9.4% calories from fat); 40g Protein; 250g Carbohydrate; 24g Dietary Fiber; 26mg Cholesterol; 2294mg Sodium.

Variation: Set machine on dough cycle. When cycle is complete, form dough into a loaf and place in greased 9 x 5 x 3-inch (22.5 x 12.5 x 7.5-cm) pan. Allow second rise to top of pan and bake in 350°F (180°C) oven for 35 to 40 minutes or until instant-read thermometer inserted in center registers at least 190°F (87.7°C).

50/50 Honey Wheat Bread

Made with flour that is half all-purpose, half whole wheat, this bread has a tender crumb yet a nutty texture—the best of both flours!

1 cup (235 ml) warm (105°F to 115°F [40.5°C to 46°C]) water

1^1/$_2$ tablespoons (12 g) nonfat dry milk

1 large egg

2 tablespoons (28 ml) vegetable oil, such as canola

2 tablespoons (40 g) honey

1 teaspoon (6 g) salt

3^1/2 cups (437.5 g) Hodgson Mill 50/50 Flour

1 package (^{5}/16-ounce) or 2^1/2 teaspoons (10 g) Hodgson Mill Fast-Rise Yeast

Place ingredients in bread pan according to manufacturer's directions. Set on whole wheat cycle and start the machine.

Yield: One 1^1/2-pound (682.5-g) loaf

Each with: 1901 Calories; 32g Fat (14.9% calories from fat); 69g Protein; 339g Carbohydrate; 29g Dietary Fiber; 189mg Cholesterol; 2256mg Sodium.

Variation: Set machine on dough cycle. When cycle is complete, form dough into a loaf and place in greased 9 x 5 x 3-inch (22.5 x 12.5 x 7.5-cm) pan. Allow second rise to top of pan and bake in 350°F (180°C) oven for 50 to 55 minutes or until instant-read thermometer inserted in center registers at least 190°F (87.7°C).

 ## 100 Percent Whole Wheat Bread

The trick to making 100 percent whole wheat bread in your machine is an extra knead, which gives the yeast and gluten a second chance to create a lighter loaf. When your first knead cycle is completed, simply reset the machine and start again. Some manufacturers produce home bakeries with a whole-wheat cycle; if your machine doesn't have one, our start-again method works as an easy alternative.

REGULAR LOAF

1 cup (235 ml) warm (105°F to 115°F [40.5°C to 46°C]) water

2^1/2 cups (312.5 g) Hodgson Mill Stone Ground Whole Grain Whole Wheat Graham Flour

1^1/4 tablespoons (10 g) nonfat dry milk

1 teaspoon (6 g) salt

1^1/2 tablespoons (21 g) butter

1^1/4 tablespoons (15 g) honey

1 tablespoon (7 g) Hodgson Mill Vital Wheat Gluten

2 teaspoons (13.3 g) molasses

1^1/2 teaspoons (6 g) Hodgson Mill Fast-Rise Yeast

LARGE LOAF

$1^1/2$ cups + 2 tablespoons (263 ml) warm (105°F to 115°F [40.5°C to 46°C]) water

$3^3/4$ cups (468.8 g) Hodgson Mill Stone Ground Whole Grain Whole Wheat Graham Flour

2 tablespoons (16 g) nonfat dry milk

$1^1/2$ teaspoons (9 g) salt

2 tablespoons (28 g) butter

2 tablespoons (40 g) honey

$1^1/2$ tablespoons (10.5 g) Hodgson Mill Vital Wheat Gluten

1 tablespoon (20 g) molasses

$2^1/8$ teaspoons (8.5 g) Hodgson Mill Fast-Rise Yeast

For both recipes: Place ingredients in bread pan according to manufacturer's directions. Set on whole wheat cycle and start the machine.

Yield: One 1-pound (455-g) loaf or one $1^1/2$-pound (682.5-g) loaf

Each with: 1354 Calories; 22g Fat (14.2% calories from fat); 42g Protein; 262g Carbohydrate; 42g Dietary Fiber; 48mg Cholesterol; 2371 mg Sodium.

Variation: Set machine on dough cycle. When kneading part of cycle is complete, stop machine. Reset to dough cycle for second knead and rise. When second cycle is complete, form dough into a loaf and place in greased 9 x 5 x 3-inch (22.5 x 12.5 x 7.5-cm) pan. Allow second rise to top of pan and bake in 350°F (180°C) oven for 50 to 55 minutes or until instant-read thermometer inserted in center registers at least 190°F (87.7°C). Turn out onto wire rack to cool.

3

Cakes

In cakes of all kinds—snack, stack, layer, sheet, short, cheese, Bundt, and angel food—whole grains add a welcome dimension of texture and flavor. Whole grains blend especially well with grated vegetables like carrot and zucchini, canned pineapple, fresh chopped apple or pear, pureed pumpkin or squash, and even chocolate to make moist and delicious baked goods.

For cakes, the most important step is creaming the butter and sugar together until light and fluffy, as this is where you'll create the light texture that the best cakes have. Always make sure to combine the dry ingredients together well first, then add them to the creamed mixture so you don't have mystery lumps of baking powder or spices. Once the dry ingredients have been added to the batter, mix only enough to blend the batter, as you don't want to activate the gluten in wheat flours.

To crown your baked glory, drizzle on your favorite glaze or icing, spread with your favorite frosting, dust with confectioners' sugar, or enjoy with a dollop of whipped cream.

White Whole Wheat Texas Sheet Cake

White whole wheat is the "good cowboy" in the white hat, but he's quite hidden in the velvety chocolate richness of this recipe. This cake recipe is a great way to introduce your family to whole grain baking.

FOR THE CAKE:

1 cup (2 sticks [225 g]) butter, cut into pieces

3 tablespoons (7.8 g) unsweetened cocoa powder

1 cup (235 ml) freshly brewed coffee

1 teaspoon (2.3 g) ground cinnamon

2 cups (400 g) granulated sugar

1 cup (125 g) Hodgson Mill Stone Ground Whole Grain White Whole Wheat Flour

1 cup (125 g) Hodgson Mill All-Purpose, Unbleached Naturally White Flour

1 teaspoon (6 g) salt

1 teaspoon (1.5 g) baking soda

2 large eggs

$1/2$ cup (120 ml) buttermilk (see note)

1 teaspoon (5 ml) vanilla extract

FOR THE GLAZE:

$1/2$ cup (1 stick [112.5 g]) butter

3 tablespoons (7.8 g) unsweetened cocoa powder

2 to 3 tablespoons (28 to 45 ml) 2 percent milk

1 teaspoon (5 ml) vanilla extract

1 box (16 ounce [200 g]) box confectioners' sugar

Preheat oven to 400°F (200°C). Lightly grease a 17 x 12 x 2-inch (42.5 x 30 x 5-cm) jelly-roll pan or two 13 x 9 x 2-inch (32.5 x 22.5 x 5-cm) pans.

Microwave butter, cocoa powder, coffee, and cinnamon in medium microwave-safe bowl, uncovered, on High (100 percent) power for 1 minute; stir just until butter is melted. Combine sugar, flours, salt, and baking soda in large bowl. Whisk in butter mixture, then eggs, buttermilk, and vanilla extract until smooth. Pour batter into prepared pan.

Bake 15 to 17 minutes or until toothpick inserted in center comes out clean. For glaze, microwave butter, cocoa powder, and milk in medium, uncovered, microwave-safe bowl on High (100 percent) power for 1 minute; stir just until butter is melted.

Stir in vanilla extract, then sift in confectioners' sugar and whisk until smooth. Spread glaze on top of cake with spatula.

Yield: 24 2-inch (5-cm) servings

Each with: 286 Calories; 12g Fat (37.2% calories from fat); 2g Protein; 44g Carbohydrate; 1g Dietary Fiber; 47mg Cholesterol; 270mg Sodium.

Note: If you don't have buttermilk, you can substitute by pouring 1 teaspoon (5 ml) vinegar in a $^{1}/_{2}$-cup (120-ml) measure. Fill to top with milk and let sit for 2 minutes, then use in recipe.

Variation: For a snack cake, cut recipe in half and bake in a greased 13 x 9-inch (32.5 x 22.5-cm) baking pan for 15 to 17 minutes, or until toothpick inserted near center comes out clean.

Yield: 13 3-inch (7.5-cm) pieces.

Gluten-Free Chocolate Cheese Cake

Who can resist cheesecake? Enjoy this gluten-free version of an American classic.

FOR THE CRUST:
$^{1}/_{2}$ cup (62.5 g) Hodgson Mill Whole Grain Apple Cinnamon Muffin Mix with Milled Flax Seed

$^{1}/_{2}$ cup (75 g) hazelnuts, pecans, or almonds (or use $^{1}/_{4}$ cup [31.3 g] more of muffin mix)

$^{1}/_{2}$ cup (115 g) brown sugar

1 tablespoon (8 g) gluten-free unsweetened cocoa powder

4 tablespoons ($^{1}/_{2}$ stick [55 g]) butter or margarine, softened

FOR THE FILLING:
1 package (12 ounces [262.5 g]) gluten-free semi-sweet chocolate chips

$^{1}/_{2}$ cup (120 ml) freshly brewed hot coffee

2 packages (8 ounces [115 g] each) cream cheese, softened, or silken tofu

1 cup (200 g) sugar

$^{1}/_{4}$ teaspoon (1.5 g) salt

4 large eggs or equivalent egg substitute

2 teaspoons (10 ml) gluten-free vanilla extract

FOR THE TOPPING:
Whipped cream, optional

Fresh strawberries for garnish

Preheat oven to 325°F (170°C). Lightly grease a 10-inch (25-cm) springform pan.

For crust, process muffin mix and nuts in bowl of food processor until nuts are ground. Add brown sugar, cocoa powder, and butter and pulse until crumbly and completely blended. Press into bottom and partly up sides of prepared pan. Bake 8 minutes. While crust bakes, prepare filling by melting chocolate chips with coffee in bowl in microwave in medium, uncovered, microwave-safe bowl on HIGH (100 percent) power for 1 minute; stir just until morsels are melted. Beat cream cheese, sugar, salt, eggs, and vanilla together until smooth.

Beat in chocolate mixture. Remove crust from oven. Pour filling into partially baked crust.

Bake 55 minutes or until toothpick inserted in center comes out clean. Let cool in pan. When ready to serve, remove sides of pan. Dollop whipped cream over cheesecake and garnish with fresh strawberries.

Yield: 9 wedge-shaped servings

Each with: 628 Calories; 41 g Fat (55.9% calories from fat); 10g Protein; 63g Carbohydrate; 4g Dietary Fiber; 152mg Cholesterol; 311 mg Sodium.

Note: To make this recipe dairy- and egg-free, use margarine, egg substitute, and silken tofu.

Variation: You can top this cheesecake with any type of fruit that goes well with chocolate, such as raspberries or oranges; simply sweeten to taste as needed.

 ## Upside-Down Almond Peach Cake

This peachy take on the traditional pineapple upside-down cake comes out of the oven juicy and golden.

FOR THE FILLING:

2 cups (200 g) peaches, fresh or canned (drained)

2/3 cup (86 g) nonfat dry milk

2 tablespoons (16 g) Hodgson Mill Pure Corn Starch

1 cup (150 g) almonds, chopped

FOR THE CRUST:

1 cup (125 g) Hodgson Mill Organic Whole Grain Whole Wheat Pastry Flour

1 teaspoon (1.5 g) baking powder

$^1/_2$ cup (1 stick [112 g]) butter, melted

2 large eggs, beaten

$^1/_2$ cup (115 g) low-fat cottage cheese

$^1/_4$ cup (50 g) sugar

Preheat oven to 350°F (180°C). Line a 9-inch (22.5-cm) pan with wax or parchment paper and lightly grease paper.

For filling, mix together and spread out peaches, nonfat dry milk, corn starch, and almonds. For crust, mix together flour, baking powder, melted butter, eggs, cottage cheese, and sugar in bowl until well blended. Spread crust batter over filling.

Bake 30 minutes. Cool in pan 15 minutes. Invert onto plate and peel off wax paper. Chill before serving.

Yield: 9 wedge-shaped servings

Each with: 335 Calories; 20g Fat (52.0% calories from fat); 11 g Protein; 31 g Carbohydrate; 4g Dietary Fiber; 71 mg Cholesterol; 271 mg Sodium.

Orange-Glazed Sweet Potato Pound Cake

If you're new to whole grain baking, using white whole wheat flour in place of some all-purpose flour is a great idea. Then, every time you make this luscious cake, add more white whole wheat flour and less all-purpose, until all 3 cups (375 g) are white whole wheat. If batter is too stiff, add 1 to 2 tablespoons (15 to 28 ml) of water.

$1^1/_2$ cups (187.5 g) Hodgson Mill Stone Ground Whole Grain White Whole Wheat Flour

$1^1/_2$ cups (187.5 g) Hodgson Mill All-Purpose, Unbleached Naturally White Flour

2 teaspoons (3 g) baking powder

$^1/_2$ teaspoon (0.7 g) baking soda

2 teaspoons (4.6 g) ground cinnamon

1 teaspoon (2.3 g) ground allspice

$^1/_2$ teaspoon (3 g) salt

1 cup (235 ml) vegetable oil

3 large eggs

3 cups (600 g) sugar

1 can (15 ounce [420 g]) sweet potatoes, mashed or pureed

^{1}/2 cup (75 g) chopped walnuts or pecans, optional

^{1}/2 cup (72.5 g) raisins or Zante currants, coated with a little flour

FOR THE ORANGE GLAZE:

1 cup (100 g) confectioners' sugar

2 to 3 tablespoons (28 to 45 ml) orange juice

1 teaspoon (1.7 g) grated orange zest

Preheat oven to 350°F (180°C). Lightly grease and flour a tube or Bundt pan.

Sift flours, baking powder, baking soda, spices, and salt together. Beat oil, eggs, and sugar together in large bowl until smooth. Mix in dry ingredients until batter is smooth. Mix in mashed sweet potatoes until smooth. Fold in nuts and raisins. Spoon batter into prepared pan.

Bake 1 hour or until toothpick inserted near center comes out clean. Carefully invert on wire rack to cool, then turn right side up. For glaze, whisk ingredients together and drizzle over cooled cake.

Yield: 16 wedge-shaped servings

Each with: 449 Calories; 17g Fat (32.9% calories from fat); 5g Protein; 72g Carbohydrate; 3g Dietary Fiber; 35mg Cholesterol; 198mg Sodium.

 ## *White Whole Wheat Banana Layer Cake*

Moist and delicious, this layer cake is delicious with a penuche (recipe follows), Lemon Cream Cheese Frosting (page 109), or Cream Cheese Frosting (page 125).

^{1}/2 cup (1 stick [112 g]) butter, softened

1^1/2 cups (300 g) sugar

^{1}/2 cup (120 ml) buttermilk or substitute (see note)

1^1/2 teaspoons (2.3 g) baking soda

1^3/4 cups (218.8 g) Hodgson Mill Whole Grain White Whole Wheat Flour

1 cup (225 g) mashed banana (about 2 medium)

Preheat oven to 350°F (180°C). Grease and flour two 8-inch (20-cm) cake pans.

Cream butter and sugar together with electric mixer until light and fluffy. Whisk buttermilk and baking soda together in small bowl. Add buttermilk mixture, alternating with flour, to creamed mixture. Mix in banana. Spoon batter into prepared pans.

Bake 25 to 28 minutes or until toothpick inserted in center comes out clean.

Yield: 9 wedge-shaped servings

Each with: 326 Calories; 11g Fat (28.9% calories from fat); 4g Protein; 56g Carbohydrate; 3g Dietary Fiber; 28mg Cholesterol; 329mg Sodium.

Note: If you don't have buttermilk, substitute by pouring 1 teaspoon (5 ml) vinegar or lemon juice in a $^1/_2$-cup (120-ml) measure. Fill to top with milk and let sit 2 minutes, then use in recipe.

Add It: To make a penuche frosting, melt $^1/_2$ cup (112 g) butter or margarine in saucepan over medium heat. Stir in 1 cup (225 g) packed light or dark brown sugar. Cook and stir until mixture bubbles. Remove from heat and whisk in $^1/_4$ cup (60 ml) 2 percent milk, then $3^1/_2$ cups (700 g) confectioners' sugar until thick and creamy. Position bottom layer of cake on serving platter. Spread frosting over bottom cake layer, then place second layer on top and spread frosting over top and sides.

 ## *Gluten-Free Rice Flour Layer Cake*

Happy Birthday! This special occasion layer cake has all the flavor of the traditional layer cake, but with slightly more texture. Frost with your favorite gluten-free frosting or with Easy Buttercream Frosting (recipe follows).

FOR THE CAKE:

1 cup (2 sticks [225 g]) butter or soy margarine, softened

$^1/_2$ cup (100 g) sugar

2 large eggs or equivalent egg substitute

2 teaspoons (10 ml) gluten-free vanilla extract

$1^1/_4$ cups (156.3 g) Hodgson Mill Stone Ground Whole Grain Brown Rice Flour

$^1/_4$ cup (32.5 g) Hodgson Mill Pure Corn Starch

1 teaspoon (1.5 g) gluten-free baking powder

FOR THE EASY BUTTERCREAM FROSTING:

$^1/_2$ cup (1 stick [112 g]) butter, softened, or soy margarine

1 teaspoon (5 ml) gluten-free vanilla extract

$^1/_8$ teaspoon (0.8 g) salt

1 package (16 ounces [200 g]) confectioners' sugar

3 to 4 tablespoons (45 to 60 ml) 2 percent milk or soy milk

Preheat oven to 350°F (180°C). Grease two 8-inch (20-cm) round cake pans.

Cream butter and sugar until light and fluffy. Add eggs and vanilla, beating with a wire whisk. Add flour, corn starch, and baking powder and continue to beat until well mixed. Pour batter into prepared pans.

Bake 27 to 30 minutes or until toothpick inserted in center comes out clean. Turn out onto wire racks to cool.

For frosting, mix butter, vanilla, and salt together in medium bowl with electric mixer. Add confectioners' sugar, $1/2$ cup (50 g) at a time, over low speed. Add enough milk to make a smooth, spreadable frosting. Position bottom layer of cake on serving platter. Spread frosting over bottom cake layer, then place second layer on top and spread frosting over top and sides.

Yield: 9 wedge-shaped servings

Each with: 617 Calories; 32g Fat (46.3% calories from fat); 3g Protein; 81 g Carbohydrate; 1g Dietary Fiber; 125mg Cholesterol; 412mg Sodium.

Note: To make this recipe dairy- and egg-free, use margarine, egg substitute, and soy milk. If you choose this version—which produces a moister cake because there's more liquid in the margarine—you'll have better results making cupcakes. Line cupcake pans with paper liners. Fill each liner $3/4$ full. Bake for 12 to 15 minutes or until a toothpick inserted in center of cupcake comes out clean.

Add It: You can make an Easy Chocolate Buttercream Frosting by melting the butter and mixing in 3 tablespoons (24 g) unsweetened cocoa powder, then proceed with rest of recipe.

 ## Gluten-Free Carrot Zucchini Cupcakes

Rice flour and ground flax seed give these cupcakes body and texture while also providing omega-3 fatty acids.

$1/2$ cup (70 g) Hodgson Mill Milled Flax Seed

$1/2$ cup (120 ml) vegetable oil, such as canola

$1/2$ cup (100 g) sugar

$1/4$ cup (60 g) unsweetened applesauce

2 large eggs or equivalent egg substitute

1 cup (125 g) Hodgson Mill Stone Ground Whole Grain Brown Rice Flour

$3/4$ teaspoon (1 g) baking soda

1 teaspoon (2.3 g) ground cinnamon

$^1/_8$ teaspoon (0.8 g) salt

2 medium carrots, grated

$^1/_2$ medium zucchini, grated

$^1/_2$ cup (75 g) chopped walnuts, optional

FOR THE LEMON CREAM CHEESE FROSTING:

1 package (8 ounces [115 g]) cream cheese, softened, or silken tofu

$1^2/_3$ cups (166 g) confectioners' sugar

1 teaspoon (1.7 g) grated lemon zest

2 teaspoons (10 ml) fresh lemon juice

Preheat oven to 400°F (200°C). Line 12-cup muffin tin with paper liners.

In a large mixing bowl, beat oil with sugar and applesauce. Add eggs. In a separate bowl, mix together ground flax seed, rice flour, baking soda, cinnamon, and salt. Add to the applesauce mixture. Fold in carrots, zucchini, and nuts (if using). Spoon into prepared muffin cups, filling $^3/_4$ full.

Bake 20 to 25 minutes or until toothpick inserted in center comes out clean. Invert onto wire rack to cool. For frosting, beat softened cream cheese with confectioners' sugar. Add lemon zest and juice. Frost cooled cupcakes.

Yield: 12 cupcakes

Each with: 354 Calories; 21g Fat (52.3% calories from fat); 6g Protein; 37g Carbohydrate; 3g Dietary Fiber; 52mg Cholesterol; 171mg Sodium.

Note: To make this recipe dairy- and egg-free, use vegetable oil, egg substitute, and silken tofu.

 ## *New Generation Hummingbird Cake* (See photo on page 232.)

Dainty as a hummingbird, this well-loved cake provides a sweet and light finish to any meal. This version has more flavor, more texture, and more health benefits—good reasons for a new generation to love it, too!

2 cups (250 g) Hodgson Mill All-Purpose, Unbleached Naturally White Flour

1 cup (125 g) Hodgson Mill Stone Ground Whole Grain White Whole Wheat Flour

$1^3/_4$ cups (350 g) sugar

1 teaspoon (6 g) salt

1 teaspoon (1.5 g) baking soda

1 teaspoon (2.3 g) ground cinnamon

3 large eggs, beaten

3/4 cup (185 g) unsweetened applesauce

1 cup (235 ml) vegetable oil, such as canola

2 teaspoons (10 ml) vanilla extract

1 cup (250 g) crushed pineapple with its own juice (do not drain)

2 cups (200 g) toasted pecans, chopped

2 cups (450 g) ripe bananas, chopped (about 4 medium)

FOR THE CINNAMON GLAZE:

2 cups (200 g) confectioners' sugar

1/2 teaspoon (1 g) ground cinnamon

1 teaspoon (5 ml) vanilla extract

3 to 4 tablespoons (45 to 60 ml) 2 percent milk

Preheat oven to 350°F (180°C). Lightly grease a 9 x 13 x 2-inch (22.5 x 32.5 x 5-cm) baking dish.

Combine flours, sugar, salt, soda, and cinnamon in a large bowl. In separate bowl, beat eggs with applesauce, oil, vanilla, and pineapple until well combined. Add egg mixture to dry ingredients, stirring well. Add pecans and bananas, mixing well, until all ingredients are combined. Spoon batter into prepared dish.

Bake 50 to 60 minutes or until toothpick inserted in center comes out clean. Let cool in pan. For glaze, whisk confectioners' sugar with cinnamon in medium bowl. Whisk in vanilla and milk until smooth. Pour glaze over cooled cake, then spread evenly using rubber spatula. Let glaze set before serving.

Yield: 20 2-inch (5-cm) servings

Each with: 382 Calories; 19g Fat (43.0% calories from fat); 4g Protein; 52g Carbohydrate; 2g Dietary Fiber; 28mg Cholesterol; 180mg Sodium.

Variation: Frost cake with Lemon Cream Cheese Frosting (page 109).

Gluten-Free Honey Cake

This sweet, moist, and delicious loaf cake tastes great with poached pears or fresh berries.

1$^1/_2$ cups (187.5 g) Hodgson Mill Stone Ground Whole Grain Brown Rice Flour

$^1/_2$ cup (65 g) Hodgson Mill Pure Corn Starch

$^1/_2$ cup (80 g) potato flour

1 teaspoon (7 g) xanthan gum

1 teaspoon (1.5 g) baking soda

1 teaspoon (1.5 g) gluten-free baking powder

1 teaspoon (2.3 g) ground cinnamon

2 large eggs or equivalent egg substitute

$^3/_4$ cup (255 g) honey

1 cup (200 g) sugar

$^1/_2$ cup (120 ml) vegetable oil, such as canola

1 cup (235 ml) strong, brewed coffee

$^1/_2$ cup (75 g) chopped nuts (e.g., walnuts, almonds), optional

Preheat oven to 325°F (170°C). Lightly grease a 9 x 5 x 3-inch (22.5 x 12.5 x 7.5-cm) loaf pan.

Combine flour, corn starch, potato flour, xanthan gum, baking soda, baking powder, and cinnamon in medium bowl. Beat eggs with honey and sugar in large bowl with electric mixer until light and creamy. Beat in oil and coffee. Beat in dry ingredients, 1 cup (225 g) at a time, until batter is smooth. Stir in nuts (if using). Spoon batter into prepared pan.

Bake 1 hour or until toothpick inserted in center comes out clean.

Yield: 8 1-inch (2.5-cm) servings

Each with: 554 Calories; 20g Fat (31.3% calories from fat); 7g Protein; 92g Carbohydrate; 2g Dietary Fiber; 47mg Cholesterol; 238mg Sodium.

Note: To make this recipe dairy- and egg-free, use vegetable oil and egg substitute.

Add It: Serve this cake sliced and topped with sautéed apples, poached pears, sliced oranges, or fresh berries.

Orange Cranberry Walnut Cake

This crackly-top cake is full of good things—dried fruit, nuts, and white whole wheat flour. Moist and flavorful, this cake is great to take along on a hike, tailgating, or on a weekend jaunt.

Grated zest of 1 orange (about 2 tablespoons [10 g])

1 cup (120 g) sweetened, dried cranberries

1 cup (150 g) chopped walnuts

1/2 cup (1 stick [112 g]) butter, softened

1 cup (200 g) sugar

2 large eggs

1 cup (125 g) Hodgson Mill All-Purpose, Unbleached Naturally White Flour

1 cup (125 g) Hodgson Mill Stone Ground Whole Wheat White Whole Wheat Flour

1/2 teaspoon (3 g) salt

1 cup (235 ml) buttermilk or substitute (see note)

1 teaspoon (1.5 g) baking soda

1 teaspoon (5 ml) vanilla extract

FOR THE GLAZE:

1/3 cup (80 ml) orange juice

1 cup (200 g) sugar

Preheat oven to 350°F (180°C). Lightly grease a 13 x 9 x 2-inch (32.5 x 22.5 x 5-cm) baking pan.

Finely grind orange zest, cranberries, and walnuts in food processor. In large bowl, beat butter and sugar together with electric mixer until light and fluffy. Beat in eggs. Add flours and salt and beat until combined. Stir buttermilk and baking soda together in small bowl until dissolved. Beat buttermilk mixture into cake batter. Stir in ground orange mixture and vanilla. Spoon batter into prepared pan. For glaze, whisk together orange juice and sugar.

Bake 30 minutes or until toothpick inserted near center comes out clean. Remove cake from oven and drizzle with glaze. Return cake to oven and bake 8 to 10 minutes more or until glaze is bubbly. Cool in pan on wire rack.

Yield: 16 3-inch (7.5-cm) servings

Each with: 266 Calories; 11g Fat (35.9% calories from fat); 5g Protein; 39g Carbohydrate; 2g Dietary Fiber; 39mg Cholesterol; 227mg Sodium.

Note: If you don't have buttermilk, substitute by pouring 2 teaspoons (10 ml) vinegar or lemon juice in a 1-cup (235-ml) measure. Fill to top with milk and let sit for 2 minutes, then use in recipe.

 ## *Gluten-Free Strawberry Cheese Cake*

Luscious cheesecake with fresh strawberries is an unbeatable combination.

FOR THE CRUST:
> 1/2 cup (62.5 g) Hodgson Mill Whole Grain Apple Cinnamon Muffin Mix with Milled Flaxseeed
>
> 1/2 cup (75 g) hazelnuts, pecans, or almonds (or use 1/4 cup [31.3 g] more of muffin mix)
>
> 1/2 cup (115 g) brown sugar
>
> 4 tablespoons (1/2 stick [112 g]) butter or margarine, softened

FOR THE FILLING:
> 2 packages (8 ounces [230 g] each) cream cheese, softened, or silken tofu
>
> 2 large eggs or equivalent egg substitute
>
> 2 tablespoons (40 g) honey
>
> 2 teaspoons (10 ml) gluten-free vanilla extract

FOR THE TOPPING:
> 1 jar (12 ounces [480 g]) good quality gluten-free strawberry preserves, room temperature
>
> Fresh strawberries for garnish

Preheat oven to 350°F (180°C). Lightly grease 10-inch (25-cm) springform pan.

For crust, process muffin mix and nuts in bowl of food processor until nuts are ground. Add brown sugar and butter and pulse until crumbly and completely blended. Press into bottom of prepared pan. Bake 8 minutes.

While crust bakes, prepare filling by beating cream cheese, eggs, honey, and vanilla together until smooth. Remove crust from oven. Spoon filling into partially baked crust.

Bake 20 to 25 minutes or until toothpick inserted in center comes out clean. Let cool in pan. Chill for several hours.

When ready to serve, remove sides of pan. Carefully spread strawberry preserves over cheesecake and garnish with fresh strawberries.

Yield: 9 wedge-shaped servings

Each with: 442 Calories; 28g Fat (55.0% calories from fat); 7g Protein; 44g Carbohydrate; 1g Dietary Fiber; 111mg Cholesterol; 250mg Sodium.

Note: To make this recipe dairy- and egg-free, use margarine, egg substitute, and silken tofu.

Variation: Use any type of jam or preserve and matching fruit as a topping for this cheesecake. Simply sweeten to taste.

 ## *Gluten-Free Upside-Down Peach and Corn Meal Cake*

Adapted from a French bistro dessert recipe by Patricia Wells, this gluten-free version is every bit as good as the original.

> 3 to 4 ripe peaches, peeled, pitted, and thinly sliced
> 1/4 cup (50 g) sugar
> 1/2 cup (1 stick [112 g]) unsalted butter or margarine
> 2 large eggs or equivalent egg substitute
> 1 1/2 teaspoons (7.5 ml) gluten-free almond extract
> 1/4 cup (36 g) Hodgson Mill Stone Ground Yellow or Stone Ground Whole Grain White Corn Meal, Plain
> 1/2 cup (62.5 g) Hodgson Mill Stone Ground Whole Grain Brown Rice Flour

Preheat oven to 325°F (170°C). Grease a 10-inch (25-cm) springform pan.

Arrange peach slices in a circle, slightly overlapping, on bottom of pan. Sprinkle peaches with 1 tablespoon (13 g) of the sugar. Place remaining sugar and butter in bowl and cream together with electric mixer. Beat in eggs and extract, then corn meal and rice flour. Spoon batter on top of peaches (batter will cover peaches while baking).

Bake 45 to 50 minutes or until browned and firm to touch. Let cool in pan. To serve, remove sides of pan and unmold onto serving plate. Cut into wedges.

Yield: 12 wedge-shaped servings

Each with: 136 Calories; 9g Fat (55.7% calories from fat); 2g Protein; 14g Carbohydrate; 1g Dietary Fiber; 52mg Cholesterol; 10mg Sodium.

Note: To make this recipe dairy- and egg-free, use vegetable margarine and egg substitute.

Variation: Use apples or pears in place of peaches, 1 teaspoon (2.3 g) cinnamon in place of almond extract.

 ## *Upside-Down Peach and Corn Meal Cake*

Adapted from a French bistro dessert recipe by Patricia Wells, this moist and fragrant cake has the delicious crunch of corn meal.

   3 to 4 ripe peaches, peeled, pitted, and thinly sliced

   $^1/_2$ cup (100 g) sugar

   $^1/_2$ cup (1 stick [112 g]) unsalted butter

   2 large eggs

   1 teaspoon (5 ml) almond extract

   $^1/_4$ cup (36 g) Hodgson Mill Stone Ground Whole Grain Yellow or White Corn Meal, Plain

   $^1/_2$ cup (62.5 g) Hodgson Mill All-Purpose, Unbleached Naturally White Flour

Preheat oven to 325°F (170°C). Grease a $10^1/_2$-inch (26.3-cm) springform pan.

Arrange peach slices in a circle, slightly overlapping, on bottom of pan. Sprinkle peaches with 1 tablespoon (13 g) of the sugar. Place remaining sugar and butter in bowl and cream together with electric mixer. Beat in eggs and extract, then corn meal and flour. Spoon batter on top of peaches (batter will cover peaches while baking).

Bake 45 minutes or until browned and firm to touch. Let cool in pan. To serve, remove sides of pan and unmold onto serving plate. Cut into wedges.

Yield: 9 wedge-shaped servings

Each with: 201 Calories; 11g Fat (49.3% calories from fat); 3g Protein; 24g Carbohydrate; 1g Dietary Fiber; 69mg Cholesterol; 14mg Sodium.

Add It: Serve each slice with a dollop of whipped cream.

Variation: Use apples or pears in place of peaches and 1 teaspoon (2.3 g) cinnamon in place of almond extract.

Moist and Delicious Coconut Snack Cake

Drizzle this textured cake with warm Chocolate Ganache (recipe follows) for a fabulous finish.

1/3 cup (66 g) sugar

3 tablespoons (42 g) butter, softened

3 large eggs

1 (14 ounce [425 ml]) can coconut milk (or light coconut milk)

3/4 cup (94 g) Hodgson Mill Stone Ground Whole Grain White Whole Wheat Flour

3/4 cup (94 g) Hodgson Mill All-Purpose, Unbleached Naturally White Flour

1 tablespoon (4.5 g) baking powder

1 cup (70 g) sweetened, flaked coconut

Preheat oven to 350°F (180°C). Grease a 8 x 8 x 2-inch (20 x 20 x 5-cm) baking pan.

Cream together sugar and butter until light and fluffy. Beat in eggs and coconut milk. Add flours, baking powder, and coconut and beat until batter is mostly smooth (a few lumps is okay). Pour into prepared pan.

Bake 40 to 45 minutes or until toothpick inserted in center comes out clean. Cut into squares to serve.

Yield: 16 4-inch (10-cm) servings

Each with: 164 Calories; 10g Fat (54.9% calories from fat); 3g Protein; 16g Carbohydrate; 1g Dietary Fiber; 41 mg Cholesterol; 139mg Sodium.

Add It: Drizzle each slice with Warm Chocolate Ganache. To make Ganache, heat 1 cup (235 ml) cream in saucepan until boiling. Add 1 cup (175 g) chocolate chips, remove from heat, and let rest for 5 minutes to melt chocolate. Then whisk until glossy and dark brown.

 ## Gluten-Free Coconut Snack Cake

A wonderfully moist and delicious cake. Serve with fresh pineapple, papaya, or mango—or with a decadent chocolate glaze (recipe follows).

1/3 cup (66 g) sugar

3 tablespoons (42 g) butter or margarine

3 large eggs or equivalent egg substitute

1 (14 ounce [425 ml]) can coconut milk (can use light coconut milk)

1 cup (125 g) Hodgson Mill Stone Ground Whole Grain Brown Rice Flour

1/4 cup (32.5 g) Hodgson Mill Pure Corn Starch

1 tablespoon (4.5 g) gluten-free baking powder

1 cup (70 g) desiccated coconut, shredded or flakes (available at health food stores or Asian markets)

Preheat oven to 350°F (180°C). Grease a 8 x 8 x 2-inch (20 x 20 x 5-cm) baking pan.

Cream together sugar and butter until light and fluffy. Beat in eggs and coconut milk. Add flour, corn starch, baking powder, and coconut and beat until batter is mostly smooth (a few lumps is okay). Pour into prepared pan.

Bake 40 to 45 minutes or until toothpick inserted in center comes out clean. Cut into squares to serve.

Yield: 16 4-inch (10-cm) servings

Each with: 175 Calories; 11g Fat (55.4% calories from fat); 3g Protein; 18g Carbohydrate; 1g Dietary Fiber; 41 mg Cholesterol; 143mg Sodium.

Note: To make this recipe dairy- and egg-free, use margarine and egg substitute. Light coconut milk will give a more delicate coconut flavor.

Add It: Make a simple chocolate glaze by melting 2 ounces (55 g) semisweet chocolate in a metal bowl over simmering water. Whisk in 1 cup (100 g) confectioners' sugar until smooth, then drizzle over cake.

 ## *Gluten-Free Fresh Pear Torta*

A torta is an Italian cake, and in this case, one with fabulous fresh pear flavor enlivened with a bit of lemon.

5 to 6 ripe Bartlett pears, peeled, cored and thinly sliced

2/3 cup (82.5 g) Hodgson Mill Whole Grain Multi Purpose Baking Mix or Stone Ground Stone Ground Brown Rice Flour

1 teaspoon (1.5 g) gluten-free baking powder

1/2 teaspoon (3 g) salt

1 cup (200 g) sugar

1/2 cup (1 stick [112 g]) butter, melted, or 1/2 cup (120 ml) vegetable oil

3 large eggs or equivalent egg substitute

2 teaspoons (10 ml) gluten-free vanilla extract

1 teaspoon (1.7 g) grated lemon zest

Confectioners' sugar for dusting, optional

Place pears in a saucepan over medium heat and cook until softened, about 10 minutes. Cool slightly.

Preheat oven to 375°F (190°C). Lightly grease a 9-inch (22.5-cm) round cake pan.

Mix together baking mix, baking powder, salt and sugar until well blended. Stir in melted butter, eggs, vanilla, and lemon zest until smooth batter. Fold in cooked pears and their juices. Spoon batter into prepared pan.

Bake 30 to 35 minutes or until toothpick inserted in center comes out clean. Cut into wedges and serve.

Yield: 8 wedge-shaped servings

Each with: 333 Calories; 14g Fat (36.6% calories from fat); 4g Protein; 52g Carbohydrate; 4g Dietary Fiber; 101mg Cholesterol; 332mg Sodium.

Note: To make this recipe dairy- and egg-free, use vegetable oil and egg substitute.

Add It: Dust each serving with confectioners' sugar before serving, if desired.

 ## *Gluten-Free Cheery Cherry Batter Cake*

This French dessert, also known as clafouti, tastes wonderful made with sweet cherries. It is best eaten warm—right out of the oven.

1/2 cup (62.5 g) Hodgson Mill Whole Grain Multi Purpose Baking Mix
   or Stone Ground Whole Grain Brown Rice Flour

1/4 cup (32.5 g) Hodgson Mill Pure Corn Starch

1/2 teaspoon (3 g) salt

1/2 cup (100 g) sugar

4 large eggs, beaten, or equivalent egg substitute

1 cup (235 ml) 2 percent milk or soy milk

1 1/2 teaspoons (7.5 ml) gluten-free almond extract

2 cups (310 g) pitted fresh or frozen and thawed sweet cherries

Confectioners' sugar for dusting, optional

Preheat oven to 400°F (200°C). Grease a 10 x 16-inch (25 x 40-cm) baking pan.

Pour baking mix and corn starch into bowl. Stir in salt and sugar to blend. Whisk in eggs, milk, and extract until smooth batter. Stir in cherries. Pour batter into prepared pan.

Bake 32 to 35 minutes until toothpick inserted in center comes out clean. Cut into squares to serve.

Yield: 12 servings, about $1/3$ cup (80 ml) each

Each with: 115 Calories; 2g Fat (17.8% calories from fat); 3g Protein; 21 g Carbohydrate; 1g Dietary Fiber; 64mg Cholesterol; 118mg Sodium.

Note: To make this recipe dairy- and egg-free, use egg substitute and soy milk.

Add It: Dust each serving with confectioners' sugar before serving, if desired.

 ## *Gluten-Free Apple Stack Cake*

This is a very easy but tasty cake that features two thin layers with a cinnamon-scented fruit filling.

- 1 box (7.6 ounce [212.8 g]) Hodgson Mill Whole Grain Apple Cinnamon Muffin Mix with Milled Flax Seed
- 3 to 4 tablespoons (39 to 52 g) sugar (sweeten to taste)
- 2 tablespoons (28 g) butter or margarine
- $1/2$ cup (120 ml) 2 percent milk or soy milk
- 1 large egg or equivalent egg substitute
- $1/2$ cup chopped walnuts (optional)

FOR THE FILLING:

- 3 large apples or pears, peeled, cored, and sliced
- 1 cup (225 g) packed brown sugar
- 1 teaspoon (2.3 g) ground cinnamon

Preheat oven to 400°F (200°C). Line baking sheet with parchment paper.

Pour mix and sugar into mixing bowl; cut in butter, add milk and egg. Mix well until moist. Spoon and spread batter into two 5-inch (12.5-cm) diameter circles on baking sheet, about 3 inches (7.5 cm) apart. If using nuts, lightly press $1/4$ cup over surface of each circle.

Bake for 10 minutes or until firm to touch. Let cool on pan.

For filling, combine ingredients in saucepan and cook over medium heat until fruit is soft and syrupy. Cool briefly.

Assemble cake by placing one apple cinnamon layer on serving platter. Spread with half of cooked apple filling. Add second cake layer and top with remaining apple filling. Cut into wedges to serve.

Yield: 8 wedge-shaped servings

Each with: 337 Calories; 9g Fat (23.7% calories from fat); 7g Protein; 62g Carbohydrate; 4g Dietary Fiber; 32mg Cholesterol; 115mg Sodium.

Note: To make this recipe dairy- and egg-free, use margarine, soy milk, and egg substitute.

 ## *Appalachian Apple Gingerbread Stack Cake*

This is a very easy but tasty cake that features two thin layers with a cinnamon-scented fruit filling.

    1 box (15 ounce [420 g]) Hodgson Mill Whole Wheat Gingerbread Mix
    2 egg whites or equivalent egg substitute
    1 cup (235 ml) 2 percent milk
    4 tablespoons butter or margarine, softened

FOR THE FILLING:

    3 large apples or pears, peeled, cored, and sliced
    1 cup (225 g) packed brown sugar
    1 teaspoon (2.3 g) ground cinnamon

Preheat oven to 375°F (190°C). Line baking sheet with parchment paper.

Pour mix into mixing bowl. Stir in egg whites, milk, and butter. Beat with electric mixer for 1/2 minute at low speed, 3 minutes on high. Spread batter into 2 5-inch (12.5-cm) diameter circles on baking sheet, about 3 inches (7.5 cm) apart.

Bake 10 minutes or until firm to touch. Let cool in pan.

For filling, combine ingredients in saucepan and cook over medium heat until fruit is soft. Cool.

Assemble cake by placing one gingerbread layer on serving platter. Spread with half of apple filling. Add second gingerbread layer and top with remaining apple filling. Cut into wedges to serve.

Yield: 8 wedge-shaped servings

Each with: 400 Calories; 7g Fat (14.8% calories from fat); 6g Protein; 79g Carbohydrate; 5g Dietary Fiber; 18mg Cholesterol; 559mg Sodium.

Gluten-Free Angel Food Cake

Homemade angel food cake tastes so much better than any you can buy. You can dress it up with a special frosting, drizzle it with chocolate glaze, and serve with fresh fruit, or simply enjoy a plain (but tasty!) slice.

1/2 cup (62.5 g) Hodgson Mill Stone Ground Whole Grain Brown Rice Flour

1/2 cup (65 g) Hodgson Mill Pure Corn Starch

1 1/2 cups (300 g) sugar

12 large egg whites or equivalent egg white substitute

1/2 teaspoon (3 g) salt

1 1/2 teaspoon (4 g) gluten-free cream of tartar

1 teaspoon (5 ml) gluten-free vanilla or almond extract

Preheat oven to 325°F (170°C). Lightly grease angel food cake or tube pan.

Combine flour, corn starch, and 3/4 cup (150 g) sugar in a small bowl and stir until thoroughly mixed. Set aside. Whip egg whites, salt, and cream of tartar together until foamy at low speed using electric mixer. Increase speed to high and gradually add remaining 3/4 cup (150 g) sugar and vanilla extract until stiff peaks form. Sprinkle 1/3 of the flour mixture over the beaten whites and fold in carefully using a rubber spatula. Fold in second 1/3 of flour mixture. Add last third and fold only until it is thoroughly mixed. Spoon into prepared cake pan.

Bake 1 hour or until toothpick inserted near center comes out clean and cake has shrunk from sides of pan. Invert pan on wire rack to cool, then carefully remove cake.

Yield: 12 wedge-shaped servings

Each with: 169 Calories; trace Fat (0.9% calories from fat); 4g Protein; 38g Carbohydrate; trace Dietary Fiber; 0mg Cholesterol; 144mg Sodium.

White Whole Wheat Angel Food Cake

Made with white whole wheat flour, this version of angel food cake has an appealing light and airy yet nubby texture.

$3/4$ cup (94 g) Hodgson Mill Stone Ground Whole Grain White Whole Wheat Flour

$1/4$ cup (32.5 g) Hodgson Mill Pure Corn Starch

$1^{1}/2$ cups (300 g) sugar

12 large egg whites

$1/2$ teaspoon (3 g) salt

$1^{1}/2$ teaspoons (4 g) cream of tartar

1 teaspoon (5 ml) vanilla or almond extract

Preheat oven to 325°F (170°C). Lightly grease angel food cake or tube pan.

Combine flour, corn starch, and $3/4$ cup (150 g) sugar in a small bowl and stir until thoroughly mixed. Set aside. Whip egg whites, salt, and cream of tartar together until foamy at low speed using electric mixer. Increase speed to high and gradually add remaining $3/4$ cup (150 g) sugar and vanilla extract until stiff peaks form. Sprinkle $1/3$ of the flour mixture over the beaten whites and fold in carefully using a rubber spatula. Fold in second $1/3$ of flour mixture. Add last third and fold only until it is thoroughly mixed. Spoon into prepared cake pan.

Bake 1 hour or until toothpick inserted near center comes out clean and cake has shrunk from sides of pan. Invert pan on wire rack to cool, then carefully remove cake.

Yield: 12 wedge-shaped servings

Each with: 158 Calories; trace Fat (0.7% calories from fat); 5g Protein; 35g Carbohydrate; 1g Dietary Fiber; 0mg Cholesterol; 144mg Sodium.

Caramel Bran Cake

This snack cake packs a double helping of bran—in the cake and the crunchy broiled topping.

$1^{1}/4$ cups (295 ml) very hot water

1 cup (100 g) Hodgson Mill Wheat Bran, Unprocessed

$1/2$ cup (1 stick [112 g]) butter

$1/2$ cup (50 g) granulated sugar

$1/2$ cup (115 g) packed light or dark brown sugar

2 large egg whites

1 teaspoon (5 ml) vanilla

1 cup (125 g) Hodgson Mill Stone Ground Whole Grain White Whole Wheat Flour

1 cup (125 g) Hodgson Mill All-Purpose, Unbleached Naturally White Flour

1 teaspoon (2.3 g) ground cinnamon

1 teaspoon (1.5 g) baking soda

$1/4$ teaspoon (1.5 g) salt

FOR THE TOPPING:

3 tablespoons (42 g) butter, melted

$1/4$ cup (60 g) packed light or dark brown sugar

$1/2$ cup (75 g) chopped walnuts or mixed nuts

$1/4$ cup (25 g) Hodgson Mill Wheat Bran, Unprocessed

Preheat oven to 350°F (180°C). Lightly grease a 9 x 9 x 2-inch (22.5 x 22.5 x 5-cm) pan.

Pour water over bran in bowl and let soften for 2 to 3 minutes. Cream butter and sugars together with electric mixer in bowl until light and fluffy. Beat in egg whites, vanilla, and bran mixture. Add flours, cinnamon, baking soda, and salt. Mix well. Pour into prepared pan.

Bake 30 to 35 minutes or until toothpick inserted in center comes out clean.

For topping, combine ingredients and spread on hot cake. Broil until bubbly, about 2-3 minutes.

Yield: 9 3-inch (7.5-cm) servings

Each with: 390 Calories; 18g Fat (39.7% calories from fat); 7g Protein; 55g Carbohydrate; 6g Dietary Fiber; 38mg Cholesterol; 363mg Sodium.

 ## *Whole Wheat Gingerbread*

A square of this moist and spicy cake with a warm cup of tea is the perfect snack on a cold day.

1 box (15 ounce [420 g]) Hodgson Mill Whole Wheat Gingerbread Mix

2 egg whites or equivalent egg substitute

4 tablespoons (55 g) butter or margarine, softened

1 cup (235 ml) 2 percent milk

Preheat oven to 375°F (190°C). Lightly grease a 8 x 8 x 2-inch (20 x 20 x 5-cm) square pan.

Pour gingerbread mix into mixing bowl. Stir in egg whites, butter, and milk. Beat with electric mixer for $1/2$ minute at low speed, then 3 minutes on high. Spread batter in pan.

Bake 35 to 40 minutes or until toothpick inserted in center comes out clean.

Yield: 9 large ($2^1/2$-inch [6.3-cm]) or 12 small (2-inch [5-cm]) servings

---

Each with: 236 Calories; 6g Fat (22.3% calories from fat); 5g Protein; 39g Carbohydrate; 3g Dietary Fiber; 16mg Cholesterol; 487mg Sodium.

Note: This snack cake is moist and freezes well for up to 3 months.

Add It: This cake is delicious served warm as is or topped with whipped cream, ice cream, yogurt, or lemon sauce. Or sauté fresh apple or pear slices in butter and serve with warm gingerbread.

 ## *Spicy Pumpkin Cake*

Along with whole grain goodness, enjoy a boost of beta-carotene from the pumpkin in this moist and fragrant cake.

> 1 box (15 ounce [420 g]) Hodgson Mill Whole Wheat Gingerbread Mix
> 2 large eggs or equivalent egg substitute
> 1 can (15 ounce [420 g]) pumpkin (not pumpkin pie filling)
> $1/2$ cup (120 ml) 2 percent milk

Preheat oven to 375°F (190°C). Lightly grease a 8 x 8 x 2-inch (20 x 20 x 5-cm) square pan.

Pour gingerbread mix into mixing bowl. Stir in eggs, pumpkin, and milk. Beat with electric mixer for $1/2$ minute at low speed, then 3 minutes on high. Spread batter in prepared pan.

Bake 35 to 40 minutes or until toothpick inserted in center comes out clean.

Yield: 9 large ($2^1/2$-inch [6.3-cm]) or 12 small (2-inch [5-cm]) servings

---

Each with: 211 Calories; 1 g Fat (6.1 % calories from fat); 5g Protein; 42g Carbohydrate; 5g Dietary Fiber; 43mg Cholesterol; 431 mg Sodium.

Note: This snack cake is moist and freezes well for up to 3 months.

Add It: For a special occasion, crown this cake with a Cream Cheese Frosting. Beat together one 8 ounce (230 g) package Neufchâtel cheese and 2 tablespoons (28 g) softened butter until creamy. Beat in 1 cup (100 g) confectioners' sugar and 1 teaspoon (5 ml) vanilla. Spread the frosting over the top of the cooled cake.

Apple Ginger Cake

Enjoy this snack cake with sautéed apples for breakfast, brunch, or snacktime.

1 box (15-ounce [420 g]) Hodgson Mill Whole Wheat Gingerbread Mix
2 large eggs
2 cups (490 g) unsweetened applesauce
$1/2$ cup (120 ml) 2 percent milk

Preheat oven to 375°F (190°C). Lightly grease a 8 x 8 x 2-inch (20 x 20 x 5-cm) square pan.

Pour gingerbread mix into mixing bowl. Stir in eggs, applesauce, and milk. Beat with electric mixer for $1/2$ minute at low speed, then 3 minutes on high. Spread batter in pan. Pour into prepared pan.

Bake 35 to 40 minutes or until toothpick inserted in center comes out clean.

Yield: 9 large ($2^1/2$-inch [6.3-cm]) or 12 small (2-inch [5-cm]) servings

Each with: 218 Calories; 1g Fat (5.4% calories from fat); 5g Protein; 45g Carbohydrate; 4g Dietary Fiber; 43mg Cholesterol; 430mg Sodium.

Note: This snack cake is moist and freezes well for up to 3 months.

Add It: For a great presentation, place an 8-inch (20-cm) round paper doily on top of the cooled cake. Sift confectioners' sugar over the doily so that it makes a decorative pattern on top of the cake. Carefully remove the doily and serve!

Banana Brunch Cake

This cake is moist and delicious like banana bread, only better for you!

  2^1/2 cups (312.5 g) Hodgson Mill Whole Wheat Buttermilk Pancake Mix, Whole
    Grain Buckwheat Pancake Mix, or Multi Grain Pancake Mix

  ^{3}/4 cup (170 g) packed brown sugar

  1^1/2 teaspoons (3.5 g) ground cinnamon

  1^1/2 cups (338 g) mashed bananas (about 3 medium)

  ^{3}/4 cup (175 ml) 2 percent milk

  1 large egg

  ^{1}/2 cup (60 ml) vegetable oil

FOR THE TOPPING:

  ^{1}/2 cup (75 g) chopped nuts

  ^{1}/4 cup (60 g) packed light or dark brown sugar

  2 tablespoons (28 g) butter, melted

Preheat oven to 350°F (180°C). Lightly grease a 13 x 9-inch (32.5 x 22.5-cm) baking pan.

Pour pancake mix into mixing bowl and stir in brown sugar and cinnamon. Add banana, milk, egg, and oil. Mix well. Spread into prepared pan. For topping, combine nuts, brown sugar, and butter in a bowl. Sprinkle evenly over batter.

Bake 30 minutes or until golden brown and toothpick inserted in center comes out clean.

Yield: 12 3-inch (7.5-cm) servings

Each with: 317 Calories; 16g Fat (42.0% calories from fat); 5g Protein; 44g Carbohydrate; 4g Dietary Fiber; 22mg Cholesterol; 241mg Sodium.

 ## *Insta-Bake Blueberry Buckle* (See photo on page 230.)

The somewhat nutty flavor of whole wheat goes well with the fresh taste of blueberry for breakfast, brunch, snack, or dessert. Using the Insta-Bake Mix makes this recipe very easy—the mix combines whole wheat and all-purpose flours, along with leavening.

  ^{3}/4 cup (150 g) sugar

  ^{1}/4 cup (^{1}/2 stick [55 g]) butter

1 large egg

$^1/2$ cup (120 ml) 2 percent milk

$1^1/2$ cups (187.5 g) Hodgson Mill Whole Wheat Insta-Bake Mix

2 cups (290 g) fresh blueberries, or 1 package (12 ounces [340 g]) frozen (thawed)

FOR THE TOPPING:

$^1/2$ cup (100 g) sugar

$^1/3$ cup (41.6 g) Hodgson Mill Whole Wheat Insta-Bake Mix

$^1/2$ teaspoon (1.6 g) ground cinnamon

$^1/4$ cup ($^1/2$ stick [55 g]) softened butter

Preheat oven to 375°F (190°C). Lightly a grease 9 x 9 x 2-inch (22.5 x 22.5 x 5-cm) pan.

Cream butter and sugar with electric mixer in bowl until light and fluffy. Beat in egg and milk. Add mix to creamed mixture, $^1/2$ cup (120 ml) at a time, until smooth. Fold in blueberries. For topping, combine ingredients to form crumb mixture. Pour blueberry mixture into prepared pan. Spread crumb mixture on top of batter.

Bake 45 to 50 minutes or until toothpick inserted in center comes out clean.

Yield: 9 3-inch (7.5-cm) servings

Each with: 315 Calories; 12g Fat (32.5% calories from fat); 4g Protein; 51g Carbohydrate; 3g Dietary Fiber; 49mg Cholesterol; 296mg Sodium.

 ## *Gluten-Free Blueberry Buckle*

Cakes with the fresh taste of blueberry are great for breakfast, brunch, snack, or dessert.

$^3/4$ cup (150 g) sugar

$^1/4$ cup ($^1/2$ stick [55 g]) butter or vegetable shortening, softened

1 large egg or equivalent egg substitute

$^1/2$ cup (120 ml) 2 percent milk or soy milk

$1^1/2$ cups (187.5 g) Hodgson Mill Stone Ground Whole Grain Brown Rice Flour

2 teaspoons (3 g) gluten-free baking powder

$^1/2$ teaspoon (3 g) salt

2 cups (290 g) fresh blueberries, or 1 package (12 ounces [340 g]) frozen (thawed)

FOR THE TOPPING:

$1/2$ cup (100 g) sugar

$1/3$ cup (41.6 g) sifted Hodgson Mill Stone Ground Whole Grain Brown Rice Flour

$1/2$ teaspoon (1.6 g) ground cinnamon

$1/4$ cup ($1/2$ stick [55 g]) softened butter or margarine

Preheat oven to 375°F (190°C). Lightly grease a 9 x 9 x 2-inch (22.5 x 22.5 x 5-cm) pan.

Cream butter and sugar with electric mixer in bowl until light and fluffy. Beat in egg and milk. Combine flour, baking powder, and salt in bowl. Add to the creamed mixture, $1/2$ cup (120 ml) at a time, until smooth. Fold in blueberries. For topping, combine ingredients to form crumb mixture. Pour blueberry mixture into prepared pan. Spread crumb mixture on top of batter.

Bake 45 to 50 minutes or until toothpick inserted in center comes out clean.

Yield: 9 3-inch (7.5-cm) servings

Each with: 320 Calories; 12g Fat (32.4% calories from fat); 4g Protein; 52g Carbohydrate; 2g Dietary Fiber; 49mg Cholesterol; 346mg Sodium.

Note: To make this recipe dairy- and egg-free, use vegetable shortening, egg substitute, and soy milk.

Note: To make homemade soy milk, bring 6 cups (1.4 L) water to boil in saucepan over medium-high heat. Slowly add 1 cup (125 g) Hodgson Mill Soy Flour, stirring constantly. Strain through lined colander. Refrigerate soy milk immediately. Milk may be flavored with sweetener or vanilla as desired.

 ## *Spicy Carrot Bundt Cake* (See photo on page 231.)

With a delicious flavor and wonderful golden color, this cake deserves to be served on a special cake stand. Top with Lemon Butter Frosting (recipe follows) or a sprinkle of confectioners' sugar.

2 tablespoons (28 g) softened butter or vegetable shortening for greasing

$3/4$ cup (112.5 g) chopped pecans

$1 1/4$ cups (285 g) firmly packed light or dark brown sugar

$3/4$ cup (167 g) butter, melted

4 large eggs

1³/4 cups (218.8 g) Hodgson Mill All-Purpose, Unbleached Naturally White Flour

³/4 cup (105 g) Hodgson Mill White Corn Meal, Plain

1 tablespoon (4.5 g) baking powder

1 teaspoon (6 g) salt

1 teaspoon (2.3 g) ground allspice

1 teaspoon (2.3 g) ground cinnamon

2¹/2 cups (300 g) shredded carrots

³/4 cup (110 g) raisins

Preheat oven to 350°F (180°C). Generously grease Bundt pan with butter or shortening, then coat pan with nuts.

Beat sugar and melted butter together with electric mixer in mixing bowl. Add eggs one at a time, beating well after each addition. Combine flour, corn meal, baking powder, salt, and spices in a separate bowl. Stir into butter mixture. Add carrots and raisins. Mix well. Pour into prepared pan.

Bake 45 to 50 minutes or until toothpick inserted in center comes out clean. Immediately invert onto wire rack to cool.

Yield: 12 wedge-shaped servings

Each with: 399 Calories; 20g Fat (43.7% calories from fat); 6g Protein; 53g Carbohydrate; 3g Dietary Fiber; 99mg Cholesterol; 474mg Sodium.

Add It: To make Lemon Butter Frosting, place 2 tablespoons (28 g) melted butter in a bowl. Add 1 teaspoon (1.7 g) grated lemon zest and 1 cup (100 g) confectioners' sugar and mix until a thin, smooth icing. Drizzle or spread cooled cake with icing.

 ## *Vanilla Snack Cake*

Mellow and delicious, this cake is one that pleases children and adults alike.

2 large eggs, separated

¹/3 cup (75 g) butter or vegetable shortening, softened

³/4 cup (150 g) white sugar

¹/2 cup (65 g) Hodgson Mill Pure Corn Starch

1 cup minus 1 tablespoon (117 g) sifted Hodgson Mill
  Whole Grain Whole Wheat Pastry Flour

1 tablespoon (4.5 g) baking powder

1/2 teaspoon (3 g) salt

1/2 cup + 1 tablespoon (135 ml) 2 percent milk

1 teaspoon (5 ml) vanilla extract

Preheat oven to 350°F (180°C). Lightly grease a 9 x 9 x 2-inch (22.5 x 22.5 x 5-cm) pan.

Beat egg whites in medium mixing bowl with electric mixer until stiff; set aside. Cream butter and sugar together until light and fluffy in second large bowl. Sift together corn starch, pastry flour, baking powder, and salt in third bowl. Add the egg yolks to the butter mixture, and beat until mixture is very creamy. Beat dry ingredients into butter mixture, alternating with milk. Stir in vanilla. Fold in beaten egg whites. Spoon into prepared pan.

Bake 45 to 50 minutes or until toothpick inserted in center comes out clean. Invert cake onto wire rack to cool. Drizzle with Lemon Butter Frosting (see page 129), if desired.

Yield: 9 3-inch (7.5-cm) servings

Each with: 239 Calories; 8g Fat (30.5% calories from fat); 3g Protein; 40g Carbohydrate; 2g Dietary Fiber; 61 mg Cholesterol; 370mg Sodium.

 ## *Good-For-You Apple Cake*

Whole wheat and wheat germ pack this moist cake with great texture and nutty flavor.

2 cups (250 g) Hodgson Mill Stone Ground Whole Grain White Whole Wheat Flour

1/4 cup (50 g) Hodgson Mill Wheat Germ, Untoasted

2 teaspoons (3 g) baking soda

1 teaspoon (2.3 g) ground cinnamon

1 teaspoon (6 g) salt

1 teaspoon (3 g) freshly grated nutmeg

4 cups (600 g) diced, peeled tart cooking apples, such as Granny Smith

1 cup (200 g) sugar

1 cup (225 g) packed light or dark brown sugar

2/3 cup (155 ml) vegetable oil, such as canola

1 cup (150 g) chopped walnuts

2 large eggs, well beaten

1 teaspoon (5 ml) vanilla extract

Preheat oven to 350°F (180°C). Lightly grease a 13 x 9 x 2-inch (32.5 x 22.5 x 5-cm) baking pan.

Combine flour, wheat germ, soda, cinnamon, salt, and nutmeg in large bowl; set aside. Combine apples, sugars, oil, walnuts, eggs, and vanilla in large mixing bowl. Add flour mixture; stir gently with wooden spoon to blend well. Spoon into prepared pan.

Bake 50 minutes or until cake pulls away from sides of pan. Cool in pan on rack. If desired, sprinkle with sifted confectioners' sugar.

Yield: 12 3-inch (7.5-cm) servings

Each with: 418 Calories; 19g Fat (40.4% calories from fat); 7g Protein; 58g Carbohydrate; 4g Dietary Fiber; 31 mg Cholesterol; 404mg Sodium.

 ## *Naturally Gluten-Free Applesauce Cake*

Here's a moist and delicious cake without eggs, dairy, wheat, or corn! Just the natural goodness of whole grain flours, applesauce, and spices.

1 cup (125 g) Hodgson Mill Stone Ground Whole Grain Brown Rice Flour

3/4 cup (93.8 g) Hodgson Mill Stone Ground Whole Grain Buckwheat Flour

1/2 cup (62.5 g) Hodgson Mill Soy Flour

2 teaspoons (16 g) Hodgson Mill Pure Corn Starch

2 teaspoons (3 g) gluten-free baking powder

1 teaspoon (1.5 g) baking soda

1/2 teaspoon (3 g) salt

1 teaspoon (2.3 g) ground cinnamon

1/2 teaspoon freshly grated nutmeg

1/2 cup (120 ml) vegetable oil, such as canola

1/2 cup (100 g) sugar

1 teaspoon (5 ml) gluten-free vanilla extract

2 tablespoons (28 ml) water

1 cup (245 g) unsweetened applesauce

Preheat oven to 325°F (170°C). Lightly grease a 9 x 13 x 2-inch (22.5 x 32.5 x 5-cm) pan.

Combine flours, corn starch, baking powder, baking soda, salt, and spices together in large bowl. Make a well in center and stir in oil, sugar, vanilla, water, and applesauce until smooth. Spoon batter into prepared pan.

Bake 35 minutes or until toothpick inserted in center comes out clean. Cool in pan.

Yield: 18 2-inch (5-cm) servings

Each with: 134 Calories; 6g Fat (41.7% calories from fat); 3g Protein; 18g Carbohydrate; 2g Dietary Fiber; 0mg Cholesterol; 184mg Sodium.

 ## *Insta-Bake Strawberry Shortcakes*

Make your strawberry shortcakes with a nutritional and taste twist—the nutty, nubby flavor of whole wheat.

FOR THE FILLING:

    3 cups (330 g) fresh strawberries, hulled and sliced

    $1/2$ cup (100 g) sugar

FOR THE SHORTCAKE:

    $2^1/4$ cups (281.3 g) Hodgson Mill Whole Wheat Insta-Bake Mix

    3 tablespoons (39 g) sugar

    $1/4$ cup (60 ml) 2 percent milk

    $1/4$ cup ($1/2$ stick [55 g]) butter or margarine, melted

    1 large egg, beaten

    Whipped cream to garnish

For filling, combine strawberries and sugar in bowl. Let rest for 15 minutes or until strawberries release their juices. Use potato masher to mash half of strawberries. Combine with remaining sliced strawberries.

Preheat oven to 425°F (220°C). Line baking sheet with parchment paper.

Combine baking mix and sugar. Add milk, butter, and egg; stir to form soft dough. Turn onto a floured surface. Knead 10 strokes and roll to $3/4$-inch (1.9-cm) thick. Cut 6 to 8 circles with floured 2- or 3-inch (5- or 7.5-cm) biscuit cutter. Gather scraps, re-roll, and cut again. Place on prepared sheet about 1 inch (2.5 cm) apart.

Bake 10 minutes or until golden brown. To assemble, split shortcakes in half horizontally. Spoon strawberry mixture on bottom half of shortcake. Replace top.

Garnish with whipped cream and pass any extra strawberry mixture.

Yield: 6 2-inch (5-cm) or 8 3-inch (7.5-cm) servings

Each with: 350 Calories; 10g Fat (24.9% calories from fat); 6g Protein; 61 g Carbohydrate; 5g Dietary Fiber; 53mg Cholesterol; 420mg Sodium.

Gluten-Free Strawberry Shortcake

Celebrate summer with a delicious strawberry shortcake.

FOR THE FILLING:

3 cups (330 g) fresh strawberries, hulled and sliced

1/2 cup (100 g) sugar, or to taste

FOR THE SHORTCAKE:

2 cups (240 g) Hodgson Mill Whole Grain Multi Purpose Baking Mix

3 tablespoons (39 g) sugar

2/3 cup (158 ml) 2 percent milk or soy milk

1/2 cup (1 stick [110 g]) butter or margarine, melted

1 teaspoon (5 ml) gluten-free vanilla extract

1 large egg, beaten, or equivalent egg substitute

For filling, combine strawberries and sugar in bowl. Let rest for 15 minutes or until strawberries release their juices. Use potato masher to mash half of strawberries. Combine with remaining sliced strawberries.

Preheat oven to 425°F (220°C). Grease 8-inch (20-cm) cake pan.

Combine mix and sugar. Cut in butter until coarsely mixed. Combine milk, vanilla, and egg; add to dry mixture and stir to form soft dough. Place in prepared pan.

Bake 10 minutes or until golden brown. To assemble, cut into wedges and split shortcakes in half horizontally. Spoon strawberry mixture on bottom half of shortcake. Replace top. Garnish with whipped cream and pass any extra strawberry mixture.

Yield: 1 8-inch (20-cm) cake

Each with: 396 Calories; 19g Fat (39.8% calories from fat); 7g Protein; 58g Carbohydrate; 6g Dietary Fiber; 73mg Cholesterol; 170mg Sodium.

Note: To make this recipe dairy- and egg-free, use vegetable oil, egg substitute, and soy milk.

Note: To make homemade soy milk, see recipe note on page 128.

 ## *Low-Fat Sugarless Chocolate Cake*

Make this cake when you just have to have chocolate, but can't have fat or sugar. If you wish, use cooking spray to grease the pan and carob powder, which is stimulant-free, in place of cocoa powder.

> 1^1/2 cups (187.5 g) Hodgson Mill Stone Ground Whole Grain Whole Wheat Graham Flour
>
> ^{1}/2 cup (62.5 g) Hodgson Mill Oat Bran Flour
>
> 1 cup (25 g) Splenda Sugar Free Substitute
>
> ^{1}/2 cup (64 g) unsweetened cocoa powder
>
> 1^1/4 cups (295 ml) buttermilk or substitute (see note)
>
> 2 teaspoons (3 g) baking soda
>
> 1 large egg white
>
> 2 teaspoons (10 ml) vanilla extract

Preheat oven to 325°F (170°C). Lightly grease a 9 x 13-inch (22.5 x 32.5-cm) cake pan.

Combine flours, Splenda, and cocoa powder in bowl. Mix well. Whisk together buttermilk, baking soda, egg white, and vanilla until smooth. Make a well in center of dry ingredients and stir in buttermilk mixture until smooth. Pour into prepared pan.

Bake 30 minutes or until toothpick inserted in center comes out clean. Cool in pan on wire rack.

Yield: 12 3-inch (7.5-cm) servings

Each with: 94 Calories; 2g Fat (14.4% calories from fat); 4g Protein; 18g Carbohydrate; 4g Dietary Fiber; 16mg Cholesterol; 243mg Sodium.

Note: If you don't have buttermilk, substitute by pouring 2^1/2 teaspoons (12.38 g) vinegar or lemon juice in a 1^1/4-cup (295 ml) measure. Fill to top with milk and let sit for 2 minutes, then use in recipe.

 Pineapple Cake with Caramel Rum Sauce

It's important for the success of this cake to bring ingredients to room temperature for 30 minutes before proceeding, as softer ingredients will blend better with the textured corn meal and whole wheat pastry flour.

   1 cup (2 sticks [225 g]) butter or margarine

   2 cups (400 g) sugar

   1 teaspoon (5 ml) vanilla

   5 large eggs

   1 cup (140 g) Hodgson Mill Stone Ground Whole Grain White or Yellow Corn
      Meal, Plain

   2^1/2 cups (312.5 g) Hodgson Mill Whole Grain Whole Wheat Pastry Flour

   1 teaspoon (1.5 g) baking powder

   1 teaspoon (1.5 g) baking soda

   1 cup (245 g) pineapple-flavored yogurt

   1 can (8 ounces [200 g]) crushed pineapple, drained (reserve liquid)

FOR THE SAUCE:

   1 bottle (12 ounces [355 ml]) caramel ice cream topping

   1 tablespoon (15 ml) reserved pineapple juice

   1 to 2 teaspoons (5 to 10 ml) rum flavoring

Preheat oven to 325°F (170°C). Grease and flour Bundt or tube pan.

Cream butter with electric mixer in bowl for 30 seconds. Gradually add sugar and beat 10 minutes or until very fluffy. Add vanilla and eggs, one at a time, beating after each addition. Combine corn meal, flour, baking powder, and baking soda in bowl. Alternately add dry ingredients and yogurt to egg mixture, beating until combined. Stir in drained pineapple. Pour into prepared pan.

Bake 65 minutes or until a toothpick inserted near center comes out clean. Cool 10 minutes in pan, then invert onto wire rack to cool completely. For sauce, combine caramel ice cream topping with pineapple juice and rum flavoring. Heat just to a boil. Serve warm over sliced cake.

Yield: 18 wedge-shaped servings

Each with: 339 Calories; 12g Fat (31.9% calories from fat); 5g Protein; 55g Carbohydrate; 3g Dietary Fiber; 81 mg Cholesterol; 289mg Sodium.

 Pumpkin Snack Cake

Make this flavorful cake in the fall, when you crave the mellow flavor of pumpkin.

   1 package (7 ounces [196 g]) Hodgson Mill Whole Wheat or Whole Grain Bran Muffin Mix

   1 tablespoon (15 ml) vegetable oil, such as canola

   $1/2$ cup (120 ml) 2 percent milk

   2 large eggs

   $1/2$ cup (112.5 g) canned pumpkin (not pumpkin pie filling)

   $1/2$ teaspoon (0.7 g) ground cinnamon

   $1/4$ teaspoon freshly grated nutmeg

   $1/3$ cup (50 g) chopped pecans or walnuts, optional

Preheat oven to 375°F (190°C). Lightly grease 8 x 8 x 2-inch (20 x 20 x 5-cm) pan.

Pour mix into bowl. Blend in remaining ingredients. Spoon batter into prepared pan.

Bake 35 to 40 minutes or until toothpick inserted in center comes out clean.

Yield: 8 large (4-inch [10-cm]) or 12 small (3-inch [7.5-cm]) servings

Each with: 149 Calories; 6g Fat (35.9% calories from fat); 5g Protein; 20g Carbohydrate; 3g Dietary Fiber; 43mg Cholesterol; 112mg Sodium.

Add It: To make a quick and easy frosting, mix together 1 package (8 ounce [230 g]) cream cheese, softened; $1^2/3$ cups (166.7 g) confectioners' sugar; and 1 teaspoon (5 ml) vanilla in food processor until smooth. Frost top of cooled cake.

Whole Wheat Carrot Cake

This cake has it all—whole grains, vegetables, fruit, spice—and flavor! The verdict from testers is "very moist and very yummy!"

1^1/$_2$ cups (187.5 g) Hodgson Mill Stone Ground Whole Grain Whole Wheat Graham Flour

^{3}/$_4$ cup (75 g) sugar

1 teaspoon (1.5 g) baking powder

1 teaspoon (1.5 g) baking soda

1 teaspoon (2.3 g) ground cinnamon (or more to taste)

^{1}/$_2$ teaspoon (3 g) salt

^{2}/$_3$ cup (162 g) unsweetened applesauce

2 large egg whites

1 cup (120 g) finely shredded carrot

^{1}/$_2$ cup (100 g) juice packed pineapple (with juice)

1 teaspoon (5 ml) vanilla extract

Preheat oven to 350°F (180°C). Lightly grease a 9 x 9 x 2-inch (22.5 x 22.5 x 5-cm) pan.

Combine flour, sugar, baking powder, baking soda, cinnamon, and salt in large bowl. Make a well in center and stir in remaining ingredients until just moistened. Spoon batter into prepared pan.

Bake 30 to 35 minutes or until toothpick inserted in center comes out clean. Cool in pan on wire rack.

Yield: 9 3-inch (7.5-cm) servings

Each with: 159 Calories; trace Fat (2.1% calories from fat); 3g Protein; 37g Carbohydrate; 4g Dietary Fiber; 0mg Cholesterol; 330mg Sodium.

4

Coffee Cakes, Pastries, Donuts, and Sweet Breads

Coffee cakes, pastries, donuts, and sweet breads are more time-consuming to make, but oh so wonderful to eat. They're perfect for a special occasion, a family celebration, or a holiday.

Even special treats like these can have the goodness of whole grains, along with spices that add antioxidants, dairy that adds calcium, nuts and eggs that add protein, and pumpkin, which is full of beta-carotene.

For these special breads and pastries that need a lighter texture, it's very important to measure flour correctly. Although European bakers measure by weight to ensure the proper amount, North Americans prefer to measure by volume. But flour can compress very easily if you scoop it with the measuring cup and deposit it directly into the bowl, meaning you could end up with more flour than you need—and a heavier texture. Instead, we recommend scooping the flour from the bag or container to fill the correct measuring cup, then leveling the top using the back of a table knife before adding it to the recipe.

For these special occasion breads and pastries, it's also important to use the best ingredients—real maple syrup, butter, and extracts; fresh nuts; and good quality fillings.

And if you're going to spend the time making these wonderful treats, why not bake once, so you can enjoy twice? Make a double batch and freeze the extra to enjoy later on. Baked goods, well wrapped, can be frozen for up to 3 months. Simply thaw for a few hours or re-warm from frozen in a 350°F (180°C) oven before serving.

Lemon Berry Swirl

In this recipe, a biscuit-like dough is spread with a sweet, lemon butter, rolled up and sliced. When pastry swirls are placed over the delicious berry sauce and baked, mmmmmm!

3 cups (365 g) fresh or frozen (thawed) mixed berries, such as strawberries, blueberries, raspberries, and blackberries

FOR THE SAUCE:

$2/3$ cup (132 g) sugar

2 tablespoons (28 g) quick-cooking tapioca

$1/2$ teaspoon (1.2 g) ground cinnamon

$1/4$ teaspoon (0.6 g) freshly grated nutmeg

$1/4$ teaspoon (1.5 g) salt

1 cup (235 ml) hot water

FOR THE FILLING:

2 tablespoons (28 g) butter, softened

1 teaspoon (1.7 g) grated lemon zest

$1/4$ cup (50 g) sugar

FOR THE DOUGH:

1 cup (125 g) Hodgson Mill Whole Wheat Pastry Flour

2 teaspoons (3 g) baking powder

$1/2$ teaspoon (3 g) salt

3 tablespoons (42 g) butter

1 large egg, beaten

2 tablespoons (28 ml) 2 percent milk

Preheat oven to 425°F (220°C). Butter a 9- or 10-inch (22.5- or 25-cm) round baking pan.

Sprinkle berries over bottom of prepared pan.

For sauce, combine sugar, tapioca, spices, and salt in medium saucepan. Whisk in hot water and bring to boil over medium-high heat. Whisk while cooking until thickened, about 5 minutes. Pour hot tapioca mixture over them.

For filling, mash butter, lemon zest, and sugar together in small bowl until well combined and spreadable. Set aside.

Combine flour, baking powder, and salt in large bowl. Cut butter into mixture until it resembles coarse meal. Add egg and milk and stir to smooth dough. Turn out onto floured surface and gently knead for 1 minute.

Roll dough out on floured surface to 6 x 12-inch (15 x 30-cm) rectangle. For filling, mash butter, lemon zest, and sugar together in small bowl. Spread filling on dough, leaving 1-inch (2.5-cm) perimeter around dough. Roll up, jelly-roll style, starting with one of long sides. Cut roll into 20 slices. Place slices, cut-side (swirl-side) showing, over berries in pan. Bake 20 to 25 minutes or until dough is golden brown.

Yield: 8 to 10 servings

Each with: 239 Calories; 8g Fat (30.1% calories from fat); 3g Protein; 41 g Carbohydrate; 3g Dietary Fiber; 43mg Cholesterol; 406mg Sodium.

Add It: Pour a little cream over each serving, if you like.

 ## *Gluten-Free Apple Cinnamon Kuchen* Gluten Free

Adapted from the German kuchen, or yeast-risen coffee cake, this one has all the goodness of baked goods made from wheat flour.

    3 large eggs or equivalent egg substitute

    1 teaspoon (5 ml) cider vinegar

    3 tablespoons (45 ml) olive oil

    1/2 cup (115 g) unsweetened applesauce

    1 1/3 cups (315 ml) water

    1 cup (125 g) Hodgson Mill Whole Grain Multi Purpose Baking Mix

    1 cup (125 g) Hodgson Mill Stone Ground Whole Grain Brown Rice Flour

    1 cup (130 g) tapioca flour or potato starch

    1/2 cup (65 g) Hodgson Mill Pure Corn Starch

    4 teaspoons (28 g) xanthan gum

    3 tablespoons (45 g) packed light or dark brown sugar

    1/2 teaspoon (3 g) salt

    1 package (5/16 ounce) or 2 1/2 teaspoons (10 g) Hodgson Mill Fast-Rise Yeast

FOR THE TOPPING:

$^1/2$ cup (115 g) packed light or dark brown sugar

1 cup (125 g) Hodgson Mill Whole Grain Apple Cinnamon Muffin Mix with Milled Flax Seed

2 teaspoons (4.3 g) ground cinnamon

2 tablespoons (28 ml) melted butter or margarine

$^3/4$ cup (112.5 g) chopped pecans, optional

Whisk eggs, vinegar, and olive oil together in large bowl. Whisk in applesauce and water and pour into bread pan. Add baking mix, rice flour, tapioca flour, corn starch, xanthan gum, brown sugar, and salt. Add yeast. Select dough cycle and start machine.

When cycle is complete, stop machine. Oil two 8-inch (20-cm) round cake pans. Carefully spoon dough into prepared cake pans and smooth tops with spatula. For topping, mix ingredients together in bowl and spoon on top of batter in pans. Let rise for 15 minutes.

Preheat oven to 350°F (180°C). Bake 20 to 25 minutes or until instant-read thermometer inserted in center registers at least 190°F (87.7°C). Transfer to wire racks to cool.

Yield: 24 servings (12 servings per cake)

Each with: 173 Calories; 6g Fat (31.7% calories from fat); 3g Protein; 28g Carbohydrate; 2g Dietary Fiber; 26mg Cholesterol; 77mg Sodium.

Note: To make this recipe dairy- and egg-free, use vegetable oil and egg substitute.

Good-for-You Coffee Cake

A coffee cake that's good for you? You bet, if it's a healthy makeover of the classic sour cream coffee cake. With whole grains, omega-3s from flax seed, and beta-carotene from pumpkin, this coffee cake has all the good taste of the original, but a lot more nutrients.

$^1/2$ cup (1 stick [112 g]) butter

1 cup (200 g) sugar

1 can (15 ounce [420 g]) can pumpkin (not pumpkin pie filling)

2 large eggs

1 cup (230 g) light or regular sour cream

1 teaspoon (5 ml) vanilla extract

1 cup (125 g) Hodgson Mill Whole Grain Whole Wheat Pastry Flour

1 cup (125 g) cake flour

$^1/_2$ teaspoon (3 g) salt

$1^1/_2$ teaspoons (2.3 g) baking powder

FOR THE FILLING:

$^1/_2$ cup (115 g) packed light or dark brown sugar

1 tablespoon (7 g) ground cinnamon

$^3/_4$ cup (112. 5 g) pecan pieces

$^1/_4$ cup (70 g) Hodgson Mill Milled Flax Seed

Preheat oven to 350°F (180°C). Lightly grease tube or Bundt pan.

Cream butter and sugar together in large bowl with electric mixer. Beat in eggs, pumpkin, sour cream, and vanilla extract. Sift dry ingredients into bowl and stir together until just blended.

For filling, mix all ingredients together in bowl. Spoon half of coffee cake batter into prepared pan and sprinkle $^3/_4$ of filling over batter. Spoon remaining batter over filling. Sprinkle remaining filling on top of batter.

Bake for 55 to 60 minutes, or until toothpick inserted near center comes out clean. Let cool in pan for 10 minutes, then invert onto wire rack, remove cake pan, and set right side up to finish cooling.

Yield: 16 wedge-shaped servings

Each with: 270 Calories; 14g Fat (44.7% calories from fat); 4g Protein; 35g Carbohydrate; 3g Dietary Fiber; 45mg Cholesterol; 190mg Sodium.

Cinnamon Pecan Coffee Ring

This coffee cake, made from a biscuit-like dough, is a much quicker version of the yeast-risen Swedish tea ring, and is best served warm.

FOR THE DOUGH:

2 cups (250 g) Hodgson Mill Whole Grain Whole Wheat Pastry Flour

1 tablespoon (4.5 g) baking powder

1 teaspoon (6 g) salt

2 tablespoons (26 g) sugar

6 tablespoons (85 g) butter

1 large egg, beaten

1/2 cup (120 ml) 2 percent milk

FOR THE FILLING:

1/4 cup (4 tablespoons [55 g]) butter, softened

1/2 cup (115 g) packed light or dark brown sugar

1 tablespoon (7 g) ground cinnamon

1 teaspoon (2.3 g) ground allspice

1/2 cup (72.5 g) raisins

1/2 cup (75 g) chopped pecans

FOR THE GLAZE:

1 cup (100 g) confectioners' sugar

1/2 teaspoon (2.5 ml) vanilla extract

2 tablespoons (28 ml) 2 percent milk

Preheat oven to 425°F (220°C). Line baking sheet with parchment paper.

Combine flour, baking powder, salt, and sugar in large bowl. Cut butter into mixture until it resembles coarse meal. Add egg and milk and stir to smooth dough.

Turn out onto floured surface and gently knead for 1 minute.

Roll out to 9 x 12-inch (22.5 x 30-cm) rectangle. Spread with softened butter. Sprinkle with brown sugar, spices, raisins, and pecans, leaving 1-inch (2.5-cm) perimeter around dough. Roll up, jelly roll style, starting with one of long sides. Place seam side down on prepared pan and form a ring. Cut through ring from almost inner ring to outer edge at 2-inch (5-cm) intervals. Twist cut dough slightly to show filling.

Bake 15 minutes or until browned. While dough is baking, whisk glaze ingredients together in small bowl. When coffee ring comes out of the oven, drizzle with glaze. Cut into pieces and serve.

Yield: 16 wedge-shaped servings

Each with: 224 Calories; 10g Fat (40.3% calories from fat); 3g Protein; 32g Carbohydrate; 3g Dietary Fiber; 32mg Cholesterol; 310mg Sodium.

 ## *Strawberry Rhubarb Buttermilk Coffee Cake*

Rosy and delicious, this coffee cake could be the centerpiece of a weekend breakfast or brunch.

FOR THE TOPPING:

$1/2$ cup (100 g) sugar

$1/2$ teaspoon (1.2 g) ground cinnamon

1 tablespoon (14 g) butter, softened

FOR THE BATTER:

1 cup (125 g) Hodgson Mill Stone Ground Whole Grain White Whole Wheat or 50/50 Flour

$1^1/2$ cups (187.5 g) Hodgson Mill All-Purpose, Unbleached Naturally White Flour

1 teaspoon (1.5 g) baking soda

$1/2$ teaspoon (3 g) salt

$1^1/2$ cups (340 g) packed light or dark brown sugar

2 large eggs

1 cup (235 ml) buttermilk or substitute (see note)

$2/3$ cup (156.6 ml) vegetable oil, such as canola

1 teaspoon (5 ml) vanilla extract

1 cup (115 g) fresh or frozen (thawed) chopped rhubarb

1 cup (110 g) fresh or frozen (thawed) sliced strawberries

Preheat oven to 350°F (180°C). Lightly grease 13 x 9 x 2-inch (32.5 x 22.5 x 5-cm) pan.

For topping, combine ingredients in small bowl and set aside.

For batter, stir together flours, baking soda, and salt in large bowl. In medium bowl, whisk brown sugar, eggs, buttermilk, vegetable oil, and vanilla together. Whisk buttermilk mixture into dry mixture until smooth. Fold in rhubarb and strawberries.

Spoon batter into prepared pan. Sprinkle with topping.

Bake 40 minutes or until toothpick inserted in center comes out clean. Cool in pan on wire rack.

Yield: 16 2-inch (5-cm) servings

Each with: 280 Calories; 11g Fat (33.1% calories from fat); 3g Protein; 45g Carbohydrate; 2g Dietary Fiber; 26mg Cholesterol; 184mg Sodium.

Note: If you don't have buttermilk, substitute by pouring 2 teaspoons (10 ml) vinegar in a 1-cup (235-ml) measure. Fill to top with 2 percent milk and let sit for 2 minutes, then use in recipe.

Variation: For a snack cake, cut recipe in half and bake in a greased 13 x 9-inch (32.5 x 22.5-cm) baking pan for 15 to 17 minutes, or until toothpick inserted near center comes out clean.

 ## *Sugar and Spice Cake Donuts*

With just a hint of spice, these donuts taste wonderful hot out of the oven as a weekend treat.

2 cups (250 g) Hodgson Mill Stone Ground Whole Grain White Whole Wheat Flour

2 cups (250 g) Hodgson Mill All-Purpose, Unbleached Naturally White Flour

1/2 teaspoon (1.2 g) ground cinnamon

1/2 teaspoon (1.2 g) freshly grated nutmeg

1/2 teaspoon (3 g) salt

5 large egg yolks

1 cup (200 g) sugar

1/3 cup (80 ml) vegetable oil, such as canola, plus more for brushing

1 cup (235 ml) 2 percent milk

Confectioners' sugar for dusting

Preheat oven to 375°F (190°C). Line baking sheet with parchment paper.

Sift flour, mix, spices, and salt together in bowl. In large bowl, beat egg yolks until light and thick. Gradually add sugar, then vegetable oil. Mix in flour mixture, alternating with milk, to form smooth dough. Transfer to floured surface.

Roll out dough to $1/3$-inch (0.8-cm) thickness. Cut with donut cutter. Place donuts on prepared baking sheet. Brush donuts with vegetable oil.

Bake for 10 to 12 minutes or until lightly browned. Dust hot donuts with confectioners' sugar.

Yield: 24 donuts

Each with: 143 Calories; 4g Fat (27.3% calories from fat); 3g Protein; 24g Carbohydrate; 1g Dietary Fiber; 45mg Cholesterol; 51 mg Sodium.

Variation: Instead of confectioners' sugar, make an easy glaze by whisking 1 cup (100 g) confectioners' sugar with 2 tablespoons (28 ml) heavy cream and $1/2$ teaspoon (2.5 ml) gluten-free vanilla extract.

 ## *Gluten-Free Cinnamon Streusel Coffee Cake*

Made with baking powder, this is more of a quick bread type of coffee cake, perfect for when you want a sweet treat in a hurry.

- 1 cup (125 g) Hodgson Mill Whole Grain Apple Cinnamon Muffin Mix with Milled Flax Seed or Whole Grain Multi Purpose Baking Mix
- $1/2$ cup (65 g) Hodgson Mill Pure Corn Starch
- $1^1/2$ teaspoons (12 g) xanthan gum
- $3/4$ cup (150 g) sugar
- 2 teaspoons (3 g) gluten-free baking powder
- $1/4$ teaspoon (1.5 g) salt
- 1 cup (245 g) unsweetened applesauce or (225 g) mashed banana
- 1 large egg or equivalent egg substitute
- $1/2$ cup (120 ml) 2 percent milk or soy milk (see note)

FOR THE TOPPING:
- $1/2$ cup (115 g) packed light or dark brown sugar
- 2 tablespoons (28 g) Hodgson Mill Whole Grain Apple Cinnamon Muffin Mix with Milled Flax Seed or Whole Grain Multi Purpose Baking Mix
- 2 teaspoons (4.6 g) ground cinnamon

2 tablespoons (28 g) melted butter or margarine

3/4 cup (112.5 g) chopped pecans, optional

Preheat oven to 375°F (190°C). Grease a 9 x 9 x 2-inch (22.5 x 22.5 x 5-cm) pan.

Combine muffin mix, corn starch, xanthan gum, sugar, baking powder, and salt in large bowl. Stir in applesauce, egg, and milk until well blended. Spoon into prepared pan.

For topping, combine topping ingredients in bowl. Scatter over batter in pan.

Bake 25 to 30 minutes or until toothpick inserted in center comes out clean.

Yield: 12 2-inch (5-cm) servings

Each with: 250 Calories; 8g Fat (27.6% calories from fat); 3g Protein; 44g Carbohydrate; 2g Dietary Fiber; 22mg Cholesterol; 189mg Sodium.

Note: To make homemade soy milk, bring 6 cups (1.4 L) water to boil in saucepan over medium-high heat. Slowly add 1 cup (125 g) Hodgson Mill Soy Flour, stirring constantly. Strain through lined colander. Refrigerate soy milk immediately. Milk may be flavored with sweetener or vanilla as desired.

 ## *Blueberry Lemon Coffee Cake*

Wake up to the fresh flavor of blueberry and lemon with this coffee cake.

1 box (10 ounces [280 g]) Hodgson Mill Whole Wheat Wild Blueberry Muffin Mix with Milled Flax Seed

FOR THE TOPPING:

2 cups (290 g) fresh or frozen blueberries

2 tablespoons (26 g) sugar

2 teaspoons (10 ml) fresh lemon juice

FOR THE LEMON GLAZE:

1 teaspoon (1.7 g) grated lemon zest

1 tablespoon (15 ml) lemon juice

1 tablespoon (15 ml) water

1 cup (100 g) confectioners' sugar

Preheat oven to 350°F (180°C). Grease an 8 x 8 x 2-inch (20 x 20 x 5-cm) pan.

Prepare mix according to package directions and spoon into prepared pan. For topping, combine ingredients in bowl and spoon over batter.

Bake 25 to 30 minutes or until toothpick inserted in center comes out clean. Cool in pan on wire rack.

For glaze, whisk glaze ingredients together in bowl and drizzle over cooled coffee cake. Slice and serve.

Yield: 12 2-inch (5-cm) servings

Each with: 156 Calories; 1g Fat (4.1% calories from fat); 3g Protein; 37g Carbohydrate; 3g Dietary Fiber; 0mg Cholesterol; 137mg Sodium.

 Variation: Serve coffee cake with dollop of prepared lemon curd or blueberry or lemon yogurt instead of glaze.

Gluten-Free Apple Cinnamon Coffee Cake with Fresh Apple Topping

Apples and cinnamon combine in this fragrant coffee cake.

> 1 box (7.6 ounces [213 g]) Hodgson Mill Whole Grain Apple Cinnamon Muffin Mix with Milled Flax Seed
>
> 3 to 4 tablespoons (39 to 52 g) sugar (sweeten to taste)
>
> 2 tablespoons (28 ml) vegetable oil
>
> 1/2 cup (120 ml) 2 percent milk or soy milk (see recipe note, page 148)
>
> 1 large egg or equivalent egg substitute

FOR THE FRESH APPLE TOPPING:

> 3 large apples, peeled, cored, and sliced
>
> 1/2 cup (115 g) packed light or dark brown sugar
>
> 1 teaspoon (2.3 g) ground cinnamon
>
> Confectioners' sugar for dusting

Preheat oven to 350°F (180°C). Grease an 8 x 8-inch (20 x 20-cm) square baking pan.

Combine mix and sugar in bowl; stir in oil, milk, and egg. Mix well until moist. Spoon into prepared pan.

Bake for 30 to 35 minutes or until toothpick inserted in center comes out clean.

For topping, combine apples, brown sugar, and cinnamon in a large skillet over medium heat. Cook, stirring, until apples are soft, about 20 minutes. Let cool.

Spoon topping over coffee cake and serve, cut into squares, each dusted with confectioners' sugar.

Yield: 8 2-inch (5-cm) servings

Each with: 156 Calories; 1g Fat (4.1% calories from fat); 3g Protein; 37g Carbohydrate; 3g Dietary Fiber; 0mg Cholesterol; 137mg Sodium.

Note: To make this recipe dairy- and egg-free, use soy milk and egg substitute. To make homemade soy milk, see page 128.

Gluten-Free Cinnamon Apple Sweet Bread

This bread rises high and bakes to a golden brown, with a mellow white yeast bread flavor and tender crumb. The bonus? Luscious nuggets of cinnamon apple!

  3 large eggs or equivalent egg substitute

  1 teaspoon (5 ml) cider vinegar

  3 tablespoons (45 ml) vegetable oil

  $^1/_2$ cup (112 g) unsweetened applesauce

  1$^1/_3$ cups (315 ml) water

  1 cup (125 g) Hodgson Mill Whole Grain Multi Purpose Baking Mix

  1 cup (125 g) Hodgson Mill Stone Ground Whole Grain Brown Rice Flour

  1 cup (130 g) tapioca flour or potato starch, plus more for sprinkling

  $^1/_2$ cup (65 g) Hodgson Mill Pure Corn Starch

  4 teaspoons (28 g) xanthan gum

  3 tablespoons (42 g) packed brown sugar

  $^1/_2$ teaspoon (3 g) salt

  1 package ($^5/_{16}$ ounce) or 2$^1/_2$ teaspoons (10 g) Hodgson Mill Fast-Rise Yeast

FOR THE CINNAMON APPLE NUGGETS:

  $^1/_2$ cup (62.5 g) Hodgson Mill Whole Grain Apple Cinnamon Muffin Mix with Milled Flax Seed

  1 teaspoon (2.3 g) ground cinnamon

$^1/4$ cup (60 g) brown sugar

4 tablespoons ($^1/2$ stick [55 g]) butter or margarine, softened

Whisk eggs, vinegar, and vegetable oil together in large bowl. Whisk in applesauce and water and pour into bread pan. Start machine on dough cycle. Add baking mix, rice flour, tapioca flour, corn starch, xanthan gum, brown sugar, and salt. Add yeast.

Mix Cinnamon Apple Nuggets ingredients together in bowl. Divide mixture into 1 teaspoon (5 g) nuggets and transfer to plate. Grease 9 x 5 x 3-inch (22.5 x 12.5 x 7.5-cm) loaf pan.

When cycle is complete, stop machine. Spoon dough into bowl and stir in Cinnamon Apple Nuggets, a few at a time. Spoon dough into prepared loaf pan. Cover and let rise until doubled in bulk, about 2 hours.

Preheat oven to 350°F (180°C). Bake 45 to 50 minutes or until instant-read thermometer inserted in center registers at least 190°F (87.7°C). Turn out onto wire rack to cool.

Yield: One 1-pound (455-g) loaf

Per Recipe: 3240 Calories; 115g Fat (30.3% calories from fat); 58g Protein; 539g Carbohydrate; 26g Dietary Fiber; 685mg Cholesterol; 1903mg Sodium.

Note: To make this recipe dairy- and egg-free, use margarine and egg substitute.

 ## *Cherry Almond Babka*

This traditional Easter bread is adapted from a Russian heritage recipe, and looks as festive as it tastes.

1 package ($^5/16$ ounce) or $2^1/2$ teaspoons (10 g) Hodgson Mill
  Active Dry Yeast

$^1/2$ cup (120 ml) warm (105°F to 115°F [40.5°C to 46°C]) water

$1^1/2$ cups (187.5 g) Hodgson Mill All-Purpose, Unbleached Naturally White
  All-Purpose Flour

$1^1/2$ cups (187.5 g) Hodgson Mill Stone Ground Whole Grain White Whole
  Wheat Flour

$^1/2$ cup (100 g) sugar

$^1/2$ teaspoon (3 g) salt

1 cup (235 ml) 2 percent milk

1/2 cup (1 stick [112 g]) butter, cut into small pieces

1 teaspoon (5 ml) almond extract

4 large egg yolks

1 cup (120 g) dried cherries or sweetened, dried cranberries

FOR THE ALMOND GLAZE:

1 cup (100 g) confectioners' sugar

2 to 3 tablespoons (28 to 45 ml) 2 percent milk

1/2 teaspoon (2.5 ml) almond extract

FOR THE GARNISH:

Flaked almonds

Sprinkle yeast over water in bowl and set aside until foamy, about 5 minutes. Grease 3-quart (3.3-L) tube pan.

Mix flours, sugar, and salt together in large bowl. In saucepan or microwave, heat milk and butter until warm (120°F to 130°F [48.8°C to 54.4°C]). Gradually stir or beat in milk mixture with flour mixture. Beat in yeast mixture, then almond extract and egg yolks until smooth batter. Cover and let rise until doubled in bulk, about 30 minutes to 1 hour.

Stir batter down, then stir in dried cherries. Spoon batter into prepared pan. Cover and let rise until doubled in bulk, about 1 hour.

Preheat oven to 350°F (180°C). Bake 25 to 35 minutes or until toothpick inserted near center comes out clean. Loosen edges with knife, then invert onto wire rack and quickly turn right side up.

For glaze, whisk ingredients together until smooth. Drizzle glaze over warm babka. Garnish with flaked almonds, if desired.

Yield: 16 wedge-shaped servings

Each with: 235 Calories; 8g Fat (28.6% calories from fat); 4g Protein; 39g Carbohydrate; 2g Dietary Fiber; 70mg Cholesterol; 138mg Sodium.

Nutmeg Coffee Cake

Freshly grated nutmeg—use a small nutmeg grater or a microplane—tastes so much better than ground nutmeg in a jar. (Whole nutmegs also keep fresh much longer than ground nutmeg.) Inhale the lovely fragrance as this coffee cake bakes. Ahhhhh.

1 cup (225 g) packed dark brown sugar

1 cup (125 g) Hodgson Mill Whole Grain Whole Wheat Pastry Flour

1 cup (125 g) Hodgson Mill All-Purpose, Unbleached Naturally White Flour

2 teaspoons (3 g) baking powder

$1/4$ teaspoon (1.5 g) sea salt

1 teaspoon (1.5 g) baking soda

1 teaspoon (2.3 g) freshly grated nutmeg

$1^1/2$ sticks ($3/4$ cup [167 g]) unsalted butter, cut into small pieces

1 cup (235 ml) 2 percent milk

1 large egg

$1/2$ cup (75 g) chopped walnuts or pecans

Preheat oven to 350°F (180°C). Lightly grease a 9 x 9 x 2-inch (22.5 x 22.5 x 5-cm) square baking dish.

Combine sugar, flours, baking powder, salt, baking soda, and nutmeg in bowl. Cut butter into flour mixture until it resembles fine corn meal. Take half of dough and press into the bottom of prepared baking dish. Stir egg and milk into remaining flour mixture along with walnuts. Spoon on top of mixture in the pan.

Bake 45 to 50 minutes or until toothpick inserted in center comes out clean. Let cool in pan slightly before turning out onto wire rack to cool.

Yield: 9 3-inch (7.5-cm) servings

Each with: 381 Calories; 21g Fat (46.9% calories from fat); 6g Protein; 46g Carbohydrate; 3g Dietary Fiber; 64mg Cholesterol; 332mg Sodium.

Variation: Use cinnamon instead of nutmeg.

Whole Wheat Honey Yeast Donuts with Apricot Jelly

To serve these baked donuts for the Festival of Lights during Hanukkah, use kosher or pareve ingredients. These donuts are festive enough for a weekend morning or a winter evening's treat.

3/4 cup (175 ml) water

1/4 cup (60 ml) orange juice

1/4 cup plus 2 tablespoons (120 g) honey

2 tablespoons (24 g) Hodgson Mill Active Dry Yeast

2 cups (250 g) Hodgson Mill All-Purpose, Unbleached Naturally White Flour

1/2 cup (62.5 g) Hodgson Mill Stone Ground Whole Grain White Whole Wheat Flour

3/4 teaspoon (6 g) salt

2 large egg yolks

2 tablespoons (28 g) melted butter or margarine

Vegetable oil, such as canola, for brushing

FOR THE TOPPING:

1 cup (200 g) sugar

1 1/2 tablespoons (10.5 g) ground cinnamon

FOR THE FILLING:

1 cup (250 g) warm apricot preserves

Combine water, orange juice, and honey in small saucepan and warm to 110°F (43.3°C) over medium heat. Add yeast and stir to dissolve. Place liquid/yeast mixture in bowl of electric mixer fitted with paddle attachment.

In large bowl, sift together flours and salt. Add dry ingredients to yeast mixture and mix on low speed. Add egg yolks and melted butter and mix on low speed until soft dough is formed. Turn dough out onto well-floured surface. Place dough in oiled bowl, cover, and let rise until doubled in bulk, about 1 1/2 hours.

Lightly oil a baking sheet. Transfer dough to floured surface. Roll out to 1/2-inch (0.6-cm) thick and cut into 3-inch (7.5-cm) circles. Place circles on prepared baking sheet pan. Cover and let rise for 30 minutes.

Preheat oven to 375°F (190°C). Brush donuts with oil. Bake 8 to 10 minutes, or until golden brown.

For topping, combine sugar and cinnamon in shallow pie plate. Remove hot donuts from baking sheet and dredge in cinnamon sugar.

For filling, place apricot jelly in pastry bag fitted with a small, plain tip. Poke tip into side of each donut and gently squeeze filling evenly.

Yield: 24 donuts

Each with: 142 Calories; 1g Fat (8.9% calories from fat); 2g Protein; 32g Carbohydrate; 1g Dietary Fiber; 20mg Cholesterol; 83mg Sodium.

Variation: Fill with tart fruit jelly of your choice.

 ## *Whole Wheat Croissants*

With a cup of café au lait, you can imagine yourself at a Parisian café. Because these take a little time to prepare (but oh, how worth it!), make a double batch and keep extra in the freezer for up to 3 months. Before serving, warm in a 350°F (180°C) oven.

> 2 tablespoons (24 g) Hodgson Mill Active Dry Yeast
> $3/4$ cup (175 ml) warm (110°F to 115°F [43.3°C to 46°C]) water
> $1^1/2$ tablespoons (30 g) honey
> $1^3/4$ cups (218.8 g) Hodgson Mill Whole Grain Whole Wheat Pastry Flour
> 2 cups (4 sticks [450 g]) butter (cut into $1/2$-inch [1.2-cm] cubes)

FOR THE GLAZE:

> 1 large egg
> 1 tablespoon (15 ml) water

Sprinkle yeast in warm water in bowl and set aside until foamy, about 10 minutes.

Stir in honey and $3/4$ cup (93.8 g) flour. Whisk until smooth. Cover bowl and let stand for $1^1/2$ hours.

Combine butter pieces with remaining cup flour in large bowl. Pour in yeast batter and stir to moisten. Turn dough onto lightly floured surface, pat down, and roll into a rectangle. Fold $1/3$ of dough toward center, then fold other side of dough over first third, like folding a letter, and knead down with knuckles or the heel of your hand. Position dough rectangle at 12 o'clock position. Lift dough and scrape work surface clean. Turn dough left to 9 o'clock position, pat dough into rectangle, and repeat the folding process. Turn dough to 6 o'clock position and repeat folding process, sprinkling dough and work surface with flour as necessary. Turn dough to 3 o'clock position and repeat folding process. Dough should be stiff; if not, wrap and freeze for 45 minutes.

Press dough into rectangle. Cut into 3 equal parts. Work with 1 piece at a time, holding others in refrigerator until ready to use. Roll each part on floured surface into 1/4-inch (0.6-cm) thick rectangle. Divide rectangle in half. Cut each half diagonally to form 4 triangles. Roll from wide end to point and curve ends to form a crescent shape. Place on ungreased cookie sheets.

For glaze, beat together egg and water in small bowl. Brush croissants with glaze (reserve glaze) and let rise for 1 hour.

Preheat oven to 375°F (190°C). Brush croissants with reserved glaze once more before baking.

Bake 15 minutes or until risen and browned. Let cool slightly and serve.

Yield: 12 croissants

Each with: 351 Calories; 31g Fat (78.3% calories from fat); 4g Protein; 16g Carbohydrate; 3g Dietary Fiber; 98mg Cholesterol; 317mg Sodium.

Variation: Add 1 teaspoon (5 g) filling (chocolate chips, almond paste, raspberry, or apricot preserves) to wide end of dough triangle before rolling from wide end to point.

 ## *Gluten-Free Mashed Potato Cake Donuts*

More for snacking or "breakfast for dinner" dining, these baked donuts have a light texture and a firm "bite."

1 1/2 pounds (682.5 g [about 6 medium]) russet potatoes, peeled and quartered

1 tablespoon (14 g) butter or soy margarine

1 cup (120 g) grated mild Cheddar cheese or soy-based equivalent

1 large egg or equivalent egg substitute

1/2 teaspoon (3 g) salt

Freshly ground black pepper to taste

2 teaspoons (3 g) gluten-free baking powder

1 cup (125 g) Hodgson Mill Stone Ground Whole Grain Brown Rice Flour

Bring a pot of water to the boil over medium-high heat. Cook potatoes 20 to 25 minutes, until tender. Drain well. Mash potatoes with butter, cheese, egg, salt, and pepper. Stir in baking powder and flour. Cover and refrigerate until cold, about 2 hours.

Preheat oven to 400°F (200°C). Line baking sheet with parchment paper.

Divide potato mixture into six equal portions. Roll each portion into a 7-inch (17.5-cm) rope. Form into a donut shape, pressing to seal the circle. Place donuts on prepared baking sheet.

Bake 12 minutes or until lightly browned and firm to touch.

Yield: 6 donuts

Each with: 268 Calories; 10g Fat (31.9% calories from fat); 10g Protein; 36g Carbohydrate; 2g Dietary Fiber; 56mg Cholesterol; 493mg Sodium.

Note: To make this recipe dairy- and egg-free, use soy-based margarine, soy-based cheese, and egg substitute.

Baked Whole Wheat Cake Donuts

Measuring carefully makes all the difference in this recipe: Spoon flour into measuring cup and level top to get 1 cup (125 g), then measure 2 level tablespoons (28 g).

- 1 cup plus 2 tablespoons (153 g) Hodgson Mill Whole Grain Whole Wheat Pastry Flour
- 3/4 teaspoon (1.1 g) baking soda
- 1/2 teaspoon (1.2 g) ground cinnamon
- 1/8 teaspoon (0.7 g) salt
- 1/2 cup (100 g) sugar
- 1/3 cup plus 1 tablespoon (96.6 g) unsweetened applesauce
- 1/3 cup plus 1 tablespoon (95 ml) low-fat buttermilk or substitute (see note)
- 1 large egg
- 1 1/2 teaspoons (7.5 ml) canola oil
- 1 teaspoon (5 ml) vanilla extract

FOR THE GLAZE:

- 1 cup (100 g) confectioners' sugar
- 2 tablespoons (28 ml) apple juice, cider, or water
- 1 teaspoon (5 ml) vanilla extract

Position a rack in the center of oven and preheat to 350°F (180°C). Generously grease six 4-inch (10-cm) nonstick mini-fluted tube (Bundtlette) pans (Nordic Ware).

Whisk flour, baking soda, cinnamon, and salt in bowl until well combined. Beat sugar, applesauce, buttermilk, egg, oil, and vanilla with hand-held electric mixer on high speed until frothy, about 1^1/2 minutes. Make a well in center of the dry ingredients and pour in the applesauce mixture. Using a spoon, stir until just combined. Do not overmix.

Divide batter among prepared Bundt molds.

Bake 15 to 20 minutes or until tops spring back when pressed gently around the edges. Do not overbake. Cool in pan on wire rack for 5 minutes. Then, run knife around the inside of the molds to release the donuts. Invert onto the rack and cool completely. Place large sheet of waxed paper under rack of cooling donuts.

For glaze, whisk glaze ingredients until smooth. Drizzle over the tops of the donuts. Let stand until glaze is set, about 30 minutes.

Yield: 6 donuts

Each with: 259 Calories; 2g Fat (8.3% calories from fat); 4g Protein; 57g Carbohydrate; 3g Dietary Fiber; 32mg Cholesterol; 228mg Sodium.

Variation: Use canned pumpkin (not pumpkin pie filling) in place of applesauce.

Note: If you don't have buttermilk, substitute by pouring 2 teaspoons (10 ml) vinegar or lemon juice in a 1-cup (235-ml) measure. Fill to top with milk and let sit for 2 minutes, then use in recipe.

Maple Walnut Applesauce Coffee Cake

Top this moist, whole grain coffee cake with homemade applesauce, sautéed apples, or almond butter. For the best flavor, use real maple syrup, preferably the darker Grade B.

2 cups (250 g) Hodgson Mill Whole Grain Whole Wheat Pastry Flour

1 teaspoon (1.5 g) baking soda

2 teaspoons (4.6 g) ground cinnamon

^{1}/2 teaspoon (3 g) salt

^{1}/4 cup (60 ml) vegetable oil, such as canola

^{3}/4 cup (175 ml) maple syrup

2 large eggs

1 cup (245 g) unsweetened applesauce

1 teaspoon (5 ml) vanilla extract

1/2 cup (75 g) chopped walnuts

Preheat oven to 350°F (180°C). Lightly grease 9 x 9 x 2-inch (22.5 x 22.5 x 5-cm) square cake pan.

Combine flour, baking soda, cinnamon, and salt in medium bowl. Whisk together oil, maple syrup, eggs, applesauce, and vanilla in large bowl. Add dry ingredients and whisk until smooth and well blended. Stir in walnuts. Spoon batter into prepared cake pan.

Bake 45 to 55 minutes or until toothpick inserted in center comes out clean. Cool cake in pan on wire rack. Cut into squares to serve.

Yield: 12 servings

Each with: 212 Calories; 9g Fat (35.3% calories from fat); 4g Protein; 31 g Carbohydrate; 3g Dietary Fiber; 31 mg Cholesterol; 205mg Sodium.

Add It: Make a maple glaze by whisking together 1 cup (100 g) confectioners' sugar and 2 to 3 tablespoons (28 to 45 ml) maple syrup. Drizzle over warm cake.

 ## *German Kuchen*

If you wish, make the coffee cake dough the night before, press into the pans, cover and refrigerate. Let come to room temperature in the morning, then bake for a special weekend breakfast. If you like, freeze (up to 3 months) a baked but unglazed coffee cake.

1 package (5/16 ounce) or 2 1/2 teaspoons (10 g) Hodgson Mill Active Dry Yeast

1 cup (235 ml) warm (110°F to 115°F [43.3°C to 46°C]) water

1/4 cup (50 g) sugar

4 tablespoons (1/2 stick [55 g]) butter, softened

2 large eggs

1/2 cup (115 g) sour cream (regular or low fat)

3 cups (375 g) Hodgson Mill 50/50 Flour

FOR THE FILLING:

    2 cups (500 g) fruit spread

Sprinkle yeast over warm water in bowl. Set aside until foamy, about 5 minutes.

Beat sugar, butter, eggs, and sour cream together with electric mixer until smooth. Beat in 1 cup (125 g) flour, then yeast mixture. Beat in the remaining flour until soft dough. Cover bowl and set aside to rise until almost doubled in bulk, about 1 to $1^1/2$ hours.

Lightly grease two 8-inch (20-cm) cake pans. Divide dough in half. Press each half into prepared pan, making a 1-inch (2.5-cm) high rim of dough all around. Set aside to rise until almost doubled in bulk, about 1 to $1^1/2$ hours.

Preheat oven to 350°F (180°C). Spread each cake with half of topping.

Bake 20 to 25 minutes or until puffed and light brown around the edges. Leave in pan to cool. Slice to serve. If you wish, serve each slice with more fruit spread.

Yield: 16 servings

Each with: 235 Calories; 5g Fat (18.5% calories from fat); 4g Protein; 45g Carbohydrate; 2g Dietary Fiber; 34mg Cholesterol; 57mg Sodium.

Add It: Make Sour Cream Glaze by whisking $1/3$ cup (76.6 g) sour cream (can be low fat), 1 cup (100 g) confectioners' sugar, and 1 teaspoon (5 ml) vanilla extract together in bowl. Carefully remove coffee cake from pan. Drizzle cooled coffee cake with glaze.

Note: Fruit spreads have less sugar and more tart fruit flavor than jellies and preserves or canned fillings.

 ## *Sour Cream Apple Ginger Coffee Cake*

Enjoy this coffee cake with sautéed apples for breakfast and brunch or with after-dinner coffee.

    1 box (15 ounce [420 g]) Hodgson Mill Whole Wheat Gingerbread Mix (minus
        2 tablespoons [28 g])

    2 large eggs

    2 cups (300 g) finely chopped fresh apples (Braeburn, Gala, Pink Lady)

    1 cup (230 g) sour cream

FOR THE STREUSEL TOPPING:

2 tablespoons (28 g) Hodgson Mill Whole Wheat Gingerbread Mix

$1/4$ cup (60 g) packed light or dark brown sugar

1 tablespoon (14 g) softened butter or margarine

1 teaspoon (2.3 g) ground cinnamon

$1/4$ cup (37.5 g) chopped nuts

Preheat oven to 375°F (190°C). Lightly grease a 8 x 8 x 2-inch (20 x 20 x 5-cm) square pan.

Pour gingerbread mix into mixing bowl; remove 2 tablespoons (28 g) to another bowl for streusel topping. Combine eggs, apples, and sour cream and stir into mix. Beat with electric mixer for $1/2$ minute at low speed, then 3 minutes on high. Spoon batter into prepared pan. Mix streusel topping ingredients with remaining gingerbread mix and distribute over top of batter.

Bake 35 to 42 minutes or until toothpick inserted in center comes out clean. Cool cake on wire cooling rack 10 to 15 minutes before cutting and serving warm.

Yield: 8 large or 12 small servings

Each with: 352 Calories; 11g Fat (29.0% calories from fat); 7g Protein; 55g Carbohydrate; 5g Dietary Fiber; 63mg Cholesterol; 493mg Sodium.

Add It: Sauté apples to serve with the warm cake.

 Gluten-Free Quick Coffee Cake

Top this coffee cake with fresh fruit or fruit spread.

1 box (7.6 ounces [212.8g]) Hodgson Mill Whole Grain Apple Cinnamon Muffin Mix with Milled Flax Seed

$1/4$ cup (60 ml) vegetable oil, such as canola

1 large egg or equivalent egg substitute

3 tablespoons (60 g) honey

$1/2$ cup (120 ml) 2 percent milk or soy milk (see note)

Preheat oven to 375°F (190°C). Lightly grease 9-inch (22.5-cm) round cake pan.

Pour mix into bowl and stir in oil, egg, honey, and milk. Spoon batter into prepared pan and smooth the top.

Bake for 30 to 35 minutes or until toothpick inserted in center comes out clean. Invert coffee cake onto wire rack, then turn right side up to cool.

Yield: 12 wedge-shaped servings

Each with: 127 Calories; 6g Fat (38.9% calories from fat); 3g Protein; 17g Carbohydrate; 2g Dietary Fiber; 16mg Cholesterol; 50mg Sodium.

Note: To make this recipe dairy- and egg-free, use egg substitute and soy milk. To make homemade soy milk, see page 128.

Add It: Make a Fresh Apple Topping by peeling and coring an apple and cutting it into slices. Arrange slices on top of batter. Sprinkle apple with mixture of 1 1/2 tablespoons (19.5 g) sugar and 1 teaspoon (2.3 g) ground cinnamon.

Gluten-Free Pumpkin Coffee Cake with Streusel Topping

Golden and crunchy, this coffee cake also has beta-carotene from the pumpkin.

2 cups (250 g) Hodgson Mill Whole Grain Multi Purpose Baking Mix

2 teaspoons (3 g) gluten-free baking powder

1/4 teaspoon (1.5 g) salt

1/3 cup (115 g) honey

1/4 cup (60 ml) vegetable oil

1 large egg or equivalent egg substitute

1 teaspoon (2.3 g) ground cinnamon

1/4 cup (60 ml) 2 percent milk or soy milk

1 cup (225 g) canned pumpkin (not pumpkin pie filling)

FOR THE STREUSEL TOPPING:

2 tablespoons (28 g) Hodgson Mill Whole Grain Multi Purpose Baking Mix

1/4 cup (60 g) packed light or dark brown sugar

1 tablespoon (14 g) softened butter or margarine

1 teaspoon (2.3 g) ground cinnamon

1/4 cup (37.5 g) chopped nuts

Preheat oven to 375°F (190°C). Lightly grease a 9-inch (22.5-cm) round cake pan.

Pour mix into bowl and stir in baking powder and salt. In large bowl, mix honey, oil, egg, and cinnamon. Stir in milk, pumpkin, and dry ingredients until smooth.

Spoon batter into prepared pan and smooth top.

For topping, combine streusel topping ingredients in bowl. Sprinkle on top of batter.

Bake 30 to 35 minutes or until toothpick inserted in center comes out clean. Turn out coffee cake onto wire rack to cool.

Yield: 12 wedge-shaped servings

Each with: 200 Calories; 9g Fat (36.9% calories from fat); 4g Protein; 31 g Carbohydrate; 3g Dietary Fiber; 19mg Cholesterol; 146mg Sodium.

Note: To make homemade soy milk, see page 128.

 ## *Insta-Bake Streusel Coffee Cake*

Homemade coffee cake in 30 minutes? Yes! With the convenience of a ready-to-go baking mix but the added benefit of whole wheat, this quick coffee cake stirs together in minutes.

2 cups (250 g) Hodgson Mill Whole Wheat Insta-Bake Mix

2 tablespoons (26 g) granulated sugar

2 tablespoons (28 g) butter

1 large egg

2/3 cup (175 ml) 2 percent milk

FOR THE TOPPING:

2/3 cup (150 g) Hodgson Mill Whole Wheat Insta-Bake Mix

2/3 cup (150 g) packed light or dark brown sugar

2 teaspoons (4.6 g) ground cinnamon

4 tablespoons (1/4 cup [55g]) chilled butter

Preheat oven to 375°F (190°C). Grease a 9 x 1 1/2-inch (22.5 x 3.8-cm) round cake pan.

Combine mix and sugar in bowl and cut in butter until crumbly. Add remaining ingredients and beat for 20 strokes with wooden spoon.

Spread batter in prepared pan. Combine and mix topping ingredients together with fork. Sprinkle on top of batter in pan.

Bake 25 to 30 minutes or until toothpick inserted in center comes out clean.

Yield: 12 servings

Each with: 210 Calories; 7g Fat (29.5% calories from fat); 4g Protein; 34g Carbohydrate; 2g Dietary Fiber; 32mg Cholesterol; 268mg Sodium.

Variation: To make Sour Cream Coffee Cake, reduce milk to $1/2$ cup (120 ml) and add $3/4$ cup (172.5 g) sour cream to recipe.

 ## *Cranberry Orange Sweet Bread*

Studded with dried cranberries and subtly flavored with orange, this sweet bread helps celebrate any occasion.

2 packages ($5/16$ ounce each) or 5 teaspoons (20 g) Hodgson Mill
   Active Dry Yeast
$1/2$ cup (120 ml) warm (105°F to 115°F [43.3°C to 46°C]) water
2 cups (470 ml) 2 percent milk
$1/2$ cup (100 g) sugar
$1/2$ cup (1 stick [112 g]) butter
$1^1/2$ teaspoons (9 g) salt
1 cup (235 ml) orange juice
3 large eggs
4 cups (500 g) Hodgson Mill Stone Ground Whole Grain White Whole Wheat Flour
$4^1/2$ cups (562.5 g) Hodgson Mill All-Purpose, Unbleached Naturally White Flour
$1^1/2$ cups (180 g) dried cranberries

FOR THE GLAZE:

1 cup (100 g) confectioners' sugar
4 teaspoons (20 ml) orange juice
$1/2$ teaspoon (0.8 g) freshly grated orange zest

Sprinkle yeast over warm water in large bowl and set aside until foamy, about 10 minutes.

Scald milk in saucepan over medium-high heat until bubbles form around perimeter of pan. Stir in sugar, butter, salt, and orange juice and set aside until warm (105°F to 115°F [43.3°C to 46°C]).

Pour scalded milk mixture into yeast mixture and stir in eggs. Add 2 cups (250 g) white whole wheat flour and beat by hand until smooth or use electric stand mixer with paddle attachment. Stir in dried cranberries. Add remaining unbleached flour to make soft dough.

Turn dough out onto lightly floured surface and knead until smooth and satiny 10 minutes by hand, or 4 minutes in an electric mixer or food processor fitted with dough hook. Put dough in oiled bowl, turning to coat thoroughly. Cover and let rise until doubled in bulk, about 1 hour.

Punch down and turn out onto lightly floured surface. Divide into 3 parts and let rest for 10 minutes.

Grease three (9 x 5 x 3-inch [22.5 x 12.5 x 7.5 cm]) loaf pans. Shape dough into loaves and put into pans, seam side down. Cover with a damp cloth and let rise until dough rises just above tops of pans, about 1 hour.

Preheat oven to 375°F (190°C). Bake 35 to 40 minutes, or until instant-read thermometer inserted in center registers at least 190°F (87.7°C). Invert onto wire racks to cool.

For glaze, whisk glaze ingredients together until smooth. Drizzle over cooled loaves.

Yield: 3 loaves, 12 slices each

Each with: 158 Calories; 3g Fat (18.9% calories from fat); 4g Protein; 29g Carbohydrate; 2g Dietary Fiber; 23mg Cholesterol; 126mg Sodium.

Variation: Instead of dried cranberries, use finely snipped dried apricots or apples. Make glaze using apricot nectar or apple cider. Omit orange zest.

Braided Cinnamon Swirl Bread

Swirled with fragrant cinnamon, this bread makes fabulous cinnamon toast in the morning. Freeze an extra loaf (for up to 3 months) to enjoy later on.

   2 packages (^{5}/16 ounce each) or 5 teaspoons (20 g) Hodgson Mill Active Dry Yeast

   ^{1}/4 cup (60 ml) warm (105°F to 115°F [40.5°C to 46°C]) water

   1 cup (235 ml) 2 percent milk

   ^{1}/2 cup (100 g) sugar

   2 tablespoons (^{1}/4 cup [28 g]) butter, cut into cubes

   1^1/2 teaspoons (9 g) salt

   1^1/4 cups (295 ml) apple juice

   1 egg, slightly beaten

   3 cups (375 g) Hodgson Mill Stone Ground Whole Grain White Whole Wheat Flour

   4 cups (500 g) Hodgson Mill All-Purpose, Unbleached Naturally White Flour

FOR THE FILLING:

   ^{1}/2 cup (115 g) packed light or dark brown sugar

   1 tablespoon (13 g) sugar

   1 tablespoon (7 g) ground cinnamon

FOR THE GLAZE:

   1 cup (100 g) confectioners' sugar

   4 teaspoons (20 ml) apple juice or cider

Sprinkle yeast over warm water in large bowl and set aside until foamy, about 10 minutes.

Scald milk in saucepan over medium-high heat until bubbles form around perimeter of pan. Stir in sugar, butter, salt, apple juice, and egg, and set aside until warm (105°F to 115°F [40.5°C to 46°C]).

Stir scalded milk mixture into yeast mixture. Beat in white whole wheat flour, then 3 to 4 cups all-purpose flour or enough to form soft dough. Turn out onto floured surface and knead until smooth and satiny, 10 minutes by hand or 4 minutes in an electric mixer or food processor fitted with a dough hook. Put dough in oiled bowl, turning once to coat. Cover with a damp cloth and let rise until doubled in bulk, about 1 hour.

Lightly grease two 9 x 5 x 3-inch (22.5 x 12.5 x 7.5-cm) loaf pans. Punch dough down. Turn out onto lightly floured surface. Divide into 6 equal portions and let rest for 10 minutes.

For filling, mix together sugars and cinnamon.

Roll each dough portion into rectangle, $^1/2$-inch (1.2-cm) thick. Sprinkle each with 1 tablespoon (15 g) filling. Sprinkle each rectangle with a few drops of water and smooth with spatula. Roll each rectangle, jelly-roll style, starting with long end, into a long rope. Pinch edges closed. Braid 3 ropes together for each loaf, tucking ends under, and put in prepared pans. Cover and let rise until doubled in bulk, about 1 hour.

Preheat oven to 350°F (180°C). Bake 30 minutes or until instant-read thermometer inserted in center registers at least 190°F (87.7°C). Transfer to wire racks to cool.

For glaze, whisk glaze ingredients together until smooth. Drizzle over warm loaves.

Yield: 2 loaves, 12 slices each

Each with: 197 Calories; 2g Fat (7.1% calories from fat); 5g Protein; 43g Carbohydrate; 2g Dietary Fiber; 11mg Cholesterol; 153mg Sodium.

 ## *Chocolate Cream Coffee Cake* (See photo on page 234.)

Here's yet another good-for-you coffee cake with whole grains, antioxidants (cocoa powder), and fiber-rich almonds. With a luscious cream cheese filling, one pretty coffee cake wouldn't last 24 hours in anyone's house, so it's good that this recipe makes three!

2 packages ($^5/16$ ounce each) or 5 teaspoons (20 g) Hodgson Mill Active Dry Yeast

$^1/2$ cup (120 ml) warm (105°F to 115°F [40.5°C to 46°C]) water

$1^1/4$ cups (295 ml) 2 percent milk

8 tablespoons (1 stick [112 g]) butter

$^1/2$ cup (100 g) sugar

1 teaspoon (6 g) salt

$^1/2$ cup (64 g) unsweetened cocoa powder

2 cups (250 g) Hodgson Mill Stone Ground Whole Grain White Whole Wheat Flour

2 large eggs

2 cups (250 g) Hodgson Mill All-Purpose, Unbleached Naturally White Flour

1 cup (125 g) Hodgson Mill Best For Bread Flour

FOR THE FILLING:

    1 package (8 ounce [230 g]) cream cheese, softened

    $^1/_2$ cup (100 g) sugar

    1 teaspoon (5 ml) vanilla extract

    1 large egg

FOR THE GLAZE:

    1 cup (100 g) confectioners' sugar

    7 teaspoons (35 ml) 2 percent milk

    $^1/_2$ teaspoon (2.5 ml) vanilla extract

    $^1/_4$ cup (37.5 g) sliced almonds for garnish

Sprinkle yeast over warm water in a large bowl and set aside until foamy, about 10 minutes.

Combine milk, butter, sugar, and salt in large glass bowl or large saucepan. Heat to 135°F (57.2°C) ($1^1/_2$ minutes in a microwave or 4 minutes in saucepan over medium-high heat).

Stir in cocoa and white whole wheat flour. Spoon mixture into yeast mixture in large bowl. Mix in eggs by hand or with paddle attachment of stand mixer. Stir in remaining flours to make soft dough.

Turn dough out onto lightly floured surface. Knead dough until smooth and satiny, 10 minutes by hand or 4 minutes in electric mixer or food processor fitted with dough hook. Put dough in oiled bowl, turning once to coat thoroughly. Cover and let rise until doubled in bulk, about 1 hour.

For filling, combine cream cheese, sugar, vanilla, and egg in medium bowl until well blended. Cover and refrigerate until ready to use (can be made a day ahead).

Lightly grease three 9-inch (22.5-cm) pie pans. Transfer dough to lightly floured surface. Divide into 3 equal portions and let rest for 10 minutes.

Roll each portion into 12-inch (30-cm) circle. Drape circle over each prepared pie pan so that 1 inch (2.5 cm) of dough hangs over perimeter of pan. Spread $^1/_3$ of filling in bottom of each dough circle in pan. Cut overhanging dough at 1-inch (2.5-cm) intervals to make 2-inch (5-cm) long "fingers." Fold each dough "finger" over filling to make a fringed appearance. Do not cover and let rise until doubled in bulk, about 40 minutes.

Preheat oven to 350°F (180°C). Bake 25 minutes or until puffed and golden brown. Cool in pans on wire racks.

For glaze, whisk ingredients together and drizzle over cooled coffee cakes. Sprinkle with almonds.

Yield: 3 coffee cakes, 8 wedge-shaped servings each

Each with: 233 Calories; 9g Fat (33.9% calories from fat); 6g Protein; 34g Carbohydrate; 2g Dietary Fiber; 45mg Cholesterol; 171mg Sodium.

5

Cookies and Brownies

With a little something to sweeten, moisten, and leaven, whole grains take on an entirely new form in all-American cookies and brownies. "Cookie" is a Dutch term first used by Amelia Simmons in her 1796 cookbook. Brownies came about at the beginning of the twentieth century, when unsweetened cocoa powder and bar chocolate for baking were more widely available. In cookies, whole grains add a delightful crunchiness and a slightly nutty flavor. In brownies, they add more body.

The techniques used for making whole grain cookies and brownies are simple. Combine the dry ingredients so that the salt and baking powder are evenly dispersed in the flours, and blend the "wet" ingredients until smooth. Then, when you combine the two, stir just until the mixture is well blended. More stirring or beating can activate the gluten in the flours, which can give the cookies a tough texture.

Be sure to leave enough room for cookies to spread on the baking sheet (about 2 inches [5 cm] is right for most recipes). Once you've baked and cooled your cookies, they can be stored in an airtight container, between sheets of waxed paper, for up to 2 weeks. For longer-term storage, both cookies and brownies can be wrapped and frozen for up to 3 months.

Gluten-Free Apple Cinnamon Drop Cookies

For an after-school snack or room mother's treat, these easy cookies can be made in minutes.

$^1/2$ cup (62.5 g) Hodgson Mill Whole Grain Apple Cinnamon Muffin Mix with Milled Flax Seed

$^1/2$ cup (75 g) hazelnuts, pecans, or almonds (or use $^1/4$ cup [31.3 g] more of muffin mix)

$^1/2$ cup (115 g) packed brown sugar

4 tablespoons ($^1/2$ stick [55 g]) butter or margarine, softened

2 large eggs or equivalent egg substitute

Preheat oven to 350°F (180°C). Line 2 baking sheets with parchment paper.

Process muffin mix and nuts in bowl of food processor or blender until nuts are ground. Add brown sugar and butter and pulse until somewhat smooth. Add eggs and process until well blended.

Drop by tablespoonfuls 2 inches (5 cm) apart on prepared baking sheet.

Bake 8 minutes or until lightly browned on edges. Cool on wire racks.

Yield: 28 to 30 cookies

Each with: 54 Calories; 3g Fat (53.4% calories from fat); 1g Protein; 6g Carbohydrate; trace Dietary Fiber; 17mg Cholesterol; 26mg Sodium.

Note: To make this recipe dairy- and egg-free, use soy margarine and egg substitute.

Honey Whole Grain Cookies

These cookies provide a delicious way to add more whole grains to your diet. Pack these in a lunch, take them along on a trip, or enjoy one or two with a cup of hot herbal tea.

3 cups (375 g) Hodgson Mill Multi Grain Hot Cereal with Flaxseed and Soy, uncooked

$1^1/2$ cups (187.5 g) Hodgson Mill Whole Grain Whole Wheat Pastry Flour

$^1/2$ teaspoon (1.2 g) ground cinnamon

$^1/2$ teaspoon (1.5 g) salt

^{1}/2 teaspoon (0.7 g) baking soda

1 cup (320 g) honey

^{3}/4 cup (1^1/2 sticks [167 g]) butter or margarine, softened

^{1}/2 teaspoon (2.5 ml) vanilla extract

1 large egg

^{1}/2 cup (75 g) chopped nuts (optional)

^{1}/2 cup (72.5 g) raisins or dates (optional)

Preheat oven to 375°F (190°C). Line 2 baking sheets with parchment paper.

Combine cereal, flour, cinnamon, salt, and baking soda in large bowl. In separate bowl, mix honey, butter, vanilla, and eggs together until smooth. Stir honey mixture into dry ingredients until well blended. Add nuts and raisins (if using). Drop by rounded teaspoons onto prepared baking sheets. Flatten down into cookie shapes with slightly wet fingers or the back of a fork before baking.

Bake 10 minutes or until lightly browned at edges. Cool on wire racks.

Yield: 50 cookies

Each with: 100 Calories; 4g Fat (37.0% calories from fat); 2g Protein; 14g Carbohydrate; 2g Dietary Fiber; 11mg Cholesterol; 64mg Sodium.

 ## Gluten-Free Key Lime Cheesecake Cookies with Nut Crust

There's one word for these cookies—fabulous! The tart yet creamy filling along with a buttery nut crust make these decadent treats a true delight. Use either tiny key limes or the more common Persian limes—the ones you usually see at the grocery store.

FOR THE CRUST:

^{1}/2 cup (62.5 g) Hodgson Mill Whole Grain Apple Cinnamon Muffin Mix with Milled Flax Seed

^{1}/2 cup (75 g) hazelnuts, pecans, or almonds (or use ^{1}/4 cup [31.3 g] more of muffin mix)

^{1}/2 cup (115 g) packed brown sugar

4 tablespoons (^{1}/2 stick [55 g]) butter or margarine, softened

FOR THE FLLING:

1 package (8 ounce [230 g]) Neufchâtel cream cheese, softened, or silken tofu

1/3 cup (66.6 g) sugar

1 large egg or equivalent egg substitute

1 teaspoon (1.7 g) grated lime zest (from about 3 key limes or 1 Persian lime)

1 tablespoon (15 ml) freshly squeezed lime juice (from about 3 key limes or
1 Persian lime)

Preheat oven to 350°F (180°C). Line 36 mini muffin cups with paper liners.

For crust, process muffin mix and nuts in bowl of food processor until nuts are ground. Add brown sugar and butter and pulse until crumbly and completely blended. Press about 1 teaspoon (5 g) crumb mixture into bottom of each prepared mini muffin cup. Bake 8 minutes.

For filling, blend cream cheese, sugar, egg, lime zest, and juice together.

Remove crust from oven. Spoon 1 teaspoon (5 g) filling onto each mini muffin cup crust. Return to oven for 10 minutes or until firm. Cool in pan. Carefully lift each cookie from muffin tin to serve.

Yield: 36 cookies

Each with: 67 Calories; 4g Fat (53.8% calories from fat); 1g Protein; 7g Carbohydrate; trace Dietary Fiber; 13mg Cholesterol; 45mg Sodium.

Note: For a more intense lime flavor, use 2 teaspoons (3.4 g) lime zest.

Variation: If gluten is not a health concern, you can also make these with 1/2 cup (62.5 g) Hodgson Mill Stone Ground Whole Grain White Whole Wheat Flour or 50/50 Flour plus 1/4 teaspoon (0.6 g) ground cinnamon in place of Whole Grain Multi Purpose Baking Mix.

 ## *Raisin-Filled Whole Grain Peanut Butter Cookies*

Keep these in your cookie jar for a delicious and nutritious after-school snack or after-dinner treat.

FOR THE DOUGH:

1/2 cup (1 stick [112 g]) butter or margarine, softened

1/2 cup (130 g) peanut butter

1 cup (200 g) sugar

1 large egg

1 teaspoon (5 ml) vanilla extract

1 1/4 cups (156.3 g) Hodgson Mill Stone Ground Whole Grain White Whole Wheat Flour

1/2 teaspoon (0.8 g) baking powder

1/4 teaspoon (1.5 g) salt

FOR THE FILLING:

1 1/2 cups (217.5 g) golden raisins (or use regular raisins)

3/4 cup (175 ml) orange juice

1/3 cup (66.6 g) sugar

3/4 teaspoon (1.3 g) grated orange zest

For dough, combine butter, peanut butter, sugar, egg, and vanilla in large bowl. Beat until light and fluffy with electric mixer. Combine flour, baking powder, and salt in separate bowl. Stir into butter mixture and mix until smooth. Cover and refrigerate until firm, about 1 hour.

For filling, combine all ingredients in saucepan over medium heat. Cook, stirring frequently, until sugar dissolves and mixture thickens slightly. Cool.

Preheat oven to 350°F (180°C). Line 2 baking sheets with parchment paper.

Roll out dough on lightly floured surface to 1/8-inch (0.3-cm) thickness. Cut into 30 (2-inch [5-cm]) rounds with cookie cutter. Gather scraps, re-roll, and cut again. Place 1 teaspoon (5 g) of filling in center of half the dough rounds. Cut small circles from centers of remaining dough rounds; place on top of filled rounds. Press edges lightly together to seal. Place on prepared baking sheets.

Bake in upper third of oven 10 to12 minutes. Cool on wire racks.

Yield: 30 cookies

Each with: 131 Calories; 6g Fat (36.2% calories from fat); 2g Protein; 20g Carbohydrate; 1g Dietary Fiber; 15mg Cholesterol; 80mg Sodium.

Cranberry and Orange Corn Meal Drop Cookies

(See photo on page 235.)

You'll offer the kids a delicious, fiber-rich treat when you make these cookies.

> 1 box (7 ounces [196 g]) Hodgson Mill Whole Grain Cornbread Muffin Mix
> $^1/_4$ cup (50 g) sugar
> 1 large egg
> $^1/_2$ cup (115 g) sour cream
> 2 teaspoons (3.4 g) grated orange zest or 1 teaspoon (5 ml) orange extract
> 1 cup (120 g) sweetened, dried cranberries

Preheat oven to 350°F (180°C). Line cookie sheets with parchment paper.

Pour mix into bowl and stir in sugar. Add eggs, sour cream, and orange zest and blend to a thick batter. Fold in cranberries.

Drop by rounded teaspoonfuls, 2 inches (5 cm) apart, onto prepared cookie sheets.

Bake 10 minutes or until pale golden brown. Cool on wire rack.

Yield: 48 cookies

Each with: 26 Calories; 1g Fat (22.8% calories from fat); 1g Protein; 4g Carbohydrate; trace Dietary Fiber; 5mg Cholesterol; 30mg Sodium.

Note: For a lower-fat version, use light sour cream.

Add It: Make an Orange Glaze by mixing together 1 teaspoon (1.7 g) grated orange zest or $^1/_2$ teaspoon (2.5 ml) orange extract, 2 tablespoons (28 ml) orange juice, and 1 cup (100 g) confectioners' sugar. Drizzle warm cookies with glaze.

 ## *Citrus Corn Meal Shortbread*

Nubby-textured and buttery, these shortbread cookies are delicious with after-dinner coffee or a warm fruit compote.

> $^1/_2$ cup (1 stick [112 g]) butter, unsalted
> $^1/_2$ cup (100 g) confectioners' sugar
> 2 teaspoons (3.4 g) grated orange zest or 1 teaspoon (5 ml) orange extract
> 1 teaspoon (5 ml) vanilla extract

$^1/_2$ cup (75 g) chopped nuts, optional

Confectioners' sugar for dusting

Preheat oven to 350°F (180°C). Grease an 8 x 8 x 2-inch (20 x 20 x 5-cm) baking pan.

Place apricots in small saucepan, cover with water, and boil over medium-high heat until tender, 10 minutes. Remove from heat, drain, and cool. When cool, chop or snip into small pieces.

Combine rice flour, corn meal, corn starch, and xanthan gum in large bowl. Process butter, sugar, and 1 cup (125 g) flour mixture until crumbly in food processor. Spread mixture onto bottom of prepared pan.

Bake 25 minutes or until light brown; remove from oven, but keep oven on.

Stir baking powder and salt into remaining flour mixture. Beat in brown sugar, eggs, and vanilla until well combined. Stir in nuts and apricots; spread batter on top of crust.

Bake 30 minutes more or until lightly browned. Cool completely in baking pan on a wire rack. Cut into bars and then roll in confectioners' sugar.

Yield: 24 bars

Each with: 144 Calories; 6g Fat (36.3% calories from fat); 2g Protein; 22g Carbohydrate; 1g Dietary Fiber; 26mg Cholesterol; 90mg Sodium.

 ## *Gluten-Free Oatmeal Raisin Cookies*

Here's another classic cookie for your cookie jar, only gluten-free. While oats do not contain gluten, they do run the risk of cross-contamination, as most oat products are produced in plants that also produce wheat products. To be safe, use gluten-free oatmeal, which can be obtained through the Internet.

$^3/_4$ cup (1$^1/_2$ sticks [167 g]) butter, softened, or soy margarine
or vegetable shortening

$^3/_4$ cup (150 g) sugar

$^3/_4$ cup (170 g) packed light or dark brown sugar

2 large eggs or equivalent egg substitute

1 teaspoon (5 ml) gluten-free vanilla

$^3/_4$ cup (93.8 g) Hodgson Mill Stone Ground Whole Grain Brown Rice Flour

$^1/_4$ cup (32.5 g) Hodgson Mill Pure Corn Starch

1/4 cup (32 g) potato starch

1 teaspoon (7 g) xanthan gum

1 teaspoon (1.5 g) baking soda

1 teaspoon (2.3 g) ground cinnamon

1/2 teaspoon (3 g) salt

2 3/4 cups (220 g) organic rolled oats

1/2 cup (72.5 g) raisins

Preheat oven to 375°F (190°C). Line baking sheet with parchment paper.

Cream together butter and sugars until smooth. Beat in eggs and vanilla until fluffy. Stir together rice flour, corn starch, potato starch, xanthan gum, baking soda, cinnamon, and salt. Gradually beat into butter mixture. Stir in oats and raisins. Drop by teaspoonfuls, about 2 inches (5 cm) apart, on prepared baking sheet.

Bake 8 to10 minutes or until golden brown. Cool on wire rack.

Yield: 15 cookies

Each with: 287 Calories; 11g Fat (33.4% calories from fat); 4g Protein; 45g Carbohydrate; 2g Dietary Fiber; 50mg Cholesterol; 262mg Sodium.

Note: To make these egg- and dairy-free, use soy margarine or vegetable shortening and egg substitute.

Gluten-Free Peanut Butter Chocolate Chip Cookies

Your family might like this "fusion" cookie best of all. Make sure your peanut butter and chocolate chips are also gluten-free.

1 cup (260 g) gluten-free chunky peanut butter

1/2 cup (62.5 g) Hodgson Mill Stone Ground Whole Grain Brown Rice Flour

1/2 cup (115 g) packed light or dark brown sugar

1 large egg or equivalent egg substitute

1/2 teaspoon (2.5 ml) gluten-free vanilla extract

1 cup (175 g) gluten-free miniature chocolate chips

Preheat oven to 350°F (180°C). Line baking sheet with parchment paper.

Mix peanut butter, flour, sugar, egg, and vanilla together in bowl. Stir in chocolate chips. Using moistened hands, pinch off 1 tablespoon (15 g) dough at a time and roll into ball. Place each ball on prepared baking sheet, 2 inches (5 cm) apart.

Bake until puffed, golden on bottom, and still soft to touch in center, about 12 minutes. Cool on sheets 5 minutes. Transfer to wire racks to cool completely.

Yield: 24 cookies

Each with: 137 Calories; 8g Fat (51.1% calories from fat); 3g Protein; 15g Carbohydrate; 1g Dietary Fiber; 8mg Cholesterol; 57mg Sodium.

Note: To make this recipe egg- and dairy-free, use egg substitute.

 ## *Gluten-Free Fudge Brownies*

Make sure you use unsweetened and not semi-sweet chocolate for the best flavor. With our baking mix, these fudgy brownies assemble in minutes.

$3/4$ cup (93.8 g) Hodgson Mill Whole Grain Multi Purpose Baking Mix

$1/2$ teaspoon (0.7 g) gluten-free baking powder

$1/2$ teaspoon (1.5 g) salt

2 squares (1 ounce [56g]) gluten-free unsweetened chocolate

$1/3$ cup (75 g) butter or (80 ml) vegetable oil, such as canola

1 cup (200 g) sugar

2 large eggs or equivalent egg substitute

1 teaspoon (5 ml) gluten-free vanilla extract

$1/2$ cup (75 g) chopped nuts, optional

Preheat oven to 350°F (180°C). Lightly grease 8 x 8 x 2-inch (20 x 20 x 5-cm) square pan.

Pour baking mix into bowl and stir in baking powder and salt. Microwave chocolate and butter in glass measuring cup on High for 1 minute. Stir until chocolate is completely melted. In large bowl, mix sugar, eggs, and vanilla together, then stir in melted chocolate. Add dry ingredients and blend until smooth. Fold in chopped nuts, if desired.

Spread batter in prepared pan. Bake for 35 to 40 minutes or until toothpick inserted in center comes out clean. Cool in pan on wire rack. Cut into 2-inch (5-cm) squares and serve.

Yield: 9 brownies

Each with: 277 Calories; 16g Fat (49.3% calories from fat); 5g Protein; 33g Carbohydrate; 3g Dietary Fiber; 60mg Cholesterol; 229mg Sodium.

 ## *Spice Cookies*

Dark with molasses and fragrant with spices, these cookies get the added crunch of white whole wheat flour. You can make the dough a day ahead, then bake the cookies later on.

1^1/2 cups (187.5 g) Hodgson Mill Stone Ground Whole Grain White Whole Wheat Flour

1^1/2 cups (187.5 g) Hodgson Mill All-Purpose, Unbleached Naturally White Flour

2 teaspoons (3 g) baking soda

1^1/2 teaspoons (3.8 g) ground ginger

^{1}/2 teaspoon (1.2 g) ground cinnamon

^{1}/2 teaspoon (1.2 g) ground cloves

^{1}/4 teaspoon (1.5 g) salt

^{1}/2 cup (112 g) vegetable shortening

^{1}/2 cup (100 g) sugar

1 large egg

^{1}/2 cup (160 g) molasses

1^1/2 teaspoons (7.5 ml) cider vinegar

Sift together flours, baking soda, ginger, cinnamon, cloves, and salt in medium bowl. In large bowl, cream shortening and sugar together with electric mixer until light and fluffy. Beat in egg, molasses, and vinegar. Stir in flour mixture, 1 cup (125 g) at a time, until blended and smooth. Form dough into a ball; wrap and refrigerate for several hours or overnight.

Preheat oven to 375 °F (190°C). Line 2 baking sheets with parchment paper.

Pinch off portions of dough and roll into 1-inch (2.5-cm) balls. Place them 1 inch (2.5 cm) apart on prepared baking sheets. Use the bottom of drinking glass to flatten the balls, pressing lightly.

Bake in oven for 5 to 7 minutes or until firm. Cool on wire rack.

Yield: 36 cookies

Each with: 84 Calories; 3g Fat (32.0% calories from fat); 1g Protein; 13g Carbohydrate; 1g Dietary Fiber; 5mg Cholesterol; 88mg Sodium.

Spiced Bran Cookies

Dark, crunchy, fiber-rich, and spicy, these cookies taste great with a piece of fresh fruit.

$^1/_2$ cup (62.5 g) Hodgson Mill All-Purpose, Unbleached Naturally White Flour

$^1/_2$ cup (62.5 g) Hodgson Mill Stone Ground Whole Grain White Whole Wheat Flour

$^1/_4$ cup (50 g) sugar

$^1/_2$ teaspoon (0.7 g) baking soda

1 teaspoon (2.3 g) ground ginger

1 teaspoon (2.3 g) ground cinnamon

$^1/_2$ teaspoon (1.2 g) ground cloves

2 cups (250 g) Hodgson Mill Wheat Bran, Unprocessed

2 large eggs, well beaten

$^1/_2$ cup (160 g) molasses

$^1/_2$ cup (120 ml) 2 percent milk

$^1/_2$ cup (1 stick [112 g]) butter, melted

Preheat oven to 400°F (200°C). Line baking sheet with parchment paper.

Sift flours, sugar, baking soda, and spices together in large bowl. Add wheat bran and mix well. Combine eggs, molasses, milk, and butter in medium bowl. Stir egg mixture into wheat bran mixture until well blended. Drop by teaspoonfuls onto prepared baking sheet, 2 inches (5 cm) apart.

Bake 8 to10 minutes. Cool on wire rack.

Yield: 36 cookies

Each with: 64 Calories; 3g Fat (37.8% calories from fat); 1g Protein; 9g Carbohydrate; 2g Dietary Fiber; 18mg Cholesterol; 50mg Sodium.

Peanut Butter Oat Bran Cookies (See photo on page 237.)

This recipe gives the traditional peanut butter cookie a whole grain makeover for better taste and better nutrition.

$^1/_2$ cup (1 stick [112 g]) butter, melted

$^1/_2$ cup (100 g) sugar

$^1/_2$ cup (115 g) packed light or dark brown sugar

1 large egg or 2 large egg whites

$^1/_2$ cup (115 g) peanut butter

$^1/_2$ teaspoon (2.5 ml) vanilla extract

$^1/_2$ cup (62.5 g) Hodgson Mill Stone Ground Whole Grain White Whole Wheat Flour

$^1/_2$ cup (62.5 g) Hodgson Mill All-Purpose, Unbleached Naturally White All-Purpose Flour

$1^1/_2$ cups (187.5 g) Hodgson Mill Oat Bran Hot Cereal, uncooked

$^3/_4$ teaspoon (1.1 g) baking powder

$^1/_4$ teaspoon (0.4 g) baking soda

Preheat oven to 350°F (180°C). Line baking sheet with parchment paper.

Stir melted butter with sugars. Add egg and mix well. Beat in peanut butter and vanilla until smooth. Combine flours, cereal, baking powder, and baking soda in medium bowl. Stir in flour mixture, 1 cup (125 g) at a time, until well blended. Drop by teaspoonfuls onto prepared cookie sheet, 2 inches (5 cm) apart. Flatten by criss-crossing with the tines of a fork before baking.

Bake 10 to 12 minutes or until golden brown.

Yield: 36 cookies

Each with: 99 Calories; 5g Fat (42.6% calories from fat); 2g Protein; 13g Carbohydrate; 1g Dietary Fiber; 12mg Cholesterol; 65mg Sodium.

Organic Soy Lemon Bars

A luscious, tart, and tangy lemon bar that's good for you? Yes!

FOR THE CRUST:

$1/2$ cup (62.5 g) Hodgson Mill Stone Ground Whole Grain White Whole Wheat Flour

$1/2$ cup (62.5 g) Hodgson Mill All-Purpose, Unbleached Naturally White Flour

$1/3$ cup (41.6 g) Hodgson Mill Organic Soy Flour

$1/3$ cup (33 g) sifted confectioners' sugar

$1/2$ teaspoon (3 g) salt

$1/2$ cup (1 stick [112 g]) chilled butter, cut into pieces

FOR THE FILLING:

4 large eggs

$1^1/2$ cups (300 g) sugar

2 teaspoons (1.7 g) grated lemon zest, or to taste

$1/3$ cup (60 ml) freshly squeezed lemon juice (from about 6 lemons)

1 teaspoon (1.5 g) baking powder

1 tablespoon (8 g) Hodgson Mill Naturally White, Unbleached, All-Purpose Flour

FOR THE TOPPING:

Sifted confectioners' sugar

Preheat oven to 350°F (180°C). Lightly grease a 13 x 9 x 2-inch (32.5 x 22.5 x 5-cm) baking pan.

For crust, combine flours, confectioners' sugar, and salt in bowl or bowl of food processor. Cut in butter by hand with pastry blender or pulse in food processor until mixture is crumbly. Press mixture into prepared pan. Bake 10 minutes.

For filling, beat eggs and sugar together until smooth. Add remaining ingredients and beat until smooth. Remove baked crust from oven and pour filling on top of the hot crust. Return pan to the oven and bake an additional 18 to 20 minutes or until set. Remove pan from the oven and dust with topping. Cool on a wire rack and cut into 24 bars.

Yield: 24 bars

Each with: 123 Calories; 5g Fat (32.6% calories from fat); 2g Protein; 19g Carbohydrate; 1g Dietary Fiber; 42mg Cholesterol; 113mg Sodium.

Note: For a very tangy lemon flavor, increase the lemon zest to 1 tablespoon (5.1 g) or mix lemon and lime zest.

 ## *Organic Holiday Nut Cookies*

The combination of butter and shortening in these cookies keeps them from spreading, but if you prefer to use all butter and no shortening, just place the cookies a little farther apart when they bake.

1 cup (200 g) sugar

$^3/_4$ cup (1$^1/_2$ sticks [167 g]) unsalted butter, softened

$^1/_4$ cup (55 g) vegetable shortening

2 large egg yolks

1$^1/_2$ teaspoons (7.5 ml) vanilla extract

$^1/_4$ cup (60 ml) half-and-half

1 cup (125 g) Hodgson Mill Organic Whole Grain Whole Wheat Pastry Flour

1$^1/_4$ cups (187.5 g) Hodgson Mill Organic All-Purpose, Unbleached Naturally White Flour

$^1/_4$ teaspoon (1.5 g) salt

$^1/_4$ cup (32.5 g) Hodgson Mill Pure Corn Starch

2 teaspoons (3 g) baking powder

1 cup (150 g) ground, lightly toasted nuts, such as walnuts, almonds, or hazelnuts

Preheat oven to 350°F (180°C). Line 2 baking sheets with parchment paper.

Cream sugar, butter, and shortening until light and fluffy. Stir together egg yolks, vanilla, and half-and-half in measuring cup. Blend into creamed butter mixture.

Combine flours, salt, corn starch, and baking powder in medium bowl. Stir flour mixture, alternating with nuts, into creamed mixture on low speed until just blended. Turn dough out onto lightly floured surface and shape into soft dough. Pinch off portions of dough, roll into 1-inch (2.5-cm) balls and place on prepared baking sheets, 2 inches (5 cm) apart. Flatten balls with end of drinking glass.

Bake 15 to 17 minutes until cookies are just starting to brown at edges. Cool on wire racks.

Yield: 36 cookies

Each with: 119 Calories; 7g Fat (51.9% calories from fat); 2g Protein; 13g Carbohydrate; 1g Dietary Fiber; 23mg Cholesterol; 44mg Sodium.

 ## *Organic Holiday Chocolate Butter Cookies*

With organic, whole grain flours and the antioxidant properties of chocolate, you can feel good about baking and serving these cookies as a special treat for any holiday.

1 ounce (28 g) unsweetened chocolate

1 ounce (28 g) semi-sweet chocolate

1 cup (200 g) sugar

3/4 cup (1 1/2 sticks [167 g]) unsalted butter, softened

1/4 cup (55 g) vegetable shortening or unsalted butter

2 large egg yolks

1 1/2 teaspoons (7.5 ml) vanilla extract

1/4 cup (60 ml) half-and-half

1 cup (125 g) Hodgson Mill Organic Whole Grain Whole Wheat Pastry Flour

1 1/2 cups (187.5 g) Hodgson Mill Organic All-Purpose, Unbleached Naturally White, All-Purpose Flour

1/4 teaspoon (1.5 g) salt

2 teaspoons (3 g) baking powder

1/4 cup (32.5 g) Hodgson Mill Pure Corn Starch

Preheat oven to 350°F (180°C). Line 2 baking sheets with parchment paper.

Melt chocolate in metal bowl on top of simmering water; set aside. Cream sugar, butter, and shortening until light and fluffy. Stir together egg yolks, vanilla, and half-and-half in measuring cup. Blend egg yolk mixture and melted chocolate into creamed butter mixture.

Combine flours, salt, baking powder, and corn starch in medium bowl. Stir flour mixture, 1 cup (125 g) at a time, into creamed mixture on low speed until just blended. Turn dough out onto lightly floured surface and shape into soft dough.

Pinch off portions of dough, roll into 1-inch (2.5-cm) balls and place on prepared baking sheets, 2 inches (5 cm) apart. Flatten balls with end of drinking glass.

Bake 15 to 17 minutes until cookies are just starting to brown at edges. Cool on wire racks.

Yield: 36 cookies

Each with: 116 Calories; 6g Fat (48.5% calories from fat); 1g Protein; 14g Carbohydrate; 1g Dietary Fiber; 23mg Cholesterol; 44mg Sodium.

 ## *Organic Coconut Butter Cookies*

For a special finish, drizzle these cookies with melted chocolate.

1 cup (200 g) sugar

$^3/_4$ cup (1$^1/_2$ sticks [167 g]) unsalted butter, softened

2 tablespoons (28 g) vegetable shortening or unsalted butter

2 large egg yolks

1$^1/_2$ teaspoon (7.5 ml) vanilla extract

1 can (4 ounces [120 ml]) creamed coconut, room temperature

$^1/_4$ cup (60 ml) half-and-half

1 cup (125 g) Hodgson Mill Organic Whole Grain Whole Wheat Pastry Flour

1$^1/_2$ cups (187.5 g) Hodgson Mill Organic Naturally White, Unbleached, All-Purpose Flour

$^1/_4$ teaspoon (1.5 g) salt

$^1/_4$ cup (32.5 g) Hodgson Mill Pure Corn Starch

2 teaspoons (3 g) baking powder

$^1/_4$ cup (18 g) shredded unsweetened coconut, lightly packed, optional

$^1/_3$ cup (36.7 g) well-drained maraschino cherries, chopped, optional

Preheat oven to 350°F (180°C). Line 2 baking sheets with parchment paper.

Cream sugar, butter, and shortening until light and fluffy. Stir together egg yolks, vanilla, creamed coconut, and half-and-half in measuring cup. Blend egg yolk mixture into creamed butter mixture.

Combine flours, salt, corn starch, baking powder, and coconut in medium bowl. Stir flour mixture, 1 cup (125 g) at a time, into creamed mixture on low speed until just blended. Gently fold in cherries. Turn dough out onto lightly floured surface and shape into soft dough. Pinch off portions of dough, roll into 1-inch (2.5-cm) balls and place on prepared baking sheets, 2 inches (5 cm) apart. Flatten balls with end of drinking glass.

Bake 15 to 17 minutes until cookies are just starting to brown at edges. Cool on wire racks.

Yield: 36 cookies

Each with: 128 Calories; 7g Fat (50.4% calories from fat); 1g Protein; 15g Carbohydrate; 1g Dietary Fiber; 21 mg Cholesterol; 49mg Sodium.

White Whole Wheat Holiday Butter Cookies

If you like, use vanilla instead of almond extract. To make cookies formed with a cookie press, add a few drops of food coloring to the egg mixture before blending it in with the flour.

> 1 cup (200 g) sugar
> 1 cup (2 sticks [224 g]) unsalted butter, softened
> 2 large egg yolks
> 1 to 2 drops food coloring, optional
> 1 teaspoon (5 ml) almond extract
> $^1/_4$ cup (60 ml) half-and-half
> $1^1/_2$ cups (187.5 g) Hodgson Mill Organic Naturally White, Unbleached Flour
> 1 cup (125 g) Hodsgon Mill Stone Ground White Whole Wheat Flour
> $^1/_4$ teaspoon (1.5 g) salt
> $^1/_4$ cup (32.5 g) Hodgson Mill Pure Corn Starch
> 2 teaspoons (3 g) baking powder
> Decorative sugars and sprinkles, optional

Preheat oven to 350°F (180°C). Line 2 baking sheets with parchment paper.

Cream sugar and butter until light and fluffy. Stir together egg yolks, optional food coloring, almond extract, and half-and-half in measuring cup. Blend egg yolk mixture into creamed butter mixture.

Combine flours, salt, corn starch, and baking powder in medium bowl. Stir flour mixture, 1 cup (125 g) at a time, into creamed mixture on low speed until just blended. Turn dough out onto lightly floured surface and shape into soft dough. Fill cookie press with dough and press cookies onto prepared baking sheets, 2 inches (5 cm) apart. Decorate with optional colored sugars and sprinkles.

Bake 15 to 17 minutes until cookies are just starting to brown at edges. Cool on wire racks.

Yield: 36 cookies

Each with: 106 Calories; 6g Fat (46.6% calories from fat); 1g Protein; 13g Carbohydrate; 1g Dietary Fiber; 26mg Cholesterol; 44mg Sodium.

 ## *Healthy Jam Bars*

Use good quality fruit jam or preserves for these fiber-rich cookies.

$3/4$ cup ($1^1/2$ sticks [167 g]) butter

1 cup (225 g) packed light or dark brown sugar

$3/4$ cup (93.8 g) Hodgson Mill All-Purpose, Unbleached Naturally White Flour

$3/4$ cup (93.8 g) Hodgson Mill Stone Ground Whole Grain White Whole Wheat or Whole Grain Whole Wheat Pastry Flour

1 teaspoon (6 g) salt

$1/2$ teaspoon (0.7 g) baking soda

1 cup (125 g) Hodgson Mill Oat Bran Hot Cereal, uncooked

$1/2$ cup (62.5 g) Hodgson Mill Unprocessed Wheat Bran, Unprocessed

1 jar (12 ounces [480 g]) strawberry jam or preserves

Preheat oven to 400°F (200°C). Lightly grease a 13 x 9-inch (32.5 x 22.5-cm) baking pan.

Cream butter and sugar together until light and fluffy. Combine flours, salt, and baking soda in large bowl. Stir in oats and wheat bran. Beat cereal mixture, 1 cup (125 g) at a time, into creamed mixture to make crumbly dough. Press half of dough on bottom of prepared pan. Spread preserves on top. Sprinkle with remaining crumb mixture.

Bake 25 minutes. Cool in pan on wire rack, then cut into 10 bars.

Yield: 10 bars

Each with: 401 Calories; 15g Fat (31.9% calories from fat); 5g Protein; 68g Carbohydrate; 6g Dietary Fiber; 37mg Cholesterol; 440mg Sodium.

Whole Wheat Chocolate Chip Cookies

This just might replace the back-of-the-package cookie recipe at your house—it's that good.

2^1/4 cups (281.3 g) Hodgson Mill Whole Grain Whole Wheat Pastry Flour

1 teaspoon (1.5 g) baking powder

^{1}/2 teaspoon (0.7 g) baking soda

^{1}/4 teaspoon (1.5 g) salt

^{3}/4 cup (1^1/2 sticks [167 g]) butter, softened

^{1}/2 cup (100 g) sugar

^{1}/2 cup (115 g) packed light or dark brown sugar

1 large egg

1 teaspoon (5 ml) vanilla extract

1 package (6 ounces [131.3 g]) semi-sweet chocolate chips

Preheat oven to 375°F (190°C). Line a baking sheet with parchment paper.

Combine flour, baking powder, baking soda, and salt. Cream butter and sugars together until light and fluffy, then beat in eggs and vanilla. Add dry ingredients to creamed mixture, 1 cup (125 g) at a time, and blend well. Stir in chocolate chips. Drop by rounded teaspoonfuls, 2 inches (5 cm) apart, onto prepared baking sheet.

Bake 8 to10 minutes. Cool slightly in pan before transferring cookies to a wire rack.

Yield: 48 cookies

Each with: 63 Calories; 3g Fat (42.8% calories from fat); 1g Protein; 8g Carbohydrate; 1g Dietary Fiber; 12mg Cholesterol; 66mg Sodium.

 ## *Baker's Choice Chunky Cookies*

Made with tofu, soy margarine, and flour, these cookies have the added benefit of soy in three forms. The "choice" in the recipe title refers to the ingredients you can use to customize this cookie.

^{1}/2 cup (115 g) packed light or dark brown sugar

^{1}/2 cup (100 g) sugar

4 ounces (115 g) light silken tofu, extra firm

2 tablespoons (28 g) soy margarine

1 teaspoon (5 ml) vanilla extract

1/2 cup (62.5 g) Hodgson Mill Organic Naturally White,
     Unbleached, All-Purpose Flour

1/3 cup (41.6 g) Hodgson Mill Soy Flour

1/3 cup (41.6 g) Hodgson Mill Stone Ground Whole Grain Whole Wheat
     Graham Flour

1/3 teaspoon (3 g) salt

1/2 teaspoon (0.7 g) baking soda

3/4 to 1 cup (125 to 150 g) of your choice: raisins, dried cherries, or
     cranberries; chopped pecans or walnuts; chocolate chips, soy nuts,
     roasted sunflower seed kernels, snipped apricot, or chopped dates;
     or a mixture of any (or all) of the above

Confectioners' sugar for dusting

Preheat oven to 350°F (180°C). Line 2 baking sheets with parchment paper.

Combine sugars, tofu, margarine, and vanilla in blender or food processor and
puree until smooth. Combine flours, salt, and baking soda in separate bowl. Add to
pureed mixture and pulse to blend. Transfer dough to large bowl. Fold in "choice"
ingredients. The dough will be very stiff and chunky. Drop by rounded teaspoonfuls
onto prepared baking sheets, 2 inches (5 cm) apart. Flatten with bottom end of
drinking glass and dust with confectioners' sugar.

Bake 10 to 12 minutes or until browned, but slightly soft. Cool slightly in pan, then
transfer to wire rack to cool completely.

Yield: 24 cookies

Each with: 78 Calories; 1g Fat (13.4% calories from fat); 2g Protein; 16g Carbohydrate; 1g Dietary
Fiber; 0mg Cholesterol; 70mg Sodium.

Honey Spelt Shortbread Cookies

The trick to this recipe is not to overbake the shortbread cookies, as they can lose
their buttery flavor. These cookies are naturally low in gluten.

1 cup (2 sticks [225 g]) butter, softened

1/4 cup (80 g) honey

1/3 cup (41.6 g) Hodgson Mill Stone Ground Whole Grain Brown Rice Flour

2 cups (250 g) Hodgson Mill Stone Whole Grain Organic Spelt Flour

Line 2 baking sheets with parchment paper.

Cream butter and honey with electric mixer in medium bowl until light and fluffy. Beat in rice flour until quite soft and not grainy. Add spelt flour and mix until dough holds together (use hands if necessary). Divide into 3 equal portions. Press each portion into a 6-inch (15-cm) round about $^1/4$-inch (0.6-cm) thick. Pierce each round with tines of fork all the way through dough. Score each round into 8 wedges. Chill in refrigerator 1 hour or until set.

Preheat oven to 325°F (170°C). Bake 40 to 45 minutes or until edges are brown. wnie, add 2 tablespoons (28 ml) of water with the eggs.

Add It: Make a glaze by melting 2 tablespoons (28 g) butter in microwave, then mixing in $1^1/2$ teaspoons (3.9 g) unsweetened cocoa powder, 1 cup (100 g) confectioners' sugar, and $^1/4$ cup (60 ml) 2 percent milk until smooth. Spread over warm brownies in the pan.

Yield: 24 cookies

Each with: 113 Calories; 8g Fat (58.0% calories from fat); 2g Protein; 11g Carbohydrate; 2g Dietary Fiber; 21 mg Cholesterol; 78mg Sodium.

 ## *Whole Wheat Brownies with Milled Flax Seed*

Moist and fudgey, these brownies also have the benefit of whole wheat and omega-3 fatty acids from flax seed in the brownie mix.

$^1/4$ cup ($^1/2$ stick [55 g]) butter or margarine

$^1/4$ cup (60 ml) vegetable oil, such as canola

1 box (12 ounces [420 g]) Hodgson Mill Whole Wheat Brownie Mix with Milled Flax Seed

2 large eggs, beaten

Preheat oven to 350°F (170°C). Lightly grease an 8 x 8 x 2-inch (20 x 20 x 5-cm) baking pan.

Melt butter or margarine in microwave-safe mixing bowl in microwave on High for 5 seconds or until melted. Stir in vegetable oil and mix until just blended. Stir in eggs. Spread batter in prepared pan.

Bake 20 to 24 minutes or until toothpick inserted in center comes out clean. Cool completely in pan before cutting.

Yield: 16 brownies

Each with: 139 Calories; 7g Fat (44.3% calories from fat); 3g Protein; 18g Carbohydrate; 1g Dietary Fiber; 31 mg Cholesterol; 86mg Sodium.

Note: For a chewier brownie, add 2 tablespoons (28 ml) of water with the eggs.

Add It: Make a glaze by melting 2 tablespoons (28 g) butter in microwave, then mixing in 1^1/2 teaspoons (3.9 g) unsweetened cocoa powder, 1 cup (100 g) confectioners' sugar, and ^{1}/4 cup (60 ml) 2 percent milk until smooth. Spread over warm brownies in the pan.

Reduced-Fat Whole Wheat Brownies

Enjoy these fiber-rich, fudgey brownies that have less fat.

    4 tablespoons (^{1}/2 stick [55 g]) butter or margarine, softened
    1 box (12 ounces [420 g]) Hodgson Mill Whole Wheat Brownie Mix
        with Milled Flax Seed
    ^{1}/3 cup (81.6 g) unsweetened applesauce
    1 large egg, beaten

Preheat oven to 350°F (180°C). Lightly grease an 8 x 8 x 2-inch (20 x 20 x 5-cm) baking pan.

Melt butter or margarine in microwave-safe mixing bowl in microwave on High for 5 seconds or until melted. Stir in brownie mix and applesauce until just blended. Stir in egg. Spread batter in prepared pan.

Bake 20 to 24 minutes or until toothpick inserted in center comes out clean. Cool completely in pan before cutting.

Yield: 16 brownies

Each with: 107 Calories; 3g Fat (27.7% calories from fat); 2g Protein; 18g Carbohydrate; 1g Dietary Fiber; 19mg Cholesterol; 83mg Sodium.

Add It: Place paper doily over the top of the cooled brownies in their pan and dust with confectioners' sugar to make a pattern.

Note: For a chewier brownie, add 2 tablespoons (28 ml) water along with the egg.

Whole Wheat Graham Brownies

These brownies are almost souffle-like in texture, which depends on creaming the butter and sugar together until they are very light and fluffy. Very light, very choco-latey, very good!

2 squares (1 ounce [28 g]) squares unsweetened chocolate

1/2 cup (1 stick [112 g]) butter or margarine

1/2 cup (115 g) packed light or dark brown sugar

2 large eggs

1 teaspoon (5 ml) vanilla extract

1/2 cup (62.5 g) Hodgson Mill Stone Ground Whole Grain Whole Wheat Graham Flour

1/2 cup (75 g) chopped pecans

Preheat oven to 325°F (170°C). Lightly grease a 8 x 8 x 2-inch (20 x 20 x 5-cm) square pan.

Melt chocolate in a double-boiler (or, if double-boiler is unavailable, a metal bowl over simmering water); set aside. Cream butter and brown sugar together with elec-tric mixer until light and fluffy. Add eggs, melted chocolate, and vanilla and beat well. Stir in whole wheat flour and chopped pecans until just blended. Spread in pre-pared pan.

Bake 35 to 40 minutes or until toothpick inserted in center comes out clean. Cool in pan.

Yield: 16 brownies

Each with: 141 Calories; 11g Fat (65.1% calories from fat); 2g Protein; 11g Carbohydrate; 1g Dietary Fiber; 39mg Cholesterol; 69mg Sodium.

Add It: To make a simple chocolate icing, beat together 1 1/2 squares (1-ounce [42 g each]) melted, unsweetened chocolate; 1/4 teaspoon (1.5 g) salt; 1/2 teaspoon (2.5 ml) vanilla extract, 3 tablespoons (45 ml) milk, and about 1/2 cup (50 g) confectioners' sugar to make a good spreading consistency. Spread over cooled brownies in pan, then cut into squares.

Variation: Substitute chopped hazelnuts, almonds, or walnuts for pecans.

Honey Whole Wheat Chocolate Chip Cookies

The sweet taste of honey makes these cookies extraordinary.

$^1/_2$ cup (1 stick [112 g]) butter or margarine, softened

$^1/_3$ cup (115 g) mild-flavored honey

1 large egg

1 teaspoon (5 ml) vanilla extract

1$^3/_4$ cups (218.8 g) Hodgson Mill Stone Ground Whole Grain Whole Wheat
  Graham Flour or Whole Grain White Whole Wheat Flour

1 teaspoon (1.5 g) baking powder

1 package (6 ounces [131.3 g]) semi-sweet chocolate chips

$^1/_2$ cup (75 g) chopped pecans

Preheat oven to 400°F (200°C). Line baking sheet with parchment paper.

Cream butter with electric mixer until light and fluffy. Add honey, egg, and vanilla and beat well.

Stir whole wheat flour and baking powder together in bowl. Stir flour mixture into creamed mixture, $^1/_2$ cup (62.5 g) at a time, until well blended. Stir in chopped pecans and chocolate chips. Drop by rounded teaspoonfuls onto prepared baking sheet, 2 inches (5 cm) apart.

Bake 10 minutes or until lightly browned. Cool on wire racks.

Yield: 36 cookies

Each with: 87 Calories; 5g Fat (51.3% calories from fat); 1g Protein; 10g Carbohydrate; 1g Dietary Fiber; 12mg Cholesterol; 42mg Sodium.

 ## *White Whole Wheat Sugar Cookies*

When you're introducing your family to whole grain baking, start off by baking a batch of these yummy sugar cookies, made with mellow white whole wheat flour. They'll never realize they're eating whole grains!

1 cup (200 g) sugar, plus more for dipping

$^1/_2$ cup (1 stick [112 g]) butter or margarine, softened

2 tablespoons (28 ml) 2 percent milk

1 tablespoon (1.7 g) grated lemon zest

1 teaspoon (5 ml) vanilla extract

1 large egg white

2 cups (250 g) Hodgson Mill Stone Ground Whole Grain White Whole
Wheat Flour

1 teaspoon (1.5 g) baking powder

$^1/_2$ teaspoon (0.7 g) baking soda

$^1/_2$ teaspoon (1.4 g) freshly grated nutmeg

FOR THE TOPPING:

2 tablespoons (26 g) sugar

$^1/_2$ teaspoon (1.2 g) ground cinnamon

Preheat oven to 375°F (190°C). Line 2 baking sheets with parchment paper.

Cream butter and sugar together until light and fluffy. Beat in milk, lemon zest, vanilla, and egg white until smooth. Combine flour, baking powder, baking soda, and nutmeg in bowl. Beat flour mixture, 1 cup (125 g) at a time, into creamed mixture. Pinch off dough and roll into 1-inch (2.5-cm) balls. Place on prepared baking sheets, 2 inches (5 cm) apart. Flatten each cookie with the bottom of a glass dipped in sugar. For topping, blend sugar and cinnamon and sprinkle over cookies.

Bake 8 to 10 minutes or until lightly browned. Cool on wire racks.

Yield: 36 cookies

Each with: 71 Calories; 3g Fat (33.3% calories from fat); 1g Protein; 11g Carbohydrate; 1g Dietary Fiber; 7mg Cholesterol; 59mg Sodium.

 ## *Whole Wheat, Wheat Germ Drop Cookies*

These powerhouse cookies are packed with flavor and fiber.

$^1/_2$ cup (120 ml) vegetable oil, such as canola

1 cup (225 g) packed light or dark brown sugar

$^1/_2$ cup (120 ml) 2 percent milk

2 large eggs, beaten

2$^1/_4$ cups (281.3 g) Hodgson Mill Stone Ground Whole Grain Whole Wheat
Graham Flour

2 teaspoons (3 g) baking powder

$^1/_2$ cup (62.5 g) Hodgson Mill Wheat Germ, Untoasted

2 teaspoons (5.4 g) freshly grated nutmeg

Preheat oven to 350°F (180°C). Line baking sheet with parchment paper.

Beat oil and sugar together with electric mixer in bowl until well blended. Beat in milk and eggs. Combine flour, baking powder, wheat germ, and nutmeg in bowl. Add to egg mixture until well blended. Drop by rounded teaspoonfuls on prepared baking sheet.

Bake 5 minutes, then reduce heat to 325°F (170°C) and bake 7 additional minutes or until lightly browned. Cool on wire rack.

Yield: 36 cookies

Each with: 87 Calories; 4g Fat (36.5% calories from fat); 2g Protein; 13g Carbohydrate; 1g Dietary Fiber; 11mg Cholesterol; 34mg Sodium.

 ## *Outrageous Oat Bran Cookies*

What's outrageous about these cookies is the healthy use of whole grains and flax seed with a flavor your family will love. We call it stealth health!

$^3/_4$ cup (1$^1/_2$ sticks [167 g]) butter

1 cup (225 g) packed light or dark brown sugar

$^1/_2$ cup (100 g) sugar

$^1/_2$ cup (125 g) unsweetened applesauce

2 teaspoons (10 ml) vanilla extract

1 cup (125 g) Hodgson Mill All-Purpose, Unbleached Naturally White Flour

1 cup (125 g) Hodgson Mill Stone Ground Whole Grain White Whole Wheat Flour

1 cup (125 g) Hodgson Mill Oat Bran Hot Cereal, uncooked

$^1/_4$ cup (36 g) Hodgson Mill Milled Flax Seed or Organic Golden Milled Flax Seed

$^1/_4$ teaspoon (0.4 g) baking powder

$^3/_4$ teaspoon (1.1 g) baking soda

Preheat oven to 350°F (180°C). Line 2 baking sheets with parchment paper.

Cream butter and sugars together with electric mixer in medium bowl until light and fluffy. Beat in applesauce and vanilla and mix until well blended. Combine flours, oat bran, flax seed, baking powder, and baking soda in a large bowl. Beat dry ingredients, 1 cup (125 g) at a time, into egg mixture until a dough forms. Drop dough by tablespoonfuls onto prepared baking sheet, about $2^{1}/_{2}$ inches (6.3 cm) apart.

Bake 8 to 10 minutes until lightly browned. Cool on baking sheet about 1 minute before removing cookies to cooling rack to cool completely.

Yield: 48 cookies

Each with: 82 Calories; 3g Fat (35.1% calories from fat); 1g Protein; 13g Carbohydrate; 1g Dietary Fiber; 8mg Cholesterol; 54mg Sodium.

Variation: Add $^1/_2$ cup (75 g) of raisins, (36 g) coconut, (87.5 g) chocolate morsels, or (75 g) nuts to cookie dough.

 ## *Organic Jump-Start Cookies*

Jump-start your new healthy lifestyle, your day, your car trip, or your weekend with these crunchy, nutty-flavored, fiber-rich cookies. If the dough feels too sticky to work with, chill it for an hour and then proceed.

> 1 cup (125 g) Hodgson Mill 50/50 Flour
> $^1/_2$ cup (62.5 g) Hodgson Mill Organic Soy Flour
> $^1/_4$ cup (31.3 g) Hodgson Mill Wheat Bran, Unprocessed
> $^1/_2$ teaspoon (0.7 g) baking powder
> $^1/_2$ teaspoon (0.7 g) baking soda
> $^1/_2$ teaspoon (3 g) salt
> $^1/_2$ cup (120 ml) vegetable oil, such as soy
> $^1/_2$ cup (115 g) packed light or dark brown sugar
> 1 large egg
> $^1/_2$ teaspoon (2.5 ml) vanilla extract
> $^1/_4$ cup (60 ml) water
> $^3/_4$ cup (60 g) quick cooking rolled oats
> $^1/_4$ cup (37.5 g) chopped nuts
> 3 tablespoons (39 g) sugar

Preheat oven to 350°F (180°C). Line 2 baking sheets with parchment paper.

Combine flours, bran, baking powder, baking soda, and salt together. Mix oil and sugar together until smooth in large bowl. Add egg, vanilla, and water and blend well. Stir in flour mixture, 1 cup (125 g) at a time, until smooth. Stir oats and nuts to form soft, chunky dough.

Pinch off dough and roll into 1-inch (2.5-cm) balls. Place balls on prepared baking sheets, 3 inches (7.5 cm) apart, then flatten to $1/4$-inch (0.6-cm) thickness with bottom of drinking glass dipped in sugar.

Bake 13 to 15 minutes or until lightly browned. Cool on wire rack.

Yield: 36 cookies

Each with: 73 Calories; 4g Fat (45.1% calories from fat); 2g Protein; 9g Carbohydrate; 1g Dietary Fiber; 5mg Cholesterol; 57mg Sodium.

 ## *Insta-Bake Peanut Butter Cookies*

This is your favorite peanut butter cookie, only with whole grain goodness.

$2/3$ cup (132 g) sugar

$1/2$ cup (1 stick [112 g]) butter or margarine, softened

$3/4$ cup (195 g) peanut butter

2 cups (250 g) Hodgson Mill Whole Wheat Insta-Bake Mix

1 large egg

$1/2$ teaspoon (2.5 ml) vanilla extract

3 tablespoons (45 ml) water

Preheat oven to 375°F (190°C). Line 2 baking sheets with parchment paper.

Cream sugar, butter, and peanut butter together with electric mixer in a bowl. Beat in mix. In a separate bowl, mix egg, vanilla, and water; add to peanut butter mixture until it forms a dough. Pinch off 1 teaspoon (5 g) portions of dough and roll into 1-inch (2.5-cm) balls. Place each ball on prepared baking sheets, 2 inches (5 cm) apart. Flatten by criss-crossing with the tines of a fork.

Bake 10 to12 minutes or until lightly browned. Cool on wire racks.

Yield: 42 cookies

Each with: 80 Calories; 5g Fat (51.6% calories from fat); 2g Protein; 8g Carbohydrate; 1g Dietary Fiber; 10mg Cholesterol; 87mg Sodium.

Insta-Bake Oatmeal Raisin Cookies

These classic oatmeal raisin cookies—but with more fiber and more nutrients—will be a welcome addition to your family's cookie jar.

1 cup (225 g) packed light or dark brown sugar

^{3}/4 cup (1^1/2 sticks [167 g]) margarine or butter

^{1}/2 teaspoon (2.5 ml) vanilla extract

2 large eggs

2 tablespoons (28 ml) 2 percent milk

2 cups (250 g) Hodgson Mill Whole Wheat Insta-Bake Mix

1^1/2 cups (120 g) quick cooking rolled oats, uncooked

1^1/4 cups (187.5 g) raisins

Preheat oven to 350°F (180°C). Line 2 baking sheets with parchment paper.

Beat together brown sugar, margarine, vanilla, eggs, and milk in a bowl. Stir in mix, oats, and raisins. Drop dough by rounded teaspoonfuls onto prepared baking sheets, about 2 inches (5 cm) apart.

Bake 10 to 12 minutes or until lightly browned. Cool on wire racks.

Yield: 48 cookies

Each with: 84 Calories; 3g Fat (34.9% calories from fat); 1g Protein; 13g Carbohydrate; 1g Dietary Fiber; 16mg Cholesterol; 70mg Sodium.

Insta-Bake Chocolate Chip Cookies

Here's yet another way you can make fabulous chocolate chip cookies with whole grain taste and texture.

^{1}/3 cup (75 g) butter or margarine, softened

^{1}/2 cup (115 g) brown sugar, packed

^{1}/2 cup (100 g) sugar

^{1}/2 teaspoon (2.5 ml) vanilla extract

1 large egg

1^1/2 cups (187.5 g) Hodgson Mill Whole Wheat Insta-Bake Mix

1 tablespoon (15 ml) hot water

1 package (7 ounces [196 g]) semi-sweet chocolate chips

^{1}/2 cup (75 g) chopped nuts, optional

Preheat oven to 375°F (190°C). Line 2 baking sheets with parchment paper.

Cream butter, sugars, and vanilla together with electric mixer. Beat in egg. Add Insta-Bake and water and blend until smooth. Stir in chocolate chips and optional chopped nuts. Drop by teaspoonfuls on prepared baking sheet.

Bake 10 to 12 minutes or until golden brown. Cool on wire racks.

Yield: 48 cookies

Each with: 71 Calories; 4g Fat (42.2% calories from fat); 1g Protein; 10g Carbohydrate; 1g Dietary Fiber; 7mg Cholesterol; 43mg Sodium.

 ## *Insta-Bake Chocolate Brownies*

With a mix containing whole wheat and leavening, making homemade brownies is a snap.

   1 cup (125 g) Hodgson Mill Whole Wheat Insta-Bake Mix

   $1/3$ cup (42.6 g) unsweetened cocoa powder

   1 cup (200 g) sugar

   1 tablespoon (14 g) butter or margarine

   2 large eggs, beaten

   1 teaspoon (5 ml) vanilla extract

   3 tablespoons (45 ml) 2 percent milk

   $1/2$ cup (75 g) chopped nuts, optional

Preheat oven to 350°F (180°C). Lightly grease 8 x 8 x 2-inch (20 x 20 x 5-cm) pan.

Combine mix, cocoa powder, and sugar in bowl. Cut in butter until crumbly. Mix in eggs, vanilla, milk, and nuts. Spread in prepared pan.

Bake 23 to 28 minutes or until toothpick inserted in center comes out clean.

Yield: 16 brownies

Each with: 122 Calories; 4g Fat (29.6% calories from fat); 3g Protein; 20g Carbohydrate; 2g Dietary Fiber; 26mg Cholesterol; 71 mg Sodium.

Gluten-Free Soy Chocolate Chip Cookies

Another gluten-free version of our American classic.

$^3/_4$ cup (93.8 g) Hodgson Mill Soy Flour

$^1/_4$ cup (31.3 g) Hodgson Mill Stone Ground Whole Grain Brown Rice Flour

$^1/_2$ teaspoon (3 g) salt

$6^1/_2$ tablespoons (91 g) butter or margarine

$^3/_4$ cup (150 g) sugar

$^3/_4$ cup (170 g) packed light or dark brown sugar

1 large egg or equivalent egg substitute

$^1/_2$ teaspoon (2.5 ml) gluten-free vanilla extract

$^1/_2$ cup (87.5 g) gluten-free semi-sweet chocolate chips

$^1/_2$ cup (75 g) chopped nuts, optional

Preheat oven to 375°F (190°C). Line baking sheet with parchment paper.

Sift flours and salt into medium bowl. In large bowl, cream butter and sugars together until fluffy. Beat in egg. Stir in vanilla, then dry ingredients until smooth. Stir in chocolate chips and nuts. Drop by rounded teaspoonfuls onto prepared baking sheet, 2 inches (5 cm) apart.

Bake 10 to 12 minutes or until lightly browned. Cool on wire racks.

Yield: 24 cookies

Each with: 130 Calories; 6g Fat (39.5% calories from fat); 3g Protein; 18g Carbohydrate; 1g Dietary Fiber; 16mg Cholesterol; 82mg Sodium.

 ## Gingerbread Cookies

What a fun (and easy!) holiday baking project. Gather the kids around the table, then mix, bake, and decorate gingerbread men, ladies, Christmas trees, stars—use your imagination and your collection of cookie cutters.

1 box (15 ounces [420 g]) Hodgson Mill Whole Wheat Gingerbread Mix

2 large egg whites

$^1/_4$ cup (55 g) low-fat margarine, softened, or (60 ml) vegetable oil, such as canola

$^1/_4$ cup (60 ml) water

Pour mix into large bowl. Blend in egg whites, margarine and water until smooth and stiff batter. Cover and chill for 2 to 3 hours.

Preheat oven to 375°F (190°C). Line cookie sheets with parchment paper.

Roll dough out to $1/4$-inch (0.6-cm) thickness on lightly floured surface. Cut out with cookie cutters and place on prepared cookie sheets.

Bake 10 to 12 minutes or until lightly browned on edges. Cool on wire racks.

Yield: 24 to 36 cookies

Each with: 86 Calories; 2g Fat (24.6% calories from fat); 1g Protein; 14g Carbohydrate; 1g Dietary Fiber; 0mg Cholesterol; 158mg Sodium.

Add It: To make a simple frosting that can be left white or tinted with food coloring, whisk together 2 cups (200 g) confectioners' sugar, 2 to 3 tablespoons (28 to 45 ml) 2 percent milk, and 1 teaspoon (5 ml) vanilla extract until smooth.

 Butterscotch Brownies (See photo on page 238.)

This moist, blonde brownie pairs the goodness of soy with the deliciousness of butterscotch.

$1/2$ cup (62.5 g) Hodgson Mill Bulgur Wheat with Soy Hot Cereal, uncooked

$1/2$ cup (120 ml) hot water

2 cups (450 g) dark brown sugar, packed loosely

$1/2$ cup (120 ml) vegetable oil, such as canola or soy or $1/2$ cup (1 stick [112 g]) butter, softened

2 large eggs

1 teaspoon (5 ml) vanilla extract

$2/3$ cup (82.5 g) Hodgson Mill Stone Ground Whole Grain Whole Wheat Graham Flour

$2/3$ cup (82.5 g) Hodgson Mill Wheat Germ, Untoasted

$1/2$ cup (65 g) nonfat dry milk

2 teaspoons (3 g) baking powder

$1/2$ teaspoon (3 g) salt

1 cup (150 g) walnuts, chopped

Preheat oven to 375°F (190°C). Lightly grease 8 x 8 x 2-inch (20 x 20 x 5-cm) baking pan.

Combine cereal and hot water in bowl and leave to steep for 5 minutes.

Beat sugar, oil, eggs, and vanilla together with electric mixer in bowl. Combine flour, wheat germ, dry milk, baking powder, and salt in bowl. Add dry ingredients, 1 cup (125 g) at a time, alternating with moistened cereal and nuts until a chunky batter. Spread in prepared pan.

Bake 25 to 30 minutes or until toothpick inserted in center comes out clean. Let cool in pan on rack for 5 minutes before cutting into squares.

Yield: 9 brownies

Each with: 441 Calories; 22g Fat (43.2% calories from fat); 12g Protein; 53g Carbohydrate; 5g Dietary Fiber; 43mg Cholesterol; 288mg Sodium.

 ## *Butter Nut Cookies*

These are yummy with a glass of milk or a cup of tea.

$1/2$ cup (1 stick [112 g]) butter or margarine, softened

$3/4$ cup (168.8 g) packed brown sugar

1 large egg

2 tablespoons (28 ml) 2 percent milk

1 teaspoon (5 ml) vanilla extract

$1/2$ teaspoon (3 g) salt

$13/4$ cups (218.8 g) sifted Hodgson Mill Stone Ground Whole Grain White Whole Wheat Flour

$1/2$ cup (75 g) chopped pecans

Preheat oven to 375°F (190°C). Line 2 baking sheets with parchment paper.

Cream butter with brown sugar with electric mixer in bowl until light and fluffy. Add egg, milk, vanilla, and salt. Beat in flour until smooth. Mix in pecans. Drop by rounded teaspoonfuls onto prepared baking sheet, 2 inches (5 cm) apart.

Bake 10 minutes or until lightly browned. Cool on wire racks.

Yield: 24 cookies

Each with: 109 Calories; 6g Fat (46.7% calories from fat); 2g Protein; 13g Carbohydrate; 1g Dietary Fiber; 18mg Cholesterol; 89mg Sodium.

Buckwheat Cookies

If you like buckwheat pancakes, you'll love these cookies.

$1/2$ cup (1 stick [112 g]) butter, softened

$1/3$ cup (66.6 g) sugar

1 teaspoon (5 ml) vanilla extract

1 large egg yolk, beaten

$1/2$ cup (62.5 g) Hodgson Mill Stone Ground Whole Grain Buckwheat Flour

$1/2$ cup (62.5 g) Hodgson Mill All-Purpose, Unbleached Naturally White Flour

$1/4$ teaspoon (1.5 g) salt

Preheat oven to 325°F (170°C). Line 2 baking sheets with parchment paper.

Cream butter and sugar together with electric mixer in bowl. Add vanilla and beaten egg yolk. Combine flours and salt. Add to creamed mixture to make firm dough. Pinch off teaspoonful portions of dough and roll into 1-inch (2.5-cm) balls. Place balls on prepared baking sheets, $1^1/2$ inches (3.8 cm) apart. Flatten by criss-crossing with tines of a fork.

Bake 15 to 20 minutes or until lightly browned. Cool on wire rack.

Yield: 36 cookies

Each with: 43 Calories; 3g Fat (56.5% calories from fat); trace Protein; 4g Carbohydrate; trace Dietary Fiber; 13mg Cholesterol; 41 mg Sodium.

Gluten-Free Brown Rice Cookies

With a slightly sandy texture from the brown rice flour and walnuts, this honey- and brown sugar–sweetened cookie could become a family favorite.

1 cup (125 g) Hodgson Mill Stone Ground Whole Grain Brown Rice Flour

2 teaspoons (3 g) gluten-free baking powder

$1/4$ cup (60 g) packed light or dark brown sugar

2 tablespoons (28 g) butter or margarine

$^1/_4$ cup (80 g) honey

$^1/_2$ teaspoon (3 g) salt

1 teaspoon (5 ml) gluten-free vanilla extract

1 large egg, beaten, or equivalent egg substitute

1 cup (150 g) walnuts, ground, optional

Combine all ingredients until well blended. Cover and refrigerate several hours or overnight.

Preheat oven to 350°F (180°C). Line 2 baking sheets with parchment paper.

Shape dough into 1-inch (2.5-cm) balls and arrange on prepared baking sheets, 2 inches (5 cm) apart. Press balls flat with bottom of drinking glass.

Bake 10 to 12 minutes or until lightly browned.

Yield: 18 cookies

Each with: 93 Calories; 4g Fat (39.3% calories from fat); 2g Protein; 13g Carbohydrate; trace Dietary Fiber; 14mg Cholesterol; 131mg Sodium.

Note: To make this recipe dairy- and egg-free, use soy margarine and egg substitute.

Best Ever Snickerdoodles

With a great-tasting combination of all-purpose, soy, and whole wheat graham flour, these are the "best ever" Snickerdoodles!

$^1/_2$ cup (1 stick [112 g]) butter or margarine, softened

1 cup (200 g) sugar

1 large egg

$^1/_2$ teaspoon (2.5 ml) vanilla extract

$^1/_4$ teaspoon (0.4 g) baking soda

$^1/_2$ cup (62.5 g) Hodgson Mill All-Purpose, Unbleached Naturally White Flour

$^1/_2$ cup (62.5 g) Hodgson Mill Soy Flour

$^1/_2$ cup (62.5 g) Hodgson Mill Stone Ground Whole Grain Whole Wheat Graham Flour

$^1/_2$ teaspoon (1.2 g) baking powder

FOR THE TOPPING:

    1 teaspoon (2.3 g) ground cinnamon

    1 tablespoon (13 g) sugar

Cream butter and sugar with electric mixer in large bowl until light and fluffy. Beat in egg and vanilla until smooth. Combine baking soda, flours, and baking powder in bowl. Beat in flour mixture, 1 cup (125 g) at a time, until you have a stiff dough. Cover and refrigerate for 1 hour.

Preheat oven to 375°F (190°C). Line 2 baking sheets with parchment paper.

For topping, combine cinnamon and sugar in small bowl. Shape dough into 1-inch (2.5-cm) balls. Roll balls in topping and place on prepared sheets, 2 inches (5 cm) apart.

Bake 10 minutes or until lightly browned. Cool on a wire rack.

Yield: 24 cookies

Each with: 95 Calories; 4g Fat (37.1% calories from fat); 2g Protein; 14g Carbohydrate; 1g Dietary Fiber; 18mg Cholesterol; 65mg Sodium.

6

Flatbreads, Crackers, Sticks, and Pretzels

For snacks or casual meals—especially on the go—whole grain breadstuffs have been made since ancient times.

The most basic flatbreads are simply flour and water stirred together into a dough, flattened by hand, and grilled or baked on a griddle. Many of these types of breads come to us from cultures around the Mediterranean—Greek pita bread, Afghan herb-filled flatbread, and Armenian crisp bread, to name just a few.

There are three key techniques to making flatbreads successfully: make sure the dough is warm, the flatbreads are distributed evenly throughout the oven, and the oven is at the right temperature. You might need to wait several minutes after baking one batch before starting another to let the temperature readjust. A good oven thermometer will let you know the temperature at a glance.

To serve, simply cut flatbreads and focaccia into serving size pieces. Pitas can be opened to form pockets and stuffed with meats, fresh chopped or sautéed vegetables, or other fillings. If the pocket does not open easily, slit it open with a sharp knife.

For crackers, make sure you roll the dough as thin as the recipe indicates so they bake up crisp and delicious. For bread sticks and pretzels, cut the dough thicker for a soft, doughy result or thinner for a crispy finish.

Whole Grain Flax Seed Crackers

Delicious for snacking or to serve with cheese, these whole grain crackers have the added benefit of omega-3 fatty acids from flax seed.

$^3/_4$ cup (93.8 g) Hodgson Mill 50/50 or Stone Ground Whole Grain White Whole Wheat Flour

$^3/_4$ cup (93.8 g) Hodgson Mill All-Purpose, Unbleached Naturally White Flour

$^1/_2$ cup (70 g) Hodgson Mill Milled Flax Seed

$1^1/_4$ teaspoons (7.5 g) salt

2 tablespoons (28 g) butter, chilled

$^1/_2$ cup plus 1 tablespoon (135 ml) 2 percent milk

FOR THE TOPPING:

2 tablespoons (28 ml) olive oil

$^1/_2$ teaspoon (3 g) coarse kosher or sea salt

Mix flours, flax seed, and salt in bowl. Cut in butter with pastry blender or two knives until mixture resembles coarse crumbs. Stir in milk to make soft dough. Form dough into ball, wrap, and refrigerate 15 minutes.

Preheat oven to 375°F (190°C). Line 2 baking sheets with parchment paper.

Divide dough in half. Roll out each half on floured surface to a 10 x 12-inch (25 x 30-cm) rectangle that is $^1/_8$-inch (0.3-cm) thick. With knife or pizza wheel, cut dough into 15 rectangles. Place on prepared baking sheet.

For topping, brush rectangles with olive oil and sprinkle with salt. Bake 10 minutes or until lightly browned. Cool in pans. Store in airtight containers.

Yield: 30 crackers

Each with: 46 Calories; 2g Fat (44.5% calories from fat); 1g Protein; 5g Carbohydrate; 1g Dietary Fiber; 2mg Cholesterol; 130mg Sodium.

Variation: Substitute sesame for flax seed or sprinkle crackers with dried herbs.

Amish Cinnamon-Spiced Oat Crackers

These crackers, which originate in the Amish country around northern Ohio, are delicious for snacking. Cut them out in the shape of your choice.

1 cup (2 sticks [225 g]) butter, softened

1 cup (225 g) packed light brown sugar

1 teaspoon (2.3 g) ground cinnamon

2 large eggs, beaten

1 teaspoon (1.5 g) baking soda

3 tablespoons (45 ml) 2 percent milk

3 cups (240 g) old-fashioned or quick rolled oats (not instant)

1¹/2 cups (187.5 g) Hodgson Mill Stone Ground Whole Grain White Whole Wheat Flour

1 to 1¹/2 cups (125 to 187.5 g) Hodgson Mill All-Purpose Unbleached Naturally White Flour

Preheat oven to 350°F (180°C). Line 2 baking sheets with parchment paper.

Combine butter, brown sugar, and cinnamon in bowl and beat with electric mixer until smooth and creamy. Beat in eggs. Dissolve baking soda in milk, then beat into butter mixture. Beat in oats and flours, 1 cup (125 g) at a time, to form stiff dough.

Divide dough in half. Roll out each half on floured surface to a 9 x 12-inch (22.5 x 30-cm) rectangle, about ¹/2-inch (1.2-cm) thick. Prick dough all over with tines of fork. Cut dough into 2 x 3-inch (5 x 7.5-cm) strips or shapes, and place on prepared baking sheet, about ¹/4 inch (0.6 cm) apart.

Bake 10 minutes or until lightly browned. Cool on baking sheet or on wire rack. Store in airtight containers.

Yield: 36 crackers

Each with: 126 Calories; 6g Fat (40.9% calories from fat); 2g Protein; 17g Carbohydrate; 1g Dietary Fiber; 24mg Cholesterol; 93mg Sodium.

Sauerkraut Snack Crackers

Serve these crackers as cocktail nibbles, each spread with a hearty mustard and topped with a slice of cooked Polish or kielbasa sausage. They keep well stored in an airtight container.

1^1/2 cups (187.5 g) Hodgson Mill All-Purpose, Unbleached Naturally White Flour

1^1/2 cups (187.5 g) Hodgson Mill Stone Ground Whole Grain White Whole Wheat Flour

1 teaspoon (2.3 g) ground white pepper

^{3}/4 cup (168.8 g) vegetable shortening

2 cups (450 g) sauerkraut from a jar, drained

Preheat oven to 425°F (220°C). Line 2 baking sheets with parchment paper.

Put flours and white pepper in food processor, add shortening, and pulse until mix forms a ball.

Transfer dough to floured surface. Pinch off 1 tablespoon (15 g)-size pieces of dough, roll each piece into a ball, and place on prepared baking sheet about 2 inches (5 cm) apart. Flatten balls with bottom of drinking glass to about a ^{1}/4-inch (0.6-cm) thickness.

Bake 10 minutes, then reduce the heat to 350°F (180°C) and bake 10 to 15 minutes more, or until crackers are golden brown and crisp. Cool on baking sheet or wire rack. Store in airtight containers.

Yield: 36 crackers

Each with: 74 Calories; 4g Fat (51.6% calories from fat); 1g Protein; 8g Carbohydrate; 1g Dietary Fiber; 0mg Cholesterol; 87mg Sodium.

Gluten-Free Sesame Rice Sticks

Here is a snack stick that delivers whole grain goodness, fiber, and great taste all in one small package.

2 cups (250 g) Hodgson Mill Stone Ground Whole Grain Brown Rice Flour

2 tablespoons (9 g) gluten-free baking powder

1/2 teaspoon (3 g) salt

1/4 cup (37.5 g) Hodgson Mill Pure Corn Starch

2 large eggs, beaten, or equivalent egg substitute

1 cup (235 ml) 2 percent milk or soy milk (see recipe note, page 148)

1 tablespoon (15 ml) vegetable oil, such as canola or soy

1 teaspoon (5 ml) toasted sesame oil

1/4 cup (30 g) sesame seeds

Preheat oven to 350°F (180°C). Line baking sheet with parchment paper.

Mix flour, baking powder, salt, and corn starch in large bowl. Mix eggs, milk, vegetable oil, and sesame oil in small bowl. Pour egg mixture into dry mixture and whisk to form smooth dough.

Transfer to generously rice-floured surface and roll or pat to a 12-inch (30-cm) square. Cut into 1-inch (2.5-cm) wide sticks. Sprinkle tops with sesame seeds.

Bake 10 minutes or until golden brown. Let cool in pan.

Yield: 12 rice sticks

Each with: 144 Calories; 5g Fat (29.1% calories from fat); 4g Protein; 22g Carbohydrate; 1g Dietary Fiber; 33mg Cholesterol; 352mg Sodium.

Note: To make this recipe dairy- and egg-free, use vegetable oil, egg substitute, and soy milk.

Gluten-Free Crispy Soy-Rice Crackers

Great for snacking, these crispy crackers will keep in an airtight container for up to 2 weeks.

2 cloves garlic, minced

$1/4$ cup (60 ml) vegetable oil, such as canola

$1/2$ cup (120 ml) warm (105°F to 115°F [40.5°C to 46°C]) water

$1/4$ cup (31.3 g) Hodgson Mill Soy Flour, plus more for sprinkling

$1/2$ cup (62.5 g) Hodgson Mill Stone Ground Whole Grain Brown Rice Flour

$1/2$ teaspoon (3 g) salt

$1/2$ teaspoon (1.2 g) ground white or black pepper

$1/4$ cup (30 g) sesame or poppy seeds for sprinkling

Preheat oven to 400°F (200°C). Line baking sheet with parchment paper.

Mix garlic, oil, and water together in bowl. Stir in flours, salt, and pepper to form smooth dough. Sprinkle flat surface with soy flour. Roll out dough until paper thin. Cut into 1-inch (2.5-cm) squares and place on prepared baking sheet. Prick squares with tines of fork. Sprinkle with sesame or poppy seeds.

Bake 10 to 15 minutes or until lightly browned. Remove to wire rack to cool. Store in airtight container.

Yield: 48 crackers

Each with: 21 Calories; 2g Fat (64.1% calories from fat); 1g Protein; 1g Carbohydrate; trace Dietary Fiber; 0mg Cholesterol; 22mg Sodium.

Variation: Sprinkle cracker dough with dried herbs or grated cheese before baking.

Gluten-Free Rice Flour Wraps

Known as "dosa" in southern India, each of these rice flour flatbreads is sturdy enough to hold a savory filling or simply accompany a soup or stew. For an easy entrée or snack, prepare a gluten-free Indian entrée for the filling. If you are making Mexican food, you can use these in place of flour tortillas—just omit the ginger.

1 cup (125 g) Hodgson Mill Stone Ground Whole Grain Brown Rice Flour

2 tablespoons (16 g) Hodgson Mill Pure Corn Starch

1/2 cup (62.5 g) dry whole grain rice baby food cereal

2 tablespoons (20 g) minced onion

1 teaspoon (2 g) minced fresh ginger

1 teaspoon (2.5 g) minced fresh green chile pepper (Thai, serrano, or jalapeno)

1/2 cup (115 g) plain, low-fat yogurt or soy yogurt

1 1/4 teaspoons (7.5 g) salt

2 to 2 1/2 cups (470 to 590 ml) water

Vegetable oil for brushing

Combine rice flour, corn starch, dry rice cereal, onion, ginger, chile pepper, yogurt, salt, and enough water to make a very thin batter. Cover and let batter rest for 1 hour at room temperature.

Oil inside of 8- or 10-inch (20- or 25-cm) griddle or skillet and place over medium heat. Stir batter before griddle-baking each flatbread. Ladle 1/4 cup (60 ml) batter. Cook until small bubbles form throughout and edges are starting to turn golden. Turn flatbread over and cook 1 minute more. Oil griddle or skillet again, stir batter, ladle, and cook wraps until all batter is used. Serve folded in half, golden brown side out.

Yield: 12 wraps

Each with: 53 Calories; trace Fat (8.3% calories from fat); 2g Protein; 11 g Carbohydrate; trace Dietary Fiber; 1 mg Cholesterol; 230mg Sodium.

Note: To make this recipe dairy-free, use soy yogurt.

Savory Whole Grain Blue Cheese Crackers

(See photo on page 239.)

Make these crackers a few days ahead of time for a special occasion. They are too delicious for mindless snacking, but taste wonderful with a glass of chilled cider.

1/2 pound (1 cup [120 g]) good quality blue cheese,
    such as Maytag or Point Reyes

1/2 cup (1 stick [112 g]) unsalted butter, softened

1 tablespoon (9 g) dry mustard

1/2 teaspoon (1.2 g) cayenne

1 1/2 cups (187.5 g) Hodgson Mill Whole Grain Whole Wheat Pastry Flour

1 cup (125 g) Hodgson Mill All-Purpose, Unbleached Naturally White Flour

Salt to taste

Preheat oven to 425°F (220°C). Line baking sheet with parchment paper.

Blend cheese and butter in bowl until smooth and creamy. Add mustard, cayenne, and just enough flour to form soft yet firm dough. Form dough into two rolls, 1 1/2 inches (7.5 cm) in diameter. Wrap in waxed paper and chill until ready to use (at least 2 hours).

Cut each roll into 15 slices and arrange slices on prepared baking sheet.

Bake 12 to 15 minutes or until lightly browned. Store in airtight containers.

Yield: 30 crackers

Each with: 88 Calories; 5g Fat (53.8% calories from fat); 3g Protein; 8g Carbohydrate; 1g Dietary Fiber; 14mg Cholesterol; 106mg Sodium.

Variation: Instead of blue cheese, use Brie with the rind removed. Omit the dry mustard.

Savory Whole Wheat Crackers

With garlic and black pepper in the dough itself, these crackers go well with cheese and a piece of fruit.

1 cup (125 g) Hodgson Mill Whole Grain Whole Wheat Pastry Flour

1¼ teaspoons (7.5 cm) salt

1 teaspoon (2.3 g) ground black pepper

1 teaspoon (2.3 g) garlic powder

3 tablespoons (42 g) butter or shortening

3 tablespoons (45 ml) water

Preheat oven to 425°F (220°C). Line baking sheet with parchment paper.

Combine flour, salt, pepper, and garlic powder in bowl. Cut in butter with pastry blender until mixture resembles coarse crumbs. Add water and blend with fork to form soft dough.

Transfer dough to floured surface. Roll out to ⅛-inch (0.3-cm) thickness. Cut into 2-inch (5-cm) squares with knife or pizza wheel. Place on prepared baking sheet and prick each square with tines of fork.

Bake 13 to 15 minutes or until lightly browned. Store in airtight containers.

Yield: 36 crackers

Each with: 20 Calories; 1g Fat (44.1% calories from fat); trace Protein; 3g Carbohydrate; trace Dietary Fiber; 3mg Cholesterol; 84mg Sodium.

Variation: Instead of black pepper and garlic powder, use dried herbs such as rosemary, basil, or dill weed.

Whole Grain Rosemary Red Onion Focaccia

A caramelized onion topping gives this focaccia great flavor, but you can customize this recipe any way you like. The crust is made entirely with white whole wheat flour, so it has a nice golden color and a rich flavor without being too grainy and dense.

1 package (^{5}/16 ounce) or 2^1/2 teaspoons (10 g) Hodgson Mill
     Active Dry Yeast
1^1/2 cups (355 ml) warm (105 to 115°F [40.5 to 46°C]) water
3^1/2 cups (437.5 g) Hodgson Mill Stone Ground Whole Grain White Whole Wheat
     Flour
1^1/2 teaspoons (9 g) salt
^{1}/4 cup (60 ml) olive oil

FOR THE TOPPING:
^{1}/2 cup (120 ml) olive oil
3 pounds (1.3 kg) red onions, peeled and chopped
1 teaspoon (2 g) dried rosemary
1 teaspoon (6 g) salt

Sprinkle yeast over water in large bowl and set aside until foamy, about 5 minutes.

Stir in flour, salt, and olive oil to form soft dough. Transfer to a lightly floured surface and knead until smooth and elastic, about 5 minutes. Place dough in oiled bowl, and turn to coat. Cover and let rise 1 hour or until doubled in bulk.

For topping, heat oil in large skillet over medium heat. Add onions, rosemary, and salt and cook, reducing heat to medium-low to low, and stirring frequently, for 1 hour or until onions are very soft and golden brown. Set aside to cool to room temperature.

Lightly oil large baking sheet. Punch dough down, transfer to prepared baking sheet, and pat dough with hands to 15 x 11-inch (37.5 x 27.5-cm) rectangle. Cover and let stand 45 minutes or until risen.

Spread topping over dough. Cover and let rise again for 30 minutes. Preheat oven to 425°F (220°C).

Bake on lowest oven rack 25 minutes or until crust is golden brown and crisp. Cut into pieces with sharp knife or pizza wheel to serve.

Yield: 20 servings

Each with: 169 Calories; 9g Fat (44.0% calories from fat); 4g Protein; 21 g Carbohydrate; 3g Dietary Fiber; 0mg Cholesterol; 269mg Sodium.

Variation: Top focaccia with grilled vegetables, olive oil, and grated cheese, or pizza topping of your choice.

 ### *Gluten-Free Cheddar Crackers*

These crackers are a bit labor-intensive, but oh, so satisfying! Repeated cutting, stacking, and rolling the dough makes for a crisper, flakier cracker.

1^3/4 cups (218.8 g) Hodgson Mill Stone Ground Whole Grain Brown Rice Flour, plus more for dusting

1 teaspoon (6 g) salt

^{1}/2 teaspoon (1.2 g) cayenne pepper

1 teaspoon (3 g) gluten-free English-style mustard powder

^{3}/4 cup (6 tablespoons [85 g]) butter or soy margarine, cut into small pieces

12 ounces (1^1/2 cups [180 g]) shredded sharp Cheddar cheese

3 large egg yolks or equivalent egg substitute

2 teaspoons (10 ml) water

FOR THE TOPPING:

Coarse kosher or sea salt

Combine flour, salt, cayenne pepper, and mustard in mixing bowl or food processor. With pastry blender by hand or pulsing the food processor, cut butter into flour mixture until it resembles coarse crumbs. Cut or pulse in cheese, and blend until the cheese is evenly coated. Add the egg yolks and water and blend until dough forms ball, but is somewhat crumbly. Divide dough into two equal portions and flatten into discs; wrap each in plastic wrap and chill for about 1 hour.

Preheat oven to 375°F (190°C). Line baking sheet with parchment paper.

Transfer discs to lightly rice-floured surface. Roll out each disc to ^{1}/2-inch (1.2-cm) thick circle. Press crumbly dough together when necessary. Cut each circle into 4 wedges. Stack wedges on top of each other and roll out again. Repeat cutting, stacking, and rolling twice more. Finally, roll each disc out to a ^{1}/8-inch (0.3-cm) thick rectangle. Cut into 1-inch (2.5-cm) squares with knife or pizza wheel. Place on prepared baking sheet. Prick each square with tines of fork.

Bake 8 to 10 minutes. Remove browned crackers to wire rack. Return rest to oven to bake 5 to 8 minutes more, or until browned. Transfer to wire rack to cool.

Yield: 48 crackers

Each with: 74 Calories; 6g Fat (68.5% calories from fat); 2g Protein; 3g Carbohydrate; trace Dietary Fiber; 28mg Cholesterol; 118mg Sodium.

Note: Store in airtight container for up to 1 month.

Onion and Black Pepper Bread Sticks

Serve these with a savory soup or stew, or pass in a basket to accompany a main course salad. When you make the dough in the bread machine, the rest is easy.

   1 cup (235 ml) warm (105°F to 115°F [40.5°C to 46°C]) water
   1 tablespoon (14 g) butter, softened, or (15 ml) vegetable oil, such as canola
   1 teaspoon (6 g) salt
   1^1/2 cups (187.5 g) Hodgson Mill Best For Bread Flour
   1^1/2 cups (187.5 g) Hodgson Mill Stone Ground Whole Grain White Whole Wheat
       or 50/50 Flour
   1 tablespoon (8 g) nonfat dry milk
   1 tablespoon (13 g) sugar
   1^1/2 teaspoons (3 g) minced, dry onions
   ^{3}/4 teaspoon (1.7 g) ground black pepper
   ^{1}/4 teaspoon (0.6 g) garlic powder
   2 teaspoons (8 g) Hodgson Mill Fast-Rise Yeast

Place ingredients in bread pan according to manufacturer's instructions. Select dough cycle and start the machine.

Line baking sheet with parchment paper. When cycle is complete, transfer dough to floured surface. Roll out to ^{1}/2-inch (1.2-cm) thick rectangle. Cut into 12 strips with sharp knife or pizza wheel. Twist strips, if desired. Let rise for 30 minutes.

Preheat oven to 400°F (200°C). Bake 15 to 18 minutes or until golden brown. Transfer to wire rack to cool.

Yield: 12 bread sticks

Each with: 118 Calories; 1g Fat (8.9% calories from fat); 5g Protein; 23g Carbohydrate; 2g Dietary Fiber; 3mg Cholesterol; 194mg Sodium.

Asiago Nine Grain Rolls, page 26

Chive Rolls, page 48

Buckwheat and Banana Bread, page 66

Garlic and Sun-Dried Tomato Bread, page 87

Gluten-Free Apple Cinnamon Bread, page 93

Insta-Bake Blueberry Buckle, page 126

Spicy Carrot Bundt Cake, page 128

New Generation Hummingbird Cake, page 109

Chocolate Cream Coffee Cake, page 167

Cranberry and Orange Corn Meal Drop Cookies, page 176

Gluten-Free Apricot Bars, page 180

Peanut Butter Oat Bran Cookies, page 186

237

Butterscotch Brownies, page 206

Savory Whole Grain Blue Cheese Crackers, page 220

239

Afghan Flatbreads with Fresh Herb Filling, page 270

Easy Wheat Heart Pretzels, page 275

244

Potato Cheese Bread, page 315

Yeasty Whole Wheat Biscuits, page 331

Gluten-Free Savory Black Olive and Roasted Red Pepper Scones, page 334

Apple-Carrot Muffins, page 337

248

Strawberry Orange Muffins with Soy and Whole Wheat, page 359

Gluten-Free Oven-Baked Apple Pecan Pancake, page 423

Brownie Dessert Pizza, page 443

Sour Cream Nut Bread, page 368

Lemon-Glazed Blueberry Quick Bread, page 373

Jalapeno Cornbread, page 388

Coffee Glazed Sweet Rolls, page 21

Preheat oven to 450°F (230°C). Transfer dough to floured surface and roll out to $1/2$-inch (0.6-cm) thick, 16 x 12-inch (40 x 30-cm) rectangle. Brush with beaten egg and sprinkle with caraway seeds and salt. Cut dough into narrow ($1/2$ x 4-inch [1.2 x 10-cm]) strips with sharp knife or pizza wheel. Place strips on prepared baking sheet.

Bake 25 minutes or until golden brown.

Yield: 96 sticks

Each with: 28 Calories; 2g Fat (63.3% calories from fat); trace Protein; 2g Carbohydrate; trace Dietary Fiber; 7mg Cholesterol; 143mg Sodium.

Note: You can substitute mashed potato mix, prepared according to package directions, for the mashed potatoes in this recipe.

 ## *Rye Crackers*

These sturdy, savory crackers stand up to the thickest dip. If the dough is too wet, add a little whole wheat flour.

    2 cups (250 g) Hodgson Mill Stone Ground Whole Grain Rye Flour

    $1/2$ cup (62.5 g) Hodgson Mill Soy Flour

    $1/2$ cup (62.5 g) Hodgson Mill Wheat Germ, Untoasted

    $1/2$ cup (64 g) nonfat dry milk

    $3/4$ cup (170 g) packed dark brown sugar

    1 teaspoon (6 g) salt

    2 tablespoons (9 g) baking powder

    1 cup (2 sticks [225 g]) butter, room temperature

    $1/2$ cup (120 ml) milk

FOR THE TOPPING:

    Caraway, sesame, or poppy seeds

    Hodgson Mill Stone Ground Whole Grain Whole Wheat Graham Flour

Preheat oven to 350°F (180°C). Line baking sheet with parchment paper.

Combine flours, wheat germ, powdered milk, brown sugar, salt, and baking powder in large bowl. Cut in butter with pastry blender. Add milk and stir with fork to make rough ball.

Roll out dough on well-floured surface with well-floured rolling pin to $1/8$-inch (0.3-cm) thickness. Cut into 2-inch (5-cm) rounds and place on prepared baking sheet.

Gather scraps, re-roll, and cut again. Prick crackers lightly with tines of fork. Sprinkle with seeds of choice.

Bake 10 minutes. Turn crackers over and bake 5 more minutes. Watch crackers so they don't burn. Cool on wire racks.

Yield: 50 crackers

Each with: 73 Calories; 4g Fat (46.3% calories from fat); 2g Protein; 9g Carbohydrate; 1g Dietary Fiber; 11mg Cholesterol; 148mg Sodium.

 ## *Homemade Graham Crackers*

With deep whole grain flavor, these crackers are delicious spread with peanut butter.

> 1 cup (2 sticks [225 g]) butter
>
> 4 cups (500 g) Hodgson Mill Stone Ground Whole Grain Whole Wheat Graham Flour
>
> 1 cup (225 g) packed light or dark brown sugar
>
> 1 teaspoon (1.5 g) baking soda
>
> 1 teaspoon (3 g) cream of tartar
>
> 1 large egg, slightly beaten
>
> $1/2$ cup (120 ml) hot water

FOR THE TOPPING:
> Melted butter

Preheat oven to 350°F (180°C). Line baking sheet with parchment paper.

Cut butter into flour with pastry blender in large bowl until mixture resembles coarse crumbs. Stir in sugar, baking soda, cream of tartar, egg, and enough hot water so that dough forms a ball. Transfer dough to floured surface and roll out to $1/8$- to $1/4$-inch (0.3 to 0.6-cm) thickness. Cut into 3-inch (7.5-cm) squares and place on prepared baking sheet.

Bake 15 to 20 minutes. Cool on wire rack. Brush tops with butter.

Yield: 40 3-inch (7.5-cm) servings

Each with: 103 Calories; 5g Fat (41.4% calories from fat); 1 g Protein; 14g Carbohydrate; 2g Dietary Fiber; 17mg Cholesterol; 82mg Sodium.

Honey Graham Crackers in the Round

Sweetened with honey and spiced with cinnamon, these graham crackers taste like those found at the grocery store. If you prefer, pat the dough into a rectangle and cut into rectangular pieces.

$^2/_3$ cup (82.5 g) Hodgson Mill Stone Ground Whole Grain Whole Wheat Graham Flour

$^1/_3$ cup (41.6 g) Hodgson Mill All-Purpose, Unbleached Naturally White Flour

2 tablespoons (28 g) packed light or dark brown sugar

$^1/_2$ teaspoon (1.2 g) baking powder

2 teaspoons (4.6 g) ground cinnamon

$^1/_8$ teaspoon (0.7 g) salt

2 tablespoons (28 g) butter

2 tablespoons (40 g) honey

2 tablespoons (28 ml) 2 percent milk

Preheat oven to 350°F (180°C). Lightly grease a 12-inch (30-cm) pizza pan.

Combine flours, sugar, baking powder, cinnamon, and salt in medium bowl. Cut in butter with pastry blender until mixture resembles coarse crumbs. Whisk honey and milk together in small bowl. Sprinkle half of milk mixture over dry ingredients, then stir with fork to moisten. Form into ball. If necessary, add more milk mixture.

Press dough into prepared pizza pan. Cut dough into 20 wedge-shaped sections with knife or pizza wheel. Cut each section into 2 pieces by cutting a circle around the dough 5 inches (12.5 cm) from outside edge. Prick dough surface with tines of fork.

Bake 15 minutes or until crisp, but not brown.

Yield: 40 crackers

Each with: 22 Calories; 1g Fat (24.9% calories from fat); trace Protein; 4g Carbohydrate; trace Dietary Fiber; 2mg Cholesterol; 19mg Sodium.

Homemade Whole Wheat Snack Crackers

When you want a really healthy snack cracker, make sure you include as many organic ingredients as possible in the recipe. Use a floured pastry cloth to roll the dough out very, very thin.

$1^1/2$ cups (187.5 g) Hodgson Mill Organic Naturally White, Unbleached, All-Purpose Flour

$1/2$ cup (62.5 g) Hodgson Mill Organic Stone Ground Whole Grain Whole Wheat Graham Flour

$1/2$ cup (100 g) organic sugar

$1/4$ teaspoon (1.5 g) salt

2 tablespoons (28 g) organic butter or margarine

$2/3$ cup (170 ml) 2 percent organic milk

FOR THE TOPPING:

Garlic or onion salt

Preheat oven to 325°F (170°C). Line baking sheet with parchment paper.

Combine flours, sugar, and salt in large bowl. Cut in butter with pastry blender until mixture resembles coarse crumbs. Blend in milk with fork slowly, using only enough to form dough that will form a ball. Divide dough into 2 equal portions.

Transfer dough to floured surface or pastry cloth. Roll dough out to $1/16$-inch (0.2-cm) thickness. If desired, lightly sprinkle surface with salt and gently roll over dough with rolling pin. Cut dough into 2-inch (5-cm) squares with knife or pizza wheel. Transfer to prepared baking sheet. Prick each cracker with tines of fork 2 or 3 times.

Bake 20 to 25 minutes, or until crackers are lightly browned. Cool on wire rack.

Yield: 36 crackers

Each with: 41 Calories; 1g Fat (16.5% calories from fat); 1g Protein; 8g Carbohydrate; trace Dietary Fiber; 2mg Cholesterol; 24mg Sodium.

Gluten-Free Rice Flour Pita Bread

These mellow-tasting flatbreads can easily be used like wheat flour pita breads.
Griddle-baking is the traditional cooking method, but these won't puff up quite as
much as wheat flour pita breads.

$1/2$ cup (62.5 g) Hodgson Mill Stone Ground Whole Grain Brown Rice Flour

$1/2$ cup (80 g) potato or tapioca flour

2 teaspoons (5.3 g) Hodgson Mill Pure Corn Starch

2 teaspoons (10 ml) vegetable oil, such as canola

$1/2$ cup (120 ml) water

Combine flours and corn starch in bowl. Mix oil and water into flour mixture with
fork, then finish mixing by hand until dough forms ball.

Transfer dough to rice-floured surface and knead a few times. Divide dough into 8
equal portions. Roll each portion into a ball, then pat into disc. Sprinkle each disc
with rice flour. Place between two sheets of waxed or parchment paper and roll to
$1/8$-inch (0.3-cm) thickness.

Preheat oven to 400°F (200°C). Lightly oil a griddle or skillet and heat to medium-
high. Place baking sheet on oven rack.

Griddle-bake four flatbreads at a time for 15 to 20 seconds on each side.
Immediately put bread on baking sheet in oven and bake 3 minutes. Turn and bake
$1^1/2$ to 2 more minutes or until somewhat puffed. Repeat with remaining dough.
Cool breads on wire racks before storing in plastic bags.

Yield: 8 breads

Each with: 81 Calories; 1g Fat (16.0% calories from fat); 2g Protein; 16g Carbohydrate; 1g Dietary
Fiber; 0mg Cholesterol; 4mg Sodium.

Lebanese Pita Bread

With a more rustic texture, this version of pita bread is a good vehicle for hummus and tzatziki or yogurt dip. The warm water not only helps proof the yeast, but also softens the oat bran cereal.

- 1^1/2 cups (187.5 g) Hodgson Mill Oat Bran Hot Cereal, uncooked
- 1 package (^{5}/16 ounce) or 2^1/2 teaspoons (10 g) Hodgson Mill Active Dry Yeast
- 1 cup (125 g) Hodgson Mill 50/50 Flour
- 1 to 1^1/2 cups (125 to 187.5 g) Hodgson Mill All-Purpose, Unbleached Naturally White Flour
- 1^1/4 cups (295 ml) very warm water (115°F [46°C])
- ^{1}/4 cup (60 ml) vegetable oil, such as canola
- 1^1/2 teaspoons (9 g) salt

Process cereal in food processor until fine and flour-like, about 2 minutes. Blend processed cereal, yeast, and ^{1}/2 cup (62.5 g) of 50/50 flour in large bowl.

Combine water, oil, and salt. Pour over the flour-yeast mixture. Set aside to proof until foamy, about 5 minutes.

Beat mixture at low speed in electric mixer fitted with dough hook or in a food processor for 1 minute, scraping sides of bowl. Beat for 3 minutes at medium speed to incorporate as much of the remaining flours as possible.

Turn out onto floured surface and knead enough of remaining flours to make smooth, satiny dough, about 5 to 7 minutes. Place dough in oiled bowl and turn to coat. Cover and let rise for 30 minutes. Dough should be very warm and light to touch.

Punch down dough and divide into 12 equal portions. Cover, and let rise 15 minutes.

Preheat oven to 500°F (250°C). Lightly oil griddle or skillet and heat to medium-high. Place baking sheet on oven rack.

Roll each portion into a ball, then pat into disc. Sprinkle each disc with flour. Place between two sheets of waxed or parchment paper and roll to ^{1}/8-inch (0.3-cm) thickness.

Griddle-bake four flatbreads at a time for 15 to 20 seconds on each side. Immediately place breads on baking sheet in oven and bake 3 minutes. Turn and bake 2 to 3 more minutes or until somewhat puffed. Repeat with remaining dough.

Cool breads on wire racks before storing in plastic bags.

Yield: 12 breads

Each with: 169 Calories; 6g Fat (29.8% calories from fat); 6g Protein; 26g Carbohydrate; 4g Dietary Fiber; 0mg Cholesterol; 269mg Sodium.

 Soft Pretzels

It's easy to make your own homemade soft dough pretzel snacks with this easy recipe.

^{3}/4 cup (170 ml) warm (105°F to 115°F [40.5°C to 46°C]) water

1 package (^{5}/16 ounce) or 2^1/2 teaspoons (10 g) Hodgson Mill Fast-Rise Yeast

^{1}/2 cup (120 ml) warm 2 percent milk

2 tablespoons (28 ml) vegetable oil, such as canola

1^1/2 tablespoons (19.5 g) sugar

1 teaspoon (6 g) salt

1 cup (125 g) Hodgson Mill 50/50 Flour

2 to 2^1/2 cups (250 to 312.5 g) Hodgson Mill All-Purpose, Unbleached Naturally White Flour

^{1}/2 cup (70 g) Hodgson Mill Milled Flax Seed

FOR THE TOPPING:

1 large egg

1 tablespoon (15 ml) water

Coarse kosher salt

Combine water, yeast, milk, oil, sugar, and salt in large bowl. Stir in 2 cups (250 g) flour and flax seed until smooth. Add additional flour, ^{1}/4 cup (31.3 g) at a time, until a soft dough forms. Transfer dough to lightly floured surface and knead by hand 3 to 4 minutes or until smooth and elastic. Place dough in oiled bowl and turn to coat. Cover and let rest 15 minutes.

Preheat oven to 350°F (180°C). Line 2 baking sheets with parchment paper.

Divide dough into 10 equal portions. Roll each piece into an 18-inch (45-cm) rope. Form pretzel by bringing ends of rope together to make a heart. Twist ends together twice, then draw down to attach at 4:00 and 8:00 points on heart.

Place each pretzel on prepared baking sheet. For topping, whisk egg and water together in small bowl. Brush half of mixture on pretzels. Sprinkle with half of salt. Allow pretzels to rise for 15 minutes.

Bake 15 minutes, then remove from hot oven and brush pretzels with remaining egg mixture and sprinkle with remaining salt. Bake 10 more minutes or until golden.

Cool on wire racks.

Yield: 10 pretzels

Each with: 192 Calories; 5g Fat (22.9% calories from fat); 6g Protein; 31 g Carbohydrate; 3g Dietary Fiber; 20mg Cholesterol; 413mg Sodium.

 ## *Focaccia with Milled Flax Seed*

With whole grain and omega-3 benefits, this healthy flat bread is delicious served with grilled vegetables, lean steak or pork chops, or fish.

$1^1/2$ cups (355 ml) warm (105°F to 115°F [40.5°C to 46°C]) water

1 package (^{5}/16 ounce) or $2^1/2$ teaspoons (10 g) Hodgson Mill Fast-Rise Yeast

1 tablespoon (15 ml) olive oil

1 cup (125 g) Hodgson Mill 50/50 Flour

2 to $2^1/2$ cups (250 to 312.5 g) Hodgson Mill All-Purpose, Unbleached Naturally White Flour

1/3 cup (47 g) Hodgson Mill Milled Flax Seed

1 teaspoon (6 g) salt

2 teaspoons (10 ml) Italian seasoning

1 large egg, beaten

FOR THE TOPPING:

1 onion, sliced thin

1 tablespoon (15 ml) olive oil

1 tablespoon (18 g) coarse kosher salt

2 tablespoons (6 g) fresh chives, chopped

2 tablespoons (10 g) freshly grated Parmesan cheese

Lightly coat a $15^1/2$ x $10^1/2$ x ^{3}/4-inch (38.8 x 26.3 x 1.9-cm) baking pan with olive oil. Combine water, yeast, and oil in large bowl. Combine flours in bowl. Add 2 cups (250 g) flour mixture, flax seed, salt, and seasoning to water/yeast/oil mixture. Add beaten egg and remaining flour mixture, ^{1}/2 cup (62.5 g) at a time, until a soft dough forms. Place in oiled bowl and turn to coat. Cover and let rest 20 minutes.

For topping, saute onions in olive oil in large skillet until soft but not brown; set aside to cool. Transfer dough to lightly floured surface and knead gently for 2 to 3 minutes or until elastic. Stretch and shape dough to fit prepared baking sheet. Spread with cooled onions, then sprinkle on salt, chives, and Parmesan cheese. Cover loosely with plastic wrap and let rise for 30 to 45 minutes.

Preheat oven to 400°F (200°C). Bake 20 to 25 minutes or until top is lightly browned. Cut into pieces to serve.

Yield: 10 servings

Each with: 180 Calories; 5g Fat (22.3% calories from fat); 6g Protein; 29g Carbohydrate; 3g Dietary Fiber; 19mg Cholesterol; 803mg Sodium.

Variation: Use fresh rosemary in place of chives.

 ## *Savory Cheese Gougere*

Classic French choux pastry partly made with whole grain flour? You bet! These savory bites make delicious cocktail fare or accompaniments to a hearty soup.

> 1 cup (235 ml) milk
> 1/2 cup (1 stick [112 g]) unsalted butter
> 3/4 teaspoon (4.5 g) salt
> 3/4 teaspoon (1.7 g) ground white pepper
> 1/2 cup (62.5 g) sifted Hodgson Mill Stone Ground Whole Grain White Whole Wheat Flour
> 1/2 cup (62.5 g) sifted Hodgson Mill All-Purpose, Unbleached Naturally White Flour
> 4 large eggs
> 1 cup (100 g) grated aged pecorino or Asiago cheese

FOR THE TOPPING:
> 1 large egg
> 1/3 cup (40 g) grated Gruyère or sharp Cheddar cheese

Preheat the oven to 350°F (180°C). Line baking sheet with parchment paper.

In a large saucepan, combine milk, butter, salt, and pepper and bring to a boil. Remove from heat, add flour all at once, and whisk vigorously until smooth.

Return pan to heat and cook, stirring constantly, until batter has thickened and pulls away from sides of pan. Remove pan from heat and beat in 4 eggs, one at a time, mixing thoroughly after each addition. Beat in pecorino.

Drop by rounded tablespoonfuls of batter onto prepared baking sheet. For topping, beat remaining egg in a small bowl. Brush the tops of the gougeres with the beaten egg and sprinkle with the Gruyère.

Bake 10 to 15 minutes, or until puffed, browned, and crackled. Serve warm.

Yield: 24 pastries

Each with: 87 Calories; 7g Fat (70.7% calories from fat); 4g Protein; 3g Carbohydrate; trace Dietary Fiber; 57mg Cholesterol; 149mg Sodium.

Afghan Flatbreads with Fresh Herb Filling

(See photo on page 240.)

Known as "bolani" with the accent over the "I," these flatbreads can be baked in the oven, on a griddle, or on the grill. The fresh-tasting filling makes these breads delicious served with a salad or grilled vegetables, chicken, or beef.

FOR THE DOUGH:

$1^1/2$ cups (187.5 g) Hodgson Mill Stone Ground Whole Grain Whole Wheat Graham Flour

2 cups (250 g) Hodgson Mill All-Purpose, Unbleached Naturally White Flour

2 packages ($^5/16$ ounce each) or 5 teaspoons (20 g) Hodgson Mill Fast-Rise Yeast

1 tablespoon (20 g) honey

3 tablespoons plus 1 tablespoon (60 ml) vegetable oil, such as canola

$^1/2$ teaspoon (3 g) salt

1 cup (235 ml) warm (110°F to 115°F [43°C to 46°C]) water

FOR THE FILLING:

1 cup (160 g) finely chopped green onions

1 cup (60 g) finely chopped fresh cilantro

1 small finely chopped hot green pepper, such as Thai or jalapeno

$^1/4$ teaspoon (1.5 g) salt

1 tablespoon (15 ml) vegetable oil, such as canola

For dough, combine flours and yeast in bowl of food processor or electric mixer. Combine honey, 3 tablespoons (45 ml) of oil, salt, and water in a cup and stir to blend. Turn on food processor or mixer and pour liquid mixture through feed tube or into mixing bowl in steady stream. Process or mix until dough forms a mass and cleans sides of bowl.

Turn dough out onto a floured surface and knead by hand for 5 minutes, or until smooth and elastic. Place in large oiled bowl and turn to coat. Cover and let rise until doubled in bulk, 1 to 1$^{1}/_{2}$ hours.

For filling, combine green onions, cilantro, hot pepper, and salt in bowl; set aside for 60 minutes. Drain off any excess juice. Stir in 1 tablespoon (15 ml) oil.

Punch down dough and turn out onto floured surface. Divide dough into 4 equal portions. Roll each portion into 8 x 12-inch (20 x 30-cm) oval. Place $^{1}/_{4}$ filling in top half of each oval, leaving 1-inch (2.5-cm) perimeter at the top. Brush water along edge of each oval. Fold dough over filling and press edges together.

Heat remaining 1 tablespoon (15 ml) oil in a large non-stick griddle or skillet. Griddle-bake flatbreads on each side until golden brown. Cut each bolani in half. Serve warm or at room temperature.

Yield: 4 flatbreads

Each with: 539 Calories; 18g Fat (28.6% calories from fat); 13g Protein; 87g Carbohydrate; 9g Dietary Fiber; 0mg Cholesterol; 408mg Sodium.

Note: Afghani flatbread may also be brushed with oil and grilled on both sides until done.

Zaatar Flatbread

Zaatar is a Middle Eastern herb blend used on flatbreads for savory effect. Serve this flatbread as an appetizer or main dish, accompanied by feta cheese, black olives, hummus, cucumber, and tomatoes. You can find zaatar spice blends at better herb and spice companies or make your own in this recipe.

FOR THE DOUGH:

1 package ($5/16$ ounce) or $2^1/2$ teaspoons (10 g) Hodgson Mill
   Active Dry Yeast

2 cups (470 ml) warm (105°F to 115°F [40.5°C to 46°C]) water

2 teaspoons (26 g) sugar

2 tablespoons (28 ml) olive oil

$1^3/4$ teaspoons (10.5 g) kosher salt

2 cups (250 g) Hodgson Mill 50/50 Flour

5 cups (625 g) Hodgson Mill Best For Bread Flour

FOR THE TOPPING:

2 teaspoons (2 g) dried oregano

2 teaspoons (2 g) dried thyme

1 tablespoon (3 g) sumac (a reddish Middle Eastern herb with sour flavor)

$1/2$ cup (60 g) sesame seeds

1 teaspoon (6 g) kosher salt

Grated zest and juice of 2 lemons

$3/4$ cup (170 ml) olive oil

For dough, combine yeast, water, and sugar in large bowl and set aside until foamy, about 5 minutes.

Stir in oil and salt, then 50/50 flour and all but 1 cup (125 g) of bread flour. Stir together to form soft dough. Transfer to floured surface and knead 8 to 10 times, adding enough of remaining bread flour to make smooth, elastic dough. Place in oiled bowl. Cover and let rise until doubled in bulk, about $1^1/2$ hours.

Preheat oven to 450°F (230°C). Line 3 baking sheets with parchment paper. For topping, stir zaatar spices, salt, lemon juice, and olive oil in small bowl and set aside. Divide dough into 12 equal portions. Stretch or roll dough into irregular rectangles and brush with topping. Place on prepared baking sheets. Cover and let rest 15 minutes.

Bake flatbread 5 to 10 minutes, or until browned. Brush with additional topping if desired.

Yield: 12 flatbreads

Each with: 415 Calories; 19g Fat (39.3% calories from fat); 11 g Protein; 54g Carbohydrate; 4g Dietary Fiber; 0mg Cholesterol; 441mg Sodium.

Note: This flatbread may also be brushed with oil and grilled on both sides until done.

Roman Army Flatbread

Like pita bread, this yeasty, reddish-brown flatbread is delicious served with Mediterranean-style accompaniments, such as black olives, hummus, pesto, goat cheese, and fresh tomatoes.

  3 cups (375 g) Hodgson Mill Organic Whole Grain Spelt Flour
  1 tablespoon (7 g) Hodgson Mill Vital Wheat Gluten
  2/3 cup (160 ml) warm (105°F to 115°F [40.5°C to 46°C]) water
  1 1/2 teaspoons (9 g) salt
  3 tablespoons (45 ml) olive oil
  1 tablespoon (12 g) Hodgson Mill Fast-Rise Yeast
  Hodgson Mill Stone Ground Whole Grain Yellow Corn Meal, Plain, for sprinkling

Place flour and gluten in large mixing bowl. Whisk in remaining ingredients to form soft dough.

Transfer to floured surface and knead until elastic and firm to touch. Place in oiled bowl and turn to coat. Cover and let rise until doubled in bulk, about 1 hour.

Preheat oven to 400°F (200°C). Lightly sprinkle baking sheet with corn meal.

Divide dough into 6 portions. Roll or pat each portion into a rough circle, 5 to 6 inches (13 to 15 cm) in diameter. Place dough circles on prepared baking sheet.

Bake 12 to 15 minutes, or until puffed and browned.

Yield: 6 serving-size flatbreads

Each with: 250 Calories; 9g Fat (25.7% calories from fat); 12g Protein; 45g Carbohydrate; 11g Dietary Fiber; 0mg Cholesterol; 534mg Sodium.

Variation: Roman army cooks would have griddle-baked this bread over an open fire, so try grilling this bread. Simply brush olive oil on both sides of each flatbread. Place dough circles directly on grill grates over a hot fire until bubbles form on the surface, then turn with grill tongs and cook for a minute on the other side.

 Focaccia with Sun-Dried Tomatoes

With corn meal for a little added crunch, this focaccia is delicious dipped into your favorite olive oil. And it's so easy to make the dough in the bread machine!

FOR THE DOUGH:

$1^1/4$ cups (295 ml) water

3 tablespoons (45 ml) olive oil

2 teaspoons (6 g) chopped garlic

1 teaspoon (6 g) salt

$1/3$ cup (47 g) Hodgson Mill Stone Ground Whole Grain Yellow or White Corn Meal, Plain, plus more for sprinkling

$1^1/2$ cups (187.5 g) Hodgson Mill All-Purpose, Unbleached Naturally White Flour

$1^1/2$ cups (187.5 g) Hodgson Mill Stone Ground Whole Grain White Whole Wheat Flour

2 teaspoons (8 g) Hodgson Mill Fast-Rise Yeast

FOR THE TOPPING:

$1/4$ cup (60 ml) olive oil

$1/2$ cup (87.5 g) chopped sun-dried tomatoes

$1/3$ cup (33 g) freshly grated Parmesan cheese

Place dough ingredients in bread pan according to manufacturer's instructions. Select dough cycle and start the machine.

Preheat oven to 425°F (220°C). Sprinkle baking sheet with corn meal. When cycle is complete, press or pat dough into prepared baking sheet. For topping, brush dough with olive oil, then sprinkle with tomatoes and Parmesan.

Bake 15 to 20 minutes or until instant-read thermometer inserted in center registers at least 190°F (87.7°C). Cut into pieces to serve.

Yield: 16 servings

Each with: 150 Calories; 7g Fat (38.9% calories from fat); 4g Protein; 20g Carbohydrate; 2g Dietary Fiber; 1 mg Cholesterol; 200mg Sodium.

Variation: Before final knead in machine, add tomatoes and cheese to dough. For topping, just brush dough with olive oil and sprinkle with coarse salt.

Easy Wheat Heart Pretzels (See photo on page 241.)

There is always more than one way to do something. Try this unique, no clean-up method for making the dough.

1 cup (125 g) Hodgson Mill Stone Ground Whole Grain Whole Wheat Graham Flour

1 cup (125 g) Hodgson Mill All-Purpose, Unbleached Naturally White Flour

3 tablespoons (27 g) Hodgson Mill Milled Flax Seed

2 tablespoons (26 g) sugar

1 package ($5/16$ ounce) or $2^1/2$ teaspoons (10 g) Hodgson Mill Fast-Rise Yeast

$3/4$ cup (175 ml) warm (105°F to 115°F [40.5°C to 46°C]) water

1 tablespoon (15 ml) vegetable oil, such as canola

$1/4$ teaspoon (3 g) salt

FOR THE TOPPING:

1 large egg

1 tablespoon (15 ml) water

Poppy seeds, sesame seeds, coarse salt, or favorite topping

For dough, place all ingredients in large, sealable plastic bag. Push out as much air as possible and seal bag. Blend ingredients by squeezing and pushing on bag about 10 minutes. Dough may be removed from bag and placed on lightly floured surface for final kneading. Cover dough with inverted oiled bowl and let rest 30 minutes.

Preheat oven to 350°F (180°C). Line 2 baking sheets with parchment paper.

Divide dough into 12 equal portions. Cover and let rest about 5 minutes.

Roll each piece into a 16-inch (40-cm) rope. Form pretzel by bringing ends of rope together to make a heart. Twist ends together twice, then draw down to attach at

4:00 and 8:00 points on heart. Place each pretzel on prepared baking sheet. For topping, whisk egg and water together in small bowl.

Brush half of mixture on pretzels. Sprinkle with seeds. Allow pretzels to rise for 15 minutes.

Bake 15 to 20 minutes or until golden. Cool on wire rack.

Yield: 12 pretzels

Each with: 100 Calories; 2g Fat (18.8% calories from fat); 3g Protein; 18g Carbohydrate; 2g Dietary Fiber; 16mg Cholesterol; 206mg Sodium.

 ## *Thin and Crispy Rye Bread Sticks*

The molasses and cocoa powder turn the natural gray of rye flour to a more appealing dark brown.

1 package (^{5}/16 ounce) or 2^1/2 teaspoons (10 g) Hodgson Mill
  Active Dry Yeast

1^1/4 cups (295 ml) warm (105°F to 115°F [40.5°C to 46°C]) water

2 tablespoons (28 ml) vegetable oil, such as canola

3 tablespoons (60 g) molasses

2 tablespoons (16 g) unsweetened cocoa powder

1 teaspoon (6 g) salt

1^1/2 teaspoons (3 g) caraway seeds

1 cup (125 g) Hodgson Mill Stone Ground Whole Grain Rye Flour

2^1/2 cups (312.5 g) Hodgson Mill Best For Bread Flour

FOR THE TOPPING:

1 large egg white

1 tablespoon (15 ml) water

Coarse or kosher salt, toasted sesame seeds, poppy seeds, garlic
  or onion powder, or your favorite topping

Sprinkle yeast over water in large bowl and set aside until foamy, about 5 minutes.

Stir in oil, molasses, cocoa powder, salt, caraway seeds, and rye flour. Add bread flour and stir to form soft dough. Transfer dough to floured surface and knead by hand for 5 minutes. Place dough in oiled bowl and turn to coat. Cover and let rise until doubled in bulk, about 45 minutes.

Preheat oven to 400°F (200°C). Line 2 baking sheets with parchment paper. Divide dough in half. Turn each half out onto floured surface and roll into a rectangle about 6 x 12-inches (15 x 30-cm) and 1/2-inch (1.2-cm) thick. Cut strips about 1/2-inch (1.2-cm) wide with knife or pizza cutter and place on prepared baking sheet.

For topping, beat egg and water together. Brush egg mixture on bread sticks and sprinkle with salt and your favorite toppings. Cover and let rise for 15 minutes.

Bake 15 minutes or until crispy. Cool on wire racks.

Yield: 36 sticks

Each with: 52 Calories; 1g Fat (15.5% calories from fat); 2g Protein; 10g Carbohydrate; 1g Dietary Fiber; 0mg Cholesterol; 63mg Sodium.

Variation: Substitute bread machine yeast for active dry and make the dough in the bread machine on dough cycle. When cycle is complete, proceed with rolling, cutting, and baking steps.

 ## *Mexican Corn Tortillas*

Corn meal gives these tortillas an authentic Southwestern flavor. They are a delicious way to begin lots of great Mexican meals and make terrific taco chips, too.

    1 cup (140 g) Hodgson Mill Stone Ground Whole Grain White or Yellow Corn
        Meal, Plain
    1 cup (125 g) Hodgson Mill All-Purpose, Unbleached Naturally White Flour
    1 teaspoon (6 g) salt
    1 teaspoon (1.5 g) baking soda
    3/4 cup (175 ml) warm (105°F to 115°F [40.5°C to 46°C]) water

Combine corn meal, flour, salt, and baking soda. Stir in warm water until mixture forms a ball. Divide dough into 12 equal portions. Roll each portion into a ball. Place each ball between 2 pieces of waxed or parchment paper. With a tortilla press or a rolling pin, flatten each ball into a 5- to 6-inch (12.5- to 15-cm) diameter circle.

Oil a griddle or a large frying pan and heat over medium-high heat. Griddle-bake each tortilla 1 1/2 to 2 minutes per side until speckled and brown.

Yield: 12 tortillas

Each with: 67 Calories; trace Fat (4.2% calories from fat); 2g Protein; 15g Carbohydrate; 1g Dietary Fiber; 0mg Cholesterol; 283mg Sodium.

Variation: To make baked taco chips, preheat oven to 400°F (200°C). Line 2 baking sheets with parchment paper. Spray or brush each dough circle lightly with vegetable oil, then cut into 8 wedges with pizza wheel or sharp knife. Place on prepared baking sheets. Bake 10 minutes or until lightly browned and crisp.

Whole Wheat Flour Tortillas

Whole wheat tortillas have a much better, less bland flavor than those made with all-purpose flour. Make these when you grill fajitas. In this recipe, instead of oiling the griddle, you oil the tortilla dough, but either method works fine.

$1/2$ cup (62.5 g) Hodgson Mill All-Purpose, Unbleached Naturally White Flour

$1/2$ cup (62.5 g) Hodgson Mill Stone Ground Whole Grain Whole Wheat Graham Flour

$1/4$ teaspoon (1.5 g) salt

1 tablespoon (15 ml) vegetable oil, such as canola

$3/4$ cup (175 ml) warm (105°F to 115°F [40.5°C to 46°C]) water

Combine flours and salt in bowl. Stir in oil and water to make a soft dough. Divide dough into 12 equal portions. Shape each into a small ball. Oil hands and roll each ball in your hands. Place balls on baking sheet, cover, and let rest 15 minutes.

Heat skillet or griddle over medium-high heat. Shape each ball into a very flat 4-inch (10-cm) round disc. Roll out on a lightly floured surface to a 6-inch (15-cm) circle.

Griddle-bake each round on one side only, until bubbles form on top and underside is flecked with brown, but still flexible. Stack cooked tortillas on large plate, and cover with a dry cloth towel. Serve immediately or reheat in 350°F (180°C) oven before serving.

Yield: 12 tortillas

Each with: 43 Calories; 1g Fat (24.4% calories from fat); 1g Protein; 8g Carbohydrate; 1g Dietary Fiber; 0mg Cholesterol; 45mg Sodium.

Variation: Make whole wheat tortilla chips by cutting each griddle-baked tortilla in wedges with knife or pizza wheel. Crisp in 350°F (180°C) oven to make chips for dips or serve with melted cheese and chiles as nachos.

Multi Grain Seeded Flatbread

With a delightful crunchy topping, this flatbread goes well with soups and stews.

1 teaspoon (4 g) Hodgson Mill Fast-Rise Yeast

3/4 cup (93.8 g) Hodgson Mill 50/50 or Stone Ground Whole Grain Whole Wheat Graham Flour

3/4 cup (93.8 g) Hodgson Mill Oat Bran Flour

1/2 cup (62.5 g) Hodgson Mill Stone Ground Whole Grain Rye Flour

1/2 teaspoon (3 g) salt

1/2 teaspoon (6.5 g) sugar

1 cup (235 ml) warm (105°F to 115°F [40.5°C to 46°C]) water

FOR THE TOPPING:

1 tablespoon (15 ml) olive oil

1/4 cup (30 g) sesame seeds

1/4 cup (36 g) Hodgson Mill Milled Flax Seed

1 tablespoon (18 g) coarse kosher or sea salt

Combine yeast, flours, salt, and sugar in bowl. Stir in water until soft dough forms. Cover and let rise until doubled in bulk, about 1 1/2 hours.

Preheat oven to 375°F (190°C). Line 2 baking sheets with parchment paper.

Turn dough out onto floured surface. Divide dough in half. Roll each half out into thin, free-form rectangle, about 13 x 10-inches (32.5 x 25-cm). Transfer to baking sheets. For topping, brush each flatbread with oil and sprinkle with seeds and salt.

Bake for 12 to15 minutes, until golden.

Yield: 20 servings

Each with: 64 Calories; 2g Fat (31.6% calories from fat); 2g Protein; 10g Carbohydrate; 2g Dietary Fiber; 0mg Cholesterol; 336mg Sodium.

Thin Armenian Flatbread

The 50/50 Flour, half all-purpose and half whole wheat, really gives a taste and texture similar to stone ground wheat flours from faraway lands. But ancient recipe meets modern technique in this dough you can make in the bread machine.

> 1^1/2 cups (355 ml) warm (105°F to 115°F [40.5°C to 46°C]) water
>
> 3 tablespoons (45 ml) olive oil
>
> 1 teaspoon (6 g) salt
>
> 1 teaspoon (13 g) sugar
>
> 3^1/4 cups (406 g) Hodgson Mill 50/50 Flour
>
> 1 package (^{5}/16 ounce) or 2^1/2 teaspoons (10 g) Hodgson Mill Fast-Rise Yeast

Place ingredients in bread pan according to manufacturer's instructions. Select dough cycle and start the machine.

Preheat oven to 350°F (180°C). Line baking sheet with parchment paper.

When cycle is complete, punch dough down and transfer to floured surface. Divide dough into 4 equal portions. Roll and stretch each piece into 10 x 14-inch (25 x 35-cm) rectangle and place on prepared baking sheets.

Bake 20 minutes, or until browned. Remove from baking sheets and cool on wire racks.

Yield: 20 servings

Each with: 85 Calories; 2g Fat (21.3% calories from fat); 3g Protein; 14g Carbohydrate; 1g Dietary Fiber; 0mg Cholesterol; 107mg Sodium.

Spelt Flatbread with Roasted Red Pepper and Goat Cheese

The ancient spelt grain gives this flatbread more of a burnt sienna color and a delicious flavor.

> 1^1/2 cups (355 ml) warm (105°F to 115°F [40.5°C to 46°C]) water
>
> 3 tablespoons (45 ml) olive oil
>
> 1 teaspoon (6 g) salt
>
> 1 teaspoon (13 g) sugar
>
> 2 cups (250 g) Hodgson Mill Organic Spelt Flour

1^1/4 cups (156.3 g) Hodgson Mill 50/50 flour

1 package (^{5}/16 ounce) or 2^1/2 teaspoons (10 g) Hodgson Mill Fast-Rise Yeast

FOR THE TOPPING:

^{1}/4 cup (60 ml) olive oil

1 jar (12 ounces) roasted red pepper, drained, patted dry, cut into strips

6 ounces (112.5 g) fresh goat cheese

Place ingredients in bread pan according to manufacturer's instructions. Select dough cycle and start the machine.

Preheat oven to 350°F (180°C). Line baking sheet with parchment paper.

When cycle is complete, punch dough down and transfer to floured surface. Divide dough into 4 equal portions. Roll and stretch each piece into 10 x 14-inch (25 x 35-cm) rectangle and place on prepared baking sheets. For topping, brush flatbreads with olive oil. Arrange roasted red pepper strips and pieces of goat cheese on top.

Bake 20 minutes, or until browned. Remove from baking sheets and cool on wire racks.

Yield: 20 servings

Each with: 146 Calories; 8g Fat (46.4% calories from fat); 6g Protein; 15g Carbohydrate; 3g Dietary Fiber; 9mg Cholesterol; 137mg Sodium.

Gluten-Free Buckwheat Pita Bread

Soft and slightly chewy, this flatbread has an authentic, rustic look. Serve this with other Mediterranean foods, like hummus, tzatziki (a Greek dip of yogurt, garlic, and lemon juice), and kalamata olives.

1^1/2 teaspoons (6.5 g) sugar

1^1/4 cup (295 ml) warm (105°F to115°F [40.5°C to 46°C]) water

1 package (^{5}/16 ounce) or 2^1/2 teaspoons (10 g) Hodgson Mill
  Active Dry Yeast

1 cup (125 g) Hodgson Mill Stone Ground Whole Grain Brown Rice Flour, plus
  more for sprinkling

^{3}/4 cup (98.3 g) Hodgson Mill Stone Ground Buckwheat Flour

^{1}/4 cup (35 g) Hodgson Mill Pure Corn Starch

2 teaspoons (14 g) xanthan gum

1 teaspoon (6 g) salt

2 tablespoons (28 ml) vegetable oil, such as canola

Combine sugar and water in bowl; sprinkle yeast over mixture and set aside until foamy, about 5 minutes.

Combine flours, corn starch, xanthan gum, and salt in large bowl. Stir in yeast mixture and oil until soft dough. Cover and let rise until doubled in bulk, about 2 hours.

Transfer dough to rice-floured surface. Divide dough into 8 pieces. Roll each piece out to thin, flat 6-inch (15-cm) circle.

Oil, then heat a large griddle or skillet over medium-high heat. Griddle-bake each flatbread on one side for about 2 to 3 minutes, then flip and cook on the other side until very pale brown.

Yield: 8 flatbreads

Each with: 156 Calories; 4g Fat (24.1% calories from fat); 3g Protein; 28g Carbohydrate; 2g Dietary Fiber; 0mg Cholesterol; 268mg Sodium.

7

Handmade Breads

If you've baked your own bread before, you already know the great satisfaction that comes from tasting your creation, fresh and warm from the oven. And if the smell of fresh-baked bread brings back memories from your childhood, keep in mind that baking bread is a great activity for families. It's fun, it's rewarding, and it's a lot easier than you might think.

The basic recipe for just about any type of handmade bread consists of nine basic steps:

Step One: Choose a recipe.

Step Two: Gather your ingredients and equipment. That includes an instant-read thermometer (for checking the temperature of ingredients and for final doneness of the loaf) as well as a wooden spoon or dough whisk for mixing dough by hand. Alternatively, you can use an electric stand mixer with paddle and dough hook attachments if you want to mix the dough by machine.

Step Three: Proof the yeast. If you're using active dry yeast in the recipe, you should first test the temperature of the water with your instant-read thermometer (water at 135°F [57.2°C] kills the yeast). Then, dissolve yeast in 1/4 cup (60 ml) warm water (105 to 115°F [40.5 to 46°C]) and 1/4 teaspoon sugar. Set it aside for 5 minutes or until it begins to make a beige-colored foam. Once foamy, the yeast has proofed and it is ready for use. If you're using fast-rise yeast or bread machine yeast, you don't need to proof it in water; just stir the yeast into the dry ingredients.

Step Four: Mix the ingredients together to form a dough.

Step Five: Knead the dough on a lightly floured surface. To knead, fold the dough over toward you, then press down and away with the heel or knuckles of your hand. Turn the dough a quarter turn and repeat until the dough is smooth and elastic.

Step Six: Cover the dough with plastic wrap or a moist tea towel and let it rise in a warm (75°F to 80°F [23.8°C to 26.6°C]), draft-free location unless otherwise specified in the recipe. This could be a cabinet above your oven, the top of a radiator, a sunny (draft-free) window sill, a spot near a heating duct, or on a counter 3 feet (90 cm) from a wood stove. You can also preheat the oven to 200°F (90°C) for two minutes, put a pan of water in the bottom of the oven, turn the oven off, and put the bread inside to rise. (This is the best method if your house is air-conditioned.)

Step Seven: Punch down the dough. This means punch the dough right in the bowl to remove the air.

Step Eight: Shape the dough and allow for a second rising. This step will differ from recipe to recipe.

Step Nine: Bake the dough. All bread is done when you can insert your instant-read thermometer in the center of a loaf and the thermometer registers 190°F (87.7°C).

Interruptions: Life happens, even when you're making bread. If you happen to be interrupted during the rising process, you can allow the dough to rise a second or even third time if the dough is punched down and kneaded for a minute or two each time it rises. This will keep the dough from souring.

Onion Dill Bread

This recipe makes a hearty, flavorful bread that is perfect paired with a cheese such as Cheddar, brie, or chèvre. The dough can also be used to make delicious dinner rolls.

$3/4$ cup (175 ml) buttermilk or substitute (see note)

2 large eggs

$3/4$ cup (175 ml) warm (105°F to 115°F [40.5°C to 46°C]) water

$1/4$ cup (80 g) honey

1 tablespoon (20 g) molasses

1 package ($5/16$ ounce) or $2^1/2$ teaspoons (10 g) Hodgson Mill Active Dry Yeast

1 medium yellow onion, peeled and cut in half

$1/4$ cup (60 ml) vegetable oil, such as canola

$1^1/2$ teaspoons (9 g) salt

3 tablespoons (9 g) dried dill weed

4 cups (500 g) Hodgson Mill Best For Bread Flour, plus more if needed

2 cups (250 g) Hodgson Mill Stone Ground Whole Grain Whole Wheat Graham Flour

Heat buttermilk until warm (110°F [43.3°C]) in medium saucepan. Remove from heat and stir in eggs, water, honey, molasses, and yeast. Set aside to proof until foamy, about 5 minutes.

Purée onion with oil in food processor.

Combine salt, dill weed, and flours in large bowl. Beat yeast mixture into flour mixture, then beat in onion puree to form a firm dough by hand or with electric stand mixer.

Knead the dough 5 to 7 minutes or until shiny and elastic, adding more bread flour if necessary, in electric mixer with dough hook attachment. Or turn dough out onto a floured surface and knead by hand. Place dough in large oiled bowl and turn to coat. Cover and let rise until doubled in bulk, about 1 hour.

Grease two 9 * 5 x 3-inch (22.5 x 12.5 x 7.5-cm) loaf pans. Punch down dough and transfer to floured surface. Divide the dough in half. Form each half of the dough into a loaf and place in the prepared pans. Cover and let rise until doubled in bulk, about 1 hour.

Preheat oven to 350°F (180°C). Bake 35 to 40 minutes, or until instant-read thermometer inserted in the center registers 190°F (87.7°C). Cool in pans on wire racks.

Yield: Two 1-pound (455-g) loaves or 24 rolls

Each batch: 3495 Calories; 69g Fat (17.2% calories from fat); 112g Protein; 639g Carbohydrate; 52g Dietary Fiber; 380mg Cholesterol; 3620mg Sodium.

Note: If you don't have buttermilk, substitute by pouring 1½ teaspoons (7.5 ml) vinegar in a ¾-cup (175-ml) measure. Fill to top with milk and let sit for 2 minutes, then use in recipe.

Variation: Dill Rolls: Make the dough. Skip the kneading step and instead grease two 9-inch (22.5-cm) round pans and set aside. Punch down dough and transfer to floured surface. Divide dough in half. Cut each half into 12 pieces, and roll each piece into a ball. Place rolls in prepared pans, cover, and let rise until doubled in bulk, about 1 hour. Bake rolls at 350°F (180°C) for 10 to 15 minutes, or until they are reddish brown and sound hollow when tapped on the bottom. Cool on wire racks.

Variation: To make dough in the bread machine, substitute bread machine yeast for active dry. Add ingredients to bread pan according to manufacturer's directions. Set on dough cycle and start machine. When cycle is complete, proceed with shaping into loaves and the second rise.

Whole Wheat and Soy Bread

This dough will smell a little like bean sprouts, but that odor disappears during baking to give you a fine-textured, mild-flavored bread.

2 packages (⁵/16 ounce each) or 5 teaspoons (20 g) Hodgson Mill Active Dry Yeast

1½ cups (355 ml) warm (105°F to 115°F [40.5°C to 46°C]) water

2 large eggs, beaten

½ cup (120 ml) soy or canola oil

¼ cup (80 g) honey

2 teaspoons (12 g) salt

3 cups (375 ml) Hodgson Mill All-Purpose, Unbleached Naturally White Flour, plus more for kneading

1 cup (125 g) Hodgson Mill Soy Flour

2 cups (250 g) Hodgson Mill Stone Ground Whole Grain Whole Wheat Graham Flour

2 tablespoons (28 g) unsalted butter or soy margarine, melted

Sprinkle yeast over the warm water in large bowl and set aside to proof until foamy, about 5 minutes.

Beat in eggs, oil, honey, and salt with wooden spoon or dough whisk or paddle attachment of electric mixer. Beat in flours, 1 cup (125 g) at a time, to form a stiff dough that does not stick to the bowl. Transfer dough to an oiled surface. Oil your hands and knead the somewhat sticky dough, adding more all-purpose flour as necessary, until smooth and elastic, about 8 to 10 minutes. Place dough in a large, oiled bowl and turn to coat. Cover and let rise until doubled in bulk, about 1 hour.

Grease two 9 x 5 x 3-inch (22.5 x 12.5 x 7.5-cm) loaf pans. Punch down dough and divide in half. Shape each half into loaf and place in a prepared loaf pan. Cover and let rise until doubled in bulk, 45 to 60 minutes.

Preheat oven to 375°F (190°C). Bake 35 minutes or until an instant-read thermometer inserted in center registers 190°F (87.7°C). Brush tops of the loaves with melted butter or soy margarine and let cool in pans or on wire racks.

Yield: Two 1-pound (455-g) loaves

Each batch: 3936 Calories; 145g Fat (31.6% calories from fat); 135g Protein; 569g Carbohydrate; 70g Dietary Fiber; 436mg Cholesterol; 4391 mg Sodium.

Multi Grain Bread

Cooking the grains to soften them before adding them to the dough is an ancient technique that still works well today.

2^1/2 cups (312.5 g) Hodgson Mill Multi Grain Hot Cereal with Flaxseed and Soy, uncooked

2 cups (470 ml) boiling water

^{1}/2 cup (170 g) wildflower or other medium-colored honey

2 teaspoons (12 g) salt

2 packages (^{5}/16 ounce each) or 5 teaspoons (20 g) Hodgson Mill Fast-Rise Yeast

1 cup (235 ml) warm (105°F to 115°F [40.5°C to 46°C]) water

3 to 4 cups (375 to 500 g) Hodgson Mill Best For Bread Flour

Pour cereal in medium bowl. Pour boiling water over cereal, and set aside to soften for 15 minutes.

Stir together honey, salt, yeast and warm water with a wooden spoon or dough whisk in large bowl. Beat in 3 cups (375 g) of bread flour, then the softened grains, with wooden spoon or dough whisk or paddle attachment of electric mixer to form a moist, soft, yet heavy dough. Switch to dough hook attachment and knead the dough for 8 to 10 minutes, adding about 1 cup (125 g) more bread flour, until the dough is elastic and not sticky. Alternatively, turn dough out onto a floured surface and knead by hand. Place dough in a large, oiled bowl and turn to coat. Cover and let rise until doubled in bulk, about 1 hour.

Grease two 9 x 5 x 3-inch (22.5 x 12.5 x 7.5-cm) loaf pans or a large baking sheet and set aside. Punch down dough and turn out onto floured surface. Knead by hand a few more times. Divide the dough in half. Shape each portion into a regular or round loaf and put in the prepared loaf pans or on the baking sheet. Cover and let rise again until doubled in bulk, about 1 hour.

Preheat oven to 375°F (190°C). Bake 40 minutes, or until instant-read thermometer inserted in the center registers 190°F (87.7°C). Transfer to wire racks to cool.

Yield: Two 1-pound (455-g) loaves

Each batch: 3165 Calories; 23g Fat (6.3% calories from fat); 115g Protein; 643g Carbohydrate; 61 g Dietary Fiber; 0mg Cholesterol; 4361 mg Sodium.

Apple-Cinnamon Granola Bread

Sweet, apple-scented, and with just a slight crunch from the granola, this Wisconsin bread makes delicious toast.

1¹/2 teaspoons (6 g) Hodgson Mill Active Dry Yeast

¹/4 cup (60 ml) warm (105°F to 115°F [40.5°C to 46°C]) water

³/4 cup (175 ml) 2 percent milk

¹/2 cup (125 g) sweetened, chunky applesauce

¹/2 tablespoon (7 g) unsalted butter

³/4 teaspoon (1.7 g) ground cinnamon

2¹/2 teaspoons (15 g) salt

2 cups (250 g) Hodgson Mill Stone Ground Whole Grain White Whole Wheat Flour

1¹/2 cups (187.5 g) Hodgson Mill Best For Bread Flour, plus more if needed

³/4 cup (93.8 g) packaged or homemade granola

Sprinkle yeast over water and set aside to proof until foamy, about 5 minutes. Scald the milk in saucepan over medium-high heat until small bubbles form around the perimeter. Remove from heat and let cool to lukewarm (90°F [32.2°C]).

Combine milk, applesauce, butter, cinnamon, and salt in large bowl. Beat with wooden spoon or dough whisk or paddle attachment of electric mixer. Beat in flours, 1 cup (125 g) at a time, and granola, to form a soft dough. Switch to the dough hook and knead the dough for 3 to 4 minutes until smooth and elastic, adding more bread flour if necessary. Alternatively, turn the dough out onto a floured surface and knead by hand. Place dough in large, oiled bowl and turn to coat. Cover and let rise until doubled in bulk, about 1 hour.

Grease a 9 x 5 x 3-inch (22.5 x 12.5 x 7.5-cm) loaf pan and set aside. Punch down dough and turn out onto a floured surface. Form dough into a loaf and place in prepared loaf pan. Cover and let rise until doubled in bulk, about 1 hour.

Preheat oven to 350°F (180°C). Bake 35 to 40 minutes, or until instant-read thermometer registers 190°F (87.7°C). Cool in the pan or on a wire rack.

Yield: One 1-pound (455-g) loaf

Each batch: 2105 Calories; 38g Fat (15.7% calories from fat); 76g Protein; 388g Carbohydrate; 43g Dietary Fiber; 29mg Cholesterol; 5467mg Sodium.

Variation: To make dough in the bread machine, substitute bread machine yeast for active dry. Add ingredients to bread pan according to manufacturer's directions. Set on dough cycle and start machine. When cycle is complete, proceed with shaping into loaves and the second rise.

Cracked Wheat Bread

This bread was born when a thrifty cook decided that leftover hot breakfast cereal should not go to waste. Old-fashioned rolled oats (not instant) also work instead of cracked wheat, but this version will have a softer texture.

1 1/2 cups (187.5 g) Hodgson Mill Cracked Wheat Hot Cereal, uncooked

1/2 cup (170 g) honey or 3/4 cup (170 g) packed dark brown sugar

1/2 tablespoon (9 g) salt

1^{1}/2 tablespoons (21 g) unsalted butter

1^{2}/3 cups (390 g) boiling water

2 packages (^{5}/16 ounce each) or 5 teaspoons (20 g) Hodgson Mill Active Dry Yeast

1 cup (235 ml) warm (105°F to 115°F [40.5°C to 46°C]) water

6 to 7 cups (750 to 875 g) Hodgson Mill Best For Bread Flour

2 tablespoons (28 g) unsalted butter, melted

Combine cereal, honey, salt, and butter in bowl. Pour boiling water over the mixture, stir, and set aside for 15 minutes, or until cereal has softened, and the mixture is still warm (100°F [32.2°C]). Sprinkle yeast over warm water in large bowl and set aside to proof until foamy, about 5 minutes.

Beat 1 cup (125 g) bread flour into yeast mixture with wooden spoon or dough whisk or electric mixer. Beat in cracked wheat mixture, then add 5 additional cups of bread flour, 1 cup (125 g) at a time. Switch to dough hook and knead dough gently for 15 to 20 minutes, adding the remaining 1 cup (125 g) flour, if necessary, to form elastic dough. Or turn dough out onto floured surface and knead by hand. Place dough in large, oiled bowl and turn to coat. Cover and let rise until doubled in bulk, about 1^{1}/2 to 2 hours.

Grease two 9 x 5 x 3-inch (22.5 x 12.5 x 7.5-cm) loaf pans and set aside. Punch down dough and turn out onto floured surface. Divide the dough in half, form each half into a loaf, and place in prepared loaf pans. Cover and let rise until doubled in bulk, about 45 minutes.

Preheat oven to 350°F (180°C). Bake for 1 hour, or until instant-read thermometer inserted in center registers at least 190°F (87.7°C). Cool in the pans or on a wire rack. Brush tops of loaves with melted butter.

Yield: Two 1-pound (455-g) loaves

Each batch: 4391 Calories; 46g Fat (8.9% calories from fat); 151g Protein; 912g Carbohydrate; 60g Dietary Fiber; 109mg Cholesterol; 3369mg Sodium.

Variation: To make dough in the bread machine, substitute bread machine yeast for active dry. Add ingredients to bread pan according to manufacturer's directions. Set on dough cycle and start machine. When cycle is complete, proceed with shaping loaves and the second rise.

Wildflower Honey and White Whole Wheat Bread

White whole wheat flour is made from a variety of whole wheat with a milder flavor and lighter color, so it doesn't have to be mixed with all-purpose or bread flour to produce a delicious loaf. This recipe yields a nutty-flavored wheat bread with a tender crumb and just a touch of honey sweetness.

$2^1/4$ teaspoons (9 g) Hodgson Mill Active Dry Yeast

1 cup plus 1 tablespoon (250 ml) warm (105°F to 115°F [40.5°C to 46°C]) water

1 teaspoon (6 g) salt

$1/4$ cup (60 ml) vegetable oil

$1/2$ cup (170 g) wildflower or other amber honey

$2^1/2$ to 3 cups (312 to 375 g) Hodgson Mill Stone Ground Whole Grain White Whole Wheat Flour, plus more if needed

In a small bowl, sprinkle the yeast over the warm water and set aside to proof until foamy, about 5 minutes.

In the bowl of an electric mixer or another large mixing bowl, combine salt, oil, and honey and mix together using the paddle attachment or a wooden spoon or dough whisk. Add the flour, 1 cup (125 g) at a time, to form a soft dough.

Switch to the dough hook and knead the dough for 3 to 4 minutes until smooth and elastic, adding more flour if necessary. (Note: If the dough is too dry, add 1 tablespoon water at a time until dough softens.) Or turn the dough out onto a floured surface and knead by hand. Place the dough in a large, oiled bowl and turn to coat. Cover with plastic wrap and let rise at room temperature until doubled in bulk, about 1 hour.

Grease a 9 x 5 x 3-inch (22.5 x 12.5 x 7.5-cm) loaf pan and set aside. Punch dough down and turn out onto a floured surface. Form dough into a loaf and place in prepared loaf pan. Cover with plastic wrap sprayed with nonstick pan spray and let rise at room temperature until doubled in bulk, about 1 hour.

Preheat oven to 350°F (180°C). Bake for about 35 minutes, or until bread is golden brown on top and sounds hollow when tapped on the bottom; an instant-read thermometer should register at least 190°F (87.7°C). Cool in the pan or on a wire rack.

Yield: One 1-pound (455-g) loaf

Each batch: 2035 Calories; 60g Fat (25.1% calories from fat); 46g Protein; 353g Carbohydrate; 32g Dietary Fiber; 0mg Cholesterol; 2146mg Sodium.

 *Dakota Bread*

Adapted from a recipe by the Wheat Commissions of both North and South Dakota, this hearty combination makes a delicious round loaf—and you make this no-knead bread in the food processor! This loaf has a dense, chewy texture and a soft crumb.

> 1 tablespoon (9 g) Hodgson Mill Stone Ground Whole Grain Yellow Corn Meal or White Corn Meal, Plain
>
> 2 cups (250 g) Hodgson Mill Best For Bread Flour
>
> $1/2$ cup (62.5 g) Hodgson Mill Stone Ground Whole Grain Rye Flour
>
> $1/2$ cup (62.5 g) Hodgson Mill Stone Ground Whole Grain Whole Wheat Graham Flour or Stone Ground Whole Grain White Whole Wheat Flour
>
> $1/4$ cup (45 g) unsalted sunflower seed kernels
>
> 1 package ($5/16$ ounce) or $2^1/2$ teaspoons (10 g) Hodgson Mill Fast-Rise Yeast
>
> 1 teaspoon (6 g) salt
>
> 2 teaspoons (2 g) dried dill weed
>
> $1/2$ cup (115 g) cottage cheese
>
> 1 large egg
>
> $1/4$ cup (80 g) honey
>
> 2 tablespoons (28 ml) sunflower, canola, or other vegetable oil
>
> $1/2$ cup (120 ml) warm (105°F to 115°F [40.5°C to 46°C]) water

FOR THE TOPPING:

> 1 large egg white, beaten until foamy
>
> 2 tablespoons (30 g) unsalted sunflower seed kernels

Lightly grease a 9-inch (22.5-cm) glass pie pan and sprinkle bottom and sides with the corn meal.

Mix flours together in food processor and add sunflower seeds, yeast, salt, dill weed, cottage cheese, egg, honey, oil, and water and process until thick dough forms. Place dough in lightly oiled bowl. Cover and let rise until doubled in bulk, about 30 minutes.

Punch down dough in bowl. Transfer to floured surface and form into a round loaf. Place in prepared pie pan. Cover and let rise until doubled in bulk, about 1 hour.

Preheat oven to 350°F (180°C). Brush loaf with egg white and sprinkle on sunflower seeds.

Bake 35 to 40 minutes or until instant-read thermometer inserted in center registers 190°F (87.7°C).

Yield: One 1-pound (455-g) loaf

Each batch: 2274 Calories; 68g Fat (25.6% calories from fat); 87g Protein; 360g Carbohydrate; 34g Dietary Fiber; 383mg Cholesterol; 2754mg Sodium.

 ## Mini Wheat and Dill Loaves

How can you make homemade yeast bread in an hour? By using fast-rise yeast and smaller loaf pans.

> 3 cups (375 g) Hodgson Mill 50/50 Flour
> 1 package ($5/16$ ounce) or $2^1/2$ teaspoons (10 g) Hodgson Mill Fast-Rise Yeast
> 1 teaspoon (1 g) dried dill weed
> 1 cup (235 ml) non-alcoholic beer
> 2 tablespoons (28 g) unsalted butter, melted
> 1 large egg, beaten

Stir together flour, yeast, and dill weed in bowl with wooden spoon or dough whisk. Pour beer in microwave-safe bowl and microwave on High for $1^1/2$ minutes, or until very warm (120°F [48.9°C]). Stir beer into flour mixture, then butter and egg, to form soft dough. Turn dough out onto a floured surface, dust with more flour, and knead 3 minutes, dusting with more flour when necessary, until smooth and elastic.

Preheat oven to 375°F (190°C). Grease two 7 x 4 x 2-inch (17.5 x 10 x 5-cm) loaf pans. Cut dough in half and form each half into loaf. Place each loaf in prepared loaf pan. Cover and let rise 25 to 30 minutes, or until almost doubled in bulk.

Bake 20 to 25 minutes or until instant-read thermometer inserted in center of the loaf registers at least 190°F (87.7°C).

Yield: 2 mini loaves

Per Loaf: 797 Calories; 14g Fat (16.0% calories from fat); 29g Protein; 133g Carbohydrate; 13g Dietary Fiber; 125mg Cholesterol; 36mg Sodium.

Golden Wheat and Cheddar Loaves

With all the flavor of traditional yeast breads, these loaves can be made quickly by using fast-rise yeast and smaller loaf pans.

> 1 package ($^5/16$ ounce) or 2$^1/2$ teaspoons (10 g) Hodgson Mill Fast-Rise Yeast
>
> 2 cups (250 g) Hodgson Mill Stone Ground Whole Grain Whole Wheat Graham Flour
>
> 1 cup (125 g) Hodgson Mill 50/50 Flour
>
> 1 teaspoon (6 g) salt
>
> 1 cup (115 g) grated sharp Cheddar, plus $^1/2$ cup (58 g) more for garnish
>
> 2 cups (470 ml) warm (105°F to 115°F [40.5°C to 46°C]) water

Preheat oven to 350°F (180°C). Grease two 7 x 4 x 2-inch (17.5 x 10 x 2.5-cm) loaf pans.

Combine yeast, flours, salt, and 1 cup (115 g) Cheddar cheese in bowl with wooden spoon or dough whisk. Make a well in center and stir in water to form medium soft dough. If dough is too dry, add a little more water, one tablespoon (15 ml) at a time. If the dough is too wet, add a little more flour, one tablespoon (8 g) at a time. Divide the dough in half and press into prepared loaf pans. Cover and let rise for 15 minutes, or until dough has risen slightly.

Sprinkle remaining Cheddar cheese over tops of loaves. Bake 25 to 30 minutes or until instant-read thermometer inserted in center registers 190°F (87.7°C).

Yield: 2 mini loaves

Per Loaf: 955 Calories; 30g Fat (27.9% calories from fat); 43g Protein; 133g Carbohydrate; 21 g Dietary Fiber; 89mg Cholesterol; 1601 mg Sodium.

Gluten-Free Chocolate Bread

Unsweetened cocoa powder and naturally gluten-free buckwheat flour help turn this loaf dark and give it a deep, mysterious flavor. Because this bread has a heavy texture like European peasant breads, it makes a great sandwich.

3 large eggs or equivalent egg substitute

3 tablespoons (45 g) packed light or dark brown sugar

1 teaspoon (5 ml) cider vinegar

3 tablespoons (42 ml) canola or soy oil

1 1/2 cups + 2 tablespoons (383 ml) water

2 1/4 cups (281.3 g) Hodgson Mill Stone Ground Whole Grain Brown Rice Flour

1 cup (125 g) Hodgson Mill Stone Ground Whole Grain Buckwheat Flour

1/4 cup (32 g) gluten-free unsweetened cocoa powder

2 1/2 teaspoons (17.5 g) xanthan gum

1 1/2 teaspoons (9 g) salt

1/2 cup (65 g) nonfat dry milk or soy milk powder

1 package (5/16 ounce) or 2 1/2 teaspoons (10 g) Hodgson Mill Fast-Rise Yeast

Whisk together eggs, brown sugar, vinegar, oil, and water in large bowl. Combine flours, cocoa powder, xanthan gum, salt, milk powder, and yeast in medium bowl. Beat in flour mixture, 1 cup (125 g) at a time, to egg mixture with wooden spoon or dough whisk or electric mixer until cake batter–like consistency. Cover and let rise until doubled in bulk, about 1 hour.

Preheat oven to 350°F (180°C). Grease 9 x 5 x 3-inch (22.5 x 12.5 x 7.5-cm) loaf pan. Carefully spoon dough into prepared pan.

Bake 45 to 50 minutes or until instant-read thermometer inserted in center registers at least 190°F (87.7°C). Turn out onto wire rack to cool.

Yield: One 1-pound (455-g) loaf

Each batch: 2395 Calories; 70g Fat (25.5% calories from fat); 80g Protein; 384g Carbohydrate; 29g Dietary Fiber; 573mg Cholesterol; 3716mg Sodium.

Note: To make this recipe dairy- and egg-free, use vegetable oil, egg substitute, and soy milk powder.

Variation: To make dough in the bread machine, add ingredients to bread pan according to manufacturer's directions. Set on dough cycle and start machine. When cycle is complete, proceed with shaping into loaf and baking.

Gluten-Free Swedish Fruit Bread

This cardamom-scented yeast bread is especially delicious toasted.

3 large eggs or equivalent egg substitute

1 teaspoon (5 ml) cider vinegar

$^1/2$ cup (120 ml) vegetable oil, such as canola

$1^2/3$ cups (390 ml) water

2 cups (250 g) Hodgson Mill Stone Ground Whole Grain Brown Rice Flour

$^1/3$ cup (41.6 g) tapioca flour

$^2/3$ cup (43.3 g) Hodgson Mill Pure Corn Starch

$2^1/2$ teaspoons (17.5 g) xanthan gum

$^1/2$ cup (65 g) nonfat dry milk powder or soy milk powder

$1^1/2$ teaspoons (9 g) salt

3 tablespoons (42 g) sugar

2 teaspoons (4.6 g) ground cardamom

1 package ($^5/16$ ounce) or $2^1/2$ teaspoons (10 g) Hodgson Mill Fast-Rise Yeast

1 cup (145 g) chopped, dried fruit such as golden raisins, cherries, or apricots

Whisk together eggs, vinegar, oil, and water in large bowl. Combine flours, corn starch, xanthan gum, milk powder, salt, sugar, cardamom, and yeast in medium bowl. Beat in flour mixture, 1 cup (125 g) at a time, to egg mixture with wooden spoon or dough whisk or electric mixer until cake batter–like consistency. Fold in dried fruit. Cover and let rise until doubled in bulk, about 1 hour.

Preheat oven to 375°F (190°C). Grease 9 x 5 x 3-inch (22.5 x 12.5 x 7.5-cm) loaf pan. Carefully spoon dough into prepared pan.

Bake 45 to 50 minutes or until instant-read thermometer inserted in center registers at least 190°F (87.7°C). Turn out onto wire rack to cool.

Yield: One 1-pound (455-g) loaf

Each batch: 3443 Calories; 132g Fat (33.4% calories from fat); 70g Protein; 520g Carbohydrate; 22g Dietary Fiber; 573mg Cholesterol; 3711 mg Sodium.

Variation: To make dough in the bread machine, add ingredients to bread pan according to manufacturer's directions. Set on dough cycle and start machine. When cycle is complete, proceed with shaping into loaf and baking.

Gluten-Free French Bread

Adapted from a recipe by Tom Van Deman, this bread does approximate the taste and texture of a French baguette—even starting with a batter-like dough.

FOR THE FLAX MEAL THICKENER:

4 teaspoons (12 g) Hodgson Mill Milled Flax Seed

2 cups (470 ml) water, divided

1 teaspoon (5 ml) cider vinegar

FOR THE DOUGH:

1 cup (125 g) Hodgson Mill Stone Ground Whole Grain Brown Rice Flour

$^1/_2$ cup (62.5 g) Hodgson Mill Stone Ground Whole Grain Buckwheat Flour

$^1/_2$ cup (65 g) Hodgson Mill Pure Corn Starch

$^3/_4$ cup (97.5 g) potato starch

1 teaspoon (5 g) egg replacer (powdered form)

$3^1/_2$ teaspoons (24.5 g) xanthan gum

$1^1/_2$ teaspoons (19.5 g) sugar

1 teaspoon (6 g) salt

$^2/_3$ cup (86 g) nonfat dry milk or soy milk powder

2 packages ($^5/_{16}$ ounce each) or 5 teaspoons (20 g) Hodgson Mill Fast-Rise Yeast

1 cup (235 ml) warm (105°F to 115°F [40.5°C to 46°C]) water

$^1/_4$ cup (36 g) Hodgson Mill Stone Ground Whole Grain Yellow Corn Meal, Plain
Olive oil

For Flax Meal Thickener, whisk flax meal and 1 cup (235 ml) water in a small saucepan. Bring to boil; simmer, stirring occasionally, for about 5 minutes or until mixture thickens slightly. Whisk in vinegar and remaining water.

Combine flours, starches, egg replacer, xanthan gum, sugar, salt, dry milk powder, and yeast in large bowl. Beat in flax thickener with electric mixer, 1 cup (125 g) at a time, to form thick, cake batter–like dough. Add warm water to the flax meal mixture. Beat on high for 4 minutes.

Preheat oven to 400°F (200°C). Grease two French bread pans, then sprinkle pan with corn meal until completely dusted.

Spoon bread dough into prepared pans. Brush loaves with olive oil. Cover with plastic wrap and let rise until doubled in bulk, about 20 minutes.

Bake 35 to 40 minutes or until instant-read thermometer inserted in center registers at least 190°F (87.7°C). Cool on wire racks.

Yield: 2 baguettes

Per Loaf: 969 Calories; 5g Fat (4.7% calories from fat); 29g Protein; 211 g Carbohydrate; 9g Dietary Fiber; 14mg Cholesterol; 1300mg Sodium.

Note: To make this recipe dairy- and egg-free, use vegetable oil, egg substitute, and soy milk.

 ## Gluten-Free Soft White Bread

This bread rises high and bakes to a golden brown, with a mellow flavor and tender crumb.

3 large eggs or equivalent egg substitute

1 teaspoon (5 ml) cider vinegar

3 tablespoons (42 ml) olive oil

$1/2$ cup (125 g) unsweetened applesauce

3 tablespoons (45 g) packed light or dark brown sugar

$1 1/2$ cups (313 ml) warm (105°F to 115°F [40.5°C to 46°C]) water

1 cup (125 g) Hodgson Mill Whole Grain Multi Purpose Baking Mix

1 cup (125 g) Hodgson Mill Stone Ground Whole Grain Brown Rice Flour

1 cup (130 g) tapioca flour or potato starch

$1/2$ cup (65 g) Hodgson Mill Pure Corn Starch

4 teaspoons (28 g) xanthan gum

$1/2$ teaspoon (3 g) salt

1 ($5/16$ ounce) package or $2 1/2$ teaspoons (10 g) Hodgson Mill Fast-Rise Yeast

Whisk eggs, vinegar, and oil together in large bowl. Whisk in applesauce, sugar, and water. Combine baking mix, flour, starches, xanthan gum, salt, and yeast. Stir flour mixture, 1 cup (125 g) at a time, into egg mixture until soft batter forms. Cover and let rise until doubled in bulk, about 1 hour.

Preheat oven to 350°F (180°C). Grease 9 x 5 x 3-inch (22.5 x 12.5 x 7.5-cm) loaf pan. Carefully spoon dough into prepared pan.

Bake 30 minutes or until instant-read thermometer inserted in center registers at least 190°F (87.7°C). Turn out onto wire rack to cool.

Yield: One 1-pound (455-g) loaf

Each batch: 2448 Calories; 66g Fat (22.9% calories from fat); 48g Protein; 452g Carbohydrate; 18g Dietary Fiber; 561mg Cholesterol; 1261mg Sodium.

Variation: To make dough in the bread machine, add ingredients to bread pan according to manufacturer's directions. Set on dough cycle and start machine. When cycle is complete, proceed with shaping into loaf and baking.

Note: To make this recipe dairy- and egg-free, use vegetable oil and egg substitute.

Gluten-Free Deli "Rye" Bread

With the taste of rye bread, but without the rye (which contains gluten), this bread is great for sandwiches.

    3 large eggs or equivalent egg substitute
    1 teaspoon (5 ml) cider vinegar
    $1/2$ cup (120 ml) vegetable oil, such as canola
    3 tablespoons (60 g) molasses
    $1/4$ cup (32 g) gluten-free unsweetened cocoa powder
    $1^1/3$ cups (313 ml) warm (105°F to 115°F [40.5°C to 46°C]) water
    1 cup (125 g) Hodgson Mill Whole Grain Multi Purpose Baking Mix
    1 cup (125 g) Hodgson Mill Stone Ground Whole Grain Brown Rice Flour
    1 cup (130 g) tapioca flour or potato starch
    $1/2$ cup (65 g) Hodgson Mill Pure Corn Starch
    4 teaspoons (28 g) xanthan gum
    $1/2$ teaspoon (3 g) salt
    1 tablespoon (6.7 g) caraway seeds
    1 ($5/16$ ounce) package or $2^1/2$ teaspoons (10 g) Hodgson Mill Fast-Rise Yeast

Whisk eggs, vinegar, and oil together in large bowl. Whisk in molasses, cocoa powder, and water. Combine baking mix, flour, starches, xanthan gum, salt, caraway seeds, and yeast. Stir flour mixture, 1 cup (125 g) at a time, into egg mixture to form soft batter. Cover and let rise until doubled in bulk, about 1 hour.

Preheat oven to 350°F (180°C). Grease 9 x 5 x 3-inch (22.5 x 12.5 x 7.5-cm) loaf pan. Carefully spoon dough into prepared pan.

Bake 30 minutes or until instant-read thermometer inserted in center registers at least 190°F (87.7°C). Turn out onto wire rack to cool.

Yield: One 1-pound (455-g) loaf

Each batch: 3081 Calories; 138g Fat (38.0% calories from fat); 53g Protein; 455g Carbohydrate; 27g Dietary Fiber; 561 mg Cholesterol; 1270mg Sodium.

Variation: To make dough in the bread machine, add ingredients to bread pan according to manufacturer's directions. Set on dough cycle and start machine. When cycle is complete, proceed with shaping into loaf and baking.

Note: To make this recipe dairy- and egg-free, use vegetable oil and egg substitute.

Gluten-Free Orange Sweet Potato Bread

A lovely golden color, this bread makes delicious toast and French toast.

3 large eggs or equivalent egg substitute

1 teaspoon (5 ml) cider vinegar

3 tablespoons (42 ml) vegetable oil, such as canola

1 cup (225 g) cooked or canned sweet potato, mashed

3 tablespoons (45 g) packed light or dark brown sugar

2 teaspoons (5.4 g) freshly grated orange zest or 1 teaspoon (5 ml) orange oil

$1^{1}/3$ cups (313 ml) warm (105°F to 115°F [40.5°C to 46°C]) water

$1/2$ cup (62.5 g) Hodgson Mill Whole Grain Multi Purpose Baking Mix

1 cup (125 g) Hodgson Mill Stone Ground Whole Grain Brown Rice Flour

$1/2$ cup (70 g) Hodgson Mill Stone Ground Whole Grain Yellow Corn Meal, Plain

1 cup (130 g) tapioca flour or potato starch

$1/2$ cup (65 g) Hodgson Mill Pure Corn Starch

4 teaspoons (28 g) xanthan gum

$1/2$ teaspoon (3 g) salt

1 ($5/16$ ounce) package or $2^{1}/2$ teaspoons (10 g) Hodgson Mill
    Fast-Rise Yeast

Whisk eggs, vinegar, and oil together in large bowl. Whisk in sweet potato, sugar, orange zest, and water. Combine baking mix, flour, corn meal, starches, xanthan gum, salt, and yeast. Stir flour mixture, 1 cup (125 g) at a time, into egg mixture to form soft batter. Cover and let rise until doubled in bulk, about 1 hour.

Preheat oven to 350°F (180°C). Grease 9 x 5 x 3-inch (22.5 x 12.5 x 7.5-cm) loaf pan. Carefully spoon dough into prepared pan.

Bake 30 minutes or until instant-read thermometer inserted in center registers at least 190°F (87.7°C). Turn out onto wire rack to cool.

Yield: One 1-pound (455-g) loaf

Each batch: 2614 Calories; 65g Fat (21.3% calories from fat); 48g Protein; 489g Carbohydrate; 23g Dietary Fiber; 561mg Cholesterol; 1334mg Sodium.

Variation: To make dough in the bread machine, add ingredients to bread pan according to manufacturer's directions. Set on dough cycle and start machine. When cycle is complete, proceed with shaping into loaf and baking.

Note: To make this recipe dairy- and egg-free, use vegetable oil and egg substitute.

 ## *Crusty Italian Bread* (See photo on page 242.)

This delicious crusty bread is simply hearty but with plenty of character. The secret? Combining bread flour with the traditional blend of whole wheat and white flours. In addition, the steam from the pan of water and the water spray help create a good crust.

> 2 packages (^{5}/16 ounce each) or 5 teaspoons (20 g) Hodgson Mill Active Dry Yeast
> 4 cups (940 ml) warm (105°F to 115°F [40.5°C to 46°C]) water
> 2 tablespoons (28 ml) extra virgin olive oil
> 2 teaspoons (12 g) salt
> 6^1/2 to 7 cups (812.5 to 875 g) Hodgson Mill 50/50 Flour
> 1 cup (125 g) Hodgson Mill Best For Bread Flour

Sprinkle yeast over 1 cup (235 ml) warm water in large bowl and set aside to proof until foamy, about 5 minutes.

Stir 3 cups (705 ml) water, oil, and salt into yeast. Combine 5 cups (625 g) 50/50 flour and bread flour in medium bowl. Add flour mixture, 1 cup (125 g) at a time, to yeast mixture until stiff dough forms. Turn dough out onto floured board and knead to form smooth and elastic ball, adding more flour if necessary, about 10 minutes.

Place dough in large, oiled bowl and turn to coat thoroughly. Cover with plastic wrap, then with damp tea towel, and let rise until almost doubled in bulk, about 1 hour.

Line 2 baking sheets with parchment paper. Punch dough down. Turn dough onto floured surface. Cut dough into 4 equal portions. Form each portion into a long loaf, 12-inches (30-cm) long and 3 inches (7.5 cm) wide. Place 2 loaves on each prepared baking sheet, cover, and let rise for 1 hour.

Place a 9 x 13-inch (22.5 x 32.5-cm) pan of water on bottom rack of oven. Preheat oven to 425°F (220°C).

Spray tops of loaves with water from spray bottle and bake 15 minutes. Remove loaves from baking sheet, place directly on oven rack, and reduce oven temperature to 350°F (180°C). Repeat spraying every 10 minutes until bread has baked 20 more minutes and is golden brown.

Yield: 4 loaves, 6 servings per loaf

Per Serving: 146 Calories; 1g Fat (6.9% calories from fat); 6g Protein; 28g Carbohydrate; 3g Dietary Fiber; 0mg Cholesterol; 180mg Sodium.

Note: This dough also makes a great pizza crust.

Golden Acorn Squash Bread

Golden and delicious, this bread is wonderful for sandwiches or French toast. Save your leftover cooked acorn or butternut squash for this recipe.

> 2 packages (^{5}/16 ounce each) or 5 teaspoons (20 g) Hodgson Mill Active Dry Yeast
>
> ^{1}/2 cup (120 ml) warm (105°F to 115°F [40.5°C to 46°C]) water
>
> 1^1/4 cups (295 ml) skim milk
>
> 4 tablespoons (^{1}/2 stick [55g]) butter, softened
>
> ^{1}/2 cup (170 g) honey
>
> 1 cup (225 g) cooked or canned squash or sweet potatoes, mashed
>
> 1 teaspoon (6 g) salt
>
> 2 large egg whites
>
> 3 cups (375 g) Hodgson Mill Stone Ground Whole Grain Whole Wheat Graham Flour
>
> 2 cups (250 g) Hodgson Mill Best For Bread Flour

Whole Wheat Graham Bread

A classic whole wheat bread, this one uses sorghum as a sweetener. If you can't find sorghum, substitute honey.

    2 cups (470 ml) 2 percent milk
    1/2 cup (112 g) shortening
    1/2 cup (115 g) packed light or dark brown sugar
    1/4 cup (80 g) sorghum
    1/4 cup (80 g) honey
    1 teaspoon (6 g) salt
    4 cups (500 g) Hodgson Mill Stone Ground Whole Grain Whole Wheat
        Graham Flour
    2 packages (5/16 ounce each) or 5 teaspoons (20 g) Hodgson Mill Active Dry Yeast
    2 to 3 cups (250 to 375 g) Hodgson Mill All-Purpose, Unbleached Naturally
        White Flour

Scald milk in large saucepan over medium-high heat until bubbles form around the perimeter of pan. Remove from heat and pour into large bowl. Stir in shortening, brown sugar, sorghum, honey, salt, and 2 cups (250 g) whole wheat flour. Cool to lukewarm, 90°F (32.2°C).

Stir yeast into milk mixture and beat with electric mixer until smooth and creamy. Cover and let rest for 30 minutes.

Combine remaining wheat flour with unbleached flour in bowl. Beat in enough of flour mixture to form stiff dough. Turn dough out onto floured surface. Knead, adding more flour if necessary, about 10 minutes by hand, or 4 minutes in an electric mixer or food processor fitted with dough hook, to form smooth and elastic dough. Place in oiled bowl and turn to coat. Cover and let rise until doubled, about 1 hour.

Punch down dough and let rise again 1 hour.

Preheat oven to 325°F (170°C). Grease two 9 x 5 x 3-inch (22.5 x 12.5 x 7.5-cm) loaf pans. Turn dough out onto lightly floured surface and knead lightly several times. Divide into half and let rest 10 minutes.

Form into loaves. Place in prepared pans, cover, let rise 30 minutes.

Bake 15 minutes, then increase oven temperature to 350°F (180°C) and bake 45 minutes more or until instant-read thermometer inserted in center registers at least 190°F (87.7°C). Remove from pans and cool on wire racks.

Yield: Two 1-pound (455-g) loaves

Each batch: 4642 Calories; 121g Fat (22.7% calories from fat); 108g Protein; 824g Carbohydrate; 83g Dietary Fiber; 37mg Cholesterol; 2424mg Sodium.

Variation: For a crunchy variation, substitute 2 cups (250 g) Hodgson Mill Cracked Wheat Cereal for the all-purpose flour.

Whole Wheat French Bread

Make either two large batards or four baguettes with this whole grain recipe. This bread does a final rising in a very low oven. If your oven does not have a low temperature of 100°F (37.8°C), then place the baking sheet with the loaves on an open oven door (with the oven set to the lowest setting).

> 2 packages (^{5}/16 ounce each) or 5 teaspoons (20 g) Hodgson Mill
>   Active Dry Yeast
>
> 2 cups (470 ml) warm (105°F to 115°F [40.5°C to 46°C]) water
>
> 1 tablespoon (13 g) sugar
>
> 1^1/2 teaspoons (9 g) salt
>
> 1 tablespoon (7 g) Hodgson Mill Vital Wheat Gluten
>
> 3 cups (375 g) Hodgson Mill Stone Ground Whole Grain Whole Wheat
>   Graham Flour
>
> 3 cups (375 g) Hodgson Mill Best For Bread Flour
>
> Hodgson Mill Stone Ground Whole Grain Yellow Corn Meal, Plain, for sprinkling
>
> Hot water

FOR THE GLAZE:

> 1 large egg white
>
> 1 tablespoon (15 ml) water
>
> Poppy or sesame seeds for sprinkling, optional

Sprinkle yeast over water in large bowl and set aside to proof until foamy, about 5 minutes.

Stir in sugar, salt, gluten, and half of whole wheat and bread flours to make sponge. Cover and let rise 30 minutes.

Beat in enough of remaining flours to make dough. Turn out onto floured surface and knead until smooth and elastic, 8 to10 minutes, adding more flour if necessary. Cover and let rise until doubled in bulk.

Punch dough down, then cover and let rest 10 minutes.

Preheat oven to lowest setting, about 100°F (32.2°C). Line baking sheet with parchment paper and sprinkle with corn meal. Turn dough out onto floured surface. Divide dough in half. Roll each half to 15 x 9-inch (37.5 x 22.5-cm) rectangle. Roll each rectangle up, jelly-roll style, starting with long side. Taper ends. Place on prepared baking sheet.

Place small metal cup of hot water on lower oven rack. Place baking sheet on top rack of oven, close oven door, and let dough rise until doubled in bulk, about 30 minutes.

For glaze, beat egg white with water and brush on bread. Sprinkle with seeds (if using). Slash tops diagonally with serrated knife, about $1/2$ inch (1.2 cm) deep and $1^1/2$ inches (3.7 cm) apart.

Increase oven temperature to 425°F (220°C). Place 13 x 9-inch (32.5 x 22.5-cm) pan of hot water on lowest oven rack.

Bake 10 minutes. Reduce heat to 400°F (200°C) and bake 20 to 25 more minutes or until instant-read thermometer inserted in center registers at least 190°F (87.7°C). Cool on wire racks.

Yield: 2 large loaves or batards

Each batch: 2605 Calories; 7g Fat (2.2% calories from fat); 103g Protein; 560g Carbohydrate; 64g Dietary Fiber; 0mg Cholesterol; 3327mg Sodium.

Variation: Divide dough into 4 equal parts. Form each part into 15-inch (37.5-cm) long baguette. Bake 10 minutes, reduce heat as above, and bake 10 to 15 minutes longer or until instant-read thermometer inserted in center registers at least 190°F (87.7°C). Cool on wire racks.

Yield: 4 baguettes

Swedish Rye Bread

Traditionally, this bread is part of a smorgasbord or buffet for special occasion or holiday dinners. It makes terrific open-faced sandwiches of ham or turkey.

1 cup (235 ml) 2 percent milk

2 tablespoons (28 g) butter

2 tablespoons (40 g) molasses

1/4 cup (80 g) honey

2 teaspoons (12 g) salt

1 cup (235 ml) water

2 packages (5/16 ounce each) or 5 teaspoons (20 g) Hodgson Mill Active Dry Yeast

3 1/2 cups (437.5 g) Hodgson Mill All-Purpose, Unbleached Naturally White Flour

2 cups (250 g) Hodgson Mill Stone Ground Whole Grain Rye Flour

Hodgson Mill Stone Ground Whole Grain Yellow Corn Meal, Plain for sprinkling

Scald milk in medium saucepan over medium-high heat until bubbles form around the perimeter of pan. Remove from heat and stir in butter, molasses, honey, and salt. Cool to lukewarm, about 90°F (32.2°C). Sprinkle yeast over water in large bowl and set aside to proof until foamy, about 5 minutes.

Beat in all-purpose flour until very smooth with wooden spoon or dough whisk or electric mixer. Gradually add rye flour to form slightly stiff dough. Transfer dough to floured surface and knead until smooth and elastic, about 5 minutes. Place in oiled bowl and turn to coat. Cover and let rise until about doubled in bulk, about 2 hours.

Punch down dough, cover, and let rise again until doubled in bulk, about 1 hour.

Line baking sheet with parchment paper and sprinkle with corn meal. Transfer dough to floured surface and divide in half. Shape each half into oblong loaf. Place on prepared baking sheet. Cover with damp tea towel and let rise about 1 hour.

Preheat oven to 375°F (190°C). Bake 30 to 40 minutes or until instant-read thermometer inserted in center registers at least 190°F (87.7°C).

Yield: Two 1-pound (455-g) loaves

Each batch: 2921 Calories; 36g Fat (10.3% calories from fat); 84g Protein; 625g Carbohydrate; 58g Dietary Fiber; 80mg Cholesterol; 4645mg Sodium.

Honey Spelt Bread

Spelt is a more delicate flour than wheat and needs gentle treatment, so there's no initial kneading in this recipe. To use spelt flour in place of wheat flour, increase the amount of spelt flour by an extra tablespoon per measured cup.

    2 teaspoons (8 g) Hodgson Mill Active Dry Yeast
    1 cup (235 ml) warm (105°F to 115°F [40.5°C to 46°C]) water
    1 tablespoon (20 g) honey
    2 teaspoons (12 g) salt
    3 1/4 cups (406.3 g) Hodgson Mill Organic Whole Grain Spelt Flour
    2 tablespoons (28 ml) vegetable oil, such as canola

Sprinkle yeast over water in large bowl and set aside to proof until foamy, about 5 minutes.

Stir in honey, salt, and 1 cup (125 g) flour. Alternate adding flour and oil to form firm dough. Cover and let rise until doubled in bulk, about 1 hour.

Grease 9 x 5 x 3-inch (22.5 x 12.5 x 7.5-cm) loaf pan. Turn dough out onto floured surface. Knead, adding more flour as necessary, to form smooth and elastic dough. Place in prepared loaf pan and let rise to just over the top of the pan, about 30 minutes.

Preheat oven to 400°F (200°C). Bake 15 minutes, then lower oven temperature to 350°F (180°C) and bake 30 minutes more or until instant-read thermometer inserted in center registers at least 190°F (87.7°C). Cool in pan for 15 to 30 minutes, then turn out onto wire rack to cool completely.

Yield: One 1-pound (455-g) loaf

Each batch: 1444 Calories; 40g Fat (20.0% calories from fat); 70g Protein; 294g Carbohydrate; 66g Dietary Fiber; 0mg Cholesterol; 4271 mg Sodium.

Molasses and Brown Sugar Spelt Bread

With half spelt flour and half wheat flour, this hearty loaf has a rich color and flavor.

    1 package (5/16 ounce) or 2 1/2 teaspoons (10 g) Hodgson Mill Active Dry Yeast
    1 cup (235 ml) warm (105°F to 115°F [40.5°C to 46°C]) water
    2 tablespoons (28 ml) vegetable oil, such as canola
    2 tablespoons (40 g) molasses

2 tablespoons (30 g) packed light or dark brown sugar

1^1/2 teaspoons (9 g) salt

1^1/2 cups (187.5 g) Hodgson Mill Organic Whole Grain Spelt Flour

1^1/2 tablespoons (10.5 g) Hodgson Mill Vital Wheat Gluten

1^1/2 to 1^3/4 cups (187.5 to 218.8 g) Hodgson Mill Best For Bread Flour

Sprinkle yeast over water in large bowl and set aside until foamy, about 5 minutes.

Stir in oil, molasses, brown sugar, salt, spelt flour, and wheat gluten until well blended. Stir in enough bread flour to form soft dough. Turn dough out onto floured surface and knead until smooth, about 6 minutes. Place in oiled bowl and turn to coat. Cover and let rise until doubled in bulk, about 1 to 1^1/2 hours.

Grease 9 x 5 x 3-inch (22.5 x 12.5 x 7.5-cm) pan. Turn dough out onto floured surface and knead lightly. Shape into a loaf and place in prepared pan. Cover and let rise until dough reaches top of pan, about 1 hour.

Preheat oven to 350°F (180°C). Bake 30 minutes or until instant-read thermometer inserted in center registers at least 190°F (87.7°C). Turn out onto wire rack to cool.

Yield: One 1-pound (455-g) loaf

Each batch: 1367 Calories; 6g Fat (3.5% calories from fat); 63g Protein; 316g Carbohydrate; 37g Dietary Fiber; 0mg Cholesterol; 3253mg Sodium.

Variation: If you want this bread made with all spelt flour, use 1^1/2 cups (187.5 g) plus 1^1/2 tablespoons (12 g) spelt flour in place of bread flour and omit the first knead.

Old-Fashioned Salt Rising Bread

This bread can be tricky to make—even for experienced bread bakers—so you might want to start out with half a recipe until you get the feel of it. The trick is in the Corn Meal Starter, which attracts the natural yeast in the air to leaven the bread. The starter must ferment overnight at a constant 100°F to 110°F (37.8°C to 43.3°C) temperature (perhaps this was once accomplished in a warm bed of heated salt, hence the name). If the starter reaches 120°F (48.9°C), it will curdle and you'll have to start over. If the starter cools, it won't do the job of leavening. This bread has a distinct aroma when it is rising, similar to very ripe cheese.

FOR THE CORN MEAL STARTER:

1 cup (235 ml) 2 percent milk

$^{1}/_{2}$ cup (70 g) sifted Hodgson Mill Stone Ground Whole Grain Yellow Corn Meal, Plain

FOR THE DOUGH:

1 quart (945 ml) 2 percent milk

1 tablespoon plus $^{1}/_{2}$ cup (113 g) sugar

12 cups (1.5 kg) sifted Hodgson Mill All-Purpose, Unbleached Naturally White Flour

$^{3}/_{4}$ cup (167 g) shortening

1 tablespoon (18 g) salt

Melted butter or shortening

For Corn Meal Starter, scald milk in medium saucepan over medium-high heat until bubbles form around perimeter. Stir in corn meal and cook until thick. Place in a quart jar with top and place in warm place (such as oven on 100°F [32.2° C] or low oven with door open) to sour overnight. When bubbles form, it is ready to use.

For dough, stir milk and 1 tablespoon (13 g) sugar together in large saucepan and scald over medium-high heat until bubbles form around the perimeter. Remove from heat and cool to 100°F (32.2°C). Transfer to large bowl and stir in fermented starter. Gradually stir in 6 cups (750 g) of flour. Cover and let rise until doubled in bulk, about 2 hours.

Stir in shortening, remaining sugar, and salt. Mix well. Gradually add 6 cups (750 g) of flour and work in. Transfer dough to floured surface and knead, adding more all-purpose flour, until dough is smooth and elastic, about 20 minutes.

Grease and flour four 9 x 5 x 3-inch (22.5 x 12.5 x 7.5-cm) pans. Divide dough into four equal parts and place in prepared pans. Brush tops of loaves with melted butter or shortening and place in warm place to rise above pans, about 2 hours.

Preheat oven to 200°F (93.3°C). Put loaves in oven and bake for 15 minutes. Then increase oven temperature to 300°F (150°C) and bake 45 to 60 minutes or until instant-read thermometer inserted in center registers at least 190°F (87.7°C). Turn out onto wire racks to cool. Brush tops of loaves with more melted butter or shortening.

Yield: Four 1-pound (455-g) loaves

Each batch: 7013 Calories; 179g Fat (22.2% calories from fat); 191g Protein; 1219g Carbohydrate; 54g Dietary Fiber; 92mg Cholesterol; 7004mg Sodium.

Note: Save 1 tablespoon (15 g) of the soured Corn Meal Starter for your next batch of bread. This starter will shorten the souring time of the next corn meal mixture. Starter can be stored in the refrigerator for 2 weeks.

Orange Molasses Rye Bread

Rich with orange, molasses, and honey, this rye bread is a cousin of the traditional and beloved Swedish limpa.

2 packages (^{5}/16 ounce each) or 5 teaspoons (20 g) Hodgson Mill Active Dry Yeast

1^1/2 cups (355 ml) warm (105°F to 115°F [40.5°C to 46°C]) water

3 tablespoons (42 g) sugar

^{1}/2 cup (160 g) molasses

^{1}/4 cup (80 g) honey

2 tablespoons (28 g) shortening

2 teaspoons (12 g) salt

Finely grated zest of two oranges

2^1/2 cups (312.5 g) Hodgson Mill Stone Ground Whole Grain Whole Wheat Rye Flour

3 cups (375 g) Hodgson Mill All-Purpose, Unbleached Naturally White Flour

Hodgson Mill Stone Ground Whole Grain Yellow or White Corn Meal, Plain

Sprinkle yeast over water and sugar in bowl and set aside to proof until foamy, about 5 minutes.

Mix in molasses, honey, shortening, salt, and orange zest. Stir in rye flour and mix until smooth. Add enough all-purpose flour to make firm dough. Turn out dough onto floured surface and knead until smooth and elastic, about 5 minutes. Place in oiled bowl and turn to coat. Cover and let rise until about doubled in bulk, about 2 hours.

Line baking sheet with parchment paper and sprinkle with corn meal. Turn dough out onto floured surface and divide in half. Shape each half into round loaf and place on prepared baking sheet. Cover with damp tea towel and let rise about 1 hour.

Preheat oven to 375°F (190°C). Bake 30 to 40 minutes or until instant-read thermometer inserted in center registers at least 190°F (87.7°C).

Yield: Two 1-pound (455-g) loaves

Each batch: 3287 Calories; 36g Fat (9.1% calories from fat); 76g Protein; 736g Carbohydrate; 66g Dietary Fiber; 0mg Cholesterol; 4339mg Sodium.

Raisin Whole Wheat Bread

A sponge is a starter dough that gets the yeast going before adding more flour.

FOR THE SPONGE:

1 package (^{5}/16 ounce) or 2^1/2 teaspoons (10 g) Hodgson Mill Active Dry Yeast

2 cups (470 ml) warm (105°F to 115°F [40.5°C to 46°C]) water

2 teaspoons (10 g) packed light or dark brown sugar

2^1/2 cups (312.5 g) Hodgson Mill All-Purpose, Naturally White Unbleached Flour

FOR THE DOUGH:

3 tablespoons (42 g) butter or shortening

2 tablespoons (40 g) molasses

1^1/2 teaspoons (9 g) salt

1^1/2 cups (187.5 g) Hodgson Mill Stone Ground Whole Grain White Whole Wheat Flour

^{1}/2 teaspoon (1.2 g) ground cinnamon

1^1/2 to 2 cups (187.5 to 250 g) Hodgson Mill All-Purpose, Unbleached Naturally White Flour

1 cup (145 g) raisins

For Sponge, sprinkle yeast over water in large bowl and set aside to proof until foamy, about 5 minutes.

Stir in sugar and all-purpose flour, cover, and let rise until it looks light and bubbly, about ^{1}/2 hour.

For dough, stir butter, molasses, salt, white whole wheat flour, cinnamon, all-purpose flour, and raisins into sponge. Add enough additional flour to make a smooth dough. Turn out onto floured surface and knead until smooth and elastic, about 5 minutes. Place in oiled bowl and turn to coat. Cover and let rise until doubled in bulk, about 1 hour.

Grease two 9 x 5 x 3-inch (22.5 x 12.5 x 7.5-cm) loaf pans. Punch down dough and turn out onto floured surface. Divide dough in half. Let rest a few minutes. Form each half into loaf and place in prepared pan. Cover and let rise until dough tops pans.

Preheat oven to 400°F (200°C). Bake 25 to 30 minutes or until instant-read thermometer inserted in center registers at least 190°F (87.7°C). Remove from pans and cool on rack.

Yield: Two 1-pound (455-g) loaves

Each batch: 3316 Calories; 38g Fat (9.9% calories from fat); 87g Protein; 696g Carbohydrate; 43g Dietary Fiber; 93mg Cholesterol; 3599mg Sodium.

 ## Blue Ribbon Whole Wheat Bread

At any baking contest, this bread would win!

2 packages (^{5}/16 ounce each) or 5 teaspoons (20 g) Hodgson Mill Active Dry Yeast

^{1}/4 cup (60 ml) warm (105°F to 115°F [40.5°C to 46°C]) water

^{3}/4 cup (170 g) brown sugar

1 tablespoon (18 g) salt

^{1}/2 cup (112 g) shortening

2^1/4 cups (528.8 ml) boiling water

3 cups (375 g) Hodgson Mill Stone Ground Whole Grain Whole Wheat Graham Flour

5 cups (625 g) Hodgson Mill All-Purpose, Unbleached Naturally White Flour

Sprinkle yeast over water in small bowl and set aside to proof until foamy, about 5 minutes.

Combine sugar, salt, shortening, and boiling water in large bowl and let cool to 100°F (32.2°C). In a separate bowl, mix whole wheat and all-purpose flours.

Stir 3 cups (375 g) flour mixture into sugar mixture and beat with electric mixer for 2 minutes. Add yeast and beat another 2 minutes. Add remaining flour mixture, 1 cup (125 g) at a time, and beat by hand with wooden spoon or dough whisk. Turn out onto floured surface and knead, adding flour as necessary, until smooth and elastic, about 10 minutes. Place in oiled bowl, cover and let rise until doubled in bulk, about 1 hour.

Punch down dough and turn out onto floured surface. Divide in half. Knead lightly and let rest 10 minutes.

Grease two 9 x 5 x 3-inch (22.5 x 12.5 x 7.5-cm) loaf pans. Form into loaves and place in prepared pans. Cover and let rise until above tops of pans, about 30 minutes.

Preheat oven to 375°F (190°C). Bake 10 minutes. Reduce oven temperature to 350°F (180°C) and continue baking 27 to 30 more minutes or until instant-read thermometer inserted in center registers at least 190°F (87.7°C). Turn out onto wire racks to cool.

Yield: Two 1^1/2-pound (683-g) loaves

Per Serving: 1525 Calories; 36g Fat (20.6% calories from fat); 35g Protein; 279g Carbohydrate; 23g Dietary Fiber; 0mg Cholesterol; 2152mg Sodium.

 Potato Cheese Bread (See photo on page 245.)

This dough works best with freshly made, still-warm mashed potatoes. You can also make them from an instant potato mix, according to package directions. The potatoes add smooth texture and moisture to this whole grain bread.

    1 cup (225 g) mashed potatoes
    1 cup (235 ml) water
    3 tablespoons (42 ml) oil
    1 teaspoon (6 g) salt
    1 tablespoon (13 g) sugar
    ^{1}/2 cup (50 g) grated Asiago or Parmesan cheese
    2 cups (250 g) Hodgson Mill Organic Naturally White, Unbleached
        All-Purpose Flour
    2 cups (250 g) Hodgson Mill Organic Stone Ground Whole Grain Whole Wheat
        Graham Flour
    1 tablespoon (8 g) Hodgson Mill Vital Wheat Gluten
    1 package (^{5}/16 ounce) or 2^1/2 teaspoons (10 g) Hodgson Mill Fast-Rise Yeast

Stir together mashed potatoes, water, oil, salt, sugar, and cheese in large bowl. Combine flours, wheat gluten, and yeast in medium bowl. Stir in flour mixture, 1 cup (125 g) at a time, to form soft dough. Transfer dough to floured surface and knead until smooth and elastic, adding more all-purpose flour if necessary, about 5 minutes. Place in oiled bowl and turn to coat. Cover and let rise until doubled in bulk, about 1 hour.

Grease 9 x 5 x 3-inch (22.5 x 12.5 x 7.5-cm) pan. Punch down dough and turn out onto floured surface. Form dough into loaf and place in prepared pan. Cover and let rise until dough tops the pan, about 1 hour.

Preheat oven to 350°F (180°C). Bake 45 minutes or until instant-read thermometer inserted in center registers at least 190°F (87.7°C).

Yield: One 1-pound (455-g) loaf

Each batch: 2413 Calories; 61 g Fat (22.2% calories from fat); 78g Protein; 408g Carbohydrate; 46g Dietary Fiber; 36mg Cholesterol; 3375mg Sodium.

Variation: Use sharp Cheddar, Gruyère, or pecorino instead of Asiago cheese.

Variation: To make dough in the bread machine, set on whole wheat cycle and start machine.

Oat Flour–Potato Buttercrust Bread

With a buttery crust, a tender crumb, and mellow flavor, this bread is a winner.

   1 medium potato, peeled and diced

   2 packages (^{5}/16 ounce each) or 5 teaspoons (20 g) Hodgson Mill Active Dry Yeast

   2 tablespoons (28 g) butter or margarine

   2 tablespoons (30 g) packed light or dark brown sugar

   1 teaspoon (6 g) salt

   1 cup (235 ml) skim milk

   1 large egg

   3 cups (375 g) Hodgson Mill Oat Bran Flour Blend

   3^1/2 cups (437.5 g) Hodgson Mill Stone Ground Whole Grain Whole Wheat Graham Flour

FOR THE TOPPING:

   1 tablespoon (14 g) butter, melted

Place potato in saucepan with enough water to cover it, then cook over medium-high heat until tender, about 15 minutes.

Drain and reserve potato water in 1-cup (235-ml) measuring cup. Mash potato in pan and set aside. If necessary, add enough water to reserved potato water to equal 1 cup (235 ml). Pour potato water in small bowl and let cool to 105°F to 115°F (40.5°C to 46°C).

Sprinkle yeast over potato water and set aside to proof until foamy, about 5 minutes.

Stir together mashed potato, yeast mixture, butter, brown sugar, salt, milk, and egg until smooth with wooden spoon, dough whisk, or electric mixer. Combine flours in second large bowl. Beat in flour mixture, 1 cup (125 g) at a time, until dough cleans the bowl. Turn dough out onto floured surface and knead until smooth and elastic, about 10 minutes. Place in oiled bowl and turn to coat. Cover and let rise until doubled in bulk, about 45 minutes.

Grease two 8^1/2 x 4^1/2 x 2-inch (21.3 x 11.3 x 5-cm) loaf pans. Punch down dough and turn out onto floured surface. Divide in half. Shape each half into loaf and place in prepared pan. Cover and let rise for 30 minutes.

Preheat oven to 375°F (190°C). Bake 10 minutes. Remove loaves from oven and brush with melted butter. Return to oven and bake an additional 20 to 25 minutes or until instant-read thermometer inserted in center registers at least 190°F (87.7°C). Turn out onto wire racks to cool.

Yield: Two 1-pound (455-g) loaves

Each batch: 3436 Calories; 70g Fat (17.4% calories from fat); 103g Protein; 651 g Carbohydrate; 96g Dietary Fiber; 285mg Cholesterol; 2731 mg Sodium.

No-Knead 50/50 Wheat Bread

Stir this dough together, let it rise, then form into loaves and bake. Voila!

$5^1/2$ cups (687.5 g) Hodgson Mill 50/50 Flour

$1^1/2$ cups (120 g) quick or old fashioned rolled oats, uncooked

2 packages ($5/16$ ounce each) or 5 teaspoons (20 g) Hodgson Mill Fast-Rise Yeast

1 tablespoon (18 g) salt

$2^1/2$ cups (587.5 g) buttermilk or substitute (see note)

$1/2$ cup (160 g) molasses

$1/3$ cup (75 g) butter or margarine

2 large eggs

Vegetable oil for brushing

Measure 3 cups (375 g) 50/50 flour into measuring bowl. Add oats, yeast, and salt. Heat buttermilk, molasses, and butter together in saucepan over medium heat until warm to touch (105°F to 115°F [40.5°C to 46°C]).

Stir warm buttermilk mixture and eggs into dry ingredients. Beat by hand with wooden spoon or dough whisk or with electric mixer at low speed until well-mixed. Beat at high speed for 3 minutes, scraping bowl occasionally. Stir in remaining $2^1/2$ cups (312.5 g) flour with wooden spoon or dough whisk. Cover and let rise in warm place until doubled in bulk, about 1 hour.

Line baking sheet with parchment paper. Punch down dough. Divide dough in half, form each into round loaf, and place on prepared baking sheet. Brush tops lightly with oil. Cover and let rise until doubled in bulk, about 45 minutes.

Preheat oven to 375°F (190°C). Bake 35 to 40 minutes or until instant-read thermometer inserted in center registers at least 190°F (87.7°C). Transfer to wire racks to cool.

Yield: Two 1-pound (455-g) loaves

Each batch: 4073 Calories; 83g Fat (18.2% calories from fat); 145g Protein; 695g Carbohydrate; 59g Dietary Fiber; 561 mg Cholesterol; 7838mg Sodium.

Note: If you don't have buttermilk, substitute by pouring 5 teaspoons (25 ml) vinegar in a $2^1/2$-cup (587.5-ml) measure. Fill to top with milk and let sit for 2 minutes, then use in recipe.

Limpa

A traditional Swedish bread, this one is a favorite for holiday baking—and for serving on the smorgasbord or buffet table.

    2 cups (470 ml) 2 percent milk
    2 packages ($5/16$ ounce each) or 5 teaspoons (20 g) Hodgson Mill
        Active Dry Yeast
    $1/4$ cup (59 ml) warm (105°F to 115°F [40.5°C to 46°C]) water
    1 tablespoon (13 g) sugar
    5 to 6 cups (625 to 750 g) sifted Hodgson Mill All-Purpose, Unbleached Naturally
        White Flour
    1 cup (340 g) dark corn syrup
    $1^1/2$ teaspoons (3 g) fennel seeds
    $1^1/2$ teaspoons (3 g) anise seed
    $1/2$ cup (170 g) molasses
    $3/4$ cup (167 g) shortening
    1 tablespoon (18 g) salt
    $1/4$ cup (20 g) grated orange zest (about 2 oranges)
    8 cups (1 kg) Hodgson Mill Stone Ground Whole Grain Rye Flour

FOR THE TOPPING:

    1 teaspoon (2 g) fennel seeds
    1 teaspoon (2 g) anise seeds

Scald milk in saucepan over medium-high heat until bubbles form around perimeter of pan. Remove from heat and cool to 100°F (32.2°C). Sprinkle yeast over water in small bowl and set aside to proof until foamy, about 5 minutes.

Pour milk into large bowl. Stir in sugar and yeast, then all-purpose flour, and beat well with wooden spoon or dough whisk by hand or using electric mixer. Cover and let rise until doubled in bulk, about 1 hour.

Blend corn syrup, fennel seed, anise seed, and molasses in saucepan over medium heat and bring to boil; cook 1 minute. Remove from heat and let mixture steep for 15 minutes. Strain out seeds and mix shortening into syrup mixture. Stir syrup and shortening mixture, salt, and orange zest into dough. Beat in enough rye flour to make firm dough. Turn dough out on floured surface and knead until smooth and elastic, adding more flour if necessary, about 6 minutes.

Line 2 baking sheets with parchment paper. Divide dough into 4 equal portions. Shape each portion into round loaf and place 2 loaves on each baking sheet. For topping, press seeds on top of loaves. Cover and let rise until doubled in bulk, about 1 hour.

Preheat oven to 400°F (200°C). Bake 15 minutes, then reduce oven temperature to 350°F (180°C) and bake 45 minutes more or until instant-read thermometer inserted in center registers at least 190°F (87.7°C).

Yield: Four 1-pound (455-g) loaves

Each batch: 8410 Calories; 197g Fat (19.2% calories from fat); 194g Protein; 1673g Carbohydrate; 190g Dietary Fiber; 37mg Cholesterol; 7215mg Sodium.

 Gluten-Free Potato Cheese Bread

This is a mellow, moist bread with the tang of Cheddar cheese.

$1/2$ cup (65 g) potato starch

3 cups (375 g) Hodgson Mill Stone Ground Whole Grain Brown Rice Flour

2 teaspoons (14 g) xanthan gum

2 packages ($5/16$ ounce each) or 5 teaspoons (20 g) Hodgson Mill Fast-Rise Yeast

2 tablespoons (26 g) sugar

1 teaspoon (6 g) salt

2 tablespoons (3 g) gluten-free baking powder

1 cup (130 g) nonfat dry milk or nonfat dry soy milk

1/4 cup (56.3 g) gluten-free instant mashed potatoes, uncooked

2 cups (470 ml) warm (105°F to 115°F [40.5°C to 46°C]) water

1/4 cup (55 g) soft butter or soy margarine

4 eggs or equivalent egg substitute, beaten

1 cup (120 g) grated Cheddar or soy-based cheese

Combine potato starch, flour, and xanthan gum in bowl. Place 2 cups (250 g) flour mixture into large bowl. Add yeast, sugar, salt, baking powder, and dry milk. Mix thoroughly. Combine instant mashed potatoes and warm water; fluff lightly with fork. Add potato mixture and butter to dry ingredients in bowl. Beat 3 minutes on medium speed. Add remaining flour mixture, eggs, and cheese. Beat 3 minutes on medium speed until mixture is a thick, cake-like batter. Cover and let rise until doubled in bulk, about 1 hour.

Preheat oven to 325°F (170°C). Grease two 9 x 5 x 3-inch (22.5 x 12.5 x 7.5-cm) loaf pans. Spoon batter into prepared pans, cover and let rise 30 minutes.

Bake 30 to 35 minutes until lightly browned and instant-read thermometer inserted in center registers at least 190°F (87.7°C).

Yield: Two 1-pound (455-g) loaves

Each batch: 3324 Calories; 114g Fat (30.2% calories from fat); 137g Protein; 455g Carbohydrate; 15g Dietary Fiber; 1015mg Cholesterol; 7121mg Sodium.

Note: To make this recipe dairy- and egg-free, use soy milk powder, soy margarine, egg substitute, and soy cheese.

German Dark Rye Bread

Dark and delicious, this rye bread is great for any deli-type sandwich.

3 cups (375 g) Hodgson Mill Best For Bread Flour

1/4 cup (32 g) unsweetened cocoa powder

2 packages (5/16 ounce each) or 5 teaspoons (20 g) Hodgson Mill Fast-Rise Yeast

1 tablespoon (6.7 g) caraway seeds

8 teaspoons (16 g) Hodgson Mill Vital Wheat Gluten

2 teaspoons (12 g) salt

2 cups (470 ml) water

1/2 cup (170 g) honey

2 tablespoons (28 g) butter

3¹/2 cups (437.5 g) Hodgson Mill Stone Ground Whole Grain Rye Flour

Melted butter for brushing

Combine bread flour, cocoa, yeast, caraway seeds, gluten, and salt in large bowl. Stir to mix. Place water, honey, and butter in a saucepan over medium heat until butter melts. Let cool to 105° to 115°F (40.5°C to 46°C).

Stir butter mixture into flour mixture until moistened, then beat very hard for 3 minutes with wooden spoon or dough whisk by hand or electric mixer. Stir in enough rye flour to make soft dough. Turn dough out onto floured surface and knead 8 to 10 minutes or until smooth and elastic.

Grease two 9 x 5 x 3-inch (22.5 x 12.5 x 7.5-cm) loaf pans. Divide dough in half. Form each half into loaf and place in prepared pan. Brush tops lightly with melted butter and cover with a damp tea towel. Let rise in cold oven over pan of hot water until dough is over tops of pans, about 1 hour.

Preheat oven to 400°F (200°C). Bake 25 minutes or until instant-read thermometer inserted in center registers at least 190°F (87.7°C). Turn out on wire racks to cool.

Yield: Two 1-pound (455-g) loaves

Each batch: 3380 Calories; 41 g Fat (9.7% calories from fat); 118g Protein; 741 g Carbohydrate; 96g Dietary Fiber; 62mg Cholesterol; 4584mg Sodium.

Dark Rye Bread

With most ingredients pre-measured in the bread mix, all you do is add a few more for a deliciously dark rye bread.

1 package (16 ounces) Hodgson Mill Caraway Rye Bread Mix

1 cup minus 1 tablespoon (220 ml) warm (105°F to 115°F [40.5°C to 46°C]) water

2 tablespoons (28 ml) vegetable oil, such as canola

3 tablespoons (60 g) molasses

3 tablespoons (24 g) unsweetened cocoa powder

Yeast packet from mix

Pour contents of bread mix package into large bowl. Mix in remaining ingredients with wooden spoon or dough whisk until soft dough forms. Turn out onto floured surface and knead until smooth and elastic, about 6 to 8 minutes. Place dough in oiled bowl and turn to coat. Cover and let rise until doubled in bulk, about 1^1/2 hours.

Line baking sheet with parchment paper. Punch dough down and shape into round loaf. Cover and let rise for 1 hour.

Preheat oven to 350°F (180°C). Bake 30 to 35 minutes or until instant-read thermometer inserted in center registers at least 190°F (87.7°C). Turn out onto wire rack to cool.

Yield: One 1-pound (455-g) loaf

Each batch: 1978 Calories; 43g Fat (18.4% calories from fat); 75g Protein; 357g Carbohydrate; 48g Dietary Fiber; 0mg Cholesterol; 2645mg Sodium.

 ## Cracked Wheat Carrot Loaf Bread

Carrots add color, Vitamin D, and moistness to this cracked wheat bread.

^{1}/4 cup (62.5 g) Hodgson Mill Cracked Wheat Hot Cereal, uncooked

^{1}/2 cup (120 ml) boiling water

1 teaspoon (4 g) Hodgson Mill Active Dry Yeast

^{1}/4 cup (60 ml) warm (105°F to 115°F [40.5°C to 46°C]) water

^{1}/3 cup (78.3 ml) warm (105°F to 115°F [40.5°C to 46°C]) skim milk

4 tablespoons (^{1}/2 stick [55 g]) butter or margarine

^{1}/4 cup (60 g) packed light or dark brown sugar

1 teaspoon (6 g) salt

1 cup (120 g) shredded carrots

1 large egg

2^1/3 to 2^2/3 cups (291.6 to 333.2 g) Hodgson Mill All-Purpose, Unbleached Naturally White Flour

^{2}/3 cup (83.2 g) Hodgson Mill Oat Bran Hot Cereal, uncooked

Pour cracked wheat in bowl and pour boiling water over. Let soften 15 minutes. Sprinkle yeast over warm water in large bowl and set aside to proof until foamy, about 5 minutes.

Drain excess water from cereal. Stir milk, butter, brown sugar, salt, carrot, and egg into yeast mixture until well blended. Stir in softened cereal. Combine 1 cup (125 g) all-purpose flour and oat bran cereal and stir into yeast mixture. Add enough remaining all-purpose flour to make a moderately stiff dough. Turn out onto a lightly floured surface. Knead until dough is smooth and elastic, about 10 minutes. Shape dough into ball. Place in large, oiled bowl and turn to coat. Cover and let rise until doubled in bulk, about $1^1/2$ hours.

Grease 9 x 5-inch (22.5 x 12.5-cm) loaf pan. Punch dough down and shape into loaf. Place in prepared pan. Cover and let rise until nearly doubled in bulk, about 1 hour.

Preheat oven to 375°F (190°C). Bake 25 to 30 minutes, shielding crust with aluminum foil after 20 minutes of baking, until instant-read thermometer inserted in center registers at least 190°F (87.7°C). Remove from pan and cool on wire rack.

Yield: One 1-pound (455-g) loaf

Each batch: 2207 Calories; 60g Fat (22.9% calories from fat); 63g Protein; 388g Carbohydrate; 35g Dietary Fiber; 313mg Cholesterol; 2775mg Sodium.

Variation: Instead of Oat Bran Cereal, use Bulgur Wheat with Soy.

 ## Basic Whole Wheat Bread

Use this basic whole grain bread recipe as a template to customize your bread baking. Instead of 3 cups (375 g) of graham flour, use white whole wheat, 50/50, or 1 cup (125 g) of each.

2 packages ($^5/16$ ounce each) or 5 teaspoons (20 g) Hodgson Mill Active Dry Yeast

2 cups (470 ml) warm (105°F to 115°F [40.5°C to 46°C]) water

3 tablespoons (42 g) packed light or dark brown sugar

1 tablespoon (7 g) Hodgson Mill Vital Wheat Gluten

3 cups (375 g) Hodgson Mill Stone Ground Whole Grain Whole Wheat Graham Flour

$^1/4$ cup (60 ml) vegetable oil, such as canola

1 teaspoon (6 g) salt

3 to $3^1/2$ cups (375 to 437.5 g) Hodgson Mill Best For Bread Flour, approximately

Sprinkle yeast over water in large bowl and set aside to proof until foamy, about 5 minutes.

Stir in sugar, gluten, and whole wheat flour. Beat well until very smooth, about 200 strokes with wooden spoon or dough whisk. Beat in oil and salt. Then beat in enough bread flour to form soft dough. Turn dough out onto floured surface. Knead until smooth and elastic, 6 to 8 minutes. Place in oiled bowl and turn to coat. Cover and let rise until doubled in bulk, about 1 1/2 to 2 hours.

Punch down dough and turn out onto floured surface. Divide in half. Shape each half into ball and cover with bowl on floured surface. Let rest 15 minutes.

Grease two 9 x 5 x 3-inch (22.5 x 12.5 x 7.5-cm) loaf pans. Shape each ball into loaf. Place in prepared pan. Cover and let rise until dough tops pans, about 45 minutes.

Preheat oven to 400°F (200°C). Bake 30 to 35 minutes or until instant-read thermometer inserted in center registers 190°F (87.7°C). Remove from pan and cool on wire racks.

Yield: Two 1-pound (455-g) loaves

Each batch: 3127 Calories; 61g Fat (16.8% calories from fat); 98g Protein; 576g Carbohydrate; 63g Dietary Fiber; 0mg Cholesterol; 2222mg Sodium.

50/50 Honey Wheat Bread

Using half all-purpose and half whole wheat flour, this recipe produces a hearty wheat bread with a soft crumb.

2 packages (^{5}/16 ounce each) or 5 teaspoons (20 g) Hodgson Mill Active Dry Yeast

2 cups (470 ml) warm (105°F to 115°F [40.5°C to 46°C]) water

2 teaspoons (12 g) salt

^{1}/3 cup (113 g) honey or molasses

2 tablespoons (28 ml) vegetable oil, such as canola, or (28 g) shortening

5 to 6 cups (625 to 750 g) Hodgson Mill 50/50 Flour

FOR THE TOPPING:

Melted butter

Sprinkle yeast over water in large bowl and set aside to proof until foamy, about 5 minutes.

Stir in salt, honey, and oil until smooth. Beat in flour, 1 cup (125 g) at a time, to form stiff dough. Turn dough out onto floured surface. Knead until smooth and elastic, 8 to 10 minutes. Place in oiled bowl and turn to coat. Cover and let rise until doubled in bulk, about $1^1/2$ to 2 hours.

Punch down dough and turn out onto floured surface. Divide in half. Shape each half into ball and cover with bowl on floured surface. Let rise 15 minutes.

Grease two $8^1/2$ x $4^1/2$ x $2^1/2$-inch (21.3 x 11.3 x 6.3-cm) loaf pans. Shape each ball into loaf and shape into loaves. Place into prepared pan. Cover and let rise until double in bulk, about 1 hour.

Preheat oven to 375°F (190°C). Bake 30 to 35 minutes or until instant-read thermometer inserted in center registers 190°F (87.7°C). Remove from pan; brush top crust with melted butter and cool on racks.

Yield: Two 1-pound (455-g) loaves

Each batch: 3044 Calories; 27g Fat (8.0% calories from fat); 104g Protein; 603g Carbohydrate; 50g Dietary Fiber; 0mg Cholesterol; 4282mg Sodium.

---

100 Percent Whole Wheat Bread

This hearty wheat loaf makes a great grilled cheese sandwich.

1 package ($^5/16$ ounce) or $2^1/2$ teaspoons (10 g) Hodgson Mill Active Dry Yeast

1 cup plus 2 tablespoons (263 ml) warm (105°F to 115°F [40.5°C to 46°C]) water

$^1/4$ cup (32.5 g) nonfat dry milk

$1^1/2$ tablespoons (22.5 ml) vegetable oil, such as canola

$1^1/2$ teaspoons (9 g) salt

$2^1/2$ tablespoons (50 g) honey

1 large egg

1 tablespoon (7 g) Hodgson Mill Vital Wheat Gluten

$3^3/4$ cups (468.8 g) Hodgson Mill Stone Ground Whole Grain Whole Wheat Graham Flour

Yeasty Whole Wheat Biscuits (See photo on page 246.)

With both yeast and baking powder as leaveners, these whole wheat biscuits have nothing to do but rise, rise, rise in the oven. The result: a beautifully airy biscuit with a light and tender bite. Use shortening with no transfats.

> 1 package (^{5}/16 ounce) or 2^1/2 teaspoons (10 g) Hodgson Mill Active Dry Yeast
> 3 tablespoons (45 ml) warm (105°F to 115°F [40.5°C to 46°C]) water
> 4^3/4 cups (593.8 g) Hodgson Mill Stone Ground Whole Grain Whole Wheat Graham Flour
> ^{1}/4 cup (50 g) sugar
> 5 teaspoons (7.5 g) baking powder
> 1 teaspoon (1.5 g) baking soda
> 1 teaspoon (6 g) salt
> 1 cup (225 g) vegetable shortening
> 2^1/4 cups (530 ml) buttermilk, at room temperature, or substitute (see note)

Preheat oven to 400°F (200°C). Line 2 baking sheets with parchment paper. Sprinkle yeast over water in bowl and set aside to proof until foamy, about 5 minutes.

Combine flour, sugar, baking powder, baking soda, and salt in large bowl. Cut in shortening with pastry blender or two knives until mixture resembles coarse crumbs. Mix buttermilk with yeast mixture, then stir into dry ingredients to form soft dough.

Turn out on floured surface and knead a few times. Do not overwork. Roll out dough to ^{1}/2-inch (1.2-cm) thickness. Cut biscuits with 2-inch (5-cm) cutter. Gather scraps, re-roll, and cut again.

Bake 15 to 18 minutes or until risen and lightly browned.

Yield: 36 biscuits

Each with: 116 Calories; 6g Fat (45.9% calories from fat); 2g Protein; 14g Carbohydrate; 2g Dietary Fiber; 1mg Cholesterol; 178mg Sodium.

Note: If you don't have buttermilk, substitute by pouring 4^1/2 teaspoons (22.5 ml) vinegar in a 2^1/4-cup (530-ml) measure. Fill to top with milk and let sit for 2 minutes, then use in recipe.

Whole Wheat Scones

Scones are best eaten warm, right out of the oven, so make up a batch for breakfast or a casual supper. You can also freeze scones, unbaked, for up to 3 months. Bake from frozen for about 20 minutes or until golden brown.

1³/4 cups (218.8 g) Hodgson Mill Stone Ground Whole Grain Whole Wheat Graham Flour

3 tablespoons (42 g) sugar

2¹/2 teaspoons (3.8 g) baking powder

¹/4 teaspoon (1.5 g) salt

4 tablespoons (¹/2 stick [55 g]) butter, cut into small pieces

1 large egg, beaten

¹/2 cup (72.5 g) currants or raisins, optional

4 to 6 tablespoons (55 to 83 ml) half-and-half or cream

FOR THE GLAZE:

1 large egg, beaten

Preheat oven to 400°F (200°C).

Combine flour, sugar, baking powder, and salt in bowl. Cut in butter with pastry blender or two knives until mixture resembles fine crumbs. Stir in egg and currants and just enough half-and-half until dough pulls away from sides of bowl.

Turn dough onto lightly floured surface. Knead lightly 10 times. Roll or pat ¹/2-inch (1.2-cm) thick. Cut with floured 3-inch (7.5-cm) biscuit cutter. Gather scraps, re-roll, and cut again. Place on ungreased cookie sheet. For glaze, beat egg and brush each biscuit with beaten egg.

Bake 10 to 12 minutes or until golden brown. Serve hot.

Yield: 15 scones

Each with: 108 Calories; 4g Fat (34.8% calories from fat); 2g Protein; 16g Carbohydrate; 2g Dietary Fiber; 35mg Cholesterol; 157mg Sodium.

Variation: Pat or roll dough into ¹/2-inch (1.2-cm) rectangle and cut into diamond shapes, using two knives or pizza wheel.

Gluten-Free Scones

These scones, adapted from a recipe by Irish cookbook authors Darina Allen and Rosemary Kearney, rise to about 1^1/2 inches (3.7 cm) and have a mellow, pleasing flavor. Use this as a base recipe to create your own signature scones; you can add cherry yogurt and dried cherries for cherry-flavored scones, apricot yogurt and dried apricots for apricot-flavored scones, and so on.

1^1/3 cups (313 g) Hodgson Mill Stone Ground Whole Grain Brown Rice or Stone Ground Whole Grain Buckwheat Flour

^{2}/3 cup (86.6 g) tapioca flour or potato starch

4 teaspoons (28 g) xanthan gum

1 teaspoon (6 g) salt

2 tablespoons (26 g) sugar

1 teaspoon (1.5 g) gluten-free baking powder

^{1}/2 cup (1 stick [112 g]) butter, cut into pieces, or vegetable shortening

^{1}/3 cup (48.3 g) currants or raisins, optional

2 large eggs or equivalent egg substitute

1 carton (6 ounce [168 g]) plain yogurt or soy yogurt

Sift flours, xanthan gum, salt, sugar, and baking powder into large bowl and blend well. Cut in butter with pastry blender or two knives until mixture resembles coarse crumbs. Stir in currants.

Lightly whisk eggs and yogurt together. Make a well in the center of dry ingredients and add the egg and yogurt mixture. Mix with fork to form soft dough. Cover and refrigerate 30 minutes.

Preheat oven to 450°F (230°C). Line a baking sheet with parchment paper.

Turn out dough onto floured surface and knead lightly to shape into a round. Roll out to 1-inch (2.5-cm) thickness and cut out rounds using 2-inch (5-cm) biscuit cutter. Gather scraps, re-roll, and cut again. Place on prepared baking sheet.

Bake 12 to 15 minutes or until golden brown on top. Transfer to wire rack to cool.

Yield: 12 scones

Each with: 178 Calories; 9g Fat (45.7% calories from fat); 3g Protein; 22g Carbohydrate; 1g Dietary Fiber; 54mg Cholesterol; 312mg Sodium.

Note: You can also use the scone batter to top a fruit dessert. Bake the dessert until the topping is golden brown and the fruit filling is warmed through.

Note: To make this recipe dairy- and egg-free, use vegetable oil, egg substitute, and soy yogurt.

Variation: Use half buckwheat, half brown rice flour.

 ## *Gluten-Free Savory Black Olive and Roasted Red Pepper Scones* (See photo on page 247.)

The yogurt in this recipe helps to produce a light and tender scone. Black olives and roasted red pepper are big-flavor ingredients that turn the basic scone dough into a savory treat.

> 1^1/3 cups (166.6 g) Hodgson Mill Stone Ground Whole Grain Brown Rice or Stone Ground Whole Grain Buckwheat Flour
>
> ^{2}/3 cup (86.6 g) tapioca flour or potato starch
>
> 4 teaspoons (28 g) xanthan gum
>
> 1 teaspoon (6 g) salt
>
> 1 tablespoon (13 g) sugar
>
> 4 teaspoons (16.4 g) gluten-free baking powder
>
> ^{1}/2 teaspoon (0.7 g) dried thyme
>
> ^{1}/2 cup (1 stick [112 g]) butter, cut into pieces, or vegetable shortening
>
> ^{1}/4 cup (25 g) sliced black olives
>
> ^{1}/4 cup (25 g) pimento, drained
>
> 2 large eggs or equivalent egg substitute
>
> 1 (6-ounce [168 g]) carton plain yogurt or soy yogurt

Sift flours, xanthan gum, salt, sugar, baking powder, and thyme into large bowl and blend well. Cut in butter with pastry blender or two knives until mixture resembles coarse crumbs. Stir in black olives and pimento.

Whisk eggs and yogurt together. Make a well in the center of dry ingredients and add the egg and yogurt mixture. Mix with fork to form soft dough. Cover and refrigerate for 30 minutes.

Preheat oven to 450°F (230°C). Line a baking sheet with parchment paper.

Turn out dough onto rice-floured surface and knead lightly to shape into a round. Roll out to 1-inch (2.5-cm) thickness and cut out rounds using 2-inch (5-cm) biscuit cutter. Gather scraps, re-roll, and cut again. Place on prepared baking sheet.

Bake for 12 to 15 minutes or until golden brown on top. Transfer to wire rack to cool.

Yield: 12 scones

Each with: 167 Calories; 10g Fat (50.4% calories from fat); 3g Protein; 18g Carbohydrate; 1g Dietary Fiber; 54mg Cholesterol; 458mg Sodium.

Note: You can top a hearty pot pie or casserole with the unbaked scone batter. Bake until the topping is golden brown and pot pie or casserole filling is warmed through.

Note: To make this recipe dairy- and egg-free, use vegetable oil, egg substitute, and soy yogurt.

Variation: Use half buckwheat, half brown rice flour.

 ## Whole Wheat Wild Blueberry Muffins with Milled Flax Seed

Rise and shine to these whole grain muffins featuring a tender crumb and great blueberry flavor. The milled flax seed is already in the mix.

> 1 box (7 ounces [196 g]) Hodgson Mill Whole Wheat Wild Blueberry Muffin Mix with Milled Flax Seed
>
> 1 tablespoon (15 ml) vegetable oil
>
> 1 cup plus 2 tablespoons (263 ml) 2 percent milk
>
> 1 large egg

Preheat oven to 400°F (200°C). Line 8 to 9 muffin cups with paper liners.

Pour mix into bowl. Stir in oil, milk, and egg. Let rest for 10 minutes.

Spoon batter into prepared muffin tin.

Bake 16 minutes. Turn out muffins onto wire rack to cool.

Yield: 9 muffins

Each with: 125 Calories; 3g Fat (21.8% calories from fat); 5g Protein; 21 g Carbohydrate; 2g Dietary Fiber; 23mg Cholesterol; 148mg Sodium.

Variation: To make Whole Wheat Wild Blueberry Quick Bread, pour batter into greased 9 x 5 x 3-inch (22.5 x 12.5 x 7.5-cm) loaf pan and bake at 350°F (180°C) for 40 to 45 minutes or until toothpick inserted in center comes out clean.

Add It: Drizzle muffins with a Lemon Glaze. Whisk together 1 teaspoon (1.7 g) grated lemon zest, 1 tablespoon (15 ml) lemon juice, 1 tablespoon (15 ml) heavy cream, and 1 cup (100 g) confectioners' sugar.

 ## *Insta-Bake Whole Wheat Biscuits*

> 2 tablespoons (28 g) butter, cut into pieces
> 2 cups (250 g) Hodgson Mill Whole Wheat Insta-Bake Mix
> $^2/_3$ cup (156.6 ml) 2 percent milk

Preheat oven to 425°F (220°C).

Cut butter into Insta-Bake mix with pastry blender or two knives until mixture resembles coarse crumbs. Add milk and stir with fork to form soft dough. Mix until dough pulls away from sides of bowl.

Form dough into ball. Turn dough onto floured surface and knead 4 to 5 times. Roll dough out to $^1/_2$-inch (1.2-cm) thickness on floured surface. Cut dough with 2-inch (5-cm) biscuit cutter and place on ungreased baking sheet.

Bake 10 to 12 minutes or until golden brown.

Yield: 12 to 14 biscuits

Each with: 93 Calories; 3g Fat (25.5% calories from fat); 2g Protein; 15g Carbohydrate; 2g Dietary Fiber; 6mg Cholesterol; 171mg Sodium.

Note: Use unbaked Insta-Bake Whole Wheat Biscuits to top a hearty pot pie or casserole. Bake until the topping is golden brown and pot pie or casserole filling is warmed through.

50/50 Baking Powder Biscuits

Made with 50/50 Flour, which contains a mixture of all-purpose and whole wheat flours, these baking powder biscuits take on a slightly nutty flavor and offer more nutritional benefit. For better health, use a shortening with no transfats.

$^1/_4$ cup (55 g) shortening

2 cups (250 g) Hodgson Mill 50/50 Flour

1 tablespoon (4.5 g) baking powder

$^1/_2$ teaspoon (3 g) salt

$^3/_4$ cup (175 ml) 2 percent milk

Preheat oven to 450°F (230°C).

Cut shortening into flour, baking powder, and salt with pastry blender or two knives until mixture resembles fine meal. Stir in milk to form soft dough.

Knead lightly on floured surface about 10 times. Roll out to $^1/_2$-inch (1.2-cm) thickness and cut with a 2-inch (5-cm) round cutter. Gather scraps, re-roll, and cut again. Place close together on ungreased cookie sheet.

Bake 12 to 15 minutes, or until golden brown.

Yield: 10 to 12 biscuits

Each with: 135 Calories; 5g Fat (36.1% calories from fat); 4g Protein; 18g Carbohydrate; 2g Dietary Fiber; 1mg Cholesterol; 475mg Sodium.

Variation: Add $^1/_2$ cup (50 g) grated Parmesan or Asiago cheese to flour mixture for Cheese Biscuits.

 ## *Apple Carrot Muffins* (See photo on page 248.)

Sweetened naturally with shredded carrots and chopped apples, these muffins are great to serve for lunch with a tuna or chicken salad.

1 box (7 ounces [196 g]) Hodgson Mill Whole Wheat or Whole Grain Bran Muffin Mix

1 tablespoon (15 ml) vegetable oil

$^2/_3$ cup (156.6 ml) 2 percent milk

1 large egg

$^1/_2$ cup (60 g) shredded carrots

^{1}/2 cup (75 g) chopped apples

^{1}/2 teaspoon (1.2 g) ground cinnamon

^{1}/4 cup (37.5 g) chopped nuts, optional

Preheat oven to 400°F (200°C). Line 8 muffin cups with paper liners or grease muffin cups.

Pour mix into bowl and stir in remaining ingredients until just blended. Spoon batter into prepared muffin cups.

Bake for 18 to 20 minutes or until toothpick inserted in center comes out clean.

Yield: 8 muffins

Each with: 159 Calories; 6g Fat (30.5% calories from fat); 5g Protein; 23g Carbohydrate; 3g Dietary Fiber; 25mg Cholesterol; 124mg Sodium.

 ## *Applesauce Whole Wheat Muffins*

Fragrant with apple and cinnamon, these muffins can be a great take-with-you breakfast on your morning commute.

1 box (7 ounces [196 g]) Hodgson Mill Whole Wheat Muffin Mix

^{1}/2 cup plus 2 tablespoons (263 ml) 2 percent milk

^{1}/2 cup (125 g) applesauce

^{1}/2 teaspoon (1.2 g) ground cinnamon

Preheat oven to 400°F (200°C). Line 8 muffin cups with paper liners or grease muffin cups.

Pour mix into bowl and stir in remaining ingredients until just blended. Spoon batter into prepared muffin cups.

Bake 18 to 20 minutes or until toothpick inserted in center comes out clean.

Yield: 8 muffins

Each with: 112 Calories; 1g Fat (6.0% calories from fat); 3g Protein; 23g Carbohydrate; 2g Dietary Fiber; 1mg Cholesterol; 152mg Sodium.

Banana Apple Soy Muffins

Add a little soy to your diet with these delicious muffins.

1 cup (125 g) Hodgson Mill Organic Soy Flour

1 cup (125 g) Hodgson Mill Organic All-Purpose, Unbleached Naturally White Flour

1 cup (125 g) Hodgson Mill Organic Stone Ground Whole Grain Whole Wheat Graham Flour

2 teaspoons (3 g) cream of tartar

2 teaspoons (3 g) baking soda

1 teaspoon (2.3 g) ground allspice

1/4 cup (60 ml) apple juice

1 tablespoon (15 ml) vanilla extract

4 large eggs

1 cup (225 g) mashed banana (about 2 medium)

1/2 cup (125 g) unsweetened applesauce

1 cup (340 g) honey

1 apple, unpeeled, cored, and diced

1 cup (145 g) raisins, optional

Preheat oven to 350°F (180°C). Line 12 muffin cups with paper liners or grease muffin cups.

Combine flours, cream of tartar, baking soda, and allspice in medium bowl. In separate bowl, mix apple juice, vanilla, eggs, banana, applesauce, and honey on low speed until blended. Add dry ingredients and stir together until just moistened. With a spatula, fold in diced apple and raisins. Fill muffin cups two-thirds full.

Bake 18 to 20 minutes or until toothpick inserted in center comes out clean.

Yield: 12 muffins

Each with: 273 Calories; 2g Fat (6.1% calories from fat); 9g Protein; 60g Carbohydrate; 5g Dietary Fiber; 62mg Cholesterol; 232mg Sodium.

Banana Wheat Germ Muffins

Wheat germ is the highly nutritious core of the wheat berry. It is rich in minerals, vitamins, protein—and flavor.

1¹/2 cups (187.5 g) Hodgson Mill Stone Ground Whole Grain Whole Wheat Graham or All-Purpose, Unbleached Naturally White Flour

1 cup (112 g) Hodgson Mill Wheat Germ, Untoasted

1 tablespoon (4.5 g) baking powder

¹/2 teaspoon (3 g) salt

¹/2 cup (115 g) packed light or dark brown sugar

1 cup (225 g) mashed banana (about 2 medium bananas)

¹/2 cup (120 ml) 2 percent milk

¹/4 cup (60 ml) vegetable oil, such as canola

2 large eggs, beaten

Preheat oven to 400°F (200°C). Line 12 muffin cups with paper liners or grease muffin cups.

Combine flour, wheat germ, baking powder, and salt. Stir in sugar, banana, milk, oil, and eggs until well blended. Spoon batter into prepared cups.

Bake 20 to 25 minutes or until toothpick inserted in center of muffin comes out clean.

Yield: 12 muffins

Each with: 195 Calories; 6g Fat (29.1% calories from fat); 6g Protein; 30g Carbohydrate; 5g Dietary Fiber; 32mg Cholesterol; 229mg Sodium.

 ## *Gluten-Free Blueberry Muffins*

With a tender texture and mellow flavor, these muffins are a wonderful accompaniment to a luncheon with tuna or chicken salad.

1 cup (125 g) Hodgson Mill Stone Ground Whole Grain Brown Rice Flour

¹/2 cup (62.5 g) tapioca flour

¹/2 cup (65 g) Hodgson Mill Pure Corn Starch

2 teaspoons (14 g) xanthan gum

2¹/2 teaspoons (3.8 g) gluten-free baking powder

¹/3 cup (66.6 g) sugar

$^3/_4$ teaspoon (4.5 g) salt

$^1/_4$ cup (60 g) applesauce

Two large eggs, lightly beaten, or equivalent egg substitute

$^1/_4$ cup (60 ml) vegetable oil, such as canola

$^3/_4$ cup (97.5 g) nonfat milk or soy milk

$^1/_2$ teaspoon (2.5 ml) gluten-free vanilla extract

$1^1/_2$ cups (218 g) fresh or frozen (thawed) blueberries

FOR THE TOPPING:

1 tablespoon (13 g) sugar

Preheat oven to 400°F (200°C). Line 12 muffin cups with paper liners or grease muffin cups.

Combine flours, corn starch, xanthan gum, baking powder, sugar, and salt in large bowl. Make a well in center of mixture and add applesauce, eggs, oil, milk, and vanilla. Stir together just until moistened. Gently fold in blueberries. Spoon mixture into prepared muffin tins. For topping, sprinkle muffins with sugar.

Bake 25 minutes or until toothpick inserted in center of muffin comes out clean.

Yield: 12 muffins

Each with: 181 Calories; 6g Fat (27.5% calories from fat); 3g Protein; 31 g Carbohydrate; 1g Dietary Fiber; 31 mg Cholesterol; 253mg Sodium.

 ## *Bran Muffins*

Enjoy these delicious bran muffins as is or customize this recipe to your family's taste—with cheese, chopped fresh fruit, shredded vegetables, or dried fruit. This small batch recipe can be ready in 20 minutes.

1 box (7 ounces [196 g]) Hodgson Mill Whole Grain Bran Muffin Mix

1 tablespoon (14 g) melted butter or (15 ml) vegetable oil

$^1/_2$ cup (120 ml) 2 percent milk

1 large egg

Preheat oven to 400°F (200°C). Line 6 muffin cups with paper liners or grease muffin cups.

Pour mix into bowl. Stir in butter, milk, and egg until moist. Let rest for 10 minutes. Spoon batter into prepared muffin cups.

Bake 15 minutes or until toothpick inserted in center of muffin comes out clean.

Yield: 6 muffins

Each with: 157 Calories; 3g Fat (19.7% calories from fat); 5g Protein; 27g Carbohydrate; 3g Dietary Fiber; 38mg Cholesterol; 177mg Sodium.

Add It: To customize these muffins, add $1/2$ cup (72.5 g) raisins, chopped apples, grated Cheddar, shredded carrots, or zucchini before baking.

 ## *Gluten-Free Buckwheat Corn Muffins*

Buckwheat and corn are naturally gluten-free, so enjoy these muffins whether you have dietary restrictions or not. They're delicious spread with apple butter or other fruit spread.

  1 cup (125 g) Hodgson Mill Stone Ground Whole Grain Buckwheat Flour
  $1/2$ cup (70 g) Hodgson Mill Stone Ground Whole Grain Yellow Corn Meal, Plain
  $2 1/2$ teaspoons (3.8 g) gluten-free baking powder
  $1/4$ cup (50 g) sugar
  2 large eggs, beaten
  $1 1/4$ cups (295 ml) 2 percent milk
  $1/4$ cup (60 ml) vegetable oil, such as canola

Preheat oven to 400°F (200°C). Line 12 muffin cups with paper liners or grease muffin cups.

Combine flour, corn meal, baking powder, and sugar. In separate bowl, whisk eggs, milk, and oil together. Add to dry ingredients and stir until just moistened (batter will be thin). Fill muffin tins two-thirds full.

Bake 15 to 20 minutes or until toothpick inserted in center of muffin comes out clean.

Yield: 12 muffins

Each with: 130 Calories; 6g Fat (41.8% calories from fat); 3g Protein; 17g Carbohydrate; 2g Dietary Fiber; 33mg Cholesterol; 124mg Sodium.

Gluten-Free Carrot-Raisin Muffins

The combination of brown rice flours and corn starch provides a softer texture for these muffins, while the spices, carrots, and raisins add flavor and color

1 cup (125 g) Hodgson Mill Stone Ground Whole Grain Brown Rice Flour

$^1/_2$ cup (80 g) potato starch flour

$^1/_2$ cup (65 g) Hodgson Mill Pure Corn Starch

2 teaspoons (14 g) xanthan gum

2$^1/_2$ teaspoons (3.8 g) gluten-free baking powder

1 teaspoon (2.3 g) ground cinnamon

$^1/_2$ teaspoon (0.9 g) freshly grated nutmeg

$^1/_4$ teaspoon (0.6 g) ground cloves

$^1/_2$ teaspoon (3 g) salt

$^1/_3$ cup sugar plus 1 tablespoon (80 g)

Two large eggs, beaten, or equivalent egg substitute

$^1/_4$ cup (60 ml) vegetable oil, such as canola or soy

Two jars (4 ounces [115 g] each) gluten-free baby food strained carrots

$^1/_2$ cup (120 ml) orange juice

$^3/_4$ cup (109 g) raisins

Preheat oven to 400°F (200°C). Line 12 muffin cups with paper liners or grease muffin cups.

Stir together flours, corn starch, xanthan gum, baking powder, spices, salt, and sugar. Make a well in center and add eggs, oil, carrots, and orange juice. Stir together until ingredients are just moistened. Gently fold in raisins. Fill muffin cups three-quarters full.

Bake 25 minutes or until toothpick inserted in muffin comes out clean.

Yield: 12 muffins

Each with: 208 Calories; 6g Fat (24.0% calories from fat); 2g Protein; 39g Carbohydrate; 1g Dietary Fiber; 31 mg Cholesterol; 209mg Sodium.

Note: To make this recipe dairy- and egg-free, use vegetable oil and egg substitute.

Add It: For a special occasion, crown these muffins with Cream Cheese Frosting (see page 125).

Corn Muffins

So easy and yet so good. You can have hot-from-the-oven homemade corn muffins on the table in just 20 minutes!

  1 box (7$^1/_2$ ounces [210 g]) Hodgson Mill Whole Grain Cornbread Muffin Mix
  $^3/_4$ cup (175 ml) 2 percent milk
  1 large egg

Preheat oven to 400°F (200°C). Line 6 muffin cups with paper liners or grease muffin cups.

Pour mix into bowl and stir in milk and egg until just moistened. Fill muffin tins three-quarters full.

Bake 15 minutes or until toothpick inserted in center comes out clean.

Yield: 6 muffins

Each with: 154 Calories; 2g Fat (10.7% calories from fat); 6g Protein; 28g Carbohydrate; 3g Dietary Fiber; 33mg Cholesterol; 261 mg Sodium.

Date Nut Muffins

Spread with cream cheese or a cream cheese frosting, these easy-to-make muffins are great for work or school.

  1 box (7 ounces [196 g]) Hodgson Mill Whole Wheat or Whole Grain Bran
     Muffin Mix
  1 tablespoon (15 ml) vegetable oil, such as canola
  2 large eggs
  $^1/_2$ cup (120 ml) 2 percent milk
  $^1/_2$ cup (75 g) chopped dates
  $^1/_2$ cup (75 g) chopped nuts

Preheat oven to 400°F (200°C). Line 8 muffin cups with paper liners or grease muffin cups.

Pour mix into bowl and stir in remaining ingredients until just moistened. Fill muffin cups two-thirds full.

Oat Bran Muffins

With white whole wheat and oat bran, these muffins can start your day with more protein, fiber, vitamins, and minerals than most breakfast cereals. They also taste great with butter and tart fruit jelly or jam.

1 cup (125 g) Hodgson Mill Stone Ground Whole Grain White Whole Wheat Flour

1 cup (125 g) Hodgson Mill Oat Bran Hot Cereal, uncooked

$^1/_4$ cup (50 g) granulated sugar

3 tablespoons (4.5 g) baking powder

$^1/_2$ teaspoon (3 g) salt

$1^1/_4$ cups (295 ml) 2 percent milk

1 large egg, beaten

3 tablespoons (45 ml) vegetable oil

Preheat oven to 425°F (220°C). Line 12 muffin cups with paper liners or grease muffin cups.

Combine flour, cereal, sugar, baking powder, and salt. Stir in milk, egg, and oil until just moistened. Fill muffin cups two-thirds full.

Bake 15 minutes or until toothpick inserted in center of muffin comes out clean.

Yield: 12 muffins

Each with: 139 Calories; 5g Fat (32.3% calories from fat); 5g Protein; 21 g Carbohydrate; 3g Dietary Fiber; 17mg Cholesterol; 473mg Sodium.

 ## *Insta-Bake Bran Muffins*

A blend of all-purpose and whole wheat flours, the Insta-Bake mix produces muffins with a heartier texture and slightly nutty flavor. Wheat bran, or the outer layer of the wheat berry or kernel, is a great source of dietary fiber.

2 cups (250 g) Hodgson Mill Whole Wheat Insta-Bake Mix

$^1/_2$ cup (62.5 g) Hodgson Mill Wheat Bran, Unprocessed

$^1/_3$ cup (66.6 g) sugar

1 large egg, beaten

$^1/_2$ cup (72.5 g) raisins

^{3}/4 cup (175 ml) water

^{1}/4 teaspoon (2.5 ml) vanilla extract

Preheat oven to 400°F (200°C). Line 12 muffin cups with paper liners or grease muffin cups.

Combine mix, wheat bran, and sugar in bowl. Stir in remaining ingredients until just moistened. Fill muffin cups two-thirds full. Let muffins stand 2 minutes to soften bran.

Bake 20 minutes or until toothpick inserted in center comes out clean.

Yield: 12 muffins

Each with: 124 Calories; 4g Fat (29.0% calories from fat); 3g Protein; 19g Carbohydrate; 2g Dietary Fiber; 17mg Cholesterol; 175mg Sodium.

 ## *Insta-Bake Easy Bake Muffins*

It's this easy to make a batch of whole grain muffins—in under 30 minutes! Although these muffins stay moist for several days, you can freeze any extras for up to 3 months to warm and enjoy on a busy morning. You can also customize these muffins in a variety of ways; consider adding chopped nuts, dried fruit, or grated vegetables such as carrots or zucchini.

2^1/4 cups (281.3 g) Hodgson Mill Whole Wheat Insta-Bake Mix

2 tablespoons (26 g) sugar

1 large egg

^{3}/4 cup (175 ml) 2 percent milk

2^1/2 tablespoons (37.5 ml) vegetable oil

Preheat oven to 400°F (200°C). Line 12 muffin cups with paper liners or grease muffin cups.

Combine mix and sugar in bowl. Stir in remaining ingredients until just moistened. Fill muffin cups two-thirds full.

Bake 15 to 20 minutes or until toothpick inserted in center comes out clean.

Yield: 12 muffins

Each with: 124 Calories; 4g Fat (29.0% calories from fat); 3g Protein; 19g Carbohydrate; 2g Dietary Fiber; 17mg Cholesterol; 175mg Sodium.

Variations: Some easy variations to this recipe include:

Apple Muffins: Add $3/4$ cup (112.5 g) peeled and finely diced apple, $1/4$ teaspoon (0.6 g) ground cinnamon, and a dash of nutmeg to the batter.

Banana Muffins: Add $1/2$ cup (115 g) mashed banana (about 1 medium) and $1/4$ teaspoon (0.6 g) nutmeg to the batter.

Corn Muffins: Add $1/2$ cup (80 g) cream-style corn to the egg and milk mixture (reduce milk to $2/3$ cup [156.6 ml] before adding the mixture to the batter).

Dried Fruit Muffins: Add $3/4$ cup (109 g) cooked, finely chopped dried apricots, prunes, or raisins to the batter.

Blueberry Muffins: Add $1/2$ cup (72.5 g) canned, fresh, or frozen (thawed) blueberries, drained, to the batter.

 ## *Insta-Bake Honey Graham Muffins*

A taste of honey sweetens these easy, whole grain muffins. Choose an amber-colored honey, such as wildflower or clover, for the best flavor.

> 1 large egg
> $1/2$ cup (120 ml) 2 percent milk
> $1/2$ cup (170 g) honey
> 2 cups (250 g) Hodgson Mill Whole Wheat Insta-Bake Mix
> $1/3$ cup (41.6 g) Hodgson Mill Stone Ground Whole Grain Whole Wheat
>   Graham Flour

Preheat oven to 400°F (200°C). Line 10 muffin cups with paper liners or grease muffin cups.

Whisk together egg, milk, and honey in small bowl until smooth. Combine mix and flour in medium bowl. Stir honey mixture into dry ingredients until just moistened. Fill muffin cups two-thirds full.

Bake 15 to 18 minutes or until toothpick inserted in center comes out clean.

Yield: 10 muffins

Each with: 206 Calories; 1g Fat (4.6% calories from fat); 3g Protein; 48g Carbohydrate; 2g Dietary Fiber; 19mg Cholesterol; 181 mg Sodium.

Gluten-Free Mexican Cheese Muffins

Your tastebuds will say "Olé" to these Southwestern-flavored muffins!

    1^1/2 cups (187.5 g) sifted Hodgson Mill Stone Ground Whole Grain
        Brown Rice Flour

    ^{1}/2 cup (65 g) Hodgson Mill Pure Corn Starch or (62.5 g) Soy Flour

    1 tablespoon (4.5 g) gluten-free baking powder

    1 cup (235 ml) bottled enchilada sauce

    ^{3}/4 cup (175 ml) warm water

    2 tablespoons (28 ml) olive oil

    1 cup (225 g) grated cheese, such as Monterey Jack or Cheddar

Preheat oven to 375°F (190°C). Line 12 muffin cups with paper liners or grease muffin cups.

Combine flour, corn starch, and baking powder in bowl. Stir in remaining ingredients until just moistened. Fill muffin cups two-thirds full.

Bake 20 minutes or until toothpick inserted in center comes out clean.

Yield: 12 muffins

Each with: 172 Calories; 8g Fat (40.9% calories from fat); 4g Protein; 22g Carbohydrate; 1g Dietary Fiber; 16mg Cholesterol; 202mg Sodium.

Note: Stir this batter quickly, as the flour absorbs the liquid quickly.

Note: To make this recipe dairy- and egg-free, use vegetable oil and egg substitute.

Variation: If gluten is not a health concern, you can also make these with ^{1}/2 cup (62.5 g) Hodgson Mill All-Purpose, Unbleached Naturally White Flour in place of the Soy Flour.

 ## *Molasses Bran Muffins*

With an old-fashioned flavor, these muffins go well with a classic breakfast of ham and eggs.

    1 cup (125 g) Hodgson Mill Stone Ground Whole Grain Whole Wheat Graham
        Flour

    1 teaspoon (1.5 g) baking soda

    2 teaspoons (3 g) baking powder

    ^{3}/4 cup (175 ml) buttermilk or substitute (see note)

^{1}/2 cup (170 g) molasses

2 tablespoons (28 ml) vegetable oil, such as canola

1 large egg, beaten

1^1/2 cups (187.5 g) Hodgson Mill Wheat Bran, Unprocessed

^{1}/2 cup (72.5 g) raisins

Preheat oven to 400°F (200°C). Line 12 muffin cups with paper liners or grease muffin cups.

Combine flour, baking soda, and baking powder in bowl. Stir in remaining ingredients until just moistened. Fill muffin cups two-thirds full. Let stand 2 minutes to soften bran.

Bake 15 minutes or until toothpick inserted in center comes out clean.

Yield: 12 muffins

Each with: 135 Calories; 3g Fat (18.0% calories from fat); 3g Protein; 27g Carbohydrate; 5g Dietary Fiber; 16mg Cholesterol; 213mg Sodium.

Note: If you don't have buttermilk, substitute by pouring 1^1/2 teaspoons (7.5 ml) vinegar in a ^{3}/4-cup (175-ml) measure. Fill to top with milk and let sit for 2 minutes, then use in recipe.

Oat Bran Honey Muffins

In addition to the great taste of honey and whole grains, you can make these muffins lower in cholesterol, too, by using egg whites instead of whole eggs.

1^1/2 cups (187.5 g) Hodgson Mill Oat Bran Hot Cereal, uncooked

1^1/2 cups (187.5 g) Hodgson Mill Stone Ground Whole Grain Whole Wheat Graham Flour

1^1/2 teaspoons (2.2 g) baking powder

1^1/2 teaspoons (2.2 g) baking soda

^{1}/4 teaspoon (1.5 g) salt

4 large egg whites or 2 large eggs

1 cup (235 ml) buttermilk or substitute (see note)

2^1/2 tablespoons (37.5 ml) vegetable oil, such as canola

^{1}/2 cup (170 g) honey

Preheat oven to 400°F (200°C). Line 12 muffin cups with paper liners or grease muffin cups.

Combine cereal, flour, baking powder, baking soda, and salt in large bowl. Whisk egg whites until foamy in medium bowl, then whisk in buttermilk, oil, and honey. Stir honey mixture into dry ingredients until just moistened. Fill muffin cups two-thirds full.

Bake 20 to 25 minutes or until toothpick inserted in center comes out clean.

Yield: 12 muffins

Each with: 198 Calories; 6g Fat (23.0% calories from fat); 6g Protein; 35g Carbohydrate; 5g Dietary Fiber; 32mg Cholesterol; 295mg Sodium.

Note: If you don't have buttermilk, substitute by pouring 2 teaspoons (10 ml) vinegar in a 1-cup (235-ml) measure. Fill to top with milk and let sit for 2 minutes, then use in recipe.

 ## *Pineapple Whole Wheat Bran Muffins*

The tangy flavor of pineapple plays well off the mellow, somewhat nutty flavor of the whole wheat graham flour.

1 cup (125 g) Hodgson Mill Stone Ground Whole Grain Whole Wheat Graham Flour

1 tablespoon (4.5 g) baking powder

$1/4$ teaspoon (3 g) salt

1 large egg, beaten

$1/3$ cup (80 ml) skim milk

One (8 ounce [225 g]) can crushed pineapple with juice

$1^1/2$ tablespoons (22.5 g) packed light or dark brown sugar

1 cup (125 g) Hodgson Mill Wheat Bran, Unprocessed

$1/4$ cup (60 ml) vegetable oil, such as canola

Preheat oven to 400°F (200°C). Line 12 muffin cups with paper liners or grease muffin cups.

Combine flour, baking powder, and salt in large bowl. Stir in remaining ingredients until just moistened. Fill muffin cups two-thirds full. Let stand 2 minutes to soften bran.

Bake 20 to 25 minutes or until toothpick inserted in center comes out clean.

Yield: 12 muffins

Each with: 110 Calories; 5g Fat (38.4% calories from fat); 2g Protein; 16g Carbohydrate; 4g Dietary Fiber; 16mg Cholesterol; 175mg Sodium.

 ## *Pumpkin Muffins*

Pump it up with pumpkin! Get a healthy dose of beta-carotene along with protein and fiber from whole grains in one delicious muffin.

   1 box (7 ounces [196 g]) Hodgson Mill Whole Wheat or Whole Grain Bran Muffin Mix

   1 tablespoon (15 ml) vegetable oil, such as canola

   $1/2$ cup (120 ml) 2 percent milk

   2 large eggs

   $1/2$ cup (112.5 g) canned pumpkin (not pumpkin pie filling)

   $1/2$ teaspoon (1.2 g) ground cinnamon

   $1/4$ teaspoon (0.7 g) freshly grated nutmeg

   $1/3$ cup (50 g) chopped nuts, optional

Preheat oven to 400°F (200°C). Line 8 muffin cups with paper liners or grease muffin cups.

Combine muffin mix, oil, milk, eggs, pumpkin, cinnamon, and nutmeg in a large bowl. Stir until just moistened. Stir in nuts. Fill muffin cups two-thirds full. Let stand 2 minutes to soften bran.

Bake 18 to 20 minutes or until toothpick inserted in center comes out clean.

Yield: 8 muffins

Each with: 171 Calories; 7g Fat (35.0% calories from fat); 6g Protein; 23g Carbohydrate; 3g Dietary Fiber; 48mg Cholesterol; 126mg Sodium.

Raisin and Cracked Wheat Muffins

Tender, sweet nuggets of dried fruit and the nutty flavor of cracked wheat make these muffins worth getting up for in the morning.

3/4 cup (175 ml) water

1/4 cup (31.3 g) Hodgson Mill Cracked Wheat Hot Cereal, uncooked

2/3 cup (97 g) raisins

1 1/2 cups (187.5 g) Hodgson Mill All-Purpose, Unbleached Naturally White Flour

1 tablespoon (4.5 g) baking powder

3/4 teaspoon (4.5 g) salt

1/2 cup (100 g) sugar

2 large eggs, beaten

1/2 cup (120 ml) 2 percent milk

1/4 cup (60 ml) vegetable oil, such as canola

Preheat oven to 350°F (170°C). Line 12 muffin cups with paper liners or grease muffin cups.

Bring water and cracked wheat cereal to a boil in small saucepan over medium-high heat. Reduce heat and simmer, covered, stirring occasionally, for 7 minutes or until cracked wheat has softened. Remove from heat, stir in raisins, and let plump for 3 minutes.

Combine flour, baking powder, and salt in large bowl. Stir in cracked wheat mixture and remaining ingredients until just moistened. Fill muffin cups two-thirds full.

Bake 22 to 25 minutes or until toothpick inserted in center of muffin comes out clean.

Yield: 12 muffins

Each with: 172 Calories; 6g Fat (27.9% calories from fat); 3g Protein; 29g Carbohydrate; 1g Dietary Fiber; 32mg Cholesterol; 271mg Sodium.

Spelt Bran Muffins

An ancient grain, spelt is higher in protein, carbohydrates, iron, thiamine, riboflavin, and niacin than whole wheat. However, spelt doesn't contain as much gluten as wheat, so you'll get a muffin with a softer texture.

2^1/4 cups (281.3 g) Hodgson Mill Organic Whole Grain Spelt Flour

1 cup (100 g) Hodgson Mill Wheat Bran, Unprocessed

1 tablespoon (4.5 g) baking powder

^{1}/4 teaspoon (1.5 g) salt

1^1/4 cups (295 ml) 2 percent milk

3 large eggs, beaten

1 tablespoon (15 g) unsweetened applesauce

^{1}/4 cup (36.3 g) raisins or (37.5 g) nuts

Preheat oven to 350°F (170°C). Line 12 muffin cups with paper liners or grease muffin cups.

Combine flour, bran, baking powder, and salt in large bowl. Stir in remaining ingredients until just moistened. Fill muffin cups two-thirds full.

Bake 18 to 20 minutes or until toothpick inserted in center of muffin comes out clean.

Yield: 12 muffins

Each with: 113 Calories; 2g Fat (15.0% calories from fat); 7g Protein; 23g Carbohydrate; 6g Dietary Fiber; 49mg Cholesterol; 193mg Sodium.

 ## *Strawberry Orange Muffins with Soy and Whole Wheat* (See photo on page 249.)

The mellow, somewhat nutty flavor of whole grains is a good complement to tart fruit flavors such as strawberry and orange, as you'll see when you taste this muffin.

1 cup (170 g) chopped fresh or frozen (thawed) strawberries

^{1}/3 cup (66.6 g) sugar

1 tablespoon plus ^{2}/3 cup (172 ml) orange juice

^{1}/2 cup (62.5 g) Hodgson Mill Soy Flour

1^1/2 cups (187.5 g) Hodgson Mill Stone Ground Whole Grain Whole Wheat Graham Flour

2 teaspoons (3 g) baking powder

1 teaspoon (1.5 g) baking soda

$^1/_2$ teaspoon (1.4 g) freshly grated nutmeg

2 tablespoons (28 ml) soy oil

$1^1/_2$ teaspoons (2.6 g) freshly grated orange zest

2 large egg whites or 1 whole large egg, lightly beaten

Preheat oven to 350°F (170°C). Line 12 muffin cups with paper liners or grease muffin cups.

Mix strawberries with sugar and 1 tablespoon (15 ml) orange juice in bowl and let stand for 5 minutes.

Combine flours, baking powder, baking soda, and nutmeg in large bowl. Stir in strawberry mixture and remaining ingredients until just moistened. Fill muffin cups two-thirds full.

Bake 15 minutes or until toothpick inserted in center of muffin comes out clean.

Yield: 12 muffins

Each with: 128 Calories; 3g Fat (22.5% calories from fat); 5g Protein; 21 g Carbohydrate; 3g Dietary Fiber; 31 mg Cholesterol; 196mg Sodium.

 ## *Wheat Germ Muffins*

You'll get your whole grain wheat two different ways in this muffin—from the heart of the kernel (the wheat germ) and the whole ground kernel.

1 large egg

1 cup (235 ml) 2 percent milk

1 cup (125 g) Hodgson Mill Wheat Germ, Untoasted

$^1/_4$ cup (60 g) packed light or dark brown sugar or honey

4 teaspoons (6 g) baking powder

1 cup (125 g) Hodgson Mill Stone Ground Whole Grain Whole Wheat
    Graham Flour

$^3/_4$ teaspoon (4.5 g) salt

2 tablespoon (28 ml) vegetable oil, such as canola

Preheat oven to 400°F (200°C). Line 12 muffin cups with paper liners or grease muffin cups.

Whisk egg and milk together in large bowl. Stir in wheat germ. Let stand 2 minutes. Sift in dry ingredients. Add oil and stir until just moistened. Fill muffin cups one-half full.

Bake 15 minutes or until toothpick inserted in center of muffin comes out clean.

Yield: 12 muffins

Each with: 124 Calories; 4g Fat (27.7% calories from fat); 5g Protein; 18g Carbohydrate; 4g Dietary Fiber; 17mg Cholesterol; 312mg Sodium.

 ## *Whole Wheat, Apple 'n Flax Seed Muffins*

Loaded with flavor and nutrition, these muffins are great to take with you for breakfast on the run or to enjoy on a weekend drive.

1/4 cup (35 g) Hodgson Mill Milled Flax Seed
1 1/2 cups (187.5 g) Hodgson Mill 50/50 Flour
1/2 cup (100 g) sugar
2 teaspoons (3 g) baking powder
1/2 teaspoon (1.2 g) baking soda
1/2 teaspoon (3 g) salt
1 large egg, beaten
3 tablespoons (45 ml) vegetable oil, such as canola
1/2 cup (120 ml) 2 percent milk
1 1/2 cups (225 g) finely chopped apple
1/2 cup (75 g) chopped nuts

Preheat oven to 400°F (200°C). Line 12 muffin cups with paper liners or grease muffin cups.

Combine flax seed, flour, sugar, baking powder, baking soda, and salt in large bowl. Stir in remaining ingredients until just moistened. Fill muffin cups two-thirds full.

Bake 18 to 20 minutes or until toothpick inserted in center of muffin comes out clean.

Yield: 12 muffins

Each with: 181 Calories; 8g Fat (38.7% calories from fat); 4g Protein; 24g Carbohydrate; 3g Dietary Fiber; 16mg Cholesterol; 395mg Sodium.

Whole Wheat Muffins

Hearty yet tender-textured, these muffins taste great with butter and a tart fruit jelly or jam. Customize this basic recipe, if you wish, with an additional $1/2$ cup (115 g) of grated cheese, shredded vegetables, dried fruit, or chopped fresh fruit.

    1 box (7 ounces [196 g]) Hodgson Mill Whole Wheat Muffin Mix
    $1/4$ cup (60 ml) vegetable oil, such as canola
    $3/4$ cup (175 ml) 2 percent milk
    1 large egg

Preheat oven to 400°F (200°C). Line 6 muffin cups with paper liners or grease muffin cups.

Pour mix into bowl and stir in remaining ingredients until just moistened. Fill muffin cups two-thirds full.

Bake 18 to 20 minutes or until toothpick inserted in center comes out clean

Yield: 6 muffins

Each with: 226 Calories; 11g Fat (43.3% calories from fat); 6g Protein; 26g Carbohydrate; 3g Dietary Fiber; 33mg Cholesterol; 214mg Sodium.

Variation: Add $1/2$ cup (72.5 g) raisins, pineapple, or chopped dates. For a sweeter muffin, add 1 or 2 tablespoons (15 to 30 g) brown sugar, honey, or sorghum.

 # Big Batch Whole Wheat Pumpkin Muffins

A hearty, moist muffin with the beautiful colors and flavors of fall. Enjoy these muffins slathered with pumpkin or apple butter.

    3 cups (375 g) Hodgson Mill Stone Ground Whole Grain Whole Wheat
        Graham Flour
    $1^1/2$ teaspoons (2.2 g) baking powder
    1 teaspoon (1.5 g) baking soda
    1 teaspoon (6 g) salt
    $1/2$ teaspoon (1 g) cloves
    $3/4$ teaspoon (1.7 g) ground cinnamon
    1 teaspoon (2.7 g) freshly grated nutmeg
    2 cups (400 g) sugar
    $1/2$ cup (120 ml) vegetable oil, such as canola
    3 large eggs

9

Quick Breads

Whole grain flours make truly delicious, good-for-you quick breads in a variety of flavors—from apple, banana, cheese, and corn to strawberry or zucchini. By definition, a quick bread is one that is leavened by eggs or baking powder, not yeast, and that's what makes them "quick." These breads can be baked in loaf pans of varying sizes, baking dishes, or cast iron skillets.

Quick breads are delicious for breakfast and brunch—spread them with flavored butter, apple butter, other fruit spread, or cream cheese. They're also good for tea or dessert, as many dessert chefs can attest to. You can do likewise by toasting slices of a quick bread and topping them with ice cream and a sauce, fresh berries and whipped cream, or sauteed fruit and caramel.

From our first mill in the Ozark Mountains of Missouri, Hodgson Mill has been known for our corn meal products—yellow, white, self-rising, and organic corn meals as well as cornbread mixes. So, it's no wonder that a good portion of the quick breads in this chapter feature corn meal in some way. It seems that everyone has his or her own favorite kind of corn bread, from the hearty and crumbly to the smooth and sweet or the hot and spicy. Whatever your favorite, you'll probably find it in this chapter.

Spicy Chile-Cheese Cornbread

Olé! This is just the cornbread to go with a savory soup or stew on a cold night. Adapted from a recipe by Sarah Fertig, it's a crowd-pleasing favorite.

   2 tablespoons (28 g) butter

   2 cups (250 g) Hodgson Mill Whole Grain Jalapeno Cornbread Mix

   1 cup (155 g) cream-style corn

   1 can (4 ounces [112 g]) green chiles

   1 large egg

   $^1/_2$ cup (120 ml) 2 percent milk

   $^1/_4$ cup (56.3 g) prepared salsa

   4 ounces ($^1/_2$ of an 8-ounce package [115 g]) cream cheese, softened

   1 cup (115 g) grated Cheddar cheese

Preheat oven to 400°F (200°C). Place butter in 8 x 8 x 2-inch (20 x 20 x 5-cm) baking dish and set aside.

Combine cornbread mix, corn, green chiles, egg, and milk in bowl. In separate bowl, combine salsa, cream cheese, and Cheddar cheese.

Place baking dish in oven for 3 minutes or until the butter is bubbling slightly. Remove baking dish and pour half of cornbread batter into dish, spreading to cover the bottom. Spoon salsa mixture over batter. Pour remaining cornbread batter over salsa mixture.

Bake for 25 to 30 minutes or until edges have browned and center of cornbread springs back lightly to the touch.

Yield: 12 servings

Each with: 185 Calories; 9g Fat (43.9% calories from fat); 7g Protein; 20g Carbohydrate; 1g Dietary Fiber; 42mg Cholesterol; 407mg Sodium.

Variation: For a vegetarian main dish, add 1 (14-ounce [400-g]) can drained and rinsed pinto or black beans to cornbread batter.

^{2}/3 cup (76 g) shredded sharp Cheddar cheese

^{1}/3 cup (50 g) diced ham

Preheat oven to 400°F (200°C). Lightly grease an 8 x 8 x 1^1/2-inch (20 x 20 x 3.8-cm) baking pan.

Pour mix into bowl and blend in oil, milk, egg, cheese, and ham until just blended. Spoon batter into prepared pan.

Bake 18 to 20 minutes or until toothpick inserted in center comes out clean.

Yield: 8 servings

Each with: 175 Calories; 7g Fat (34.4% calories from fat); 7g Protein; 21 g Carbohydrate; 2g Dietary Fiber; 38mg Cholesterol; 324mg Sodium.

Variation: Instead of ham, used cooked and crumbled sausage, bacon, or soy-based breakfast sausage.

Gluten-Free Banana Bread

Adapted from a recipe by Irish cookbook authors Darina Allen and Rosemary Kearney, this bread is moist, delicious, and good for you. Be sure to use ripe bananas.

^{1}/2 cup (1 stick [112 g]) butter, softened

^{1}/2 cup (100 g) sugar

2 large eggs or equivalent egg substitute

3 large ripe bananas, mashed

1 cup (125 g) Hodgson Mill Stone Ground Whole Grain Brown Rice Flour

^{1}/2 cup (43.3 g) Hodgson Mill Pure Corn Starch

2 teaspoons (3 g) gluten-free baking powder

^{1}/2 teaspoon (3 g) salt

^{1}/2 cup (75 g) chopped walnuts or pecans, optional

Preheat oven to 350°F (180°C). Lightly grease 9 x 5 x 3-inch (22.5 x 12.5 x 7.5-cm) loaf pan.

Cream butter and sugar together until light and fluffy. Add eggs, one at a time, and beat well after each addition. Add bananas to creamed mixture. Combine rice flour, corn starch, baking powder, and salt together in bowl. Add dry ingredients, $1/2$ cup (62.5 g) at a time, to banana mixture. Stir in nuts (if using). Spoon into prepared loaf pan.

Bake $1^1/4$ to $1^1/2$ hours or until toothpick inserted in the center comes out clean. Turn out onto wire rack to cool.

Yield: 1 loaf, 8 servings

Each with: 363 Calories; 18g Fat (42.2% calories from fat); 5g Protein; 49g Carbohydrate; 2g Dietary Fiber; 78mg Cholesterol; 387mg Sodium.

Add It: Turn this bread into a dessert by toasting a slice, sprinkling fresh blueberries on top, and topping with fresh mashed banana mixed with whipped cream or banana yogurt.

 ## Gluten-Free Honey Rice Batter Bread

This quick bread is delicious as toast or as the basis for a peanut butter sandwich.

 2 cups (250 g) Hodgson Mill Stone Ground Whole Grain Brown Rice Flour
 2 tablespoons (9 g) gluten-free baking powder
 $1/2$ teaspoon (3 g) salt
 $1/4$ cup (32.5 g) Hodgson Mill Pure Corn Starch
 2 large eggs, beaten, or equivalent egg substitute
 1 cup (235 ml) 2 percent milk or soy milk
 2 tablespoons (28 ml) vegetable oil, such as canola
 2 tablespoons (40 g) honey

Preheat oven to 350°F (180°C). Lightly grease 9 x 5 x 3-inch (22.5 x 12.5 x 7.5-cm) loaf pan.

Mix flour, baking powder, salt, and corn starch together in bowl. In separate bowl, beat eggs, milk, oil, and honey together. Add dry ingredients, 1 cup (125 g) at a time, to wet ingredients to form smooth batter. Spoon batter into prepared pan.

Bake 50 minutes or until toothpick inserted in center comes out clean. Cool in pan.

Yield: 8 servings

Each with: 216 Calories; 6g Fat (24.6% calories from fat); 5g Protein; 37g Carbohydrate; 1g Dietary Fiber; 49mg Cholesterol; 528mg Sodium.

Variation: If gluten is not a health concern, you can also make this with $1/2$ cup (62.5 g) Hodgson Mill All-Purpose, Unbleached Naturally White Flour in place of the corn starch.

 ## *Boston Brown Bread*

This old-fashioned recipe makes the traditional New England brown bread, delicious sliced thin for making tea sandwiches and served with Boston baked beans. Although not technically as "quick" as the other breads in this chapter, Boston Brown Bread doesn't need the slow rising time that yeast breads do. These breads steam first on top of the stove in a pot of boiling water, then finish baking in the oven. (If you don't have 3 to 4 hours for making this bread, try the Hurry-Up Brown Bread on page 390.)

> 1 cup (125 g) Hodgson Mill Stone Ground Whole Grain Rye Flour
>
> 1 cup (125 g) Hodgson Mill Stone Ground Whole Grain Whole Wheat Graham Flour
>
> 1 cup (140 g) Hodgson Mill Stone Ground Whole Grain Yellow Corn Meal, Plain
>
> $1/2$ teaspoon (0.7 g) baking soda
>
> 1 teaspoon (6 g) salt
>
> 4 teaspoons (6 g) baking powder
>
> $3/4$ cup (250 g) molasses
>
> $1 3/4$ cups (410 ml) 2 percent milk
>
> 1 cup (150 g) chopped nuts and/or raisins, optional

Grease three clean, 1-pound coffee cans or six frozen juice cans and set aside.

Mix flours, corn meal, baking soda, salt, and baking powder together in large bowl. Add molasses and milk and blend well. Stir in nuts and raisins, if using.

Fill prepared cans two-thirds full. Cover top of each can with small piece of parchment paper and tie each cover tightly to can with kitchen string. Place cans, parchment paper-covered end upward, on trivets in large pot of boiling water; water should come about two-thirds up the can. Keep water boiling and steam, covered, for 3 hours (steam for 2 hours if using juice cans). Add more water to the pot, if necessary.

Preheat oven to 350°F (180°C).

Remove cans from pot. Remove parchment paper. Bake loaves in cans (standing up) for 15 minutes (10 minutes if using juice cans). Let cool slightly in cans, then invert onto wire racks.

Yield: 3 coffee-can size loaves, 14 servings each, or 6 juice-can loaves, 7 servings each

---

Each with: 69 Calories; 2g Fat (28.2% calories from fat); 2g Protein; 12g Carbohydrate; 1g Dietary Fiber; 1mg Cholesterol; 120mg Sodium.

Note: This is an easy bread to make ahead and freeze for up to 3 months.

50/50 Boston Brown Bread

Made with part whole wheat flour, this brown bread recipe provides even more whole grain goodness.

3^1/2 cups (437.5 g) Hodgson Mill 50/50 Flour

^{1}/2 cup (70 g) Hodgson Mill Stone Ground Whole Grain Yellow Corn Meal, Plain

1^1/2 teaspoons (9 g) salt

1^1/2 teaspoons (2.2 g) baking soda

2 cups (470 ml) 2 percent milk

2 large eggs

^{1}/2 cup (170 g) dark molasses

1 cup (225 g) packed brown sugar

^{1}/2 cup (120 ml) vegetable oil, such as canola

1^1/2 cups (217.5 g) raisins, optional

Preheat oven to 325°F (170°C). Lightly grease two 8^1/2 x 4^1/2 x 2-inch (21.3 x 21.3 x 6.3-cm) loaf pans.

Combine flour, corn meal, salt, and baking soda in large bowl. Stir in milk, eggs, molasses, brown sugar, and vegetable oil until smooth. Add raisins, if using. Spoon batter into prepared pans.

Bake 55 to 60 minutes or until toothpick inserted in center comes out clean. Cool in pans 5 to 10 minutes. Invert on wire rack to cool.

Yield: 2 loaves, 14 servings each

Each with: 173 Calories; 5g Fat (23.4% calories from fat); 3g Protein; 31 g Carbohydrate; 2g Dietary Fiber; 15mg Cholesterol; 200mg Sodium.

Banana Bran Bread

1 box (7 ounces [196 g]) Hodgson Mill Whole Grain Bran Muffin Mix

1 large egg

1/2 cup (120 ml) 2 percent milk

1/4 teaspoon (0.6 g) ground cinnamon

1 large ripe banana, mashed

1/4 cup (37.5 g) chopped nuts

Preheat oven to 375°F (190°C). Lightly grease two mini-loaf (7 x 4 x 2-inch [17.5 x 10 x 5-cm]) pans.

Pour mix into bowl and combine with remaining ingredients. Spoon batter into pans.

Bake 20 minutes or until toothpick inserted in center comes out clean. Invert onto wire rack to cool.

Yield: 2 mini-loaves, 10 servings each

Each with: 59 Calories; 2g Fat (22.3% calories from fat); 2g Protein; 10g Carbohydrate; 1g Dietary Fiber; 10mg Cholesterol; 47mg Sodium.

White Whole Wheat Banana Bread

You can make this bread three different ways, if you use different pancake mixes each time.

1 1/2 cups (187.5 g) Hodgson Mill All-Purpose, Unbleached Naturally White Flour

1/2 cup (62.5 g) Hodgson Mill Whole Wheat Buttermilk Pancake Mix, Whole Grain Buckwheat Pancake Mix, or Multi Grain Pancake Mix

1 teaspoon (1.5 g) baking soda

$^1/_4$ teaspoon (1.5 g) salt

$^1/_2$ cup (1 stick [112 g]) unsalted butter, softened

$^1/_2$ cup (115 g) packed light or dark brown sugar

$^1/_2$ cup (100 g) sugar

2 large eggs (or 4 large egg whites)

$1^1/_2$ cups (338 g) ripe banana, mashed (about 3 medium)

$^1/_3$ cup (77 g) regular or light sour cream

2 tablespoons (30 g) toasted sunflower seed kernels, optional

Preheat oven to 350°F (180°C). Lightly grease 9 x 5 x 3-inch (22.5 x 12.5 x 7.5-cm) loaf pan.

Sift flours, baking soda, and salt together in medium bowl. Cream butter and sugars together until light and fluffy in large bowl on medium speed. Add eggs and bananas and mix well. Alternate adding flour mixture and sour cream, ending with flour. Blend well. Stir in sunflower seeds, if using. Spoon batter into pan.

Bake 1 hour or until bread springs back when touched in center. Invert onto wire rack to cool.

Yield: 1 loaf, 8 servings

Each with: 388 Calories; 16g Fat (36.0% calories from fat); 6g Protein; 59g Carbohydrate; 3g Dietary Fiber; 82mg Cholesterol; 311mg Sodium.

Variation: To make muffins, line muffin cups with paper liners. Fill lined cups three-quarters full. Bake 15 to 20 minutes.

 ## *Organic Whole Wheat Banana Nut Bread*

This fragrant bread tastes wonderful toasted in the morning.

$^1/_2$ cup (210 ml) vegetable oil, such as canola

1 cup (225 g) packed light or dark brown sugar

3 large eggs

4 medium ripe bananas, mashed

1 teaspoon (5 ml) vanilla extract

2 cups (250 g) Hodgson Mill Organic Whole Grain Whole Wheat Pastry Flour

1 teaspoon (1.5 g) baking soda

1 teaspoon (6 g) salt

1 cup (150 g) chopped nuts, optional

Preheat oven to 350°F (180°C). Lightly grease 9 x 5 x 3-inch (22.5 x 12.5 x 7.5-cm) loaf pan.

Beat oil and sugar together in bowl, then beat in eggs, mashed bananas, and vanilla. Sift pastry flour, baking soda, and salt together in small bowl. Stir flour mixture into banana mixture until smooth. Add nuts (if using).

Bake 45 to 50 minutes or until toothpick inserted in center comes out clean. Turn out onto wire rack to cool.

Yield: 1 loaf, 8 servings

Each with: 514 Calories; 26g Fat (43.7% calories from fat); 9g Protein; 67g Carbohydrate; 7g Dietary Fiber; 70mg Cholesterol; 458mg Sodium.

 ## *Banana Bran Bread*

With fiber from the bran and potassium from the banana, this bread makes a great way to start your day. Look for vegetable shortening containing no transfats.

$1/2$ cup (112 g) vegetable shortening

1 cup (200 g) sugar

1 cup (225 g) mashed banana (about 2 medium)

1 tablespoon (15 g) sour cream

1 egg

2 teaspoons (3 g) baking powder

$1/2$ teapsoon (1.2 g) baking soda

$1/2$ teaspoon (3 g) salt

1 cup (125 g) Hodgson Mill All-Purpose, Unbleached Naturally White Flour

$1/2$ cup (62.5 g) Hodgson Mill Stone Ground Whole Grain Whole Wheat Graham Flour

$1/2$ cup (62.5 g) Hodgson Mill Wheat Bran, Unprocessed

$1/2$ cup (75 g) walnuts, chopped (optional)

Preheat oven to 350°F (180°C). Lightly grease and flour a 9 x 5 x 3-inch (22.5 x 12.5 x 7.5-cm) loaf pan.

Cream shortening and sugar together until light and fluffy with an electric mixer. Beat in mashed bananas, sour cream, and egg. Combine baking powder, baking soda, salt, flours, wheat bran, and nuts (if using) in large bowl. Add to banana mixture, 1 cup (125 g) at a time, until well blended. Spoon into prepared pan.

Bake 50 to 60 minutes or until toothpick inserted in center comes out clean. Cool 10 minutes in pan on wire rack. Turn out onto wire rack to finish cooling.

Yield: 1 loaf, 8 servings

Each with: 378 Calories; 18g Fat (41.6% calories from fat); 6g Protein; 52g Carbohydrate; 4g Dietary Fiber; 24mg Cholesterol; 342mg Sodium.

 ## Gluten-Free Delicious Apple Cinnamon Bread with Milled Flax Seed

This is an easy, naturally gluten-free bread to make from a great mix with flax seed.

1 box (7 ounces [196g]) Hodgson Mill Whole Grain Apple Cinnamon Muffin Mix with Milled Flax Seed

1/4 cup (60 g) packed brown sugar

2 tablespoons (28 ml) vegetable oil, such as canola

1/2 cup (120 ml) 2 percent milk or soy milk

1 egg or equivalent egg substitute

Preheat oven to 350°F (180°C). Lightly grease and flour a 9 x 5 x 3-inch (22.5 x 12.5 x 7.5-cm) loaf pan.

Combine mix with sugar, oil, milk, and egg until well blended. Spoon batter into prepared pan.

Bake 15 to 18 minutes or until toothpick inserted in center comes out clean.

Yield: 1 loaf, 8 servings

Each with: 154 Calories; 5g Fat (28.8% calories from fat); 5g Protein; 25g Carbohydrate; 2g Dietary Fiber; 25mg Cholesterol; 72mg Sodium.

Note: For dairy- and egg-free bread, use soy milk and egg substitute in place of the milk and egg. To make homemade soy milk, bring 6 cups (1.4 L) water to boil in saucepan over medium-high heat. Slowly add 1 cup (125 g) Hodgson Mill Soy Flour, stirring constantly. Strain through lined colander. Refrigerate soy milk immediately. Milk may be flavored with sweetener or vanilla as desired.

Gluten-Free Soy Quick Bread with Honey

The goodness of soy with the delicious taste of apples and honey are the hallmarks of this recipe. Because it does not contain gluten, egg, or dairy, this is a delicious bread for those with dietary concerns.

- 1 cup (125 g) Hodgson Mill Soy Flour
- 1 cup (130 g) Hodgson Mill Pure Corn Starch
- 1 cup (140 g) Hodgson Mill Stone Ground Whole Grain Yellow Corn Meal, Plain
- 1 cup (125 g) Hodgson Mill Stone Ground Whole Grain Brown Rice Flour
- 1 tablespoon (4.5 g) gluten-free baking powder
- $1/4$ cup (80 g) honey
- 1 cup (225 g) unsweetened applesauce
- $1^1/2$ cups (355 ml) apple juice, apple cider, or water

Preheat oven to 275°F (140°C). Lightly grease and flour a 9 x 5 x 3-inch (22.5 x 12.5 x 7.5-cm) loaf pan.

Mix soy flour, corn starch, corn meal, brown rice flour, and baking powder together in large bowl. Mix in honey, applesauce, and apple juice to reach consistency of cake batter. Spoon batter into prepared pan.

Bake $1^1/2$ hours or until toothpick inserted in center comes out clean. Let cool in pan for 5 minutes, then invert onto wire rack to finish cooling.

Yield: 1 loaf, 8 servings

Each with: 318 Calories; 1g Fat (2.8% calories from fat); 10g Protein; 73g Carbohydrate; 5g Dietary Fiber; 0mg Cholesterol; 185mg Sodium.

Add It: Make an Apple Glaze by whisking 1 cup (100 g) confectioners' sugar together with 2 tablespoons (28 ml) cider or apple juice. Drizzle over cooled loaf.

Insta-Bake Banana Nut Bread

Using the popular Insta-Bake, a convenient baking mix with whole wheat flour, you can mix together the banana bread batter and have banana bread warm from the oven in about 1 hour.

1 cup (200 g) sugar

$1/3$ cup (78.2 ml) canola oil

2 large eggs

$1^1/2$ cups (338 g) ripe bananas, mashed

$1/2$ teaspoon (2.5 ml) vanilla extract

2 cups (250 g) Hodgson Mill Whole Wheat Insta-Bake Mix

$1/2$ cup (75 g) chopped nuts

Preheat oven to 350°F (180°C). Lightly grease and flour a 9 x 5 x 3-inch (22.5 x 12.5 x 7.5-cm) loaf pan.

Beat sugar, oil, and eggs together in bowl with hand-held electric mixer. Add bananas and vanilla and mix gently. Stir in Insta-Bake Mix and chopped nuts. Spoon into prepared loaf pan.

Bake 55 to 70 minutes or until toothpick inserted in center comes out clean.

Yield: 1 loaf, 10 servings

Each with: 313 Calories; 13g Fat (35.8% calories from fat); 5g Protein; 47g Carbohydrate; 3g Dietary Fiber; 37mg Cholesterol; 186mg Sodium.

Insta-Bake Easy Pumpkin Bread

This easy bread tastes like pumpkin pie and is delicious spread with softened cream cheese.

$2/3$ cup (133.3 g) sugar

2 large eggs

$2^1/2$ cups (312.5 g) Hodgson Mill Whole Wheat Insta-Bake Mix

$1/2$ cup (120 ml) 2 percent milk

1 cup (225 g) canned pumpkin, not pumpkin pie filling

$2^1/2$ tablespoons (35.5 ml) vegetable oil, such as canola

$1/4$ teaspoon (0.5 g) ground cloves

1 teaspoon (2.3 g) ground cinnamon

$1/4$ teaspoon (0.7 g) freshly grated nutmeg

$1/2$ cup (75 g) chopped nuts, optional

Preheat oven to 350°F (180°C). Lightly grease and flour a 9 x 5 x 3-inch (22.5 x 12.5 x 7.5-cm) loaf pan.

Beat sugar and eggs until light and fluffy. Stir in baking mix, milk, pumpkin, oil, and spices until well blended. Stir in nuts (if using). Spoon into prepared pan.

Bake 55 to 60 minutes or until toothpick inserted in center comes out clean. Cool 10 minutes in pan on wire rack. Then invert onto wire rack to finish cooling.

Yield: 1 loaf, 8 servings

Each with: 322 Calories; 12g Fat (31.7% calories from fat); 7g Protein; 49g Carbohydrate; 5g Dietary Fiber; 48mg Cholesterol; 296mg Sodium.

Add It: To make a flavored butter to enjoy with this bread, mash $1/4$ cup ($1/2$ stick [55 g]) unsalted butter in a bowl with one of the following:

1 teaspoon (1.7 g) freshly grated orange, lime, or lemon rind; add sugar or honey to taste, if desired

1 tablespoon (20 g) honey

1 teaspoon (2.3 g) pumpkin pie spice

Insta-Bake Quick Cheese Bread

Delicious with soups or stews, this cheese bread also tastes great toasted.

$2^1/2$ cups (312.5 g) Hodgson Mill Whole Wheat Insta-Bake Mix

2 teaspoons (6 g) dry mustard

2 tablespoons (26 g) sugar

$1/4$ cup (60 ml) 2 percent milk

$2^1/2$ tablespoons (35.5 ml) vegetable oil, such as canola

2 large eggs

2 cups (450 g) shredded sharp Cheddar cheese, divided

1 tablespoon (14 g) butter, melted

Preheat oven to 350°F (180°C). Lightly grease and flour a 9 x 5 x 3-inch (22.5 x 12.5 x 7.5-cm) loaf pan.

Stir baking mix, dry mustard, and sugar together in bowl. Stir in milk, oil, eggs, and 1 1/2 cups (338 g) cheese until well blended. Spoon into prepared pan. Brush top with melted butter and sprinkle on remaining 1/2 cup (112 g) cheese.

Bake 45 to 50 minutes or until toothpick inserted in center comes out clean. Cool 10 minutes in pan on wire rack. Then invert onto wire rack to finish cooling.

Yield: 1 loaf, 8 servings

Each with: 327 Calories; 17g Fat (47.1% calories from fat); 13g Protein; 31 g Carbohydrate; 3g Dietary Fiber; 81 mg Cholesterol; 480mg Sodium.

Variation: Use mild Cheddar, Pepper Jack, Gouda, Colby, or slicing cheese of your choice.

Whole Grain Irish Soda Bread

This traditional bread tastes best eaten the day it is made, so invite friends over for an Irish tea.

> 2 cups (250 g) Hodgson Mill All-Purpose, Unbleached Naturally White Flour
> 1 cup (125 g) Hodgson Mill Stone Ground Whole Grain Whole Wheat Graham Flour
> 2 teaspoons (3 g) baking powder
> 1/2 cups (300 g) sugar
> 1/2 teaspoon (3 g) salt
> 2 large eggs
> 1 1/2 cups (355 ml) buttermilk (see note) or plain yogurt
> 3/4 cup (109 g) raisins, optional

Preheat oven to 350°F (180°C). Line baking sheet with parchment paper.

Combine flours, baking powder, sugar, and salt in large bowl. Mix together eggs and buttermilk and stir into dry ingredients. Add raisins (if using) and mix until just moistened and well blended.

Transfer dough to lightly floured board and gently knead 10 times, adding a little more all-purpose flour if necessary. Dough will be sticky. Shape into round loaf. Place on prepared baking sheet.

Bake 40 to 45 minutes or until bottom of the loaf sounds hollow when tapped.

Yield: 1 loaf, 8 servings

Each with: 275 Calories; 2g Fat (5.7% calories from fat); 8g Protein; 60g Carbohydrate; 4g Dietary Fiber; 48mg Cholesterol; 319mg Sodium.

Note: If you don't have buttermilk, substitute by pouring 3 teaspoons (15 ml) vinegar or lemon juice in a 1^1/2-cup measure. Fill to top with milk and let sit for 2 minutes, then use in recipe.

Add It: Instead of raisins, some traditional Irish soda bread recipes include about 2 teaspoons (4.2 g) caraway seed. Add these with the other dry ingredients.

 ## *Easy Jalapeno Cornbread*

Four ingredients and about 30 minutes is all it takes to make this bread, which is perfect with chili.

1 box (16 ounces [455 g]) Hodgson Mill Whole Grain Jalapeno Cornbread Mix

1^3/4 cups (410 ml) 2 percent milk

3 large eggs

^{1}/3 cup (80 ml) vegetable oil, such as canola

Preheat oven to 400°F (200°C). Lightly grease one 2-quart (1.9-L) baking dish or cast iron skillet.

Pour mix into bowl. Add milk, eggs, and oil and stir together for 1 minute.

Pour batter into prepared pan.

Bake 25 to 30 minutes or until toothpick inserted in center comes out clean.

Yield: 8 servings

Each with: 320 Calories; 13g Fat (34.7% calories from fat); 11 g Protein; 42g Carbohydrate; 2g Dietary Fiber; 74mg Cholesterol; 633mg Sodium.

Variation: You can also use this batter as a topping for a savory pot pie. Fill eight 6-ounce (168-g) oven-proof bowls two-thirds full of chili or stew. Top each with one-eighth of batter. Bake at 400°F (200°C) for 15 minutes or until cornbread topping is puffed and browned.

Jalapeno Cornbread (See photo on page 255.)

Here's another version of cornbread for anyone who loves white corn meal.

3 cups (420 g) Hodgson Mill Stone Ground Whole Grain White Corn Meal, Plain

2 teaspoons (3 g) baking powder

2^1/2 cups (587.5 ml) 2 percent milk

^{1}/2 cup (120 ml) vegetable oil, such as canola

3 large eggs, beaten

1 large onion, grated

1 cup (155 g) canned cream-style corn

1^1/2 cups (180 g) mild Cheddar or Colby cheese, grated

^{1}/4 cup (30 g) fresh, chopped jalapeno pepper

Preheat oven to 400°F (200°C). Grease a 9 x 13 x 2-inch (22.5 x 32.5 x 7.5-cm) pan.

Combine all ingredients in bowl and mix well. Pour into prepared pan.

Bake 45 minutes or until toothpick inserted in center comes out clean.

Yield: 12 servings

Each with: 299 Calories; 17g Fat (48.9% calories from fat); 10g Protein; 30g Carbohydrate; 3g Dietary Fiber; 65mg Cholesterol; 269mg Sodium.

Variation: You can use this batter as a topping for a savory pot pie. Fill 12 (6-ounce [168-g]) oven-proof bowls two-thirds full of chili or stew. Top each with one-twelfth of batter. Bake at 400°F (200°C) for 15 minutes or until cornbread topping is puffed and browned.

Variation: Instead of making the bread in a pan, try using a drop biscuit pan to make individual biscuits like the ones pictured on page 255.

Mexican Cornbread

Removing the seeds from the jalapeno takes away some of the heat.

1 box (7^1/2 ounces [210 g]) Hodgson Mill Whole Grain Cornbread Muffin Mix

^{3}/4 cup (175 ml) 2 percent milk

1 large egg

1 tablespoon (10 g) minced onion

^{1}/3 cup (75 g) shredded Cheddar cheese

Preheat oven to 400°F (200°C). Generously grease an 8 x 8 x 1¹/₂-inch (20 x 20 x 3.8-cm) baking dish.

Combine all ingredients in bowl and mix well. Pour into prepared pan.

Bake 20 to 25 minutes or until toothpick inserted in center comes out clean.

Yield: 8 servings

Each with: 135 Calories; 3g Fat (19.7% calories from fat); 6g Protein; 21 g Carbohydrate; 2g Dietary Fiber; 30mg Cholesterol; 225mg Sodium.

Variation: You can use this batter as a topping for a savory pot pie. Fill 8 (6-ounce [168-g]) oven-proof bowls two-thirds full of chili or stew. Top each with one-eighth of batter. Bake at 400°F (200°C) for 15 minutes or until cornbread topping is puffed and browned.

Old-Fashioned Cornbread

Picture a cabin in the woods, a fireplace with a cast iron skillet on the coals, and buttermilk in the churn. Choose the corn meal you like best and make up a batch of cornbread to enjoy with pinto beans or a bowl of chili.

    2 tablespoons (28 ml) vegetable oil, such as canola
    2 cups (275 g) Hodgson Mill Organic Whole Grain Yellow Corn Meal; Stone
        Ground Whole Grain Yellow Corn Meal, Plain; or Stone Ground Whole Grain
        White Corn Meal, Plain
    2 teaspoons (3 g) baking powder
    1 teaspoon (3 g) Hodgson Mill Wheat Germ, Untoasted
    1 large egg
    1 cup (235 ml) buttermilk or substitute (see note)
    1 teaspoon (1.5 g) baking soda
    1 teaspoon (6 g) salt

Pour oil into 8- or 9-inch (20- or 22.5-cm) cast iron skillet and preheat in 400°F (200°C) oven until pan is hot.

Mix remaining ingredients together in bowl until well blended. Carefully pour batter into heated skillet.

Bake 25 to 35 minutes or until bread has risen and is browned. Serve hot, cut into wedges, from skillet.

Yield: 8 servings

Each with: 152 Calories; 5g Fat (29.1% calories from fat); 5g Protein; 24g Carbohydrate; 3g Dietary Fiber; 24mg Cholesterol; 585mg Sodium.

Note: If you don't have buttermilk, substitute by pouring 2 teaspoons (10 ml) vinegar in a 1-cup (235-ml) measure. Fill to top with milk and let sit for 2 minutes, then use in recipe.

 ## Hurry-Up Brown Bread

The old-fashioned recipe for brown bread (see page 377) requires 3 hours of steaming. If you can't wait that long for a slice of brown bread, try this recipe.

1 cup (125 g) Hodgson Mill All-Purpose, Unbleached Naturally White Flour

2 teaspoons (3 g) baking soda

1 teaspoon (6 g) salt

1 cup (225 g) packed light or dark brown sugar

2 cups (250 g) Hodgson Mill Stone Ground Whole Grain Whole Wheat Graham Flour

1 tablespoon (14 g) melted butter or (15 ml) vegetable oil, such as canola

$1/4$ cup (85 g) molasses

$1^1/2$ cups (355 ml) buttermilk or substitute (see note)

1 large egg, beaten

Preheat oven to 350°F (180°C). Lightly grease a 9 x 5 x 3-inch (22.5 x 12.5 x 7.5-cm) loaf pan.

Stir all-purpose flour, baking soda, and salt together in mixing bowl. Blend in brown sugar and whole wheat flour. Add melted butter, molasses, buttermilk, and egg. Beat vigorously to form smooth batter. Pour into prepared pan. Let stand 20 minutes.

Bake 45 minutes or until toothpick inserted in center comes out clean. Turn out on wire rack to cool.

Yield: 1 loaf, 8 servings

Each with: 320 Calories; 3g Fat (7.9% calories from fat); 7g Protein; 70g Carbohydrate; 5g Dietary Fiber; 29mg Cholesterol; 665mg Sodium.

Variation: This same recipe is great when used for making muffins. Just pour batter into greased muffin tins, filling two-thirds full. Bake 20 to 25 minutes. Test for doneness.

Note: If you don't have buttermilk, substitute by pouring 1 tablespoon (15 ml) vinegar in a $1^1/_2$-cup (355-ml) measure. Fill to top with milk and let sit for 2 minutes, then use in recipe.

 ## Hearty Date Bread

With whole and cracked wheat and a touch of sweetness of applesauce, honey, and dates, this is a great bread to enjoy with tea. Slice it thin and spread with a flavored butter for a special treat!

$1^1/_2$ cups (187.5 g) Hodgson Mill All-Purpose, Unbleached Naturally White Flour

$1^1/_2$ cups (187.5 g) Hodgson Mill Stone Ground Whole Grain Whole Wheat Graham Flour

$1/_2$ cup (62.5 g) Hodgson Mill Cracked Wheat Hot Cereal, uncooked

$4^1/_2$ teaspoons (6.7 g) baking powder

1 teaspoon (6 g) salt

$1^1/_2$ cups (355 ml) 2 percent milk

$1/_2$ cup (115 g) unsweetened applesauce

3 tablespoons (42 g) butter, melted, or (45 ml) vegetable oil, such as canola

$1/_4$ cup (80 g) honey

2 large eggs

1 cup (175 g) dates, chopped

$1/_2$ cup (75 g) chopped nuts, optional

Preheat oven to 350°F (180°C). Lightly grease a 9 x 5 x 3-inch (22.5 x 12.5 x 7.5-cm) loaf pan.

Combine flours, cereal, baking powder, and salt in large bowl. Stir in milk, applesauce, butter, honey, and eggs. Stir in dates and nuts (if using). Spoon into loaf pan.

Bake 1 hour and 5 minutes or until toothpick inserted in center comes out clean. Turn out onto wire rack to cool.

Yield: 1 loaf, 12 servings

Each with: 274 Calories; 8g Fat (24.7% calories from fat); 7g Protein; 48g Carbohydrate; 5g Dietary Fiber; 41 mg Cholesterol; 416mg Sodium.

Add It: To make a flavored butter, mash $^{1}/_{2}$ cup ($^{1}/_{2}$ stick [55 g]) unsalted butter in a bowl with one of the following:

- 1 teaspoon (1.7 g) freshly grated orange, lime, or lemon rind; add sugar or honey to taste, if desired.
- 1 tablespoon (20 g) honey
- 1 teaspoon (2.3 g) pumpkin pie spice
- 1 tablespoon (15 g) reduced-sugar fruit spread, jelly, or jam

 ## Gluten-Free Rice Soy Bread

Dense and chewy with a lot of homemade flavor, this quick bread is delicious spread with apple butter. Serve it right from the pan, like cornbread.

1 cup (125 g) Hodgson Mill Stone Ground Whole Grain Brown Rice Flour
$^{1}/_{2}$ cup (62.5 g) Hodgson Mill Soy Flour
$^{1}/_{2}$ cup (65 g) Hodgson Mill Pure Corn Starch
2$^{1}/_{2}$ teaspoons (3.8 g) gluten-free baking powder
1 teaspoon (2.3 g) ground cinnamon
2 tablespoons (40 g) honey
1 cup (225 g) unsweetened applesauce
$^{1}/_{2}$ cup (120 ml) water

Preheat oven to 300°F (150°C). Lightly grease an 8 x 8 x 2-inch (20 x 20 x 5-cm) baking pan.

Combine flours, corn starch, baking powder, and cinnamon. Stir in honey, applesauce, and water to form smooth batter. Spoon into prepared pan.

Bake 40 minutes or until toothpick inserted in center comes out clean. Let cool in pan.

Yield: 1 loaf, 6 servings

Gluten-Free Southern Spoon Bread

Spoon bread is a softer cornbread, spooned from the serving dish onto your plate—and it's delicious! Typically served with a fried chicken dinner, it's equally good with "meat and three" or a main dish and three vegetables.

$2^1/2$ cups (587.5 ml) 2 percent milk or soy milk (see note)

1 cup (140 g) Hodgson Mill Stone Ground Whole Grain White Corn Meal, Plain, or Yellow Corn Meal, Plain

2 tablespoons (28 g) butter or margarine

4 large eggs or equivalent egg substitute

$1/2$ teaspoon (0.7 g) gluten-free baking powder

$1/2$ teaspoon (3 g) salt

Preheat oven to 375°F (190°C). Lightly grease $1^1/2$-quart (1.4-L) baking dish or cast iron Dutch oven.

Scald milk by heating in saucepan over medium-high heat until small bubbles form around perimeter of pan. Stir in corn meal slowly. Continue stirring until quite thick. Remove from heat and stir in butter.

Separate eggs and whip yolks until light. Stir in baking powder and salt and add to meal mixture. Whip whites until they stand in peaks, then fold into mixture. (For egg substitute, simply stir into corn meal batter.)

Spoon batter into prepared dish.

Bake 45 minutes or until puffed and brown. Serve immediately.

Yield: 8 servings

Note: To make this recipe dairy- and egg-free, use margarine, egg substitute, and soy milk. To make homemade soy milk, bring 6 cups (1.4 L) water to boil in saucepan over medium-high heat. Slowly add 1 cup (125 g) Hodgson Mill Soy Flour, stirring constantly. Strain through lined colander. Refrigerate soy milk immediately. Milk may be flavored with sweetener or vanilla as desired.

Southern Spoon Bread

One of the glories of Southern cooking, this bread is meant to be spooned from the baking dish onto your plate.

2^1/2 cups (587.5 ml) 2 percent milk

1 cup (140 g) Hodgson Mill Stone Ground Whole Grain White Corn Meal, Plain, or Yellow Corn Meal, Plain

2 tablespoons (28 g) butter

4 large eggs

^{1}/2 teaspoon (0.7 g) baking powder

^{1}/2 teaspoon (3 g) salt

^{1}/2 teaspoon (1.2 g) ground white pepper

Preheat oven to 375°F (190°C). Lightly grease 1^1/2-quart (1.4-L) baking dish or cast iron Dutch oven.

Scald milk by heating in saucepan over medium-high heat until small bubbles form around perimeter of pan. Stir in corn meal slowly. Continue stirring until quite thick. Remove from heat and stir in butter.

Separate eggs and whip yolks until light. Stir in baking powder, salt, and pepper and add to meal mixture. Whip whites until they stand in peaks, then fold into mixture.

Spoon batter into prepared dish.

Bake 45 minutes or until puffed and brown. Serve immediately.

Yield: 8 servings

Each with: 147 Calories; 7g Fat (41.9% calories from fat); 7g Protein; 15g Carbohydrate; 2g Dietary Fiber; 107mg Cholesterol; 259mg Sodium.

Southern-Style Cornbread

Southern-style means that this cornbread bakes in a very hot oven so that it's crispy on the outside and tender on the inside. Versions of this recipe have progressed from using lard to shortening, but modern recipes now use vegetable oil. A cast iron skillet heats up quickly, bakes evenly, and is the classic choice for baking cornbread.

2 cups (275 g) Hodgson Mill Whole Grain Yellow Corn Meal Mix, Self-Rising

$1/4$ cup (60 ml) vegetable oil, such as canola

1 large egg, beaten

$1^1/2$ cups (355 ml) 2 percent milk

Preheat oven to 450°F (230°C). Generously grease an 8- or 9-inch (20- or 22.5-cm) skillet and preheat in oven until hot.

Pour mix into bowl. Combine remaining ingredients and add gradually to mix, blending well. Pour into hot pan.

Bake 20 to 25 minutes or until raised and browned on top. Serve from the pan.

Yield: 8 servings

Each with: 181 Calories; 9g Fat (42.2% calories from fat); 5g Protein; 23g Carbohydrate; 3g Dietary Fiber; 27mg Cholesterol; 290mg Sodium.

Note: The classic accompaniment for this cornbread is a glass of buttermilk for dunking.

Variation: For corn muffins or corn sticks, generously grease 12 muffin cups or corn stick molds. Fill each only two-thirds full of cornbread batter. Bake 15 to 20 minutes or until bread has risen and is browned.

Gluten-Free Buckwheat Banana Bread

Mild-flavored and naturally gluten-free, this bread makes a great after-school snack or a quick and healthy breakfast option.

$1/2$ cup (87.5 g) chopped prunes or other dried fruit

$1^3/4$ cups (410 ml) buttermilk or substitute (see note)

$2^1/3$ cups (281.3 g) Hodgson Mill Stone Ground Whole Grain Buckwheat Flour

$1/2$ cup (115 g) packed light or dark brown sugar

1 teaspoon (6 g) salt

1 teaspoon (1.5 g) gluten-free baking powder

1 medium banana, mashed

Preheat oven to 325°F (170°C). Line 9 x 5 x 3-inch (22.5 x 12.5 x 7.5-cm) loaf pan with parchment or wax paper.

Place dried fruit in bowl and pour buttermilk over. Let soak for 10 minutes to plump fruit.

Combine flour, sugar, salt, and baking powder in medium bowl. Stir in buttermilk mixture and banana until well blended. Spoon batter into prepared pan and smooth top with spatula. Let stand for 10 minutes.

Bake 45 minutes or until toothpick inserted in center comes out clean. Turn pans on their sides and gently pull wax paper to slip loaves onto metal rack to cool.

Yield: 1 loaf, 8 servings

Each with: 229 Calories; 2g Fat (6.6% calories from fat); 5g Protein; 52g Carbohydrate; 5g Dietary Fiber; 2mg Cholesterol; 390mg Sodium.

Variation: This recipe will also make 2 (7 x 4 x 2-inch [17.5 x 10 x 5-cm]) loaves, which take 30 to 35 minutes to bake.

Note: If you don't have buttermilk, substitute by pouring 3 teaspoons (15 ml) vinegar in a 1³/4-cup (410-ml) measure. Fill to top with milk and let sit for 2 minutes, then use in recipe.

 ## *Spelt Banana Bread*

Spelt is an ancient grain, similar to wheat, but softer in texture.

2 cups (250 g) Hodgson Mill Organic Whole Grain Spelt Flour

¹/2 teaspoon (3 g) salt

1 teaspoon (1.5 g) baking soda

¹/2 cup (1 stick [112 g]) soft butter

1 cup (225 g) packed light or dark brown sugar

2 large eggs, beaten

2 to 3 medium, ripe bananas, mashed

¹/2 cup (75 g) chopped almonds, optional

Preheat oven to 350°F (180°C). Lightly grease 9 x 5 x 3-inch (22.5 x 12.5 x 7.5-cm) loaf pan.

Combine flour, salt, and baking soda in medium bowl. In medium bowl, cream butter and sugar until light and fluffy with hand-held electric mixer. Beat in eggs. Add dry ingredients, 1 cup (125 g) at a time, until well blended. Stir in bananas and nuts (if using).

Bake 1 hour or until toothpick inserted in center comes out clean. Turn out onto wire rack to cool.

Yield: 1 loaf, 8 servings

Each with: 400 Calories; 19g Fat (37.8% calories from fat); 9g Protein; 60g Carbohydrate; 7g Dietary Fiber; 78mg Cholesterol; 434mg Sodium.

Variation: This recipe will also make 2 (7 x 4 x 2-inch [17.5 x 10 x 5-cm]) loaves, which take 30 to 35 minutes to bake.

 ## *Tasty Cornbread*

This cornbread recipe has a softer texture, due to the mixture of all-purpose flour and corn meal.

$1^1/2$ cups (210 g) Hodgson Mill Stoone Ground Whole Grain White Corn Meal, Plain

1 cup (125 g) Hodgson Mill All-Purpose, Unbleached Naturally White Flour

$1^1/2$ teaspoons (2.2 g) baking powder

$^1/4$ teaspoon (0.4 g) baking soda

$^1/4$ cup (50 g) sugar

$^1/2$ teaspoon (3 g) salt

1 cup (235 ml) buttermilk or substitute (see note)

1 large egg, beaten

$^1/4$ cup (60 ml) vegetable oil, such as canola

Preheat oven to 400°F (200°C). Grease a 9 x 9 x 2-inch (22.5 x 22.5 x 5-cm) baking pan.

Combine corn meal, flour, baking powder, baking soda, sugar, and salt in large bowl. Mix in buttermilk, egg, and vegetable oil. Stir just until moistened. Pour into prepared pan and spread evenly.

Bake 25 to 30 minutes or until risen and golden brown.

Yield: 1 loaf, 9 servings

Each with: 205 Calories; 7g Fat (31.3% calories from fat); 5g Protein; 32g Carbohydrate; 2g Dietary Fiber; 22mg Cholesterol; 269mg Sodium.

Variation: Grease 12 muffin cups and fill three-quarters full of batter. Bake 15 to 20 minutes or until golden brown.

Note: If you don't have buttermilk, substitute by pouring 2 teaspoons (10 ml) vinegar in a 1-cup (235-ml) measure. Fill to top with milk and let sit for 2 minutes, then use in recipe.

 ## *Texas Cornbread*

Texas-style cornbread is softer and creamier than its Southern or Midwestern counterparts.

    1 large egg
    1 cup (140 g) Hodgson Mill Whole Grain Yellow Corn Meal Mix, Self-Rising
    1 can (8^1/4 ounces [230 g]) cream-style corn
    2 tablespoons (28 ml) vegetable oil, such as canola
    ^{1}/4 cup (60 ml) 2 percent milk
    1 teaspoon (13 g) sugar

Preheat oven to 450°F (230°C). Grease 8 x 8 x 2-inch (20 x 20 x 5-cm) square baking pan.

Break egg into medium bowl and beat. Add remaining ingredients; stir until blended. Pour into prepared pan.

Bake 20 to 25 minutes, or until golden brown

Yield: 8 servings

Each with: 110 Calories; 5g Fat (35.0% calories from fat); 3g Protein; 17g Carbohydrate; 2g Dietary Fiber; 24mg Cholesterol; 224mg Sodium.

Cracked Wheat and Cornbread

A hearty, dense bread full of flavor, this is delicious served with a savory soup or aged Cheddar cheese.

   1 cup (125 g) Hodgson Mill Cracked Wheat Hot Cereal, uncooked

   1 cup (140 g) Hodgson Mill Stone Ground Whole Grain Yellow Corn Meal, Plain

   $^1/_2$ cup (62.5 g) Hodgson Mill All-Purpose, Unbleached Naturally White Flour

   4 teaspoons (6 g) baking powder

   $^1/_2$ teaspoon (3 g) salt

   1 cup (235 ml) 2 percent milk

   $^1/_4$ cup (60 ml) vegetable oil, such as canola

   $^1/_4$ cup (80 g) honey

   2 large eggs, beaten

Preheat oven to 425°F (220°C). Grease a 9 x 9 x 2-inch (22.5 x 22.5 x 5-cm) baking pan.

Combine cereal, corn meal, flour, baking powder, and salt in large bowl. Stir in milk, oil, honey, and eggs and mix well. Pour batter into prepared pan.

Bake 20 to 25 minutes or until toothpick inserted in center comes out clean. Cut into squares and serve warm.

Yield: 9 to 12 servings

Each with: 227 Calories; 8g Fat (31.1% calories from fat); 6g Protein; 36g Carbohydrate; 4g Dietary Fiber; 44mg Cholesterol; 361mg Sodium.

Whole Wheat Zucchini Bread

Make this bread in the summer when zucchini is especially prolific in the garden or at the farmer's market.

   2 cups (250 g) Hodgson Mill All-Purpose, Unbleached Naturally White Flour

   1 cup (125 g) Hodgson Mill Whole Grain Whole Wheat Pastry Flour

   $^1/_2$ teaspoon (0.7 g) baking soda

   1 teaspoon (2.3 g) ground cinnamon

   $^1/_2$ teaspoon (3 g) salt

   2 teaspoons (3 g) baking powder

$^1/_2$ cup (75 g) chopped pecans

1 large egg plus 1 large egg white

1 cup (225 g) packed light or dark brown sugar

1 cup (235 ml) skim milk

$^1/_2$ cup (115 g) unsweetened applesauce

2 teaspoons (10 ml) vanilla extract

2 cups (260 g) shredded zucchini, about 1 medium

Preheat oven to 350°F (180°C). Grease 9 x 5 x 3-inch (22.5 x 12.5 x 7.5-cm) loaf pan.

Combine flours, baking soda, cinnamon, salt, and baking powder in large bowl. Add pecans (if using). Make well in center of mixture. In medium bowl, lightly beat egg and egg white. Stir sugar, milk, applesauce, and vanilla into egg mixture until blended. Stir zucchini into egg mixture. Add to dry ingredients and stir just until blended. Pour batter into prepared pan.

Bake 1 hour or until toothpick inserted in center comes out clean. Transfer to wire rack and cool in pan for 10 minutes. Invert onto wire rack, then turn right side up to cool completely.

Yield: 1 loaf, 16 servings

Each with: 170 Calories; 3g Fat (15.2% calories from fat); 4g Protein; 34g Carbohydrate; 2g Dietary Fiber; 12mg Cholesterol; 188mg Sodium.

Variation: For Chocolate Whole Wheat Zucchini Bread, add 1 cup (175 g) chocolate chips to dry ingredients in second step, and then proceed with recipe.

10

Pancakes and Waffles

Rise and shine! Griddle-baked pancakes and waffles are a great way to start the day. When your pancakes and waffles are made with whole grains, your breakfast becomes more delicious, nutritious—and filling. Drizzled with a little maple or tart fruit syrup, they are the perfect accompaniments to fresh fruit, eggs, or breakfast-style meats. Pancakes and waffles are also an easy and delicious "breakfast for dinner" evening meal.

If your weekday mornings are too busy to start from scratch, make pancakes and waffles on the weekend, then wrap and refrigerate or freeze them (for up to 3 months) to pop in the toaster or microwave later on.

The key to making pancakes and waffles is a hot griddle, skillet, or waffle iron. Pouring the batter onto a hot surface keeps the cakes tender and moist and helps prevent them from sticking. Let your stove-top griddle, skillet, or waffle iron heat up, then test it for readiness by lightly flicking several small drops of water on the surface. If the pan is ready, the drops will sizzle and disappear almost immediately. If you have an electric griddle, skillet, or waffle iron, just set and check the temperature gauge.

Add It: To make a flavored butter, mash $1/4$ cup ($1/2$ stick [55 g]) unsalted butter in a bowl with one of the following:

1 teaspoon (1.7 g) freshly grated orange, lime, or lemon rind; add sugar or honey to taste, if desired.

1 tablespoon (20 g) honey

1 teaspoon (2.1 g) pumpkin spice

1 tablespoon (20 g) reduced-sugar fruit spread, jelly, or jam

Add It: To make a naturally flavored fruit syrup, bring 2 cups (470 ml) fruit juice (cherry, cranberry, pineapple, pomegranate, apple juice, cider, etc.) to a boil and cook until it has reduced by half and has thickened slightly, about 10 minutes. If desired, add a squeeze of fresh lemon juice and honey to taste. Serve right away or keep, covered, in the refrigerator, for up to 1 week.

 ## *Gluten-Free Whole Grain Belgian Waffles*

These waffles rise as high and taste as great as those made with wheat. For the best waffle texture, the batter (minus the eggs) needs to rest for 8 hours. So mix it up the night before, cover and refrigerate, then add the eggs and make the waffles the next morning.

1 cup (125 g) Hodgson Mill Stone Ground Whole Grain Brown Rice Flour

1/2 cup (62.5 g) Hodgson Mill Whole Grain Multi Purpose Baking Mix or Hodgson Mill Apple Cinnamon Muffin Mix

1/2 cup (65 g) Hodgson Mill Pure Corn Starch

2 teaspoons (14 g) xanthan gum

2 tablespoons (26 g) sugar

1 teaspoon (2.3 g) ground cinnamon

1 teaspoon (6 g) salt

2 cups (470 ml) warm (105°F to 115°F [40.5°C to 46°C]) 2 percent milk or soy milk (see note)

1/2 cup (1 stick [112 g]) melted butter or vegetable oil, such as canola

2 teaspoons (8 g) Hodgson Mill Active Dry Yeast

3 large eggs or equivalent egg substitute

Maple syrup as accompaniment

Stir together flour, mix, corn starch, xanthan gum, sugar, cinnamon, and salt until well blended in large bowl. In separate bowl, whisk together milk, butter, and yeast. Set yeast mixture aside until foamy, about 5 minutes.

Whisk yeast mixture into flour mixture. Cover with plastic wrap and let stand at room temperature for 8 hours or overnight.

When ready to cook, whisk in eggs.

Heat and grease waffle iron according to manufacturer's directions.

Pour $^1/_2$ cup (120 ml) batter at a time onto waffle iron and cook until golden and crisp. Remove with fork. Serve drizzled with maple syrup.

Yield: 12 waffles

Each with: 204 Calories; 10g Fat (43.6% calories from fat); 5g Protein; 25g Carbohydrate; 1g Dietary Fiber; 70mg Cholesterol; 290mg Sodium.

Note: You can wrap and freeze leftover waffles for up to 3 months. Pop them, frozen, in the toaster, toaster oven, microwave, or a 350°F (180°C) oven until warmed through.

Note: To make this recipe dairy- and egg-free, use soy milk, vegetable oil, and egg substitute.

Note: To make homemade soy milk, bring 6 cups (1.4 L) water to boil in saucepan over medium-high heat. Slowly add 1 cup (125 g) Hodgson Mill Soy Flour, stirring constantly. Strain through lined colander. Refrigerate soy milk immediately. Milk may be flavored with sweetener or vanilla as desired.

Add It: Add fresh berries, chopped nuts, or finely sliced bananas to the batter.

Whole Grain Belgian Waffles

With more fiber and a pleasantly nutty texture, these waffles taste wonderful with real maple or tart fruit syrup. For the best waffle texture, the batter (minus the eggs) needs to rest for 8 hours. So mix it up the night before, cover and refrigerate, then add the eggs and make the waffles the next morning. Top these waffles with maple syrup.

2 cups (470 ml) warm (105°F to 115°F [40.5°C to 46°C]) 2 percent milk

$^1/_2$ cup (1 stick [112 g]) melted butter

2 teaspoons (8 g) Hodgson Mill Active Dry Yeast

1 cup (125 g) Hodgson Mill Stone Ground Whole Grain White Whole Wheat Flour or 50/50 Flour

1 cup (125 g) Hodgson Mill All-Purpose, Unbleached Naturally White Flour

2 tablespoons (26 g) sugar

1$^1/_4$ teaspoons (7.5 g) salt

3 large eggs

Stir together milk, butter, and yeast in large bowl. Set aside until foamy, about 5 minutes.

Whisk in flours, sugar, and salt. Cover with plastic wrap and let stand at room temperature overnight.

When ready to cook, whisk in eggs.

Heat and grease waffle iron according to manufacturer's directions.

Pour 1/2 cup (120 ml) batter at a time onto waffle iron and cook until golden and crisp. Remove with fork. Serve drizzled with maple syrup.

Yield: 12 waffles

Each with: 182 Calories; 10g Fat (47.0% calories from fat); 6g Protein; 19g Carbohydrate; 1g Dietary Fiber; 70mg Cholesterol; 334mg Sodium.

Note: You can wrap and freeze leftover waffles for up to 3 months. Pop them, frozen, in the toaster, toaster oven, microwave, or a 350°F (180°C) oven until warmed through.

Add It: Add fresh berries, chopped nuts, or finely sliced bananas to the batter.

 ## *Hearty Sour Rye and Corn Meal Pancakes*

Tart, tangy, and rich with whole grain flavor, these hearty pancakes are perfect when the weather turns cool. Add smoky ham, bacon, or sausage and homemade applesauce as accompaniments.

  Vegetable oil, such as canola, for oiling

  2 cups (470 ml) buttermilk or substitute (see note)

  1 large egg

  1 cup (125 g) Hodgson Mill Stone Ground Whole Grain Rye Flour

  1 cup (140 g) Hodgson Mill Stone Ground Whole Grain Yellow or White Corn Meal, Plain

  1/2 cup (170 g) molasses

  1 teaspoon (1.5 g) baking soda

  1 teaspoon (1.5 g) baking powder

  1 teaspoon (3 g) salt

Heat griddle or large skillet over medium-high heat or to 375°F (190°C). Oil lightly. Griddle is ready when small drops of water sizzle and disappear almost immediately.

Mix all ingredients together to form smooth batter.

Pour pancake batter onto hot griddle, using 1/4-cup (60-ml) measure. Cook until small bubbles form on the edge of the pancakes. Turn pancakes over and cook until golden brown.

Yield: 8 pancakes

Each with: 183 Calories; 2g Fat (9.5% calories from fat); 6g Protein; 39g Carbohydrate; 4g Dietary Fiber; 26mg Cholesterol; 563mg Sodium.

Note: You can wrap and freeze leftover pancakes for up to 3 months. Pop them, frozen, in the toaster, toaster oven, microwave, or a 350°F (180°C) oven until warmed through.

Note: If you don't have buttermilk, substitute by pouring 4 teaspoons (20 ml) vinegar in a 2-cup (470-ml) measure. Fill to top with milk and let sit for 2 minutes, then use in recipe.

 ## *Ozarks Sour Cream Corn Cakes*

These corn cakes are delicious drizzled with a tart fruit syrup.

> Vegetable oil, such as canola, for griddle
> 1 box (7 ounces [196 g]) Hodgson Mill Whole Grain Cornbread Muffin Mix
> 3/4 cup (175 ml) 2 percent milk
> 1 large egg
> 1/2 cup (115 g) sour cream

Heat griddle or skillet over medium heat or to 350°F (180°C). Oil lightly.

Pour mix into bowl and stir in milk, egg, and sour cream until smooth.

Pour pancake batter onto hot griddle, using 1/4-cup (60-ml) measure. Cook until small bubbles form on the edge of the pancakes. Turn pancakes over and cook until golden brown.

Yield: 6 to 8 (6-inch [15-cm]) pancakes

Each with: 187 Calories; 6g Fat (28.1% calories from fat); 6g Protein; 27g Carbohydrate; 3g Dietary Fiber; 42mg Cholesterol; 255mg Sodium.

Variation: Use regular or light sour cream.

Note: You can wrap and freeze leftover waffles for up to 3 months. Pop them, frozen, in the toaster, toaster oven, microwave, or a 350°F (180°C) oven until warmed through.

 ## *Gluten-Free Banana Blueberry Pancakes*

Vegetable oil, such as canola, for griddle

1^1/4 cups (156.3 g) Hodgson Mill Stone Ground Whole Grain Multi Purpose Baking Mix

1 teaspoon (2.3 g) ground cinnamon

^{1}/2 cup (120 ml) 2 percent milk or soy milk

1 large egg or equivalent egg substitute

1 tablespoon (15 ml) vegetable oil

2 tablespoons (40 g) honey

1 large banana, mashed

1 cup (145 g) fresh or frozen and thawed blueberries

Heat griddle or skillet over medium heat or to 350°F (180°C). Oil lightly.

Pour mix into bowl and stir in cinnamon, milk, egg, oil, honey, and banana until smooth. Stir in blueberries.

Pour pancake batter onto hot griddle, using ^{1}/3-cup (80-ml) measure. Cook until small bubbles form on the edge of the pancakes. Turn pancakes over and cook until golden brown.

Yield: 6 to 8 (6-inch [15-cm]) pancakes

Each with: 179 Calories; 5g Fat (23.3% calories from fat); 5g Protein; 34g Carbohydrate; 4g Dietary Fiber; 33mg Cholesterol; 21 mg Sodium.

Note: To make this recipe dairy- and egg-free, use soy milk and egg substitute.

Add It: Serve these pancakes with more sliced banana and fresh blueberries.

Gluten-Free Rice Flour Waffles

Quick to make and delicious to eat, these waffles have a mellow, satisfying flavor.

> Vegetable oil, such as canola, for griddle
> $3/4$ cup (93.8 g) Hodgson Mill Stone Ground Whole Grain Multi Purpose Baking Mix
> $3/4$ cup (93.8 g) Hodgson Mill Stone Ground Whole Grain Brown Rice Flour
> 1 cup (235 ml) 2 percent milk or soy milk (see note)
> 1 large egg or equivalent egg substitute
> $1/2$ cup (125 g) unsweetened applesauce
> 1 tablespoon (15 ml) vegetable oil
> 2 tablespoons (26 g) sugar
> 1 teaspoon (2.3 g) ground cinnamon

Preheat waffle maker according to manufacturer's directions. Oil lightly.

Pour mix and flour into bowl and stir in milk, egg, applesauce, oil, sugar, and cinnamon to form smooth batter.

Pour batter onto hot waffle iron, using a $1/3$-cup (80-ml) measure. Cook until steam stops and waffle is crisp. Remove with fork.

Yield: 2 large waffles

Each with: 596 Calories; 17g Fat (23.4% calories from fat); 19 g Protein; 105 g Carbohydrate; 9g Dietary Fiber; 103mg Cholesterol; 90mg Sodium.

Add It: Stir in 1 sliced banana and $1/4$ cup (37.5 g) chopped walnuts.

Note: To make this recipe dairy- and egg-free, use soy milk and egg substitute.

Note: To make homemade soy milk, see page 128.

 ## *Gluten-Free Pancakes*

Top these with gluten-free syrup or fresh fruit.

> Vegetable oil, such as canola, for griddle
> $3/4$ cup (93.8 g) Hodgson Mill Whole Grain Multi Purpose Baking Mix
> $3/4$ cup (93.8 g) Hodgson Mill Stone Ground Whole Grain Brown Rice Flour
> 1 cup (235 ml) 2 percent milk or soy milk (see note)
> 1 large egg or equivalent egg substitute
> $1/2$ cup (125 g) unsweetened applesauce

1 tablespoon (15 ml) vegetable oil, such as canola

2 tablespoons (26 g) sugar

1 teaspoon (2.3 g) ground cinnamon

Heat griddle or skillet over medium heat or to 350°F (180°C). Oil lightly.

Pour mix and flour into bowl and stir in milk, egg, applesauce, oil, sugar, and cinnamon to form smooth batter.

Pour batter onto hot griddle, using a 1/4-cup (60-ml) measure. Cook until small bubbles form on the edge of the pancakes. Turn pancakes over and cook until golden brown.

Yield: 6 to 8 (4-inch [10-cm]) pancakes

Each with: 182 Calories; 5g Fat (24.3% calories from fat); 6g Protein; 31 g Carbohydrate; 2g Dietary Fiber; 34mg Cholesterol; 30mg Sodium.

Add It: Stir in 1 sliced banana and 1/4 cup (37.5 g) chopped walnuts.

Note: To make this recipe dairy- and egg-free, use soy milk and egg substitute.

Note: To make homemade soy milk, see page 128.

 ## *Whole Wheat Blueberry Pancakes with Milled Flax Seed*

With milled flax seed in the mix, you get even more nutrition in these hearty, tasty pancakes.

Vegetable oil, such as canola, for griddle

1 box (10 ounces [280 g]) Hodgson Mill Whole Wheat Wild Blueberry Muffin Mix with Milled Flax Seed

1 1/2 cups (355 ml) 2 percent milk

1 large egg

1 tablespoon (15 ml) vegetable oil, such as canola

Heat griddle or skillet over medium heat or to 350°F (180°C). Oil lightly.

Pour mix into bowl. Stir in milk, egg, and oil to form smooth batter.

Pour batter onto hot griddle, using 1/4-cup (60-ml) measure. Cook until small bubbles form on the edge of the pancakes. Turn pancakes over and cook until golden brown.

Yield: 6 to 8 (4-inch [10-cm]) pancakes

Each with: 252 Calories; 5g Fat (18.5% calories from fat); 10g Protein; 45g Carbohydrate; 5g Dietary Fiber; 36mg Cholesterol; 310mg Sodium.

Note: You can wrap and freeze leftover pancakes for up to 3 months. Pop them, frozen, in the toaster, toaster oven, microwave, or a 350°F (180°C) oven until warmed through.

Add It: Add fresh blueberries to the batter.

 ## *Naturally Gluten-Free Buckwheat Blini*

Blini are small, yeast-leavened buckwheat pancakes that hail from Russia and Eastern Europe. Traditionally, they are served with sour cream and applesauce, but they also taste great topped with butter and syrup.

> 1 package ($^5/16$ ounce) or $2^1/2$ teaspoons (10 g) Hodgson Mill Active Dry Yeast
>
> $^1/2$ cup (120 ml) very warm (115°F to 125°F [46°C to 51.6°C]) 2 percent milk or soy milk
>
> 1 cup (230 g) plain low-fat dairy or soy yogurt, room temperature
>
> $^1/2$ teaspoon (3 g) salt
>
> 2 cups (125 g) Hodgson Mill Stone Ground Whole Grain Buckwheat Flour
>
> 1 cup (235 ml) warm (105°F to 115°F [40.5°C to 46°C]) water
>
> 3 large egg whites or equivalent egg substitute

Sprinkle yeast over very warm milk. Stir and set aside until foamy, about 5 minutes.

Blend yogurt with salt in medium bowl. Stir yeast mixture into yogurt mixture. Add buckwheat flour and warm water and whisk by hand or with electric mixer until batter is smooth. Cover bowl and let stand in warm, draft-free place for 20 minutes.

Meanwhile, whip egg whites until soft peaks form. Fold egg whites into batter and let stand another 10 minutes.

Preheat oven to 250°F (120°C). Spray a blini pan or a 6-inch (15-cm) crêpe pan with cooking spray. Heat crêpe pan over medium-high heat or electric pan to 365°F (180°C). Pour scant $^1/2$ cup (60 ml) blini batter onto hot pan and cook until top is firm and bubbly. Turn blini and cook until crisp and golden brown, about 5 minutes. Keep warm in oven until ready to serve.

Yield: 18 blini

Each with: 68 Calories; 2g Fat (19.3% calories from fat); 3g Protein; 11 g Carbohydrate; 1g Dietary Fiber; 32mg Cholesterol; 81 mg Sodium.

Note: You can store blini, covered, in the refrigerator for up to 3 weeks or wrap and freeze them for up to 3 months. To reheat, microwave each blini for 20 seconds (on High), or heat in a 350°F (180°C) oven for 5 minutes.

 ## *Country French Buckwheat Crêpes*

Want to try fast food, French-style? Then make these paper-thin crêpes, folded over an egg, ham, and cheese filling. You may never drive through again!

3/4 cup (93.8 g) Hodgson Mill Stone Ground Whole Grain Buckwheat Flour

1/4 cup (31.3 g) Hodgson Mill All-Purpose, Unbleached Naturally White Flour

1/2 teaspoon (3 g) salt

3 large eggs

1/4 cup (1/2 stick [55 g]) butter, melted

1 1/4 cups (295 ml) whole milk

Vegetable oil, such as canola, for oiling pan

Combine flours and salt in medium bowl. Whisk in eggs, melted butter, and milk to form smooth batter. Cover and let rest for 2 hours, or overnight in the refrigerator.

Oil large skillet or crêpe pan and place over medium-high heat. Ladle batter, 1/4 cup (60 ml) at a time, into skillet. Lift and tilt skillet to swirl batter to 8-inch (20-cm) diameter. Cook until edges turn opaque, about 1 minute, then turn and cook other side for 20 seconds. Transfer to plate. Cover each crêpe with waxed or parchment paper until ready to serve.

Yield: 8 to 10 crêpes

Each with: 149 Calories; 9g Fat (53.6% calories from fat); 4g Protein; 13g Carbohydrate; 1g Dietary Fiber; 91 mg Cholesterol; 231mg Sodium.

Add It: To fill crêpes, place about 1/4 cup (37.5 g) of filling (scrambled eggs, shredded cheese, chopped ham, or all three) down the center of each crêpe. Fold sides over and serve seam-side down.

Gluten-Free Apple Cinnamon Pancakes with Milled Flax Seed

Fragrant apple paired with cinnamon and the nutritional benefits of omega-3s in the flax seed make these pancakes a healthy way to start the day, and the flax seed is already in the mix.

Vegetable oil, such as canola, for griddle

1 box (7^1/2 ounces [210 g]) Hodgson Mill Whole Grain Apple Cinnamon Muffin Mix with Milled Flax Seed

1^1/4 cups (295 ml) 2 percent milk or soy milk

1 large egg or equivalent egg substitute

3 to 4 tablespoons (39 to 52 g) sugar, or to taste

1 tablespoon (15 ml) vegetable oil, such as canola

Heat griddle or skillet over medium heat or to 350°F (180°C). Oil lightly.

Pour mix into bowl. Stir in milk, egg, sugar, and oil to form smooth batter.

Pour pancake batter onto hot griddle, using a ^{1}/4-cup (60-ml) measure. Cook until small bubbles form on the edges of the pancakes. Turn pancakes over and cook until golden brown.

Yield: 6 to 8 (4-inch [10-cm]) pancakes

Each with: 199 Calories; 5g Fat (23.1% calories from fat); 8g Protein; 33g Carbohydrate; 3g Dietary Fiber; 35mg Cholesterol; 113mg Sodium.

Note: For thinner pancakes, add more milk; for thicker pancakes, add less milk.

Variation: Replace sugar with honey and add 1 teaspoon (2.3 g) ground cinnamon.

Add It: To make Fresh Apple Sauce: Peel, core, and chop two Golden Delicious apples. Cook apples in saucepan over medium heat until apples soften, about 7 minutes. Stir in 1 tablespoon (20 g) honey, 1 teaspoon (5 ml) fresh lemon juice, and ^{1}/2 teaspoon (1.2 g) ground cinnamon. Serve each pancake with a dollop of warm sauce.

Gluten-Free Blueberry Corn Meal Pancakes

Serve these pancakes with fresh blueberries or Fresh Blueberry Sauce (recipe follows) for great flavor and a boost of antioxidants.

Vegetable oil, such as canola, for griddle

2 cups (280 g) Hodgson Mill Organic Whole Grain Yellow Corn Meal or Stone Ground Whole Grain Yellow Corn Meal, Plain

1/2 teaspoon (3 g) salt

11/2 teaspoons (2.2 g) gluten-free baking powder

1/4 cup (50 g) sugar

1 teaspoon (5 ml) gluten-free vanilla extract

3 tablespoons (45 ml) vegetable oil, such as canola

2 large egg whites or equivalent egg substitute

11/2 cups (355 ml) 2 percent milk or soy milk

2 cups (290 g) fresh blueberries

Place corn meal, salt, baking powder, and sugar in a medium mixing bowl and blend well. In separate bowl, whisk together vanilla, oil, egg whites, and milk. Pour wet mixture over dry ingredients and blend just until moistened. Fold in blueberries.

Heat griddle over medium-high heat or to 375°F (190°C). Oil lightly. Griddle is ready when small drops of water sizzle and disappear almost immediately.

Pour pancake batter onto hot griddle using a 1/3-cup (80-ml) measure. Cook pancakes until they are puffed and a few bubbles appear on top, about 3 minutes. Turn and cook until both sides are a dark golden brown.

Yield: 12 pancakes

Each with: 146 Calories; 5g Fat (27.8% calories from fat); 4g Protein; 24g Carbohydrate; 3g Dietary Fiber; 2mg Cholesterol; 176mg Sodium.

Add It: To make Fresh Blueberry Sauce: Place 2 cups (290 g) fresh or frozen and thawed blueberries in saucepan over medium heat. Cook until blueberries release juice, about 7 minutes. Stir in 1 tablespoon (20 g) honey, 1 teaspoon (5 ml) fresh lemon juice, and 1/2 teaspoon (1.2 g) ground cinnamon. Serve each pancake with a spoonful of warm sauce.

Gluten-Free Old-Fashioned Blueberry Corn Meal Pancakes

Naturally gluten-free, these tasty pancakes are also low in cholesterol when you use egg whites instead of whole eggs.

Vegetable oil, such as canola, for griddle

2 cups (280 g) Hodgson Mill Stone Ground Whole Grain Yellow Corn Meal, Plain

$1/3$ teaspoon (3 g) salt

$1^1/2$ teaspoons (2.2 g) gluten-free baking powder

$1/4$ cup (50 g) sugar

1 teaspoon (5 ml) gluten-free vanilla extract

3 tablespoons (45 ml) vegetable oil, such as canola

2 large egg whites or equivalent egg white substitute

$1^1/2$ cups (355 ml) 2 percent or soy milk

2 cups (290 g) fresh blueberries

Place corn meal, salt, baking powder, and sugar in a medium mixing bowl and blend well. In a separate bowl, whisk together vanilla, oil, egg whites, and milk. Pour wet mixture over dry ingredients and blend just until moistened. Fold in blueberries.

Heat griddle on medium-high heat or to 375°F (190°C). Oil lightly. Griddle is ready when small drops of water sizzle and disappear almost immediately.

Pour batter onto hot griddle using $1/3$-cup (80-ml) measure. Cook pancakes until they are puffed and a few bubbles appear on top, about 3 minutes. Turn and cook until both sides are a dark golden brown.

Yield: 12 pancakes

Each with: 146 Calories; 5g Fat (27.8% calories from fat); 4g Protein; 24g Carbohydrate; 3g Dietary Fiber; 2mg Cholesterol; 146mg Sodium.

Add It: Top these cakes with Fresh Blueberry Sauce (see page 412).

Buckwheat Waffles

Hearty and rib-stickin' good, these waffles are a great way to increase your daily allowance of whole grains and dietary fiber.

$1^1/4$ cups (156.3 g) Hodgson Mill Stone Ground Whole Grain Whole Wheat Graham Flour

$1/2$ cup (62.5 g) Hodgson Mill Stone Ground Whole Grain Buckwheat Flour

$1/4$ cup (35 g) Hodgson Mill Wheat Germ, Untoasted

2 tablespoons (26 g) sugar

2 teaspoons (3 g) baking powder

$1/2$ teaspoon (3 g) salt

3 large eggs, beaten

$1^1/2$ cups (355 ml) 2 percent milk

4 tablespoons ($1/4$ cup [55 g]) melted butter

Vegetable oil, such as canola, for waffle iron

Mix together flours, wheat germ, sugar, baking powder, and salt in large bowl. Stir eggs into flour mixture. Add milk and mix until batter is smooth. Stir in melted butter.

Heat waffle iron according to manufacturer's directions. Oil lightly.

Pour about $1/4$ cup (60 ml) batter at a time onto center of waffle iron. Close and cook until golden brown. Remove with fork. Serve hot with syrup or honey.

Yield: 10 4-inch (10-cm) waffles

Each with: 170 Calories; 7g Fat (37.7% calories from fat); 6g Protein; 21 g Carbohydrate; 3g Dietary Fiber; 71 mg Cholesterol; 286mg Sodium.

Gluten-Free Buttermilk Buckwheat Pancakes

Wake up to a breakfast complete with calcium, protein, and whole grains with this deliciously mellow pancake. Buckwheat is a naturally gluten-free grain, so this is a good choice if you have food intolerances.

1 cup (125 g) Hodgson Mill Stone Ground Whole Grain Buckwheat Flour

2 tablespoons (26 g) sugar

1 teaspoon (1.5 g) gluten-free baking powder

$^1/_2$ teaspoon (3 g) salt

1 teaspoon (1.5 g) baking soda

1 egg, beaten, or equivalent egg substitute

1 cup (235 ml) buttermilk or substitute (see note)

2 tablespoons (28 g) melted butter or (28 ml) vegetable oil

Vegetable oil, such as canola, for griddle

Mix together flour, sugar, baking powder, salt, and baking soda in large bowl. Stir egg into flour mixture. Add buttermilk and mix until batter is smooth. Stir in melted butter.

Heat griddle or large skillet over medium-high heat or to 375°F (190°C). Oil lightly. Griddle is ready when small drops of water sizzle and disappear almost immediately.

Pour $^1/_4$ cup (60 ml) batter at a time onto hot griddle. Cook 1 to $1^1/_2$ minutes, turning when edges look cooked and bubbles begin to break on surface. Continue to cook 1 to $1^1/_2$ minutes or until golden brown.

Yield: 6 pancakes

Each with: 144 Calories; 6g Fat (33.7% calories from fat); 4g Protein; 21 g Carbohydrate; 2g Dietary Fiber; 43mg Cholesterol; 560mg Sodium.

Note: If you don't have buttermilk, substitute by pouring 2 teaspoons (10 ml) vinegar in a 1-cup (235-ml) measure. Fill to top with milk and let sit for 2 minutes, then use in recipe.

 ## *Gingerbread Waffles with Fresh Pear Sauce*

Dark and spicy waffles paired with a fresh pear sauce is a match made in heaven. Make the sauce first, keep it warm, then serve atop the fragrant waffles.

FOR THE FRESH PEAR SAUCE:

1 large, ripe pear, peeled, cored and chopped

$^1/_4$ cup (80 g) honey

2 teaspoons (10 ml) fresh lemon juice

FOR THE WAFFLES:

1 cup (125 g) Hodgson Mill Whole Wheat Gingerbread Mix

1 cup (235 ml) 2 percent milk

2 large eggs

$^1/_4$ cup (60 ml) vegetable oil, such as canola, plus more for waffle iron

For sauce, combine pear, honey, and lemon juice in large saucepan over medium-high heat. Cook, stirring, until pear softens and forms chunky sauce, about 10 minutes. Set aside.

Heat waffle iron according to manufacturer's directions. Oil lightly.

Combine all waffle ingredients in a bowl and mix well.

Pour $^1/_3$ cup (80 ml) batter at a time onto center of hot waffle iron. Bake until steam stops and waffle is golden brown. Remove with fork. Serve hot with warm Fresh Pear Sauce.

Yield: 8 waffles

Each with: 192 Calories; 9g Fat (39.9% calories from fat); 4g Protein; 26g Carbohydrate; 2g Dietary Fiber; 49mg Cholesterol; 160mg Sodium.

 ## *Golden Dipped French Toast*

Now, this is French toast! With a golden dip of whole grain pancake mix, any bread can make this delicious morning feast.

$^3/_4$ cup (93.8 g) Hodgson Mill Whole Wheat Buttermilk Pancake Mix, Whole Grain Buckwheat Pancake Mix, or Multi Grain Pancake Mix

2 large eggs

$^3/_4$ cup (175 ml) 2 percent milk

$^1/_4$ teaspoon (0.7 g) freshly ground nutmeg

$^1/_2$ teaspoon (2.5 ml) vanilla extract

9 slices day-old bread, cut in half diagonally

2 tablespoons (28 g) butter

confectioners' sugar for sprinkling

Heat skillet over medium-high heat or to 375°F (190°C).

Place pancake mix, eggs, milk, nutmeg, and vanilla in bowl. Beat to form smooth batter. Cut bread slice in half diagonally. Dip into batter.

Melt butter in skillet. When butter is sizzling, add French toast and cook until golden brown, turning once. To serve, sprinkle with confectioners' sugar or butter and jelly.

Yield: 6 servings (three $1/2$ slices each)

Each with: 218 Calories; 8g Fat (31.0% calories from fat); 7g Protein; 31 g Carbohydrate; 2g Dietary Fiber; 75mg Cholesterol; 395mg Sodium.

 ## *Insta-Bake Pancakes*

With an easy baking mix containing whole wheat, you can whip up these pancakes in no time.

> Vegetable oil, such as canola, for griddle
>
> 2 cups (250 g) Hodgson Mill Whole Wheat Insta-Bake Mix
>
> 2 large eggs
>
> $1^{1}/4$ cups (295 ml) 2 percent milk
>
> 2 tablespoons (28 ml) vegetable oil, such as canola, plus more for skillet
>
> 2 tablespoons (26 g) sugar, optional

Heat griddle or large skillet over medium-high heat or to 375°F (190°C). Oil lightly. Griddle is ready when small drops of water sizzle and disappear almost immediately.

Combine all ingredients in a mixing bowl until smooth.

Pour $1/4$ cup (60 ml) batter at a time onto hot griddle. Cook until dry around the edges and bubbles begin to break on the surface. Turn once and cook until golden brown.

Yield: 10 to 12 pancakes

Each with: 145 Calories; 5g Fat (29.3% calories from fat); 5g Protein; 21 g Carbohydrate; 2g Dietary Fiber; 40mg Cholesterol; 200mg Sodium.

Note: For thinner pancakes, add milk to batter as needed to thin consistency.

 ## *Insta-Bake Waffles*

By using an easy baking mix that contains whole wheat, you can make homemade waffles in minutes.

> 2 cups (250 g) Hodgson Mill Whole Wheat Insta-Bake Mix
>
> 2 eggs, slightly beaten

1¹/3 cups (315 ml) milk

¹/4 cup (60 ml) vegetable oil, such as canola, plus more for waffle iron

Heat waffle iron according to manufacturer's directions. Oil lightly.

Combine all ingredients in a bowl and mix well.

Pour ¹/3 cup (80 ml) batter at a time onto center of hot waffle iron. Bake until steam stops and waffle is golden brown. Remove with fork. Serve hot.

Yield: 8 waffles

Each with: 205 Calories; 10g Fat (43.3% calories from fat); 6g Protein; 24g Carbohydrate; 2g Dietary Fiber; 52mg Cholesterol; 251 mg Sodium.

Add It: Serve with warm Fresh Pear Sauce (see page 415).

 ## *Gluten-Free Apple Cinnamon Waffles with Milled Flax Seed*

With the omega-3 benefits of flax seed in the mix and the fragrant flavors of apple and cinnamon, these waffles will become family favorites.

2 cups (250 g) Hodgson Mill Whole Grain Apple Cinnamon Muffin Mix with Milled Flax Seed

2 large eggs, slightly beaten or equivalent egg substitute

1¹/3 cups (315 ml) milk

¹/4 cup (60 ml) vegetable oil, such as canola, plus more for waffle iron

Heat waffle iron according to manufacturer's directions. Oil lightly.

Combine all ingredients in bowl and mix well.

Pour ¹/3 cup (80 ml) batter at a time onto center of hot waffle iron. Bake until steam stops and waffle is golden brown. Remove with fork. Serve hot.

Yield: 8 waffles

Each with: 222 Calories; 11g Fat (41.1% calories from fat); 8g Protein; 27g Carbohydrate; 3g Dietary Fiber; 52mg Cholesterol; 114mg Sodium.

Add It: Serve with warm Fresh Pear Sauce (see page 415).

Multi Grain Pancakes and More

These hearty pancakes, with four sources of whole grains plus soy, will really stick with you through the morning. For a real pioneer flavor, use any sourdough starter or 1 cup (235 ml) reserved batter from the Old Fashioned Yeast-Raised Buckwheat Pancake recipe—in place of some or all of the buttermilk—to make these pancakes.

1 cup (125 g) Multi Grain Pancake Mix (recipe follows)
$1^{1}/4$ cup (295 ml) buttermilk or substitute (see note)
2 tablespoons (28 ml) vegetable oil, such as canola
1 large egg, beaten

Heat griddle or large skillet over medium-high heat or to 375°F (190°C). Oil lightly. Griddle is ready when small drops of water sizzle and disappear almost immediately.

Combine all ingredients in a mixing bowl until smooth.

Pour $1/4$ cup (60 ml) batter at a time onto hot griddle. Cook until dry around the edges and bubbles begin to break on the surface. Turn once and cook until golden brown.

Yield: 10 to 12 pancakes

Each with: 87 Calories; 4g Fat (40.1% calories from fat); 3g Protein; 10g Carbohydrate; 1g Dietary Fiber; 20mg Cholesterol; 147mg Sodium.

Note: If you don't have buttermilk, substitute by pouring $1^{1}/2$ teaspoons (7.5 ml) vinegar in a $1^{1}/4$-cup (295-ml) measure. Fill to top with milk and let sit for 2 minutes, then use in recipe.

Multi Grain Pancake Mix

It's easy to make your own whole grain pancake mix to have on hand for busy mornings.

$1^{3}/4$ cups (218.8 g) Hodgson Mill Stone Ground Whole Grain Whole Wheat Graham Flour
1 cup (125 g) Hodgson Mill All-Purpose, Unbleached Naturally White Flour
$3/4$ cup (93.8 g) Hodgson Mill Oat Bran Hot Cereal, uncooked
$1/2$ cup (70 g) Hodgson Mill Stone Ground Whole Grain Yellow Corn Meal, Plain
$1/2$ cup (62.5 g) Hodgson Mill Soy Flour
$1/4$ cup (50 g) sugar or (60 g) packed light or dark brown sugar

2 teaspoons (3 g) baking powder

1¹/2 teaspoons (9 g) salt

1 teaspoon (1.5 g) baking soda

¹/4 cup (37.5 g) finely chopped sunflower kernels or nuts, such as walnuts or pecans, optional

Mix all ingredients together and keep them on hand in an airtight container for up to four weeks.

Yield: 5 cups (625 g) baking mix

Each with: 2224 Calories; 32g Fat (12.1% calories from fat); 93g Protein; 438g Carbohydrate; 72g Dietary Fiber; 0mg Cholesterol; 5442mg Sodium.

 ## *Naturally Gluten-Free Old-Fashioned Yeast-Raised Buckwheat Pancakes*

The flavor develops slowly in these pioneer-style pancakes, so make up the batter and refrigerate overnight. If you wish, keep 1 cup (235 ml) of batter, covered, in the refrigerator for up to 3 days and use this in place of the yeast mixture for the next batch of pancakes.

¹/2 cup (210 ml) warm (105°F to 115°F [40.5°C to 46°C]) water

1 package (⁵/16 ounce) or 2¹/2 teaspoons (10 g) Hodgson Mill Active Dry Yeast

3¹/2 cups (822.5 ml) milk, scalded, and lukewarm (105°F to 115°F [40.5°C to 46°C])

1 teaspoon (4 g) granulated or turbinado sugar

1 teaspoon (6 g) salt

3 cups (375 g) Hodgson Mill Stone Ground Whole Grain Buckwheat Flour

1 tablespoon (20 g) molasses

¹/4 teaspoon (0.4 g) baking soda

1 tablespoon (15 ml) vegetable oil, such as canola, or melted butter

Sprinkle yeast over water and set aside until foamy, about 5 minutes.

Stir yeast mixture, sugar, and salt into lukewarm milk. Stir in flour until smooth. Cover and let stand 30 minutes.

Stir batter again to remove bubbles, then cover and refrigerate overnight. In the morning, if desired, transfer 1 cup (235 ml) batter at a time into a covered container and refrigerate. Let remaining batter warm to room temperature, then stir in molasses, baking soda, and oil. Stir until smooth.

Heat griddle or large skillet over medium-high heat or to 375°F (190°C). Oil lightly. Griddle is ready when small drops of water sizzle and disappear almost immediately.

Pour $^1/4$ cup (60 ml) batter at a time onto hot griddle. Cook until dry around the edges and bubbles begin to break on the surface. Turn once and cook until golden brown.

Yield: 18 pancakes

Each with: 108 Calories; 3g Fat (24.2% calories from fat); 3g Protein; 18g Carbohydrate; 2g Dietary Fiber; 6mg Cholesterol; 160mg Sodium.

Variation: To make pancakes from 1 cup (235 ml) starter stored in the refrigerator, use $3^1/2$ cups (437.5 g) of lukewarm milk (do not scald). Combine sugar, salt, baking soda, and buckwheat flour in bowl; add milk, water, molasses, and the starter to dry ingredients. Stir to form smooth batter. Cook as directed in main recipe.

 Orange Whole Wheat Pancakes

Enjoy your morning orange juice—in a pancake for a change! These are wonderful served with an orange-flavored butter and fresh blueberries.

> 2 large eggs
> $^1/4$ cup (60 ml) vegetable oil, such as canola, plus more for griddle
> 2 cups (250 g) Hodgson Mill Stone Ground Whole Grain Whole Wheat Graham Flour
> 2 teaspoons (3 g) baking soda
> $^1/2$ teaspoon (3 g) salt
> $1^1/2$ cups (355 ml) orange juice

Heat griddle or large skillet over medium-high heat or to 375°F (190°C). Oil lightly. Griddle is ready when small drops of water sizzle and disappear almost immediately.

Beat eggs and oil together. Sift together dry ingredients; add to egg mixture, mixing well. Add orange juice; use more if batter is too stiff. Fry $^1/4$ cup (60 ml) batter at a time on medium-hot griddle until golden brown, turning once.

Yield: 12 pancakes

Each with: 132 Calories; 6g Fat (37.7% calories from fat); 3g Protein; 18g Carbohydrate; 3g Dietary Fiber; 31 mg Cholesterol; 308mg Sodium.

Add It: To make Orange-Flavored Butter, mash $^1/4$ cup ($^1/2$ stick [55 g]) unsalted butter in bowl with 1 teaspoon (1.7 g) freshly grated orange zest; add sugar or honey to taste, if desired.

 ## *Oven-Baked Apple Pecan Pancake*

Add whole grain goodness to this traditional Dutch apple pancake recipe for a delicious flavor and nutrition twist.

$^3/4$ cup (93.8 g) Hodgson Mill Whole Wheat Buttermilk Pancake Mix, Whole Grain Buckwheat Pancake Mix, or Multi Grain Pancake Mix

$^1/2$ cup (120 ml) 2 percent milk

3 large eggs

$^1/3$ cup (66.6 g) sugar

3 large tart cooking apples, such as Granny Smith, peeled, cored, and thinly sliced

4 tablespoons ($^1/4$ cup [55 g]) butter, melted

$^1/2$ cup (75 g) chopped pecans

1 teaspoon (2.3 g) ground cinnamon

Preheat oven to 450°F (230°C).

Combine pancake mix, milk, eggs, and 1 teaspoon (4 g) sugar and mix well. In a 10-inch (25-cm) oven-proof casserole dish, saute apples in melted butter over medium high heat until tender. Remove from heat and sprinkle with nuts. Pour batter evenly over apples and nuts. Combine remaining sugar and cinnamon and sprinkle over batter. Cover skillet with lid or foil.

Bake for 10 to 12 minutes or until pancake is puffed and sugar is melted. Loosen side of pancake from skillet, cool slightly. Cut into wedges and serve with butter and syrup or eat plain.

Yield: 4 servings

Each with: 460 Calories; 26g Fat (48.9% calories from fat); 9g Protein; 53g Carbohydrate; 6g Dietary Fiber; 174mg Cholesterol; 355mg Sodium.

Note: This large pancake can be made ahead and frozen. Thaw before heating or putting in microwave.

Gluten-Free Oven-Baked Apple Pecan Pancake

(See photo on page 250.)

Enjoy a traditional breakfast recipe, but gluten-free.

$3/4$ cup (93.8 g) Hodgson Mill Whole Grain Multi Purpose Baking Mix

$1/4$ cup (60 ml) 2 percent milk or soy milk

$1/4$ cup (60 g) unsweetened applesauce

3 large eggs or equivalent substitute

$1/3$ cup (66.6 g) sugar

3 large tart cooking apples, such as Granny Smith, peeled, cored, and thinly sliced

4 tablespoons ($1/4$ cup [55 g]) butter, melted, or (60 ml) vegetable oil, such as canola

$1/2$ cup (75 g) chopped pecans

1 teaspoon (2.3 g) ground cinnamon

Preheat oven to 450°F (230°C).

Combine mix, milk, applesauce, eggs, and 1 teaspoon (4 g) sugar and mix well. In a 10-inch (25-cm) oven-proof casserole dish, saute apples in melted butter over medium-high heat until tender. Remove from heat and sprinkle with nuts. Pour batter evenly over apples and nuts. Combine remaining sugar and cinnamon and sprinkle over batter. Cover skillet with lid or foil.

Bake for 10 to 12 minutes or until pancake is puffed and sugar is melted. Loosen side of pancake from skillet, cool slightly. Cut into wedges and serve with butter and syrup or eat plain.

Yield: 4 servings

Each with: 466 Calories; 27g Fat (48.7% calories from fat); 9g Protein; 55g Carbohydrate; 7g Dietary Fiber; 172mg Cholesterol; 167mg Sodium.

Note: This large pancake can be made ahead and frozen. Thaw before heating or putting in microwave.

Note: To make this recipe dairy- and egg-free, use soy milk, egg substitute, and vegetable oil.

 ## Spelt Pancakes

Made with an ancient grain, these pancakes have a reddish-brown color and mellow flavor.

2 cups (250 g) Hodgson Mill Organic Whole Grain Spelt Flour

2 tablespoons (9 g) baking powder

$1/2$ teaspoon (3 g) salt

1 large egg

$1^3/4$ cups (410 ml) water

1 teaspoon (5 ml) maple syrup (optional)

3 tablespoons (45 ml) vegetable oil, such as canola, plus more for griddle

Heat griddle or large skillet over medium heat or to 350°F (180°C). Oil lightly.

Mix all ingredients together to form smooth batter.

Pour $1/4$ cup (60 ml) batter at a time onto hot griddle. Cook until dry around the edges and bubbles begin to break on the surface. Turn once and cook until golden brown.

Yield: 12 pancakes

Each with: 95 Calories; 4g Fat (34.8% calories from fat); 4g Protein; 15g Carbohydrate; 3g Dietary Fiber; 16mg Cholesterol; 338mg Sodium.

 ## Sweet Orange Rye Pancakes

These pancakes, with the fresh flavor of orange, are a tasty change from buttermilk.

$3/4$ cup (93.8 g) Hodgson Mill All-Purpose, Unbleached Naturally White Flour

$1/2$ cup (62.5 g) Hodgson Mill Stone Ground Whole Grain Rye Flour

$2^1/2$ teaspoons (3.8 g) baking powder

2 to 3 tablespoons (26 to 39 g) sugar or to taste

$3/4$ teaspoon (4.5 g) salt

2 teaspoons (3.4 g) freshly grated orange zest

1 large egg

$1^1/4$ cups (295 ml) 2 percent milk

1 tablespoon (14 g) melted butter, or (15 ml) vegetable oil, such as canola, plus more for griddle

Heat griddle or large skillet over medium heat or to 350°F (180°C). Oil lightly.

Mix all ingredients together to form smooth batter.

Pour $1/4$ cup (60 ml) batter at a time onto hot griddle. Cook until dry around the edges and bubbles begin to break on the surface. Turn once and cook until golden brown.

Yield: 12 pancakes

Each with: 75 Calories; 2g Fat (22.2% calories from fat); 3g Protein; 13g Carbohydrate; 1g Dietary Fiber; 20mg Cholesterol; 262mg Sodium.

 ## *Whole Grain Waffles*

Hearty and substantial, these whole grain waffles will see you through the morning.

$1^1/4$ cups (156.3 g) Hodgson Mill Stone Ground Whole Grain Whole Wheat Graham Flour

1 cup (140 g) Hodgson Mill Stone Ground Whole Grain Yellow Corn Meal, Plain

$1/2$ cup (62.5 g) Hodgson Mill Oat Bran Hot Cereal, uncooked

1 package ($5/16$ ounce) or $2^1/2$ teaspoons (10 g) Hodgson Mill Active Dry Yeast

$1/2$ teaspoon (3 g) salt

$1^3/4$ cups (410 ml) 2 percent milk

2 large eggs

$1/3$ cup (80 ml) vegetable oil, such as canola

1 teaspoon (5 ml) vanilla extract, or to taste

Combine flour, corn meal, oat bran, yeast, and salt in large bowl. Add milk, eggs, oil, and vanilla. Beat with rotary beater or electric mixer on medium speed for 1 minute or until batter is thoroughly combined. Cover batter loosely and refrigerate for 2 to 24 hours or until mixture is bubbly and slightly thickened. Or, to make waffles without chilling overnight, cover and let mixture stand for 1 hour at room temperature or till bubbly and slightly thickened.

Before using, allow refrigerated batter to stand at room temperature for 1 hour.

Heat waffle iron according to manufacturer's directions. Oil lightly.

Stir batter. Pour $1/3$ cup (80 ml) batter onto waffle iron. Close lid. Cook until steaming stops and waffles are crisp. Remove with fork. Serve hot immediately with fruit syrup or another syrup.

Yield: 12 waffles

Each with: 181 Calories; 9g Fat (40.5% calories from fat); 6g Protein; 22g Carbohydrate; 4g Dietary Fiber; 34mg Cholesterol; 116mg Sodium.

Whole Wheat Pastry Flour Pancakes

With finely ground pastry flour, these pancakes have whole wheat goodness with a finer texture than those made with regular whole wheat flour.

> 1 cup (235 ml) buttermilk or substitute (see note)
>
> 1 teaspoon (1.5 g) baking soda
>
> 2 cups (250 g) Hodgson Mill Whole Grain Whole Wheat Pastry Flour
>
> 1 large egg, beaten
>
> 1/4 cup plus 2 tablespoons (120 g) molasses
>
> Vegetable oil, such as canola, for griddle

Dissolve baking soda in buttermilk in large bowl. Mix in flour, egg, and molasses until just combined. Add additional milk, 1 tablespoon (15 ml) at a time, if batter is too thick to pour.

Heat griddle or large skillet over medium heat or to 350°F (180°C). Oil lightly.

Pour 1/4 cup (60 ml) batter at a time onto hot griddle. Cook until dry around the edges and bubbles begin to break on the surface. Turn once and cook until golden brown. Serve with hot maple syrup.

Yield: 16 pancakes

Each with: 81 Calories; 1 g Fat (7.2% calories from fat); 2g Protein; 17g Carbohydrate; 2g Dietary Fiber; 12mg Cholesterol; 101mg Sodium.

Note: If you don't have buttermilk, substitute by pouring 2 teaspoons (10 ml) vinegar in a 1-cup (235-ml) measure. Fill to top with milk and let sit for 2 minutes, then use in recipe.

Whole Wheat and Wheat Germ Waffles

Rev up the nutrition—and nutty flavor—in traditional waffles by using whole wheat graham flour and wheat germ, as in this recipe.

1 cup (125 g) Hodgson Mill Stone Ground Whole Grain Whole Wheat Graham Flour

1/4 cup (31.3 g) Hodgson Mill Wheat Germ, Untoasted

2 teaspoons (3 g) baking soda

2 tablespoons (28 ml) vegetable oil, such as canola, plus more for waffle iron

1 1/2 cups (355 ml) buttermilk or substitute (see note)

1 egg, beaten

Combine dry ingredients in a medium-size bowl. Blend oil, buttermilk, and egg together in a small bowl. Add to dry ingredients. Mix until combined. Do not beat.

Heat waffle iron according to manufacturer's directions. Oil lightly.

Pour 1/3 cup (80 ml) batter onto waffle iron. Close lid. Cook until steaming stops and waffles are crisp. Remove with fork. Serve with applesauce or fresh fruit topping.

Yield: 3 to 4 waffles

Each with: 322 Calories; 13g Fat (35.7% calories from fat); 13g Protein; 40g Carbohydrate; 8g Dietary Fiber; 67mg Cholesterol; 986mg Sodium.

Note: If you don't have buttermilk, substitute by pouring 1 tablespoon (15 ml) vinegar in a 1 1/2-cup (355-ml) measure. Fill to top with milk and let sit for 2 minutes, then use in recipe.

 *Whole Wheat Waffles*

Beaten egg whites make these whole wheat waffles extra fluffy and tender.

  2 large egg yolks

  1 cup (235 ml) 2 percent milk

  $^1/_4$ cup (60 ml) vegetable oil, such as canola, plus more for griddle

  $^3/_4$ teaspoon (4.5 g) salt

  2 teaspoons (3 g) baking soda

  1$^1/_3$ cups (315 ml) Hodgson Mill Stone Ground Whole Grain Whole Wheat
    Graham Flour

  2 large egg whites, stiffly beaten

  2 tablespoons (9 g) baking powder

Heat waffle iron according to manufacturer's directions. Oil lightly.

Beat egg yolks well; add milk and oil. Combine salt, baking soda, and flour. Add to egg yolk mixture. Beat until smooth. Fold in stiffly beaten egg whites. Sift baking powder lightly over the mixture and fold in quickly.

Pour $^1/_3$ cup (80 ml) batter onto waffle iron. Close lid. Cook until steaming stops and waffles are crisp. Remove with fork. Serve with applesauce or fresh fruit topping.

Yield: 3 to 4 waffles

Each with: 434 Calories; 24g Fat (48.3% calories from fat); 12g Protein; 46g Carbohydrate; 7g Dietary Fiber; 148mg Cholesterol; 2429mg Sodium.

11

Sweet and Savory
Tarts and Turnovers

Tarts and turnovers, both sweet and savory, are even better when made with whole grains—think enhanced texture, nuttier flavor, and healthier nutritional profile. Pizzas—from breakfast to dessert and everything else in between— also taste great when made with whole grain dough.

Tarts, turnovers, and pizza can be leavened with yeast or baking powder (for a bread-like crust) or not leavened at all for a pastry-like crust. After a yeast-leavened dough has risen, you can just pat or roll it out to make a tart, pizza crust, or individual filled "pockets."

Pastry dough, however, is a little trickier. Keep these three important tips in mind when working with pastry dough. First, add as little water as possible when making the dough. You should be able to gather the dough into a ball using your hands, but the dough should not be sticky. Second, let the dough chill for 30 minutes before rolling it out, and try rolling the dough between two sheets of parchment or wax paper. And third, always use light strokes to roll the dough from center of the circle outward, like the spoke of a wheel.

If you're making a tart, just transfer the pastry dough to the pan. Loosely fit the pastry onto the bottom and up the sides of the pan, then use your rolling pin to roll off extra pastry from the fluted edge of the pan. For a pie, fit the pastry into the pan, but leave 1 inch (2.5 cm) of dough around the edge of the pie pan. Fold this extra dough under and pinch or flute it to create a decorative edge.

Savory Sweet Potato, Apple, and Red Onion Galette

A galette is a free-form tart with a wonderful, rustic appearance. You simply make the dough, roll it into a circle, place the filling in the center, and fold the edges of the dough over to partially enclose the filling.

FOR THE DOUGH:

 1¼ cups (156.3 g) Hodgson Mill Stone Ground Whole Grain White Whole
    Wheat Flour

 ½ teaspoon (3 g) salt

 ½ cup (1 stick [112 g]) butter, cut into small pieces

 1 large egg, beaten

FOR THE FILLING:

 1 large Granny Smith apple, peeled, cored, and sliced

 1 can (15 ounces [420 g]) sweet potatoes, drained and patted dry

 1 medium red or Spanish onion, peeled and cut into 8 wedges

 1 teaspoon (1.2 g) dried rosemary

 3 tablespoons (45 ml) olive oil

 Salt and pepper to taste

Combine flour and salt in bowl. Cut butter into flour using pastry blender or 2 knives until mixture resembles coarse crumbs. Stir in egg until mixture forms stiff dough. Add 1 tablespoon (15 ml) water, if necessary. Form dough into ball, cover with plastic wrap, and refrigerate for 30 minutes.

Preheat oven to 400°F (200°C). Line baking sheet with parchment paper.

For filling, combine apple, vegetables, and rosemary in large bowl. Drizzle with olive oil, season to taste with salt and pepper, and toss to coat.

Transfer dough to floured surface. Pat or roll dough to 12-inch (30-cm) circle. Transfer to baking sheet. Arrange filling in center of dough, leaving 2-inch (5-cm) perimeter. Fold and pleat edges of dough over, but do not enclose filling.

Bake 45 to 50 minutes or until crust and vegetables have browned. Cut into wedges to serve.

Yield: 6 servings

Each with: 370 Calories; 23g Fat (55.6% calories from fat); 5g Protein; 37g Carbohydrate; 5g Dietary Fiber; 73mg Cholesterol; 372mg Sodium.

Add It: During last 5 minutes of baking, sprinkle ¹/₂ cup (25 g) shredded Parmesan or Asiago cheese over tart and continue baking until melted.

 Sweet Stone Fruit Galette (See photo on page 251.)

Use your favorite stone fruit—peaches, plums, or nectarines—for this sweet version of a galette, or free-form tart.

FOR THE DOUGH:

1¹/₄ cups (156.3 g) Hodgson Mill Stone Ground Whole Grain White Whole Wheat Flour

2 teaspoons (8 g) sugar

¹/₂ teaspoon (3 g) salt

¹/₂ cup (1 stick [112 g]) butter, cut into small pieces

1 large egg, beaten

1 tablespoon (15 ml) ice water, or less, as needed

FOR THE FILLING:

3 cups (675 g) peeled and pitted peaches, nectarines, or plums (or a mix of each), fresh or unsweetened frozen

1 teaspoon (2.3 g) ground cinnamon

1 tablespoon (13 g) sugar

3 tablespoons (42 g) melted butter

Combine flour, sugar, and salt in bowl. Cut butter into flour using pastry blender or 2 knives until mixture resembles coarse crumbs. Stir in egg until mixture forms stiff dough. Add 1 tablespoon (15 ml) water, if necessary. Form dough into ball, cover with plastic wrap, and refrigerate for 30 minutes.

Preheat oven to 400°F (200°C). Line baking sheet with parchment paper.

For filling, combine fruit, cinnamon, and sugar in large bowl. Drizzle with melted butter.

Transfer dough to floured surface. Pat or roll dough to 12-inch (30-cm) circle. Transfer to baking sheet. Arrange filling in center of dough, leaving 2-inch (5-cm) perimeter. Fold and pleat edges of dough over, but do not enclose filling.

Bake 45 to 50 minutes or until crust and fruits have browned. Cut into wedges to serve.

Yield: 6 servings

Each with: 332 Calories; 22g Fat (58.3% calories from fat); 5g Protein; 31 g Carbohydrate; 4g Dietary Fiber; 88mg Cholesterol; 402mg Sodium.

Note: If frozen, unsweetened fruit or very juicy fresh fruit is used, add 1 to 2 tablespoons (8 g to 16 g) Hodgson Mill Pure Corn Starch to fruit mixture to prevent juice from running out of crust.

Add It: Serve warm with vanilla ice cream.

 ## Reuben Rye Pockets

These savory sandwiches are great to take on a tailgating weekend, on a hike, or to make for a weeknight dinner with the help of an automatic bread machine. Set your machine so that the dough is ready when you get home from work, then make the pockets and bake.

FOR THE DOUGH:

1 package (16 ounces [448 g]) Hodgson Mill Caraway Rye Bread Mix

1 cup (230 g) plain yogurt or sour cream (light or regular)

1 cup (235 ml) warm (105°F to 115°F [40.5°C to 46°C]) water

Yeast packet from bread mix

Hodgson Mill All-Purpose, Unbleached Naturally White Flour for dusting

FOR THE FILLING:

^{1}/2 cup (112.5 g) sauerkraut (fresh or in glass jar), drained

^{1}/2 cup (112.5 g) finely chopped corned beef

^{1}/2 cup (55 g) shredded Swiss cheese

2 tablespoons (28 ml) bottled Thousand Island dressing

For dough, place mix, yogurt, water, and yeast packet in bread pan of automatic bread machine in order listed, set on dough cycle, and start machine. To make by hand, blend bread mix and yeast together in large bowl. Stir in yogurt and water to form soft dough. Cover and let rise at room temperature until about doubled in bulk, about 2 hours.

For filling, combine sauerkraut, corned beef, Swiss cheese, and dressing in bowl.

Line baking sheet with parchment paper. Sprinkle flat surface with all-purpose flour. Turn out dough onto floured surface and cut into 12 pieces. Flour rolling pin and roll out each piece to 6-inch (15-cm) circle. Put 2 tablespoons (28 g) filling in center of dough circle, moisten perimeter of dough circle with water, then fold over to make half moon, pressing edges closed. Place on prepared baking sheet. Cover and let rise for 1 hour.

Preheat oven to 350°F (180°C). Bake rolls 20 to 25 minutes or until risen and browned.

Yield: 12 pockets

Each with: 188 Calories; 5g Fat (24.8% calories from fat); 10g Protein; 27g Carbohydrate; 4g Dietary Fiber; 13mg Cholesterol; 335mg Sodium.

Add It: Brush dough pockets with milk, then sprinkle with coarse salt before baking.

Variation: To make Ham, Cheddar, and Broccoli Pockets: Substitute packaged broccoli slaw for sauerkraut, ham for corned beef, Cheddar for Swiss cheese, and Dijon mustard for Thousand Island dressing.

 ## *Wheat Country Bierocks*

Bierocks are traditional rich bread dough "turnovers" that enclose a savory beef, onion, and cabbage filling. Originally meant as "on-the-go" food for farmers harvesting wheat, they're just as great today as sandwich alternatives. Make the dough in the bread machine for a modern update on an old Russian Mennonite recipe.

FOR THE DOUGH:

$1^1/2$ cups (355 ml) warm (105°F to 115°F [40.5°C to 46°C]) water

$1/2$ cup (65 g) nonfat dry milk

$1/2$ cup (1 stick [112 g]) butter, softened

$1/3$ cup (66.6 g) sugar

$1/2$ teaspoon (3 g) salt

2 large eggs

1 cup (125 g) Hodgson Mill White Whole Wheat or 50/50 Flour

3 cups (375 g) Hodgson Mill All-Purpose, Unbleached Naturally White Flour

1 package ($^5/16$ ounce) package or $2^1/2$ teaspoons (10 g) Hodgson Mill Fast-Rise Yeast

FOR THE FILLING:

> 1 pound (455 g) ground beef
>
> 2 cups (140 g) shredded cabbage
>
> 1 large onion, peeled and chopped
>
> Salt and pepper to taste

Place dough ingredients in pan of bread machine according to manufacturer's directions. Set on dough cycle.

To make filling: brown ground beef over medium-high heat in large skillet. Add cabbage and onion and cook, stirring, until cabbage has wilted and onion is transparent, about 7 minutes. Season to taste.

Preheat oven to 350°F (180°C). Line 2 baking sheets with parchment paper.

Turn dough out onto floured surface. Divide dough into 4 portions. Divide each portion into 6 pieces. Form each piece into a ball. Flatten each ball into 6-inch (15-cm) diameter circle. Spoon $1/3$ cup filling into center of each circle. Fold edges up to meet and pinch closed. Place each bierock seam-side down on prepared baking sheet.

Bake 15 to 18 minutes or until puffed and golden brown. Transfer to wire rack to cool. Serve hot or room temperature.

Yield: 24 bierocks

Each with: 189 Calories; 9g Fat (43.8% calories from fat); 7g Protein; 20g Carbohydrate; 1g Dietary Fiber; 43mg Cholesterol; 116mg Sodium.

 Gluten-Free Bierocks

Made with a combination of soy, garbanzo bean (chickpea), and millet in the baking mix along with brown rice flour and potato and corn starch, this dough rises and tastes like wheat bread. In this recipe, we use it to enclose a savory beef, onion, and cabbage filling. Because the dough is batter-like, use muffin cups to make the "turnovers."

FOR THE DOUGH:

> 3 large eggs or equivalent egg substitute
>
> 1 teaspoon (5 ml) cider vinegar

Yield: 8 servings

Each with: 460 Calories; 23g Fat (44.0% calories from fat); 21 g Protein; 45g Carbohydrate; 3g Dietary Fiber; 169mg Cholesterol; 877mg Sodium.

Variation: Try canned black beans, cooked taco-style ground beef, cooked chorizo sausage, or grilled vegetables instead of scrambled eggs.

 ## *Mexican-Style Jalapeno Cornbread Tartlets*

Watch these miniature tarts disappear when you serve them as appetizers! They pack in all the great Southwest flavors with the goodness of whole grains.

1 box (16 ounces [448 g]) Hodson Mill Whole Grain Jalapeno Cornbread Mix
$1^3/4$ cups (410 ml) 2 percent milk
3 large eggs
$1/3$ cup (80 ml) vegetable oil

FOR THE TOPPING:

1 cup (225 g) chunky salsa
1 cup (200 g) grilled chicken, cut into bite-size pieces
1 cup (230 g) sour cream, regular or light
$1/2$ cup (30 g) chopped fresh cilantro

Preheat oven to 400°F (200°C). Line large baking sheet with parchment paper.

Pour mix into bowl. Add milk, eggs, and oil and stir together for 1 minute.

Pour batter into prepared pan and spread to rectangle measuring 12 x 16 inches (30 x 40 cm).

Bake 10 minutes or until firm to touch in center. Let cool in pan.

Cut out tartlets with 2-inch (5-cm) biscuit cutter. Top each tartlet with a spoonful of salsa, a piece of chicken, a dollop of sour cream, and a sprinkling of cilantro.

Yield: 20 servings

Each with: 169 Calories; 8g Fat (40.8% calories from fat); 7g Protein; 18g Carbohydrate; 1g Dietary Fiber; 41 mg Cholesterol; 321mg Sodium.

Variation: Try canned black beans, cooked taco-style ground beef, cooked chorizo sausage, or grilled vegetables instead of chicken.

Sauerkraut and Sausage Tart in a Caraway Rye Crust

For a casual supper or a game-time snack, this savory German-style "pizza" satisfies hearty appetites. If you like, prepare the dough a day ahead of time and keep, covered, in an oiled bowl in the refrigerator.

FOR THE DOUGH:

$^1/_2$ cup (120 ml) 2 percent milk

$1^1/_2$ cups (355 ml) warm (105°F to 115°F [40.5°C to 46°C]) water

$1^1/_2$ tablespoons (21 g) butter

1 tablespoon plus 2 teaspoons (21 g) sugar

1 package ($^5/_{16}$ ounce) or $2^1/_2$ teaspoons (10 g) Hodgson Mill Active Dry Yeast

2 cups (250 g) Hodgson Mill Stone Ground Whole Grain Rye Flour or Organic Stone Ground Whole Grain Rye Flour

2 cups (250 g) Hodgson Mill All-Purpose, Unbleached Naturally White Flour Unbleached, plus more for kneading

$2^1/_2$ teaspoons (15 g) salt

3 tablespoons (20 g) caraway seeds

FOR THE TOPPING:

$^1/_2$ cup (125 g) Dijon mustard

2 cups (450 g) sauerkraut (in a jar), drained and patted dry

1 pound (455 g) cooked bratwurst, smoked sausage, or ham, cut into bite-size pieces

$^1/_2$ cup (80 g) chopped green onion

2 cups (160 g) grated Swiss or Gruyere cheese

For the dough, place milk, 1 cup (235 ml) of water, butter, and 1 tablespoon (13 g) of sugar in a saucepan over medium-high heat and scald until bubbles form around the perimeter. Let cool slightly.

Pour remaining $^1/_2$ cup (120 ml) water in small bowl, stir in the remaining 2 teaspoons (8 g) sugar, and sprinkle yeast over mixture. Let stand until foamy, about 5 minutes.

Combine flours, salt, and caraway seeds together in a large bowl. Stir in milk mixture, then yeast mixture, to form stiff dough. (Add more water if necessary.) Knead several times in bowl. Cover and let rise in warm place until doubled in bulk, about 1 to 1¹/2 hours.

Preheat oven to 350°F (180°C). Lightly oil large baking sheet or round pizza pan.

Punch down dough and turn out onto floured surface. Press or roll out to 10-inch (25-cm) circle and place in prepared pan. Spread surface with mustard, then sauerkraut. Dot with sausage and green onion and sprinkle with cheese.

Bake 15 to 20 minutes or until cheese has melted. Cut into wedges to serve.

Yield: 8 servings

Each with: 541 Calories; 27g Fat (42.9% calories from fat); 25g Protein; 56g Carbohydrate; 9g Dietary Fiber; 67mg Cholesterol; 1666mg Sodium.

 ## *Gluten-Free Apple Cinnamon Breakfast Pizza*

Rise and shine to a gluten-free breakfast.

  1 box (10 ounces [283.5 g]) Hodgson Mill Whole Grain Apple Cinnamon Muffin Mix with Milled Flax Seed
  1 tablespoon (15 ml) vegetable oil, such as canola
  1 cup plus 2 tablespoons (263 ml) 2 percent milk or soy milk
  1 large egg or equivalent egg substitute

FOR THE TOPPING:

  3 cartons (6 ounces [168 g] each) plain or vanilla yogurt or soy-based yogurt
  2 large bananas, peeled and sliced
  1 cup (145 g) blueberries

Preheat oven to 400°F (200°C). Line large baking sheet with parchment paper.

Pour mix in bowl. Stir in oil, milk, and egg. Let rest for 10 minutes.

Spoon batter into middle of baking sheet and spread to 10-inch (25-cm) circle.

Bake 10 minutes or until firm to the touch. Spread yogurt over pizza, top with banana slices, and sprinkle with blueberries. Cut into 12 wedges with pizza cutter or sharp knife and serve.

Yield: 12 servings

Note: The breakfast pizza will spread to 11-inch (27.5-cm) diameter when it bakes.

Variation: Use whatever flavor yogurt (banana, apple, blueberry) or variety of fruit (finely chopped apple or pear) your family likes.

Blueberry Whole Wheat Breakfast Pizza

Fragrant with blueberries and cinnamon yet fortified with whole wheat, this breakfast pizza makes a healthy and delicious breakfast for kids.

1 box (10 ounces [283.5 g]) Hodgson Mill Whole Wheat Wild Blueberry Muffin Mix with Milled Flax Seed

1 tablespoon (15 ml) vegetable oil

1 cup plus 2 tablespoons (263 ml) 2 percent milk

1 large egg

FOR THE TOPPING:

3 cartons (6 ounces [168 g] each) vanilla yogurt

2 large bananas, peeled and sliced

1 cup (145 g) blueberries

Preheat oven to 400°F (200°C). Line large baking sheet (with sides) with parchment paper.

Pour mix in bowl. Stir in oil, milk, and egg. Let rest for 10 minutes.

Spoon batter into middle of baking sheet and spread to 10-inch (25-cm) circle.

Bake 10 minutes or until firm to the touch. Spread yogurt over pizza, top with banana slices, and sprinkle with blueberries. Cut into 12 wedges with pizza cutter or sharp knife and serve.

Yield: 12 servings

Note: The breakfast pizza will spread to 11-inch (27.5-cm) diameter when it bakes.

Variation: For the crust, use Hodgson Mill Bran or Whole Wheat Muffin Mix instead of Whole Wheat Wild Blueberry. Use whatever flavor yogurt (banana, apple, blueberry) or variety of fruit (finely chopped apple or pear) your family likes.

 ## *Brownie Dessert Pizza* (See photo on page 252.)

A dessert like this one can be good for you and taste great, too. Chocoholics will definitely approve.

> 1 box (12 ounces [336 g]) Hodgson Mill Whole Wheat Brownie Mix
>   with Milled Flax Seed
> $^1/_4$ cup (60 ml) vegetable oil, such as canola
> 4 tablespoons ($^1/_2$ stick [55 g]) butter or margarine, melted
> 2 large eggs
> 2 tablespoons (28 ml) water

FOR THE TOPPING:

> 1 cup (320 g) seedless raspberry jam, preserves or fruit spread
> 2 cups (220 g) fresh raspberries
> Whipped cream to garnish

Preheat oven to 350°F (180°C). Line a large baking sheet with parchment paper.

Pour mix into bowl. Stir in oil, butter, eggs, and water until smooth.

Spoon batter into middle of baking sheet and spread into 10-inch (25-cm) circle.

Bake 17 minutes or until toothpick inserted in center comes out clean. Let cool 5 minutes.

Spread raspberry jam over warm crust. Scatter fresh berries. Cut into 12 wedges with pizza cutter or sharp knife and serve. Serve each slice with a dollop of whipped cream.

Yield: 12 servings

Each with: 260 Calories; 10g Fat (31.7% calories from fat); 4g Protein; 43g Carbohydrate; 3g Dietary Fiber; 42mg Cholesterol; 126mg Sodium.

Note: The brownie pizza will spread to an 11-inch (27.5-cm) diameter when it bakes.

Variation: Instead of the raspberry jam, frost with a thin layer of Cream Cheese Frosting: Beat together 1 (8-ounce [230 g]) package Neufchâtel cheese and 2 tablespoons (28 g) softened butter until creamy. Beat in 1 cup (100 g) confectioners' sugar and 1 teaspoon (5 ml) vanilla. Spread the frosting over the top of the cooled pizza, and then arrange the berries on top.

 ## *Gingerbread Dessert Pizza*

This dark, spicy "pizza" also tastes wonderful with apple or pumpkin butter and whipped cream.

> 1 box (15 ounces [420 g]) Hodgson Mill Whole Wheat Gingerbread Mix
>
> 4 tablespoons (^{1}/2 stick [55 g]) butter or margarine, melted
>
> 2 large egg whites
>
> 1 cup (235 ml) 2 percent milk

FOR THE TOPPING:

> 1 package (8 ounces [230 g]) Neufchâtel cheese
>
> 2 tablespoons (28 g) softened butter
>
> 1 cup (100 g) confectioners' sugar
>
> 1 teaspoon (5 ml) vanilla
>
> 2 cups (300 g) finely sliced fresh apple or pear

Preheat oven to 350°F (180°C). Line a large baking sheet with parchment paper.

Pour mix into bowl. Stir in butter, egg whites, and milk until smooth.

Spoon batter into middle of baking sheet and spread into 10-inch (25-cm) circle.

Bake 15 to 17 minutes or until toothpick inserted in center comes out clean. Let cool.

For topping, beat together Neufchâtel cheese and butter until creamy. Beat in confectioners' sugar and vanilla until smooth. Spread over top of cooled pizza. Scatter fresh fruit on top. Cut into 12 wedges with pizza cutter or sharp knife and serve.

Yield: 12 servings

Each with: 294 Calories; 11g Fat (33.1% calories from fat); 6g Protein; 43g Carbohydrate; 3g Dietary Fiber; 31 mg Cholesterol; 461mg Sodium.

Note: The gingerbread pizza will spread to an 11-inch (27.5-cm) diameter when it bakes.

Nacho-Style Pizza

Rethink taco night by serving this fiber-rich "pizza" with all of your favorite nacho ingredients.

1 box (7^1/2 ounces [210 g]) Hodgson Mill Whole Grain Cornbread Muffin Mix

1 tablespoon (15 ml) vegetable oil

^{3}/4 cup (175 ml) 2 percent milk

1 large egg

FOR THE TOPPINGS:

1 cup (224 g) black beans or refried beans

1 cup (200 g) grilled chicken, cut into strips

^{3}/4 cup (60 g) finely chopped canned jalapeno pepper

1 cup (180 g) finely chopped tomato

^{3}/4 cup (40 g) finely chopped onion

^{3}/4 cup (30 g) finely chopped fresh cilantro

Preheat oven to 400°F (200°C). Line a large baking sheet with parchment paper.

Pour mix into bowl. Stir in oil, milk, and egg until smooth.

Spoon batter into middle of baking sheet and spread into 10-inch (25-cm) circle.

Bake 10 minutes or until lightly browned. Let cool 5 minutes.

Spread black beans and chicken pieces over pizza. Sprinkle on jalapeno pepper, tomato, onion, and cilantro. Dot spoonfuls of sour cream over pizza. Cut into 12 wedges with pizza cutter or sharp knife and serve.

Yield: 12 servings

Each with: 171 Calories; 3g Fat (15.2% calories from fat); 10g Protein; 26g Carbohydrate; 4g Dietary Fiber; 27mg Cholesterol; 142mg Sodium.

Note: The nacho pizza will spread to an 11-inch (27.5-cm) diameter when it bakes.

Variation: Add other Mexican-inspired toppings as desired, such as guacamole, shredded cheese, or shredded pork.

Gluten-Free Pat-in-the-Pan Pastry

This single-crust, pat-in-the-pan pastry is a great base for pumpkin, sweet potato, custard, chocolate, banana cream, or maple walnut pies—and cheesecakes, too.

$^1/_2$ cup (62.5 g) Hodgson Mill Whole Grain Apple Cinnamon Muffin Mix with Milled Flax Seed

$^1/_2$ cup (75 g) hazelnuts, pecans, or almonds (or use $^1/_4$ cup [31.3 g]) more of muffin mix)

$^1/_2$ cup (115 g) packed light or dark brown sugar

4 tablespoons ($^1/_2$ stick [55 g]) butter or margarine, softened

Preheat oven to 350°F (180°C).

Combine mix, nuts, and brown sugar in bowl. Blend with butter (Note: The mix will have small pieces of dried apple). Press into bottom and up sides of 8- or 9-inch (20- or 22.5-cm) pie pan.

To blind bake pie shell, carefully line pie plate with parchment paper and fill with pie weights or baking beans. Bake for 10 minutes, or until golden brown. Let cool. Carefully remove paper and weights.

Yield: 1 single-crust pie shell

Each with: 1503 Calories; 93g Fat (52.7% calories from fat); 20g Protein; 168g Carbohydrate; 10g Dietary Fiber; 124mg Cholesterol; 673mg Sodium.

Add It: For a Gluten-Free Pumpkin Pie, prepare unbaked pie shell. Mix together 1 (8-ounce [230-g]) package cream cheese or silken tofu, $^1/_2$ cup (100 g) sugar, one 15-ounce [420-g] can of pumpkin puree, 2 eggs or equivalent egg substitute, and 1 teaspoon (2.3 g) pumpkin pie spice. Pour into shell and bake for 1 hour or until knife inserted near center comes out clean. (To make this recipe dairy- and egg-free, use vegetable shortening, silken tofu, and egg substitute.)

 ## *Spelt Pastry*

Colored a "burnt Sienna" from the crayon box, this pastry makes a beautiful counterpoint to golden fillings such as squash, sweet potato, or pumpkin. If you wish, freeze the other pastry half for up to 3 months to use at a later date.

2 cups (250 g) Hodgson Mill Organic Whole Grain Spelt Flour

1 teaspoon (6 g) salt

$^1/_2$ cup (1 stick [112 g]) butter

6 tablespoons (90 ml) cold water

Sift flour and salt into bowl. Cut in butter with a pastry blender or 2 knives until mixture resembles coarse crumbs. Sprinkle water, 1 tablespoon (15 ml) at a time, over the mixture, stirring with fork until dough forms a ball. Cover with plastic wrap and refrigerate for 30 minutes.

Roll out dough between two sheets of parchment or wax paper.

Yield: 1 single-crust pastry

Each with: 1493 Calories; 100g Fat (51.8% calories from fat); 41 g Protein; 168g Carbohydrate; 40g Dietary Fiber; 248mg Cholesterol; 3071 mg Sodium.

Note: This dough rolls better if chilled.

Add It: For Fruit Turnovers, prepare 1 recipe pastry dough. Preheat oven to 350°F (180°C). For filling, place $^1/_4$ cup (75 g) chopped and peeled apple, peach, plum, or nectarine in bowl. In small bowl, combine 1$^1/_2$ teaspoons (6 g) sugar, $^1/_4$ teaspoon (0.6 g) ground cinnamon, and $^1/_4$ teaspoon (0.6 g) Hodgson Mill Pure Corn Starch or instant tapioca. Roll pastry and cut 4 (3-inch [7.5-cm]) circles. Place 1 tablespoon (15 g) filling in center of each circle. Moisten dough perimeter with water, fold dough over to form half moon, and press edges to seal. Place on baking sheet lined with parchment paper. Bake 15 to 20 minutes or until lightly brown and filling is bubbling.

 ## *Whole Wheat Pastry*

Hodgson Mill Whole Wheat Pastry Flour is a finer grind of whole wheat flour and makes a flakier pie crust. Graham flour is more coarsely ground but will also make a nice crust with more texture.

1$^1/_2$ cups (187.5 g) Hodgson Mill Whole Grain Whole Wheat Pastry Flour, Stone Ground Whole Grain Whole Wheat Graham Flour, or Stone Ground Whole Grain White Whole Wheat Flour

$^1/_2$ teaspoon (3 g) salt

$^1/_2$ cup (1 stick [112 g]) chilled butter, cut into pieces

4 tablespoons (60 ml) cold water

Sift together flour and salt. Cut in butter with pastry blender or fork until pieces resemble small peas. Sprinkle 1 tablespoon (15 ml) water over mixture. Gently toss with fork, and then push to one side of bowl. Sprinkle next tablespoon of water over dry portion and mix lightly; put to moistened part at side. Repeat until all mixture is moistened and dough forms a ball. Cover with plastic wrap and refrigerate for 30 minutes.

On lightly floured surface (or between 2 pieces of parchment or wax paper), roll out pastry to $^1/_8$-inch (0.3-cm) thickness.

Yield: 1 single-crust pastry

Each with: 1413 Calories; 95g Fat (58.6% calories from fat); 19g Protein; 132g Carbohydrate; 24g Dietary Fiber; 248mg Cholesterol; 2004mg Sodium.

Note: To make pastry extra tender and flaky, divide butter in half. Cut in first half until mixture looks like corn meal. Then cut in remaining half until pieces look like small peas.

Add It: For a Lemon Tart, prepare 1 recipe single crust pastry and line 9- or 10-inch (22.5- or 25-cm) tart pan. Carefully line tart with parchment paper and fill with pie weights or baking beans. Bake at 350°F (180°C) for 15 minutes, or until golden brown. Let cool. Carefully remove paper and weights. Spoon 2 cups (480 g) prepared lemon curd into tart shell and smooth top. Refrigerate for 2 hours or until completely chilled. Garnish with fresh berries and whipped cream and serve.

 ## Insta-Bake Pastry

Insta-Bake is easy to work with and gives pastry a delicious, mellow flavor.

    1 cup (125 g) Hodgson Mill Whole Wheat Insta-Bake Mix
    $^1/_3$ cup (75 g) chilled butter, cut into pieces
    $^1/_4$ cup (60 ml) cold water

Place mix in bowl. Cut in butter with pastry blender or 2 knives until crumbly. Gradually add water, 1 tablespoon (15 ml) at a time, mixing with fork just until dough holds together. Turn onto floured surface and knead 5 times. Roll dough out to $^1/_8$-inch (0.3-cm) thickness.

Yield: 1 single-crust pastry

Each with: 956 Calories; 64g Fat (59.2% calories from fat); 13g Protein; 87g Carbohydrate; 9g Dietary Fiber; 166mg Cholesterol; 1496mg Sodium.

Add It: To make an Easy Chocolate Pudding Pie: Prepare 1 recipe single crust pastry in pie shell. To blind bake, preheat oven to 450°F (230°C). Line tart or pie pan with pastry. Prick bottom with tines of fork. Line pastry with parchment paper or aluminum foil and fill with pie weights or baking beans. Bake 8 to 10 minutes or until golden brown. Let cool. Carefully remove paper and pie weights. Spoon 2 cups (500 g) prepared chocolate pudding into pie shell and garnish with chopped nuts or chocolate sprinkles.

 Calzones

Make these hearty, filled Italian pastries to take to work or school for lunch, on a car trip, or to a tailgate party.

FOR THE DOUGH:

1 cup (235 ml) warm (105°F to 115°F [40.5°C to 46°C]) water

1/2 teaspoon (2 g) sugar

1 package (5/16 ounce) or 2 1/2 teaspoons (10 g) Hodgson Mill Active Dry Yeast

3 cups (375 g) Hodgson Mill 50/50 Flour

2 tablespoons (28 ml) vegetable oil, such as olive

1/2 teaspoon (3 g) salt

FOR THE FILLING:

1 package (12 ounces [336 g]) shredded mozzarella cheese

1 package (2 ounces [56 g]) finely grated Parmesan cheese

1 package (3 ounces [84 g]) sliced prosciutto, cut into strips

3 tablespoons (9 g) chopped fresh chives

1 tablespoon (9 g) minced garlic

FOR THE TOPPING:

1 tablespoon (15 ml) vegetable oil, such as olive

1/4 cup (20 g) finely grated Parmesan cheese

Pizza sauce for serving, optional

For dough, combine warm water and sugar in bowl in medium mixing bowl. Sprinkle yeast over mixture and set aside to proof until foamy, about 5 minutes.

Mix in 1¹/2 cups (187.5 g) flour, and knead until smooth. Add oil and salt, and gradually blend in remaining flour to make firm dough. Turn out onto lightly floured surface and knead until smooth and satiny. Place dough in oiled bowl, turn to coat, and let rise until almost doubled in bulk, about 1 hour.

Line baking sheet with parchment paper. Knead down dough and divide into 3 pieces. On lightly floured surface, roll each piece to 9-inch (22.5-cm) circle. Place ¹/3 of mozzarella cheese, ¹/3 of Parmesan cheese, and ¹/3 of prosciutto on each circle of dough. Top with garlic and chives. Moisten perimeter of dough circle with water and fold over to form half moon and enclose filling, pressing edges to seal.

Place on prepared baking sheet, cover lightly with plastic wrap, and allow to rise until dough has risen slightly, about 35 minutes.

Preheat oven to 375°F (190°C).

Bake 30 to 35 minutes, or until calzones are browned. For topping, remove from oven and brush with oil. Sprinkle with grated Parmesan cheese. Serve warm with pizza sauce, if desired.

Yield: 3 large calzones

Each with: 1071 Calories; 52g Fat (43.5% calories from fat); 61g Protein; 91g Carbohydrate; 8g Dietary Fiber; 141mg Cholesterol; 2069mg Sodium.

Variation: Use crumbled, cooked Italian sausage or grilled vegetables in place of prosciutto.

Focaccia Bread with Sun-Dried Tomatoes

Focaccia bread can be similar to pizza if you spread it with toppings, then bake. This one features sun-dried tomatoes for extra flavor.

FOR THE DOUGH:
> 1¹/4 cups (295 ml) water
>
> 3 tablespoons (45 ml) olive oil
>
> 2 teaspoons (6 g) chopped garlic
>
> 1 teaspoon (1.2 g) dried rosemary
>
> 1 teaspoon (6 g) salt

$1/3$ cup (46.6 g) Hodgson Mill Stone Ground Whole Grain Yellow Corn Meal, Plain, plus more for sprinkling

3 cups (375 g) Hodgson Mill 50/50 Flour

1 package ($5/16$ ounce) or $2^1/2$ teaspoons (10 g) Hodgson Mill Fast-Rise Yeast

FOR THE TOPPING:

2 tablespoons (28 ml) olive oil

1 tablespoon (18 g) coarse kosher or sea salt

$1/2$ cup (75 g) chopped sun-dried tomatoes

$1/2$ cup (40 g) freshly grated Parmesan cheese

Place water, oil, garlic, rosemary, salt, corn meal, flour, and yeast in bread pan of automatic bread machine. Select dough cycle and start machine.

Preheat oven to 425°F (220°C). Sprinkle baking sheet with corn meal.

Turn dough out onto baking sheet and roll or pat into 10-inch (25-cm) circle. Brush with olive oil, sprinkle with salt, scatter with tomatoes, and sprinkle with cheese.

Bake 15 to 20 minutes or until golden brown. Let cool in pan, then slice and serve hot or room temperature.

Yield: 9 servings

Each with: 246 Calories; 9g Fat (32.7% calories from fat); 8g Protein; 34g Carbohydrate; 4g Dietary Fiber; 3mg Cholesterol; 1006mg Sodium.

 Easy Insta-Bake Pizza Crust

When you're teaching your children how to cook, this is the way to introduce them to pizza dough before you move on to yeast doughs.

2 cups (250 g) Hodgson Mill Whole Wheat Insta-Bake Mix

2 tablespoons (28 ml) olive oil

$1/2$ cup (120 ml) cold water

Toppings of your choice

Preheat oven to 425°F (220°C).

Pour mix into bowl. Stir in olive oil and water to form soft dough. Roll or pat into 12-inch (30-cm) circle on ungreased cookie sheet; pinch edge, forming $1/2$-inch (1.2-cm) rim. Top with desired ingredients.

Bake 20 to 25 minutes or until crust is golden.

Yield: 8 servings

Each with: 133 Calories; 4g Fat (27.3% calories from fat); 3g Protein; 22g Carbohydrate; 2g Dietary Fiber; 0mg Cholesterol; 218mg Sodium.

 ## *Whole Wheat Graham Pizza Dough*

Hearty and full of texture, this pizza dough recipe has the darkest color and chewiest crust.

   1 package (^{5}/16 ounce) or 2^1/2 teaspoons (10 g) Hodgson Mill Active Dry Yeast

   1 cup (235 ml) warm (105°F to 115°F [40.5°C to 46°C]) water

   2 cups (250 g) Hodgson Mill Stone Ground Whole Grain Whole Wheat
      Graham Flour

   1 cup (125 g) Hodgson Mill All-Purpose, Unbleached Naturally White Flour

   2 tablespoons (28 ml) olive oil

   1 teaspoon (6 g) salt

   Hodgson Mill Stone Ground Whole Grain Yellow Corn Meal, Plain for sprinkling

   Toppings of your choice

Sprinkle yeast over water in large bowl and set aside until foamy, about 5 minutes.

Combine flours in medium bowl. Stir half of flour mixture into yeast mixture until smooth. Stir in olive oil and salt, then stir in enough remaining flour to form soft dough. Transfer dough to lightly floured surface and knead until smooth and elastic, about 8 to 10 minutes. If dough becomes sticky, sprinkle with a little flour. Transfer dough to lightly oiled large bowl. Cover and let rise until doubled in bulk, about 1 hour.

Preheat oven to 425°F (220°C). Sprinkle baking sheet with corn meal. Roll or pat dough to form 12-inch (30-cm) circle on baking sheet. Cover and let rest 15 to 20 minutes.

Add toppings and bake 15 to 20 minutes or until crust is browned and toppings are bubbling.

Yield: 9 servings

Each with: 169 Calories; 4g Fat (18.0% calories from fat); 5g Protein; 31 g Carbohydrate; 4g Dietary Fiber; 0mg Cholesterol; 238mg Sodium.

Variation: Substitute Hodgson Mill 50/50 Flour for both whole wheat graham and all-purpose flour, then proceed with recipe.

Wave the Wheat Pizza Dough

This is a very easy, homemade pizza dough with white wheat added for better nutrition—and flavor. Add your favorite healthy toppings such as grilled vegetables, roasted red peppers, kalamata olives, and grated low-fat Italian cheese blend and you've got a pizza with extra nutritional pizzazz. You can make this dough up to a day ahead of time and keep it, covered, in the refrigerator until you're ready to roll or pat it out to make pizza.

> $1^3/4$ cups (218.8 g) Hodgson Mill All-Purpose, Unbleached Naturally White Flour
> $1^1/2$ cups (187.5 g) Hodgson Mill Stone Ground Whole Grain White Whole Wheat Flour
> 1 package ($5/16$ ounce) or $2^1/2$ teaspoons (10 g) Hodgson Mill Fast-Rise Yeast
> $1^1/2$ cups (355 ml) warm water (or more, if necessary)
> 1 tablespoon (20 g) honey
> 1 tablespoon (15 ml) olive oil plus more for brushing
> $1/2$ teaspoon (3 g) salt

Combine flours and yeast in large bowl. In a large measuring cup, combine water, honey, olive oil, and salt. Pour water mixture into the flour mixture and stir together until a soft dough. Add a little more water, if necessary.

Turn dough out onto floured surface and knead for 5 minutes, adding additional flour, if necessary, until elastic. Place in large, oiled bowl and turn to coat. Cover with plastic wrap and keep in the refrigerator or let rise at room temperature for 1 to $1^1/2$ hours or until doubled in bulk.

Yield: Dough for 17 x 12-inch (42.5 x 30-cm) sheet pan or 16 servings

---

Each with: 94 Calories; 1g Fat (9.4% calories from fat); 3g Protein; 19g Carbohydrate; 2g Dietary Fiber; 0mg Cholesterol; 67mg Sodium.

Add It: To make pizza, preheat oven to 375°F (190°C). Line a 17 x 12-inch (42.5 x 30-cm) sheet pan with parchment paper. Roll with a rolling pin or press the dough with your hands to fit prepared pan. Brush dough with olive oil. Sprinkle on toppings of your choice. Bake for 15 to 17 minutes, or until the pizza dough has risen and the toppings have browned.

Gluten-Free Pastry

Adapted from a technique by Irish cookbook authors Darina Allen and Rosemary Kearney, this gluten-free pastry has more texture than wheat pastry, but has a similar mellow flavor. Resist the urge to add more water to the dough, even though the dough will be easier to work with, as this can result in tough pastry.

$1/2$ cup (62.5 g) Hodgson Mill Stone Ground Whole Grain Brown Rice Flour

$1/2$ cup (46.6 g) Hodgson Mill Stone Ground Whole Grain Yellow Corn Meal, Plain

$1/2$ cup (80 g) potato flour, plus extra for dusting

$1^1/4$ teaspoons (8.8 g) xanthan gum

$1/2$ teaspoon (3 g) salt

4 tablespoons ($1/2$ stick [55 g]) chilled butter or shortening

1 large egg

2 tablespoons (15 ml) water

Sift flour, corn meal, potato flour, xanthan gum, and salt into bowl and mix well. Cut shortening in with a pastry blender or 2 knives until crumbly. Beat egg and water together in a small bowl. Stir egg mixture into dry ingredients with fork until moistened. Gather pastry into a ball.

On very lightly rice-floured surface, gently knead dough 10 times or to form smooth ball. Divide in half, flatten each half slightly, cover in plastic wrap and refrigerate 30 minutes. (This will make pastry easier to roll.)

Roll each dough portion out between two sheets of parchment paper to $1/8$-inch (0.3-cm) thickness.

Yield: Double crust pastry for 2 (8-inch [20-cm]) pies or tarts

Each with: 1206 Calories; 55g Fat (39.8% calories from fat); 25g Protein; 162g Carbohydrate; 13g Dietary Fiber; 311mg Cholesterol; 1621mg Sodium.

Variation: To bake, preheat oven to 350°F (180°C). To bake blind, line pastry-lined pan with parchment paper and fill with baking beans. Chill pastry for 15 minutes, then bake for 15 minutes or until pale golden.

Gluten-Free Summer Tomato and Pesto Tart

This recipe, which makes two appetizer or light luncheon tarts, has all the fresh taste of summer.

1 recipe Gluten-Free Pastry (page 454)

FOR THE TOPPING:

1 jar (7 ounces [196 g]) prepared gluten-free pesto or 1 cup (260 g) homemade pesto

1 cup (120 g) roasted red pepper strips (from jar)

1 cup (100 g) pitted kalamata or black olives, chopped

1 cup (180 g) finely diced tomato

1 cup (80 g) finely shredded Parmesan, Asiago, Pecorino Romano, or soy-based cheese

For dough, on very lightly rice-floured surface, gently knead dough 10 times or to form smooth ball. Divide in half, flatten each half slightly, cover in plastic wrap, and refrigerate for about 30 minutes. (This will make pastry easier to roll.)

Preheat oven to 400°F (200°C).

Roll each dough portion out between two sheets of parchment paper to 1/8-inch (0.3-cm) thickness. Line 2 (8-inch [20-cm]) tart pans. Spread bottom of each pastry-lined tart pan with pesto, then layer on remaining ingredients, ending with sprinkled cheese.

Bake for 20 to 25 minutes or until browned and bubbling. Let rest for 5 minutes, then cut into wedges to serve.

Yield: 2 (8-inch [20-cm]) tarts, 12 servings each

Each with: 118 Calories; 9g Fat (70.2% calories from fat); 4g Protein; 5g Carbohydrate; 1g Dietary Fiber; 12mg Cholesterol; 317mg Sodium.

Gluten-Free Fruit Turnovers

You can make the dough for these turnovers up to 2 days ahead of time and keep it covered in the refrigerator. Then make the filling and bake these tempting treats on the day you want to serve them!

   1 recipe Gluten-Free Pastry (page 454)

FOR THE FILLING:

   1 cup (150 g) finely chopped apple, peach, nectarine, or plum

   $^1/_2$ teaspoon (1.2 g) ground cinnamon

   1 tablespoon (13 g) sugar

   $^1/_2$ teaspoon (1.3 g) gluten-free Hodgson Mill Pure Corn Starch or instant tapioca

For dough, on very lightly rice-floured surface, gently knead dough 10 times or until it forms a smooth ball. Divide in half, flatten each half slightly, cover in plastic wrap, and refrigerate for about 30 minutes. (This will make pastry easier to roll.)

Preheat oven to 350°F (180°C). Line baking sheet with parchment paper.

For filling, place fruit in small bowl. In another bowl, combine cinnamon, sugar, and tapioca until well blended. Toss cinnamon mixture with fruit.

Roll each dough portion out between two sheets of parchment paper to $^1/8$-inch (0.3-cm) thickness. Cut into 8 (3-inch [7.5-cm] diameter) circles. Gather scraps, re-roll, and cut again. Place 1 tablespoon (15 g) filling in center of each circle. Moisten perimeter of dough circle with water and fold dough over to make half moon. Press edges to seal. Place on prepared baking sheet.

Bake 15 to 20 minutes or until pastry is light golden and fruit filling is bubbling.

Yield: 8 turnovers

Each with: 92 Calories; 4g Fat (32.9% calories from fat); 2g Protein; 14g Carbohydrate; 1g Dietary Fiber; 19mg Cholesterol; 101mg Sodium.

Index